American Oriental Society

MIDDLE WEST BRANCH

Semi-Centennial Volume

ASIAN STUDIES RESEARCH INSTITUTE
DENIS SINOR, DIRECTOR
ORIENTAL SERIES, No. 3

AMERICAN ORIENTAL SOCIETY

MIDDLE WEST BRANCH

SEMI-CENTENNIAL VOLUME

a collection of original essays edited by

DENIS SINOR

INDIANA UNIVERSITY PRESS « BLOOMINGTON » LONDON

for the International Affairs Center

Library of Congress catalog card number: 69-63000

Manufactured in the United States of America

Preface

IN DISCUSSIONS and private conversations held during the forty-ninth annual meeting of the Middle West Branch of the American Oriental Society in Detroit it was generally felt that it would be meet to mark the oncoming fiftieth anniversary of the Branch with some appropriate tribute. The idea of publishing a semi-centennial anniversary volume presented itself quite naturally and was accepted by all. This book is the embodiment of a suggestion then made. I consider it an honor to have been entrusted with its editorship, and I am happy that I could include it in the *Oriental Series* of the recently founded Asian Studies Research Institute of Indiana University.

As will be seen from Professor Grayson's unpretentious survey of the Branch's history (p. 269), cordial informality, a sincere desire to meet colleagues and exchange ideas, have long been the hallmarks of the Branch's annual gatherings. They have never degenerated into a labor exchange nor have they become the stamping ground of some of the less savory figures of academic life. Those who have come to these meetings have done so solely because of their wish to meet colleagues and listen to what they have to say about their work.

The meeting in Detroit was the first of the Branch's gatherings that I, a newcomer to the American Middle West, had attended. When the proposal to publish a semi-centennial volume was accepted, I wondered momentarily whether, overburdened as we all are, my regional colleagues would be willing to make the extra effort necessary to contribute to this commemorative venture. My fears turned out to be unfounded; the response to my appeal was generous, and there was no need for me to use persuasion to induce anyone to join in the celebration of the semi-centennial anniversary. With some slight exaggeration one could even say that the response was spontaneous; in fact, more articles were proposed than could be included in this volume. I hope every reader will understand why at least one article had to be omitted. As editor I felt that there was no need for my name to appear twice in this volume which contains eighteen articles, in addition to Professor Grayson's survey, written by scholars representing eight middle-western institutions.

These articles cover a wide spectrum of Oriental studies and represent various disciplines. This is as it should be, in full keeping with the tradition of the Middle West Branch and also of the mother Society. I regret that the coverage in time, space, and discipline could not be made even more comprehensive.

In recent years it has again become fashionable to question the use of the terms "Oriental" or "Asian" in a scholarly context. The question may be apposite but it is not new, as no lesser man than Herodotus himself doubted the validity of the terms "Europe" and "Asia." Speaking of Europe, Asia, and Lybia (the last of these terms referred to Africa), he said: "For my part I cannot conceive why three names, and women's names especially, should ever have been given to a tract which is in reality one" (Bk. IV, 45). I think, however, that I can safely follow in his illustrious footsteps and declare as he did: "Let us quit these matters. We shall ourselves continue to use the names which custom sanctions."

The proof of the pudding is in the eating. If, in the pages that follow, the reader finds enjoyment and intellectual enrichment, the publication of this volume will be justified. If, however, his verdict is negative, fifty years hence someone will have to do some hard thinking before embarking on the publication of the Centennial Anniversary Volume. . .

DENIS SINOR

Asian Studies Research Institute
Indiana University

Contents

American Oriental Society

MIDDLE WEST BRANCH

Semi-Centennial Volume

OBSERVATIONS ON THE USE OF BROKEN PLURALS IN MODERN ARABIC PROSE

by Salih J. Altoma
Indiana University

THE aim of the present paper is to outline the status of broken plurals as they are used in modern Arabic prose, and to point to any possible deviations which their modern usage may reflect in comparison with earlier practices. In view of this stress on usage, the method of counting plurals as cited by dictionaries was avoided in favor of examining their occurrences in sources pertaining to modern Arabic prose. The sources, the lists connected with them and other procedural matters are described briefly below.

1. SOURCES AND LISTS

1.1. *Advanced Arabic Readers.*[1] These are two anthologies of works selected from modern Arabic novels, short stories and essays. The first consists of an introductory chapter, and eleven selections from Arabic fiction written by leading writers from Egypt, Iraq, Jordan (Palestine) and Lebanon. The second comprises twenty-four selections from the writings of seventeen authors representing different views on Arabic culture, Arab nationalism and Islam. Each anthology has an extensive glossary of items, including a considerable number of broken plurals.[2]

1.2. *A Word Count of Modern Arabic Prose.*[3] Landau's list is the product of a word count of modern Arabic prose combining both Brill's count of 136,089 running words in Arabic newspapers and his own count of an equal number of words drawn from sixty books representing various genres or fields. The combined list consists of 12,400 specific words. Although Landau's objective was to include in his list all items occurring in a specified number of

[1] William M. Brinner, and Mounah A. Khouri, *Advanced Arabic Readers*, 2 vols. (Berkeley, 1961/1962).

[2] Ibid., I, pp. 147-228; II, pp. 193-272.

[3] Jacob M. Landau, *A Word Count of Modern Arabic Prose* (New York, 1959); Moshe Brill, *The Basic Word List of the Arabic Daily Newspaper* (Jerusalem, 1940).

pages of the selected books, an examination of three books[4] shows that not all broken plurals were recorded or given their contextual meanings.[5] In spite of such omissions, and other inaccurate listings which will be mentioned later, the list with its extensive coverage serves to illuminate various questions pertinent to the use of broken plurals in Arabic prose.

1.3. *A Selected Word List of Modern Literary Arabic.*[6] According to its authors, this list was compiled with a view to providing students of Arabic with high frequency items encountered in the language of newspapers, books, periodicals and in the conversation of educated people. The list does reflect a special emphasis on the usage and functional value of the items compiled, and, as a result, it includes usages which the classicists regard as unacceptable, either because they belong to spoken colloquials, or because they represent new developments inconsistent with traditional rules.

1.4. *A Reader in Modern Literary Arabic.*[7] This reader contains thirty-four selections from the works of prominent writers representing the modern literary style in Egypt, Iraq, Jordan, Lebanon and Syria. Its extensive glossary of about 5,048 items contains a large number of broken plurals as they are used in the texts.

2. PROCEDURES

In compiling and classifying broken plurals, the following procedures were observed.

---

[4] These are: Ṭahā Ḥusayn, *al-ʔAyyām*, I (Cairo, n.d.); A. Amīn, *Ẓuḥā Al-Islām*, I (Cairo, 1961); N. Maḥfūẓ, *Kifāḥ Ṭība* (Cairo, 1962).

[5] Among the plurals not listed in Landau's work are: /niyām/ "asleep", /suruj/ "lamps", /diyaka/ "cocks", /ʔawjāl/ "fears", /jirār/ "jars" (see Ḥusayn, op. cit., pp. 7, 8, 9) /ṣulaḥāʔ/ "virtuous", /ḥurafāʔ/ "customers", /ʔaʕlāj/ "infidels", /niḥal/ "sects", /ʔafrāx/ "young birds", /taʔālīf/ "writings, books", /ḥawāʔij/ "needs", /zuhhād/ "ascetics", /fajāʔiʕ/ "tragedies", /ʔaʕrāq/ "origins", /jurun/ and /ʔajruna/ "barns" (see Amīn,*op. cit.*, pp. 5, 6, 7, 8, 399, 403, 404, 404, 408, 408), /farāʕīn/ "Pharaohs", /šumm/ "haughty", /ğunn/ "lush", /ḍuxm/ "huge" (see Maḥfūz, op. cit., pp. 6, 8). Examples of incomplete listing of meanings include: /ʔaqṭār/ means "countries" but is also used to mean "corners, sections" (see Ḥusayn, p. 7), /ḥarāʔir/ means "silks" but it has another important meaning, "free born women" (see Amīn, p. 9).

[6] Middle East Centre for Arab Studies, *A Selected Word List of Modern Literary Arabic* (Beirut, 1959 ?).

[7] Farhat J. Ziadeh, *A Reader in Modern Literary Arabic* (Princeton, 1964).

a) Every instance of broken plurals given in the four lists was written down; then an attempt was made to record their respective singular forms as they are cited in the lists or in two modern dictionaries, *A Dictionary of Modern Written Arabic* (referred to in this article as Wehr)[8] and *Al-Muʿjam Al-Wasīṭ* (MW).[9] For example, /ʔahdāb/ "eyelashes", Sing. Forms /hudb/ and /hudub/; /ʔamθāl/ "examples, like", Sing. Forms /miθl/ "like", /maθal/ "example".

b) The plurals were grouped according to their types, and each type in turn was subdivided into its singular forms. The traditional types given in standard works[10] were followed, with the exception of minor deviations. A few plural and singular forms were transcribed according to their actual shape rather than their traditional hypothetical forms: i.e. /qudāh/ "judges" is represented by */fuʿāh/* instead of */fuʿala/*. The same can be said of triliteral singular forms which have a medial long vowel. Thus /bāb/ "door" is represented by */fāl/* rather than the traditional */faʿal/*.

c) The findings of two statistical studies covering broken plurals in earlier Arabic literature were summarized in a tabular form, and compared with those of the present paper. These studies are: Murtonen's *Broken Plurals*, drawn from[11] Lane's *Arabic-English Lexicon*, and Abū Ḥadīd's study of the broken plurals used in forty pre-Islamic and early Islamic works (mostly of poetry).[12]

3. FINDINGS

3.1. The total number of running plurals was found to be 3583, divided among the four lists as follows: Landau 1460, Middle East Centre for Arab Studies 1052, Brinner and Khouri 548, and Ziadeh 523. The approximate number of specific plurals recorded was 1870.

---

[8] Hans Wehr, *A Dictionary of Modern Written Arabic,* ed. J Milton Cowan (Wiesbaden, 1961).

[9] Majmaʿ Al-Luğa Al-ʿArabiyya, *Al-Muʿjam Al-Wasīṭ,* 2 vols. (Cairo, 1960/1961).

[10] Note for example: William Wright, *Arabic Grammar,* I (Cambridge, 1962), pp. 199-230; Henri Fleisch, *Traité de philologie Arabe,* I (Beirut, 1961), pp. 470-494).

[11] A. Murtonen, *Broken Plurals: Origin and Development of the System* (Leiden, 1964).

[12] M. F. Abū Ḥadīd, "Naẓarāt fī jumūʿ ath-thulāthī", *Majalla majmaʿ al-luğa al-ʿArabiyya* (MMLA), IX, (1957) pp. 53-60; and also "Jumūʿ ğayr ath-thulāthī," ibid., XI, (1959) pp. 79-88.

TABLE I

BROKEN PLURALS AND THE NUMBER OF THEIR RESPECTIVE SINGULAR FORMS IN MODERN ARABIC PROSE

Plural Type	*Rate of Frequency*	*No. of Singular Forms*
1. ʔafʿāl	333	17
2. fuʿūl	199	8
3. mafāʿil	199	20
4. fawāʿil	143	12
5. faʿāʔil	102	11
6. fiʿāl	99	17
7. ʔafʿila	63	13
8. faʿālīx	59	15
9. fuʿal	59	5
10. fuʿalāʔ	48	6
11. faʿālix	47	15
12. fiʿal	43	3
13. mafāʿīl	38	6
14. fuʿʿāl	37	2
15. faʿālā (faʿāyā)	35	11
16. fuʿul	31	12
17. ʔafāʿīl	31	7
18. ʔafʿilāʔ	25	2
19. fiʿlān	23	11
20. fuʿl	22	10
21. faʿālixa	22	17
22. tafāʿīl	22	4
23. fuʿlān	20	10
24. fuʿāh	20	2
25. fawāʿīl	17	5
26. faʿala	16	4
27. ʔafʿul	15	4
28. ʔafāʿil	12	9
29. faʿālī(n)	11	7
30. faʿlā	10	4
31. faʿʿāla	5	1
32. fiʿla	5	5
33. faʿīl	5	4
34. tafāʿil	4	1
35. fiʿala	4	2
36. fāʿila	4	3
37. ʔafāʿiyy	3	1
38. fuʿūla	2	2
39. fuʿʿal	2	2
misc.	29	—
Total	1870	

TABLE II

SELECTED TRILITERAL PLURALS AND THEIR SINGULAR FORMS

Sing. Forms / Plurals	ʔafʿāl	fuʿūl	fawāʿil	faʿāʔil	fiʿāl	ʔafʿila	fuʿal	fuʿalāʔ	fiʿal	fuʿʿāl	faʿālā	fuʿul	ʔafʿilāʔ	fiʿlān	fuʿl	faʿālixa	fuʿlān	fuʿāh	faʿala	ʔafʿul	ʔafāʿil	faʿālī	faʿlā	fiʿla	faʿīl	fiʿala	fāʿila	fuʿūla	fuʿʿal	faʿāh	fuʿālā
faʿl	96	148	1		30	4						1		2			1			11		3			2			1			
faʿīl	7			13	21	11		40		1	2	4	16	3	1		9						6								
fāʿil	2	1	56					4		37							2		13								1		1		
faʿal	94	6			7							1			2	1															
fiʿl	68	30			4	1														1						3		1			
faʿīla				81	3			1			3	4					1								1						
fāʿila			69	2																											
fuʿla					6		53		1																						
fuʿl	51	9			2		1																		1	1					
fiʿāl						23						14					2			2					1		2				
fiʿla					2		1		40																						
faʿla	2	1			19		2		2													2									
ʔafʿal								1				1			16		1				8		1								
faʿāl				1	1	17		1				2												1			1				
fāʿī			1			2								1				20													
faʿlāʔ					2						1				13		1														
fāl	9				1									4	1		1														
faʿiyy													9	2			1							1						1	
fūl	11														2																
fīl	9				3																										
faʿil	6	2				1		1				2																			
fuʿul	9																														
faʿlā						1					6											2									
fuʿāl						6								2			1														
fayyil	3				1														1				1								
faʿūl				3	1	1						1																			
faʿlān											4												2								1
fāʿal			5																										1		
faʿul					3																										
faʿala					3																										

TABLE III

BROKEN PLURALS AND THE NUMBER OF THEIR SINGULAR FORMS AS GIVEN BY MURTONEN

		No. of occurrences	*Singular Types*
1.	ʔafʿāl	1308	36
2.	fiʿāl	748	37
3.	fuʿūl	710	25
4.	mafāʿil	640	32
5.	fawāʿil	558	27
6.	fuʿul	522	29
7.	faʿāʔil	447	31
8.	fuʿl	428	25
9.	fuʿal	306	22
10.	ʔafʿila	295	20
11.	mafāʿīl	220	32
12.	ʔafʿul	203	16
13.	fiʿal	202	13
14.	fuʿlān	191	25
15.	fiʿlān	171	26
16.	fuʿʿal	168	15
17.	fuʿalāʔ	157	13
18.	fuʿʿāl	142	13
19.	ʔafāʿīl	139	23
20.	faʿālīx	137	24
21.	faʿālix	131	39
22.	ʔafāʿil	123	27
23.	fiʿala	116	16
24.	faʿala	90	10
25.	faʿāʿīl	88	24
26.	faʿāʿil	84	18
27.	faʿālā	68	11
28.	faʿla(y)	69	7
29.	faʿāla(y)	78	21
30.	ʔafʿilāʔ	66	6
31.	fawāʿīl	57	11
32.	faʿāliyy	50	17
33.	faʿal	49	more than 3[13]
34.	faʿālīl	46	8
35.	fuʿāl	38	16
36.	fuʿāt	37	4
37.	fuʿīl	32	13
38.	faʿla	31	6
39.	fuʿālixa	31	15
40.	fuʿūla	31	6
41.	faʿālin	30	17
42.	faʿālīn	27	8
43.	fiʿil	26	9
44.	fuʿāla(y)	25	13
45.	fiʿāla	25	9
46.	tafāʿīl	23	10
47.	faʿl	22	3
48.	ʔafʿil	21	6

[13] Only three singular forms are given in conjunction with the number of their occurrences, but the occurrence of other forms is implied. See Murtonen, pp. 3, 37.

TABLE IV

THE DISTRIBUTION OF BROKEN PLURALS
IN EARLY ARABIC LITERARY TEXTS

Plural Type	*Frequency*	*Plural Type*	*Frequency*
1. ʔafʿāl	365	16. faʿlā	13
2. fuʿūl	207	17. ʔafʿilāʔ	11
3. fuʿl	118	18. faʿl	9
4. fuʿal	116	19. faʿala	8
5. fiʿāl	83	20. fiʿala	4
6. fiʿal	78	21. Plurals with no singulars	26
7. fuʿʿal	65	22. faʿ(ʔ)l[14]	158
8. fuʿʿāl	64	23. 15 others not specified plural types	187
9. ʔafʿul	46	24. Plurals having /ā/ after the second radical	Not specified but their total frequency is 6078
10. fuʿala (= fuʿāh)	44		
11. ʔafʿila	43		
12. faʿal	23		
13. fiʿlān	22		
14. fuʿalāʔ	21		
15. fuʿlān	17		

These plurals are given in Table I according to their types and the number of their singular forms. Table II summarizes the distribution of major triliteral, mostly non-prefixed, plurals and their singular forms,[15] whereas Tables III and IV provide a summary of Murtonen's[16] and Abū Ḥadīd's findings with regard to the frequency of plural types and, as in the case of the former, the number of their singular forms.

3.2. An overall comparison between Table I and Table III yields a number of observations. First, certain plural types share a high rate of frequency. Eight out of the ten most frequent types occur in both tables. These are *ʔafʿāl, mafāʿil, fuʿūl, fawāʿil, faʿāʔil, fiʿāl, ʔafʿila* and *fuʿal.* To these may be added *faʿālīx* as a ninth common type if all the variants listed separately in Table III (nos. 20, 25, 34 and 42) are grouped into a single type. Second,

[14] This form was not fully vocalized in the original text. See Abū Ḥadīd (1959) p. 81.

[15] Plurals of non-triliteral roots or of patterns which are fairly predictable were not included.

[16] It was not essential for this study to include all plural types cited by Murtonen; however, Table III lists all types which were given a frequency of 20 or more.

others which rank relatively high in Table III seem to have become marginal in modern Arabic prose. Of special significance is the rare use of *fuʿʿal* and *fiʿala*. On the other hand, *fuʿāl*, for which Murtonen gives sixteen singular types, does not occur at all, unless /qumāš/ "cloth, trash" is viewed as a plural of /qamš/ "trash".[17] The type does not occur in Table IV, nor does it receive more than a marginal treatment in the accounts of early grammarians;[18] it therefore can be regarded as archaic or a dialectal feature which seldom occurred in early literature.

Third, Table I suggests that fewer singular forms are being used in modern Arabic for many of the plural types. Taking eight of the most frequent plurals in Tables I and III as an illustration, a considerable discrepancy in the number of singular forms can be noted.

	No. of Sing. Forms (Murtonen)	*No. of Sing. Forms (Modern Arabic)*
ʔafʿāl	36	17
mafāʿil	32	20
fuʿūl	25	8
fawāʿil	27	12
faʿāʔil	31	11
fiʿāl	37	17
ʔafʿila	20	13
fuʿal	22	5

This can be partly attributed to a tendency in modern usage to limit the number of singular forms for each plural (see for example, Table II), but in interpreting the significance of this difference, two other factors should not be overlooked. The first is the fact that Murtonen's study is based on more extensive dictionary materials which cover not only a greater number of plurals and possible singular forms, but also a substantial number of disused or rarely used forms. The other is the possibility that Murtonen's

[17] Landau lists one occurrence of /qumāš/ but assigns to it two different meanings. See op. cit., p. 245. If it is taken to denote "trash", then it can be considered as a plural of /qamš/; see MW, II, p. 764.

[18] See for example, Wright, op. cit., I, p. 202, Abū Al-Ḥasan, Al-Ušmūnī, *Manhaj as-Sālik ilā alfiyya Ibn Mālik*, III (Cairo, 1955), p. 697. The latter cites only one example /ðuʔār/ "nurses", but MW excludes it when listing its singular and other plurals. Charles A. Ferguson seems to favor its treatment as a feature peculiar to the Arabic koine; see "The Arabic Koine", *Language*, 35 (1959), p. 627.

criteria for defining singular forms tend to yield more forms, although the traditional scheme of forms was more or less applied in a similar manner in both studies.

3.3. *Observations on major plural types.*

a) *ʔafʿāl*. This type is still the most common plural in Arabic. Of its 333 instances, two singular forms, *faʿl* and *faʿal*, have the highest frequency (96 and 94, respectively), followed by *fiʿl* (68), *fuʿl* (51) and thirteen other forms which occur eleven times or less. The first four singular forms are identical with those of Murtonen's study, but arranged in a slightly different order: *faʿl*, *fiʿl*, *faʿal* and *fuʿl*.

What seems of special significance is *faʿl's* high rate of frequency in both studies, which contradicts a widely held notion that *ʔafʿāl* is rarely used as plural of *faʿl* if the latter has a consonant in medial position.[19] In contrast to eight examples recorded and regarded as irregular by Abū Ḥadīd, more than forty *ʔafʿāl* plurals of medially sound *faʿl* were found in the materials examined, including: /alf/ "thousand", /baḥθ/ "study, research", /jafn/ "eyelid", /ḥajm/ "size", /samʿ/ "hearing", /šakl/ "form", /šaxṣ/ "person", /fard/ "individual", /nahr/ "river", /zahr/ "flower", /ward/ "blossom, flower".

The plural /ʔawrād/ "flowers" of the last example seems to have occurred in medieval literature, but was not regarded as a correct usage.[20] The same attitude prevails today,[21] although /ʔawrād/ is encountered frequently in modern literature.

In addition, modern usage tends to restrict the use of this plural type for *fāʿil* and *faʿīl* forms. Of the former, only two instances were found: /ṣāḥib/ "companion" and /nāṣir/ "helper", and the latter had several examples, some of which represent rare occur-

---

[19] See Wright, op cit., I. p. 211. Sībawayh and other grammarians maintained that the use of *ʔafʿāl* type as a plural of medially sound *faʿl* was restricted to a few instances, and the same view has been held by most modern grammarians. See MMLA, IV (1937), p. 1; Aḥmad, Al-Iskandarī, "Jumūʿ at-taksīr al-qiyāsiyya", *MMLA*, IV (1937), p. 187; and Abū Ḥadīd (1957), p. 56. An exceptional case is Al-Kirmilī's view maintaining that *faʿl* as a singular of *ʔafʿāl* occurs more often than other forms. ʿAbbās Ḥasan, *an-Naḥw al-Wāfī*, IV (Cairo, 1963), p. 475.

[20] Edward W. Lane, *Arabic-English Lexicon* (New York, 1955/1956), p. 2935; referred to as "Lane."

[21] As an indication of this attitude, one may point to the fact that neither Wehr nor MW list /ʔawrād/ as a plural of /ward/.

rences: /naðīl/[22] "base", /najīb/ "noble". The others include: /ḥabīb/ "beloved", /naṣīr/ "helper", /šarīf/ "noble", /yamīn/ "oath", /yatīm/ "orphan".

b) *fuʿūl.* This is the second most frequent type used in modern Arabic and was similarly ranked in Abū Ḥadīd's study.[23] It is used primarily as a plural of *faʿl* form, but still employed in association with other forms as illustrated below: *faʿl* 148, *fiʿl* 30, *fuʿl* 9, *faʿal* 6, *faʿil* 2, *fāʿil* 1 and *faʿla* 1. Murtonen gives a slightly different order of distribution: *faʿl* 399, *fiʿl* 122, *fuʿl* 50, *fāʿil* 35, *faʿal* 33, *faʿla* 13, *faʿīl* 12 and eighteen others have 6 or less occurrences. The figures cited above indicate that the use of *fiʿl*/*fuʿūl* is not restricted to a few examples, as was the case in early Arabic literature.[24] Among the instances where *fuʿūl* is used in modern prose are: /jild/ "skin, leather", /ṣinf/ "kind", /ḥiṣn/ "fortress", /ʿilm/ "science, knowledge", /qirš/ "piaster", /qišr/ "cover, bark", /jism/ "body", /ʿiṭr/ "perfume", /niðr/ "vow", /sijn/ "prison", /libs/ "apparel", /jisr/ "bridge", /ʿirq/ "root, vein", /ḍilʿ/ "rib", /sidl/ "curtain".

Forms having a long vowel, such as *fāʿil* and *faʿīl*, tend to take other than *fuʿūl* type in modern usage: only one instance of *fāʿil*/*fuʿūl* was recorded, /šuhūd/, plural of /šāhid/ "witness". However, with *faʿl*, *fuʿl* or *fiʿl* forms, there is a tendency to extend the use of *fuʿūl*, as in /ward/ "flower", /zahr/ "rose, flower", /duhn/ "oil".[25]

c) *mafāʿil.* Of its 199 instances, 93 have *mafʿal* as their singular form. Other forms include *mafʿala* 32, *mafʿil* 31, *mifʿal* 24; and the remaining eighteen forms have 7 or less. Apart from a few exceptions, this type is used as a plural of singulars having a /m-/ prefix and a short vowel in pre-final position, or a pre-final long vowel in the case of medially or finally defective roots. The examples compiled do not exhibit significant deviation from older practices, except in the use of *mafāʿil* for *mufʿila;* e.g., /muškila/ "problem",

[22] MW cites /ʔanðāl/ as its plural, but Wehr gives /nuðālāʔ/ and /niðāl/, i.e., types which are normally used in association with *faʿīl* nouns.

[23] Of the plurals based on triliteral singulars, this type was found to constitute about 30%; Abū Ḥadīd op. cit., (1957), p. 56.

[24] Abū Ḥadīd found only eight examples of *fiʿl*/ *fuʿūl*; (1957, p. 57).

[25] Although /wurūd/ "flowers", /zuhūr/ "flowers" and /duhūn/ "oil" are encountered in modern Arabic, they are not cited in standard Arabic dictionaries. See, for example, Lane and MW.

/mašākil/ plural, /mudrika/ "sense", /madārik/ plural,[26] /muhimma/ "task", /mahāmm/ plural.

However, not all instances of *mafāʿil* stand for /m-/ prefixed forms or currently used singulars; e.g., /malāmiḥ/ "features", for which /lamḥa/ "look, feature" is given as an irregular singular; /maḥāsin/ "merits" for which are given /ḥusn/ and /maḥsana/,[27] /matāʿib/[28] "difficulties, hardships", /mabāhij/[29] "joys" and /maxāṭir/[30] "dangers". In addition, an observation should be made of Landau's listing of /majāhid/ "efforts". Although the formation of this plural is theoretically possible, the word /majāhid/ does not occur in other sources, and its listing seems to have resulted from an oversight in vocalization, for it should read /mujāhid/ "fighter", as cited by Brill.[31]

d) *fawāʿil*. The main singular forms of this type are *fāʿila* 69, and *fāʿil* 56. Other forms occur five times or less, e.g., *fāʿal* 5 and *fawʿal* 4. The traditional rules governing the formation of *fawāʿil* are generally observed in modern Arabic. Thus, as in earlier usages, *fawāʿil* is rarely applied to nouns of *fāʿil* form if they refer to men: /bāsil/ "brave", /bawāsil/ plural, /tābiʿ/ "follower", /tawābiʿ/ plural. Of the instances which are not regarded as acceptable are /nawāqiṣ/ plural of /nāqiṣ/ "deficient, shortage"; not given in any of the five dictionaries consulted (see footnotes), /ṣawānī/ plural of /ṣīniyya/ "tray, plate" and /ʿawāʔid/ a plural of /ʿāda/ "habit, custom" for which /ʿādāt/ functions as the normal plural.

---

[26] This plural is given without its singular form in both MW and Wehr, but Al-Bustānī cites both /mudrika/ and /madārik/ or /mudrikāt/; see Abdullah Al-Bustānī, *Al-Bustān*, 2 vols., I (Beirut, 1927/1930), p. 764.

[27] MW gives /ḥusn/ as its irregular singular; Wehr lists /maḥsana/, whereas Al-Bustānī, op. cit., I, p. 692, suggests that this plural has no singular.

[28] Lane, p. 307, traces it to /matʿab/ "the place of tiredness or hardship", used as a synonym of /taʿab/ "tiredness, hardship".

[29] Neither MW nor Lane list this plural, but Wehr cites it as a plural of /mabhaja/ "a moment of joy".

[30] Not listed in MW but given without its singular in Wehr. However, its origin may be sought in an early occurrence of /muxṭira/ "perilous" (Lane, p. 765), which probably led to the modern use of /maxāṭir/ "perils" analogous to /muškila/ "problem", /mudrika/ "sense" and /muhimma/ "task".

[31] The combined frequency of /majāhid/ is 22 according to Landau, pp. 53, 363, of which 21 are attributed to Brill whose text lists /mujāhid/ "fighter". See Brill, p. 16.

[32] Wehr cites both /ʿawāʔid/ and /ʿādāt/ as plurals of /ʿāda/, as Lane does, though lexicographers in general favor the sound feminine plural; Lane, p. 2191.

e) *faʿāʔil.* All the 102 occurrences of this type, with the exception of four, are derived from singulars which have a long vowel after the second consonant. Most examples belong to *faʿīla* 81, and others to *faʿīl*, *fiʿāla*, *faʿāla* and *faʿūl.* The exceptions are /wāsiṭa/ "means", /xāṣiyya/[33] "feature, quality", /junayna/ "garden" and /ḥurra/ "free born woman". The rule that *faʿāʔil* is a plural of feminine quadriliterals[34] seems to be undergoing a process of modification in modern usage. Early grammarians did refer to rare cases of its use for masculine quadriliterals, but modern Arabic offers an increasing number of such examples: /ḥarīr/ "silk", /ḥarīq/ "fire", /ḥašīš/ "grass", /dalīl/ "proof", /šarīṭ/ "tape", /ḍamīr/ "pronoun, conscience", /ʿajīb/ "wondrous thing", /ʿaḏ̣īm/ "great", /fatīl/ "gauze, wick", /qalīl/ "little", /madīḥ/ "praise", /nasīm/ "breeze", /zabūn/ "customer".

f) *fiʿāl.* Ranked second most frequent plural in Murtonen's work, but sixth in modern Arabic, this type is still divided unevenly, as in early usage, between its singular forms. Of the 17 singular forms, *faʿal* occurs 30 times, *faʿīl* 21, *faʿla* 19, *faʿal* and *fiʿl* 7 each, *fuʿla* 5 and the remaining forms 3 or less. The six forms cited above are arranged in a slightly different order in Murtonen's study:[35] *faʿl*, *faʿla*, *faʿīl*, *fiʿl*, *faʿal* and *fuʿla*. This may be attributed to a modern tendency to apply *fiʿāl* to *faʿīl* in a larger number of examples, e.g., /qilāl/ "little" plural of /qalīl/ cited neither by Lane nor MW.

On the other hand, modern use of *fiʿāl* for *fāʿil* singulars is highly restricted. The only example found in the materials is /niyām/ "asleep", plural of /nāʔim/, in contrast to Murtonen's reference to thirty occurrences of *fāʿil/fiʿāl.*[36] However, such use seems to have been restricted even in early literature (7th and 8th centuries), as suggested by Abū Ḥadīd's exclusion of *fāʿil* as a regular singular form.[37]

g) *ʔafʿila.* The major singular forms of this type are identical with those given by Murtonen: *fiʿāl* 23, *faʿāl* 17, *faʿīl* 11, *fuʿāl* 6

---

[33] The plural /xaṣāʔis/ "features" is primarily associated with its singular /xaṣīṣa/ "a feature" but modern Arabic extends it to /xāṣiyya/ "trait", note Wehr, p. 242.

[34] Note Wright, op cit., I, p. 215, Al-Ušmūnī, op. cit., III, pp. 693-694, and Ḥasan, op. cit., IV, p. 490.

[35] Murtonen, pp. 2-3.

[36] Murtonen, p. 3; for more examples, see Wright, op. cit., I, p. 204.

[37] Abū Ḥadīd (1959), p. 85. See also Al-Ušmūnī, op. cit., I, p. 686.

and *faʿl* 4. Aside from two instances, the modern use of *ʔafʿila* does not show any significant deviation. The exceptional instances are: /ʔafdina/ plural of /faddān/ "a square measure"; and /ʔakbida/ plural of /kabid/ or /kibd/ "liver". The former is given in Wehr but not in MW whereas the latter is not cited.

h) *fuʿal*. This type is primarily associated with the *fuʿla* form which occurs in 53 examples, but is used with other forms in isolated instances: *faʿla* 2, *fiʿla* 2, *fuʿl* 1 and *fuʿa* 1. As Murtonen pointed out,[38] *fuʿal* is not used as a plural of *fuʿl* singular if the latter has no nominal unit, i.e., a *fuʿla* variant. The single example of *fuʿl/fuʿal* noted in the materials is /lujj/ "depth of the sea" which has a *fuʿla* variant beside it, i.e., /lujja/.

i) *fuʿālāʔ*. This type stands primarily as a plural of *faʿīl*. Out of 48 instances, *faʿīl* occurs 40, *fāʿil* 4, *faʿīla*, *faʿil*, *afʿal* and *faʿāl* once each. Aside from the limited number of its singular forms (totaling 6, in contrast to 13 given by Murtonen), the use of *fuʿālāʔ* shows no signs of significant deviation in modern Arabic. However, reference should be made to two examples of *fuʿālāʔ*: /θuxanāʔ/ "thick", plural of /θaxīn/, which seems of recent origin,[39] and /ʿutāqāʔ/ "old, ancient", plural of /ʿatīq/, which does not represent an acceptable usage.[40]

j) *faʿālīx and related types*. The singulars for which *faʿālīx* is employed share in this study a pattern consisting of four radicals and a pre-final long vowel. The major forms are: *fuʿlāx* 16, *fiʿlāx* 11, *fuʿlūx* 7, *faʿlūx* 5, *faʿlāx* 5, *fiʿlīx* 5. An exceptional case is the use of /ʿarqala/ "obstacle" as a singular of /ʿarāqīl/. Other plural types *ʔafāʿīl*, *tafāʿīl* and *mafāʿīl* have mostly singulars of a similar pattern, e.g., *ʔufʿūla*, *ʔufʿūl*, *ʔafʿāl*, *ʔifʿīl* and *ʔifʿāl*; all related to *ʔafāʿīl*; *tafʿīl*, *tafʿīla*, *tifʿīl* and *tifʿāl*, singular forms of *tafāʿīl*. Two examples, as cited by Wehr, deviate from this pattern: /bāṭil/ "false", /sirār/ "facial expression" given instead of /ʔubṭūla/ and /ʔasrār/ as singulars of /ʔabāṭīl/ and /ʔasārīr/. The other plural

---

[38] Murtonen, p. 54 points to only one possible instance of *fuʿal* as a plural of *fuʿl* without a noun unit.

[39] Lane gives only /θixān/, whereas Wehr cites both this and /θuxanāʔ/.

[40] The plural occurs in the word list of the Middle East Centre for Arab Studies, p. 53, but neither Wehr nor MW list it, nor can it be traced to an earlier usage. The usual plural of /ʿatīq/ "old" is /ʿitāq/ whereas /ʿutaqāʔ/ implies a different meaning, i.e., "freed slaves".

type, *mafāʿīl*, is divided between 6 singular forms, in contrast to 32 given by Murtonen; *mifʿāl* 20, *mafʿūl* 13, *mafʿūla*, *mafʿīl*, *mifʿīl* and *mafʿila* occurring once each. Only the last form does not follow the general pattern. Of special significance is the non-occurrence of *mufʿil* as a singular form of *mafāʿīl*. According to Murtonen, it was found in 25 instances and therefore was ranked third after *mifʿāl* and *mafʿūl*.[41] Although isolated examples like /mufṭir/ "one who breaks his fast", /mafāṭīr/[42] plural, may take place in modern Arabic, the general rule observed calls for the formation of sound plurals in such cases.

k) *Other types*. Apart from minor observations regarding specific examples, modern use of other types does not call for a special treatment. All tend to have fewer singular forms than those recorded by Murtonen (see Tables I, II, III). Several cases of plurals as cited in the materials seem to represent incorrect usage or have resulted from misreading of the original texts. Landau lists /judur/ "fitting, suitable", /jurs/ "bells", /ʔaḍāliʿ/ "robust", /ʔaḍ̱lām/ "oppressions", /kuḥūl/ "kohls, eye-paints",[43] apparently as plurals of /jadīr/, /jaras/, /ʔaḍlaʿ/, /ḍ̱ulm/ and /kuḥl/ "eye-paint". None of these plurals occurs in the dictionaries which have been extensively used in this study. The usual plurals given for the first three are /judarāʔ/, /ʔajrās/ and /ḍulʿ/, and the item /kuḥūl/ is used to signify "alcohol, spirit". Two examples of *faʿala* type are attributed to singulars for which no such plural is usually given: /kaðaba/ "liars" for /kaððāb/ "liar"[44] and /ǧafala/ "unmindful", plural for /ǧāfil/.[45] The broken plurals attested to the latter are /ǧufūl/ and /ǧuffal/,[46] whereas /kaðaba/ occurs as a plural of /kāðib/ "a liar".

---

[41] Murtonen, p. 6. For additional information on mafʿūl/mafāʿīl see ʿĀrif an-Nakadī "Mafʿūl/Mafāʿīl" *Majalla al-Majmaʿ al-ʿIlmī al-ʿArabī* 40 (1965) 109-116.

[42] This plural is not listed in MW nor in Wehr, but is given along with others in Wright, op. cit., II, p. 229. See also Al-Bustānī, op. cit., II, p. 1860. Additional examples cited by both Wehr and MW include: /mūsir/ "prosperous" /mayāsīr/ /muflis/ "bankrupt" /mafālīs/.

[43] Landau, see pp. 43, 45, 173, 184, 251.

[44] Middle East Centre for Arab Studies, p. 66.

[45] Brinner and Khouri, op. cit., I, p. 200.

[46] See Lane, MW, Wehr, Al-Bustānī and R. Dozy, *Supplément aux dictionnaires arabes*, 2nd ed., 2 vols. (Leiden-Paris, 1927).

4. THE USE OF MULTIPLURALS

The occurrence of two or more broken plurals for the same singulars is still noticeable in modern Arabic prose. An examination of the materials collected reveals that in at least 121 cases, two or more plurals denoting identical meaning were used. The largest number of these multiplurals, as Table V indicates, belong to the four types known as "the plurals of paucity", *ʔafʿāl, ʔafʿul, ʔafʿila* and *fiʿla*, used in association with other types, "plurals of abundance."[47]

In view of the fact that these examples are not examined in their contexts, it is not possible to determine the extent to which they reflect a deliberate observation of the traditional distinction between the two categories of plurals. However, not all instances of multiplurals result from such possible distinction, for there are cases in which two or more "plurals of abundance" are used: /nuqqād/ and /naqada/ "critics", /ṭullāb/ and /ṭalaba/ "students", /rifāq/

TABLE V

DISTRIBUTION OF MULTIPLURALS

1.	ʔafʿāl in association with other types		44
	with fuʿūl	19	
	with fiʿāl	8	
	with ʔafʿul	3	
	with ʔafʿila	1	
	with others	13	
2.	ʔafʿila with 10 other types		19
3.	ʔafʿul		16
	with fuʿūl	11	
	with ʔafʿāl	3	
	with fiʿāl	2	
4.	fiʿla with fiʿlān	4	4
5.	fuʿʿāl with faʿala	9	9
6.	fuʿalāʔ with fiʿāl	6	6
7.	fiʿāl with others		13
8.	other pairs		14
	Total (not counting repetitions)		121

[47] Wright, op. cit., I, p. 234, H. Fleisch, "Djamʿ", *Encyclopaedia of Islam,* II, (Leiden-London, 1965), p. 409. See also Ibrāhīm Anīs, "Taʿaddud aṣ-ṣiyaǧ fī al-luǧa al-ʿarabiyya," *MMLA,* 13 (1961), 159-165, for his attempt to assign a primary role to "mistaken analogy" in the use of multiplurals.

and /rufaqāʔ/ "companions", /kirām/ and /kuramāʔ/ "generous". Besides, there are a few examples of nouns having two "plurals of paucity": /ʔalsun/ and /ʔalsina/ "tongues", /ʔanhār/ and /ʔanhur/ "rivers", /ʔaḍlūʕ/ and /ʔaḍlāʕ/ "ribs".

This phenomenon raises two other questions which need further investigation: How freely can a member of the same group of plurals function as a substitute for others? Are they of equal functional value in terms of frequency?

Although the multiplurals of the same singular can in theory be used interchangeably, there are situations which restrict the substitution of one plural for the other: e.g., both /kuramāʔ/ and /kirām/ "generous, distinguished" can be used in /kānū.../ "they were generous" but are not interchangeable in /al-mustamiʕūn al-kirām/ "honorable listeners". One possible reason for this restriction stems from the fact that a member of the same group acquires additional meaning which differentiates it from the rest in certain situations.

As for the second question, it appears that whenever two or more plurals exist for the same singular, there is a tendency to use one of them as a primary plural, as the following examples suggest.[48]

Plural		*No. of occurrences*
/kuttāb/		48
/kataba/	writers, secretaries	5
/wurrāθ/		1
/waraθa/	heirs	4
/kubarāʔ/		10
/kibār/	important, great	79

CONCLUSIONS

The observations made in this study point to the need for additional investigation into the system of broken plurals in modern Arabic. They also show that modern usage deviates somewhat from the rules prescribed by early grammarians and modern accounts based on such rules. Salient among these deviations are two noticeable tendencies: (1) to limit the number of singular forms used for most types, and (2) to extend the use of certain types (see

[48] These examples and their rate of frequency are drawn from Landau.

sections a-j) to singulars or forms with which they were not associated. As a result of such modifications, and in the light of the findings of this study, the traditional approach generally followed in the study and teaching of the broken plurals seems both inadequate and to a certain extent misleading.

SOME FURTHER REMARKS ON THE MONGOL BUDDHIST TERMS OF NON-TIBETAN ORIGIN

by F. A. Bischoff
Indiana University

THE so-called second conversion of the Mongols to Buddhism during the 16th and 17th centuries under Altan and Ligdan Khan was, in fact, only a change from Red to Yellow Lamaism.[1] Three arguments support this conclusion:

1) A period of 150-200 years, from the time of the expulsion of the Yüan in 1367, until the era of Altan Khan (1507–1582 ?), is indeed a very short time in which to witness the disappearance of a religion—unless one assumes that prior to 1367 Buddhism had not really become established in Mongolia. In fact, the following second argument would seem to contradict this assumption.

2) The followers of the Red Sect were, and still are, mainly to be found in areas as remote as the northern corner of the Khentei province—the homeland of Chingis Khan—in Northeastern Mongolia. This place possesses all the characteristics of a *Rückzugsgebiet*. It may, therefore, be concluded that the Yellow Sect, spreading over the country from the south, pushed the "Old Believers" into the less accessible areas of the north.

3) The Mongol *Kanjur-Tanjur* in its final form—which it took under Ligdan Khan, and in which it was printed in Peking

[1] The present article resumes the arguments previously expounded in my "Une incantation lamaïque anti-chinoise," *Central Asiatic Journal*, X, No. 2 (June 1965), pp. 128 ff. Professor Siegbert Hummel kindly notified me that he had already mentioned this incantation in an article entitled "Tāranātha und der Schwarze Mañjuśrī," *Zeitschrift für Missionswissenschaft und Religionswissenschaft*, XXXVI, 1, pp. 67 ff. The incantation is attributed to Tāranātha (Kun dga' sñiṅ po) who composed it during his sojourn on the Wu-t'ai shan. Two similar texts are in Leipzig, Mus. Nr. F. III 48 and F. III 50. Colophon: *rje bcun Ta-ra-na-tha'i Ri-bo-rce-lṅa phebs su bris pa'o*, "Upon his arrival at Mount Wu-t'ai, the Reverend Tāranātha composed it"; *rje bcun Ta-ra-na-tha'i daṅ Ri-bo-rce-lṅa la mjad pa'i gsuṅs par bris pa'o*, "The Reverend Tāranātha, on request, composed it at Mount Wu-t'ai". These indications, for which I am most grateful to Professor Hummel, confirm the great popularity of the text.

in the 18th century—appears as a *verbatim* translation from the Tibetan.[2] This close relationship between the Mongol and the Tibetan versions stands somewhat in contradiction to the vocabulary of the Mongol version which contains a great number of non-Tibetan terms (e.g., Mong. *sudur*, Sk. *sūtra*, Tib. *mdo;* Mong. *dandr-a*, Sk. *tantra*, Tib. *rgyud;* Mong. *ubadini*, Sk. *upādhyāya*, Tib. *mkhan po*, etc.). Many of these words are attested in texts of the 12th century (cf. Appendix II). They appear firmly established in Mongol Buddhist terminology and were adopted by the editorial committee of Ligdan Khan. As no terminology can survive without an uninterrupted tradition—oral or written—Buddhism could not have disappeared entirely from Mongolia during the 15th century.

To these three arguments one must add a fourth: the testimony (most relevant in the present case) of the *Kanjur*-Colophons. They never mention an "extinction" of the Religion, but refer only to times when the Religion was "darkened", "decayed" (as in col. 183: *čulčaki-kelegei;* col. 746 & 765: *čülüyideǰü*).[3]

The third of these four arguments reveals much more than is apparent at a first glance; since the same argument can be applied also to the activities of the Ligdan Khan Committee and to 'Phags pa, it must be concluded that Buddhism was introduced among the Mongols prior to the period of Emperor Khubilai and of 'Phags pa.

One of the main characteristics of the Tibetan method of translating the Scriptures from their Indian originals is the integral rendering of technical terms in plain Tibetan—and the exclusion of Sanskrit loan words.

In fact, this strict rule represented one of the major difficulties encountered by the *locchāvas:* they had to render a most differentiated religious, metaphysical and philosophical terminology in a language which, until then, could deal adequately only with matters pertaining to cattle-breeding, war and magic. But the *locchāvas* solved the problem by means of word-compounds or circumlocutions which express in simple Tibetan words the etymological or the actual meaning of the Indian terms.

---

[2] Cf. my "Der Zauberritus der Ucchuṣmā", *Central Asiatic Journal*, III, No. 3 (Sept. 1962), esp. p. 207.

[3] Cf. L. Ligeti, *Catalogue du Kanǰur mongol imprimé* (Budapest 1942–1944, Bibliotheca Orientalis Hungarica III), p. 58, 1. 2; p. 167, 1. 7; p. 182, 1. 4 of §2.

Initially the Mongol translators were facing the same problem that had confronted their Tibetan colleagues. They had to correct the inadequacies of their language in order to render Buddhism properly. Had they made their first translations from Tibetan versions, their problem would already have been solved. The Tibetan equivalents of Indian technical terms could easily have been translated into Mongol. For example, it would have been easier, and, at the same time, more meaningful, to translate the Tibetan term *lhuṅ bzed* (*lhuṅ ba*, "to beg"[4]; *bzed*, "the bowl") as "begging-bowl", than to take the Sanskrit word *pātra* from the *Mahāvyutpatti*, and to transliterate it by Mongol *badir* (cf., moreover, Appendix II).

Whatever value one may give to the argument of practicality, the fact remains that a Tibetan like 'Phags pa would not have disregarded any basic rule of Tibetan translating technique. Had 'Phags pa been the man to set the first pattern for the translation of the Scriptures into Mongol, he would certainly not have permitted the use of Sanskrit loan words.

Consequently it must be concluded that, not unlike the Ligdan Khan Committee three centuries later, 'Phags pa had at his disposal a fairly elaborate Buddhist terminology. This terminology must therefore be prior to the 13th century. It would follow that the first Mongol Buddhist translations were made before the time of Khubilai and from non-Tibetan originals. It would, however, be premature, if not altogether erroneous, to conclude that these translations were made directly from Indian originals. One would have to search rather for Uighur, Tokharian or some other Inner Asian prototypes.

In conclusion, it is possible to summarize the argumentation in the simple form of a syllogism:

major premise: Tibetan tradition informs Mongol Buddhism from the time of Khubilai.

minor premise: Tibetan tradition forbids the use of Sanskrit loan words.

---

[4] This verb is not listed in the dictionaries of Das, Jäschke and Desgodins. It was set forth by my native informer. If, however, he is wrong, and if Das (*lhuṅ*, pf. of *ltuṅ ba*, "to fall") is right, then the *locchāvas* would have misetymologized Sk. *pātra* from PAT; and this is unlikely. The correct etymology is PĀ, "to drink", which would require Tib. *'thuṅ ba* and thus induce the philologist to look in *lhuṅ* for a secondary form of this *'thuṅ ba*.

conclusion: Sanskrit loan words are introduced into Mongol before Khubilai: *quod erat demonstrandum.*

APPENDIX I

"The Yüan Dynasty had its beginnings in the north and, since ancient times, had always been dedicated to Buddhism." This statement of the *Yüan Shih*[5] should not be disregarded.

One certainly cannot deduce very much from the Uighur inscription which, as early (or as late) as 1326, refers to Chingis Khan as a "Bodhisattva in his late birth".[6] At that time, Buddhism had been established in Inner Asia for about a millenium, and the inscription may bear witness to the Uighurs' faith, rather than that of Chingis Khan. But taking into consideration the fact that the Mongols had always lived in close contact with the Turks, it is hard to imagine how Buddhism could not have spread among them.

To me this argument seems compelling—more compelling than any written testimonies such as those just mentioned, or "facts and figures" such as the temple Chao-lin in the northwest of Dolon-nor, in the circumscription of Karakorum, attested as early as 1255.[7] Indeed, one must be most cautious about the actual relevance of such material. The only valid argumentation, in the present case, seems therefore to be the *cum verisimilitudine.*

It is most likely that the type of Buddhism to which the "Yüan dynasty had, since ancient times, always been dedicated", in the remote northeastern corner of Mongolia, was a special brand of Shamanism rather than anything comparable to the reformed state religion of later ages. Nonetheless, the orthodox tradition reflected in the colophon of the *Yum* (late 16th to early 17th centuries), and according to which Buddhism was first introduced into Mongolia by Chingis Khan, sounds like an anachronism aimed at attributing great *puṇya* to the founder of the dynasty. Unless one really sticks to the words of the colophon and interprets them

---

[5] K. 202, fol. 4 b; cf. also G. Tucci, *Tibetan Painted Scrolls* (Rome, 1949), p. 31; for early contacts of the Yüan Dynasty with Buddhism, cf. O. Franke, *Geschichte des Chinesischen Reiches* (Berlin, 1930–1952), vol. IV, p. 332 and vol. V, p. 173.

[6] Cf. E. Conze, *Buddhism: Its Essence and Development* (New York, 1959), p. 75.

[7] Ed. Chavannes, "Inscriptions et pièces de chancellerie chinoises de l'époque mongole," *T'oung Pao*, Ser. 2, V (1904), p. 374.

restrictively in the way that Chingis Khan introduced to the Mongols Tibetan Buddhism itself.

Here is a translation of the first five stanzas of the *Yum* colophon:[8]

[1] After one had translated the Jewel-Law, the Religion, from the Indian into the Tibetan language, had spread it extensively, and thus procured advantage to many beings, the Law and Religion spread among the people here in the following way:

[2] Qormusda, the king of the gods, comparable to an ocean of milk, inhabitant of the splendid, big city called Sudarśana and located on the highest top of Mount Sumeru, was born, transformed into mighty, exalted Chingis Khan.

[3] With might and power he brought under his domination the completely wild, arrogant, selfish people in this most large northern country, and he spread greatly the holy, good Law.

[4] At the time of the incomparable Sečen Khan and Külüg Khan, who both were issued from the Golden family of this (Chingis) Khan, the exalted Law, the Religion, was spread in a most eminent way. After these pious princes, at the time of princes with a small merit of virtue,

[5] the Law and Religion of the admirable Buddha decayed. Therefore, Altan, the king of the Law, who out of kind compassion for all beings lost in dark night, came into being as a transformation, invited the Dalai Lama, the sun of all, to come, and exalted the Religion . . .

APPENDIX II

The following list contains the Sanskrit loan words occurring in *The Mongolian Monuments in ḣP'ags pa Script* by Nicholas Poppe and John R. Krueger,[9] together with their Sanskrit and Tibetan equivalents. The second list contains the words of Tibetan origin contained in the same source. Close observation will reveal that—with the possible exception of *arabnas* which, after all, may be a special, Tibetan type of ceremony—all Tibetan loan words concern things in some way peculiar to Tibet and her tradition, whereas the Indian loan words are plain religious terms. One will also notice that the Sanskrit loan words show a much stronger dialectical alteration than the words borrowed from Tibetan, and

[8] L. Ligeti, *Catalogue du Kanjur mongol imprimé*, p. 166, col. no. 746.

[9] *Göttinger Asiatische Forschungen*, Band 8, 1957.

must therefore, have a longer history: *galbavaraš* is not simply a misspelling! Sanskrit proper names (of monks) like Ananda t'uvaǰa širi, or ritual formulas like *su̯asti* prove that words could be spelled fairly correctly, if only one intended to. The question about the actual Sanskrit knowledge of the Mongol translators is therefore irrelevant. Nevertheless, one can possibly conceive that, since numerous loan words were already introduced into Mongol by the pre-Tibetan tradition, later translators (although they normally followed the Tibetan tradition) may have occasionally picked some new loan words from the *Mahāvyutpatti*. Such borrowings do not lack a certain amount of preciosity that might have been intended to illustrate a high standard of erudition (just as do the Sanskrit monk-names).

As for a supposed impossibility that would have compelled the Tibetan *locchāvas* to translate the Buddhist terms instead of transliterating them, it should be enough to point out that it is equally easy to write in Tibetan script *śa-kya-mu-ni* and *śa-kya-thub-pa*, to write *su-tra* and *mdo*, and that there was no difficulty in compiling a Sanskrit-Tibetan dictionary in Tibetan script, the *Mahāvyutpatti*.

SANSCRIT LOAN WORDS

Abida—Amitābha—'Od dpag med
adišdid—adhiṣṭhita—byin gyis brlabs pa
Aq[šobi]—Akṣobhya—Mi bskyod pa
Ašugi—Aśoka—Mya ṅan med
badhira lama: Poppe etymologized tentatively: vajra lama—rdo rǰe bla ma; personally, I would have opted for: badhira lama = Mong. badarči lama = a lama carrying the alms bowl (Sk. pātra, Mong. badir), Tib. lhuṅ bzed 'čhaṅ pa
bodhisivid, bodisivid, bodisi·ud, bothisivid—bodhisattva—byaṅ čhub sems dpa'
batira galb—bhadra-kalpa—bskal bzaṅ po
buyan— ? puṇya—bsod nams
č'akiravard—cakravartin—'khor lo bsgyur
divib—dvīpa—gliṅ
galbavaraš—kalpavṛkṣa—bskal pa'i śiṅ
mandalnu·ud—maṇḍala, pl.—dkyil 'khor (rnams)
maqaraŋnu·ud—mahārāja, pl.—rgyal po čhen po (rnams)
sarvavit (i)—sarvavid—thams čad mkhyen pa (?)
sudur—sūtra—mdo
su̯asti—svasti—svasti, dge ba
Šagemuni—Śākyamuni—Śā-kya thub pa
šarir—śarīra—riṅ bsrel
Vač'irabani—Vajrapāṇi—Lag na rdo rǰe
viyagirid—(viyakṛta) vyākaraṇa—luṅ bstan

TIBETAN LOAN WORDS

arabnas—rab gnas—pratiṣṭā: the consecration of a temple, picture, etc.
dhišhi (yer)— ? sde srid: an administrative district, an administrator
Dor-rǰi—Rdo rǰe: a proper name (the ritual object is called včir)
gabšes, gebshi—dge bśes: a gelong who mastered metaphysics
gecunis (pl.)—dge bcun: a devotee (who took just the basic vows)
kžis ga—gźis ka: an estate
la ma—bla ma: a lama
sku žaŋ—sku źaṅ: uncle, a title

THEORY OF LIGHT IN AL-GHAZZALI'S *MISHKĀT AL-ANWĀR*

by Vincent Cantarino
Indiana University

In the numerous studies dedicated to the topic of Light in the Western tradition, Abu Hamid Mohammed ibn Mohammed al-Ghazzali—the Algazel of the Latins—(1059-1111) is only seldom mentioned, and then only *en passant*. Yet during the late years of his life he wrote a remarkable little treatise which bears the suggestive title of *Mishkāt al-anwār* ("The Niche of Lights")[1] and is a clear and detailed exposition of the neoplatonic doctrine of illumination.[2]

It is, indeed, difficult to ascertain and evaluate in precise terms the influence this particular book actually exerted on Western Muslim and Jewish thought and the importance it had in the development of Latin philosophical doctrines of Light. Nevertheless, the fact that the *Mishkāt* was given special attention by Muslim, Jewish and Christian thinkers[3] alike supports its further consideration in studies on Light speculation.

[1] See Brockelmann, *Geschichte der arabischen Literatur* (Leiden, 1943), v. I, p. 423, n. 4; also *Supplement*, v. I, p. 751. English translation by W.H.T. Gairdner, *Niche for Lights* (Royal Asiatic Society, London, 1924; reprinted Lahore, 1952). The text was recently published by Abu l-ʿAla ʿAfifi (Cairo, 1964), whose edition we follow.

[2] "Parmi les traités de Ghazzālī, le *Mishkāt* est celui qui montre son néoplatonisme de la façon la plus détaillée et la plus claire," A.J. Wensinck, *La pensée de Ghazzālī* (Paris, 1940), p. 10. On al-Ghazzali's dependence on Plotinus' *Enneads*, see p. 14 and pp. 24 ff. of Wensinck's work, and the same author's "Ghazali's *Mishkāt al-Anwār*," in *Semitische Studien* (Leiden, 1941).

[3] The *Mishkāt* was mentioned less than a century after al-Ghazzali's death by Ibn Tufail (1105-1185) in his *Ḥayy ibn Yaqẓān* (quoted by Gairdner, op. cit., p. 21, n. 1), and by Ibn Rushd in his *al-Kashf ʿan manāhij al-adilla* (Cairo ed. p. 59); also quoted by Gairdner, pp. 17, 21; and in his *Tahāfut* (*Destructio*, f. 386), as quoted by G. Quadri, *La philosophie arabe dans l'Europe médiévale* (Paris, 1947), p. 133. The Christian scholar Raymund Martin (d. 1284) also referred to it with the title *lampas luminum* in his *Pugio fidei*, p. 1a, c. 2, par. 4, quoted by M. Asin Palacios, *La espiritualidad de Algazel y su sentido cristiano* (Madrid and Granada, 1941), v. IV, *Crestomatía algazeliana*, p. 249. On its fate among Jewish scholars and their translations, see Moritz Steinschneider, *Die hebraeischen Übersetzungen des Mittelalters und die Juden als Dolmetscher* (Berlin 1893), §196.

Modern scholarship has exhibited a tendency to approach the *Mishkāt* only as a part of al-Ghazzali's monumental literary production, and therefore to study its content in connection with the more consistent patterns in al-Ghazzali's doctrinal system. In this perspective, the modest size of our treatise has proven to be detrimental to the attention granted to it in most studies of al-Ghazzali's thought. In fact, the interpretation of the doctrinal content of the *Mishkāt* has always been subordinated to the general and comprehensive interpretation of al-Ghazzali's entire intellectual work.[4]

This is, no doubt, the method to be followed whenever the investigation aims to study the doctrines of a given author and to evaluate his contribution to the intellectual achievements of man. However, in the study of cultural exchanges such as took place between Muslim, Jewish and Latin Christian cultures during the European Middle Ages, we are faced with a different problem which must be solved by using a different approach. In order to measure the influence of a writer, not his entire intellectual production but only that part of it which brought him in contact with other cultures must be taken into consideration. Thus, in regard to the fortune encountered by the *Mishkāt* and the influence it had on the development of Western Muslim, Jewish and Christian thought, this book must be approached in itself.

In philosophical or theological matters, the medieval thinker did not respond to entire systems or even to authors as such when confronted by Muslim or Jewish thought, but responded rather to specific ideas which appealed to him and which he then incorporated into his own intellectual system. A statement was thus frequently accepted not on the authority of the writer purporting it but on the basis of its content only. This consideration, as elementary as it may sound, has often been disregarded, yet it is essential in the problem of cultural exchanges. We need renewed study of the Muslim works which were known in the Latin West, as a first step in the evaluation of their contribution and cultural impact.

Greater attention has been given to al-Ghazzali's use of esoteric symbolism in the *Mishkāt*, to the detriment of the first part of the

[4] This is the tendency in, for example, the otherwise excellent studies by Wensinck (op. cit., n. 2) and Farid Jabre (*La notion de la ma'arifa chez Ghazali*, Beyrouth, 1958).

treatise, the part that deals with Light *in se.*[5] The order of importance should be reversed. The particular forms that Light symbolism adopted in the *Mishkāt* were based on Koranic and *Ḥadīth* expressions: thus they were considered irrelevant by Jewish and Christian readers, who could only see in them a topic peculiar to Muslim religion in which they were not directly interested.[6] Their main interest was in the philosophical premises underlying this symbolism, and for these the first part of the *Mishkāt* is essential.

For this reason, we shall in the following paragraphs concentrate on an analysis of al-Ghazzali's concept of Light and on his philosophical doctrine in this book, leaving aside his other works and doctrines.

The themes to be dealt with in the *Mishkāt* are presented by the author in the introductory pages in the form of a rhetorical question. This question concerns: (1) the interpretation of the Koranic verse, "God is the Light of Heavens and Earth";[7] and (2) the meaning and symbolic use of Light in connection with the words Niche, Glass, Lamp, etc., as they appear in this verse and in connection with the so-called "Veils ḥadīth."[8]

---

[5] The same attitude can be seen in the lengthy introduction given by Gairdner to his translation of the *Mishkāt* (n. 1).

[6] The spiritual conflict in medieval Europe, which arose from the ambivalent attitude towards Muslim and Jewish scholars, cannot be overemphasized: on the one hand, the impact of their cultural and scientific achievements was generally admitted and admired; on the other, the "dangers" which this very influence represented for the purity of the Christian faith had to be combated. This problem, as important as it is, has been touched upon only in passing by Ugo Monneret de Villard, *Lo studio dell' Islam in Europa nel XII e nel XIII secolo* (Citta del Vaticano, 1944), Studi e testi, 110. See my further comments on Monneret's approach in "Dante and Islam: History and Analysis of a Controversy," in *A Dante Symposium* (University of North Carolina Series in the Romance Languages and Literatures; Chapel Hill, 1965), p. 184. See also N.A. Daniel, *Islam and the West, The Making of an Image* (Edinburgh, 1960), and James Kritzeck, *Peter the Venerable and Islam* (Princeton Oriental Series, no. 23; Princeton, 1964).

[7] S. XXIV, 35: "Allah is the Light of Heavens and Earth. The similitude of His Light is, as it were, a Niche wherein is a Lamp: the Lamp within a Glass: the Glass, as it were, a pearly star" (Gairdner, p. 76, n. 1). On the traditional interpretation of this verse, see Regis Blachère, *Le Coran* (Paris, 1951), v. II, pp. 1003 and 1012.

[8] "Allah hath Seventy Thousand Veils of Light and Darkness; were He to withdraw them, the splendor of His Aspect would surely consume everyone who apprehended Him with his sight" (Afifi ed., p. 39; Gairdner, p. 76).

This divides the treatise into two main parts: one consists of an exegetical interpretation; the other deals with the use and meaning of Light symbolism. These two aspects, however, are not always consistently separated throughout the *Mishkāt*, although they are usually referred to as first and second part. Quite frequently, the reader finds that they can be distinguished only as two different levels of thought, with both using the same or similar arguments, though directed toward the different ends of exegesis and symbolism.

Al-Ghazzali's inquiry into the Koranic statement implies a process which we must understand as a search for the hidden reality of the Divine. *Ta'wīl*[9] is in this case a hermeneutical turn from the external (exoteric) form of the revealed expression (*ẓawāhir al-āyāt*) toward the inner meaning to which it refers (*mā yushīru ilayhi*). Here, al-Ghazzali's main concern is to establish the fact that he is not dealing with religious allegories, but divine realities.

In the *Mishkāt*, Light attributed to God is the expression of a reality. It is not a symbol, at least no more of a symbol than any word is a symbol. God is, in fact, Light in the real sense of the word. He is real—ontologically real—Light (*an-nūr al-ḥaqq*). In comparison to this reality, any other attribution of Light is a change in the philosophical significance we give to our words, it is a "going over," a meta-phor, indeed a pure metaphor (*majāz makhḍ*), precisely on the basis that the latter lacks this ontological reality (*lā ḥaqīqa lahu*).

In the second part of al-Ghazzali's inquiry, he turns to the relation, the ontological equivalence God-Light, with its symbolic expressions. The process by which this relation is manifested (*tamthīl*) should not be understood as an allegorization: the very fact that God is not metaphorically but really Light creates here an unbreakable connection between the symbol and the symbolized.[10]

From this point of view, al-Ghazzali's approach in his *Mishkāt* becomes a uniform one, and although it embodies the two different

---

[9] Afifi ed. p. 39; Gairdner, p. 75. On the concept of *Ta'wīl* see Henry Corbin, *Avicenna and the Visionary Recital* (New York, 1960), pp. 28 ff.

[10] To the study of symbolism in general and specifically to the problem of the connection between symbol and symbolized, al-Ghazzali dedicated some pages in the *Mishkāt* (Afifi ed. pp. 65 ff.; Gairdner, pp. 121 ff.) which likewise deserve special attention. See also Corbin, op. cit., p. 29, n. 9.

aspects imposed by the very nature of the statements under discussion, he is, in fact, only concerned with the reality of the Divine and Its manifestation through symbols. Both parts of al-Ghazzali's inquiry show intellectual attitudes which are worth noting. In the first, he is trying to adopt a hermeneutical method of Koranic interpretation based exclusively on empirical and rational premises. He is, in fact, applying the scholastic principle of "fides quaerens intellectum,"[11] and he bases a philosophical system of illuminative emanation on the revealed statement on God as Light. In the second, however, we witness rather a religious application of a philosophical doctrine, namely his doctrine of Light. Light, therefore, is the concept we must try to understand in order to grasp in its whole significance the basic religious and philosophical content of al-Ghazzali's *Mishkāt*.

Al-Ghazzali's treatment of light follows the syllogistic patterns of a logical presentation. It also attempts an inductive method: from the consideration of material light he proceeds to that of Light divine; in logical terms, we may say that his argumentation tries to analyze the concept of light from its use *lato sensu* by the majority to its use *stricto sensu* by a very select—initiated—minority.[12] This approach, however, is more apparent than real, for the concept of Light divine underlies his whole argumentation.

"The real Light is God... the name light attributed to other than Him is a pure metaphor and conveys no real meaning," says al-Ghazzali in the introduction to the first part.[13] From this point, al-Ghazzali's treatment of light is moved from the phenomenological and empirical to the metaphysical level, since with this statement he makes the divine Reality the term of reference in his exegetical analysis. God is no longer to be explained in terms based on the nature of material light, but, on the contrary, material light is the notion which must be explained on the basis of the Divine.

---

[11] His point of departure is given by faith which leads to the acceptance of revelation. From that point, al-Ghazzali's inquiry is based on reason only as applied to elucidate the revealed Truth. Ibn Rushd rightly pointed to this as being al-Ghazzali's method in the *Mishkāt*: "et apparet ex libris dedicatis eis quod reversus est in scientiis divinis ad opiniones Philosophorum et ex magis apparentibus de eis in hoc et verior in confirmatione eius est liber eius, appellatus Fenestra luminarium" (*Destructio*, f. 381b, as quoted by Quadri, op. cit., p. 133, n. 3.

[12] Afifi ed., p. 41; Gairdner, p. 79.

[13] Afifi ed., p. 41; Gairdner, p. 79.

In a most general way, light is defined as "an expression for that which is visible by itself and by which other things become visible."[14] In accordance with this definition, the essential aspect of light is the fact of "appearance." Thus it is a "relative term" (*'amr iḍāfī*), for it necessitates the notion of a second member to which it refers, a member to which things can become visible.

> Since the very essence of light is appearance to perception; and this perception is dependent upon the existence not only of light but of the perceiving eye as well; thus light is that which appears and causes to appear.[15]

In this respect both the percipient spirit (*ar-rūḥ al-bāṣira*) and the preceptible light (*an-nūr az-ẓāhir*) are equally necessary elements of perception. This "percipient spirit" is in fact the most important of the two and *qua talis* the only essential, for:

> the percipient spirit is that which perceives and through which the perception takes place.[16]

The importance granted by al-Ghazzali to the so-called "percipient spirit" is based on the fact that it must be considered in reality as the actualizing principle of all perceptions. In this respect and for the above mentioned reasons, al-Ghazzali must conclude, as he does, that in the world of material perception:

> the eye deserves more justly the name light than the so-called light,[17]

for the eye is the percipient spirit which apprehends and thus realizes the phenomenon of visual perception.

The importance of this argument becomes more obvious if we consider that with it al-Ghazzali has come to define light as an ontological relationship between percipient and the object of perception. From this point of view, only the percipient is essential, since he alone can establish this relationship.

Once this notion has been established, al-Ghazzali proceeds to apply the same principles of reasoning to the spiritual perception

---

[14] Afifi ed., p. 42; Gairdner, p. 81.
[15] Afifi ed., p. 42; Gairdner, p. 81.
[16] Afifi ed., p. 42; Gairdner, p. 81.
[17] Afifi ed., p. 48; Gairdner, p. 91.

of the intelligence (*'aql*).[18] It is worth noting that here al-Ghazzali shows himself unconcerned with the technicalities of a given terminology:

> Know that there is in the heart of man an eye ... which is called sometimes intelligence (*al-'aql*), some other times spirit (*ar-rūḥ*), and also at times human soul (*an-nafs al-insānī*). And let us overlook the various terms ... and let us call it intelligence (*'aql*) following the current terminology.[19]

In al-Ghazzali's opinion, the intelligence deserves the name light more than the phenomenal light and more even than the eye, for better than the other two it fulfills the essential prerequisites established for the concept of manifestation and perception.[20] In this connection, he speaks of the "seven defects" of the visual perception of the eye when compared with the spiritual perception of the intelligence. This comparison is only logical within the frame of al-Ghazzali's argumentation, since it does not correspond to a simple comparison of two things, each in its own nature and activity, but he is comparing material perception in terms imposed by the spiritual, as mentioned above. From this point of view, it is obvious that the eye cannot offer the same spiritual perfection as the intelligence; thus he concludes:

> that the intelligence is worthier of the name light than the eye. More-

---

[18] F. Jabre (op. cit. p. 102, n. 4) analyses al-Ghazzali's concept of *'aql* in the first chapter of the *Mishkāt*, and concludes that "Elle (the intelligence) est la réalisation plus parfaite de la lumière qui dérive de Dieu et qui constitue les êtres. Cela veut dire que tous les êtres sont eux-mêmes des vérités connues ou à connaître, et donc pour Ghazali, des lumières." Jabre has rightly pointed to the ontological character of Light in the *Mishkāt*. It is not clear, however, what Jabre means by the intentionality of being. If that refers to the *'aql* only, the statement does not seem acceptable. However, if it refers to God primarily, the beings are "des vérités connues" only; for, when dealing with the problem of existence, we refer to the metaphysical, not to the actual. What God does not know does not exist and never will exist, because He is the measure of Being.
For Ibn Gabirol's solution to a similar problem, see my "Ibn Gabirol's Metaphysic of Light," in *Studia Islamica* (1967).

[19] Afifi ed., p. 43; Gairdner, p. 83.

[20] The same argument was used two centuries later by the Christian theologian Thomas Aquinas (1225–1274): "Dicitur enim lux in spiritualibus illud quod ita se habet ad manifestationem intellectivam, sicut se habet lux corporalis ad manifestationem sensitivam. Manifestatio autem verius est in spiritualibus" (*Sent.* II, d. 13, q. i a. 2 ad 1).

> over, between the two there is such a difference that it should be said that it alone deserves this name.[21]

That is, intelligence alone deserves the name light metaphorically, for it is the actualizing principle of perception at the spiritual level and it transcends the natural shortcomings and necessary limits of the material.

From the consideration of the metaphorical uses of Light, al-Ghazzali goes on to the real object of the inquiry, which is, as we have seen, light *stricto sensu*, the real Light which is God alone:

> You know that He is Light and there is no Light beside Him; that He is every Light and that He is the universal Light.[22]

The singular aspect in al-Ghazzali's *Mishkāt* is not so much the fact of this identification of Light with God, but the very argument by which he substantiates his statement. The metaphorical uses of Light previously referred to were of phenomenological nature in the material perception, and of psychological in the intellectual perception. Now, the role of God as Light and His function in the divine perception and manifestation is ontological and refers to the basic and most elementary roots of Being, namely the very fact of its existence.[23] Therefore, we must bear in mind that, at this point, al-Ghazzali is not speaking of three different levels of perception and manifestation—or of light for that matter—since the divine Light as such necessarily includes the other two, for they also are covered by the notion of Being. Thus, these two, the material and intellectual lights, which were considered so far as being metaphors only, can now be considered real as a part of the ontological universality of the divine illumination.

Light "is summed up in appearing and manifesting."[24] This concept, which is intended as a summary of all preceding discussion

---

[21] Afifi ed., p. 48; Gairdner, p. 91.

[22] Afifi ed., p. 59; Gairdner, p. 109.

[23] In this respect Wensinck's summary of the *Mishkāt* as "un traité sur la lumière spirituelle—la seule lumière essentielle—qui émana de Dieu et qui se répand de Lui sur le monde céleste, puis sur le monde sublunaire jusque le cœur de l'homme" (op. cit., p. 10, n. 2) is clearly insufficient, yet it is usually accepted as definitive. For light there is not only intellectual light, nor does it presuppose the object of the divine illumination. Light is spiritual, but it has an ontological meaning that transcends the intellectual functions of the human intellect, namely, that it is light creative.

[24] Afifi ed., p. 55; Gairdner, p. 102.

and, at the same time, as an introduction to that of God-Light, must be understood in terms of the divine. For God now is considered as the Creator and Preserver of all:

> The real Light is He in whose hand lies Creation and its destiny; and He from whom first the illumination originates and then its preservation.[25]

There cannot be any doubt that in this respect, this very divine illumination is for al-Ghazzali the creative act of God. It is His illumination of the World into existence. Whatever remains beyond the range of this illumination does not exist.

> There is no darkness more intense than the concealment of the non-existing, for a dark thing is called dark because no one can perceive it . . . that which has no existence for others nor for itself, how could that rightly deserve (another qualification) than that of being the extreme of darkness?[26]

Therefore the "appearing and manifesting" must be referred to the coming out from the "darkness of not-being" into the light of existence through God's illuminative and creative act. By the same token, God's illumination is such that it does not require the pre-existence of an object, for it creates its own object. Thus the basis of the ontological relationship between God and the illuminated object is the very fact that it exists.

A further consideration of this argumentation is that the opposite of "darkness" is not "illumination" but "light," as the opposite of "not being" is not "creation" but "being." Thus we must also conclude with al-Ghazzali that:

> in contrast with it (darkness) is Being (*al-wujūd*) which is therefore light.[27]

This equation of being and light brings us to the most important points in al-Ghazzali's inquiry. On the one hand, there is the notion that only in God these two concepts of Being and Light find a complete and perfect—ontologically real—realization:

> Real Being is God most high; as the real Light is also God.[28]

---

[25] Afifi ed., p. 54; Gairdner, p. 102.
[26] Afifi ed., p. 55; Gairdner, p. 103.
[27] Afifi ed., p. 55; Gairdner, p. 103.
[28] Afifi ed., p. 55; Gairdner, p. 103.

On the other hand, there is also the concept that the ontological relationship of Being to its own existence is the most basic distinction in the Cosmos, since the reason for this distinction is to be found in the nature of Being itself:

> Being is itself divided into that which exists in itself and that which exists because of something else.[29]

God only is the real Light, Being in itself; that which exists because of something other than itself is the Cosmos in its entirety, the material and the spiritual Creation, which is brought into existence by God's creative illumination. In the metaphorical use of light we have seen that the illuminative process necessarily presupposed the object of the illumination; thus the relationship between the actualizing principle and the illuminated object was by necessity an accidental one, for it must be considered as additional to the complete essence and nature of both. In the divine action, there is, as we have mentioned above, no object of the illuminative act previous to the action; the very act of illumination creates its object and maintains it in existence, in so far and as long as the creative illumination lasts. Should it stop, the World would then return to the "darkness of not-being." In this process of creation and preservation, the relationship between Creator and created is not accidental, for it is based on the very essence of both. In the Creator, as God, there can be nothing accidental; in the created, everything can be accidental but its relation of dependence upon God.

Along with the problem of the philosophical nature of God's illuminative act, al-Ghazzali also tries to solve a problem which is common to all theologians of the divine creation, the problem of how one single act of the essentially One can produce multiplicity and diversity in the created. Al-Ghazzali has obviously chosen the doctrine of illuminative emanation. Thus this illuminative process must also be understood as ontological.

The divine creative illumination, therefore, is not an act proceeding from God in each individual case. It is a process of creative emanation, which only ultimately originates from and depends on God as its primal source. Not only do the lower degrees of being receive their illumination from the higher and more spiritual ones, but these too are to be considered as part of

[29] Afifi ed., p. 55; Gairdner, p. 103.

the ontological structure of the divine illumination which ends in God:

> These lights do have an order, but know that it does not form an infinite series, but rises to a primal fountain which is Light in and by Himself; on Him no light comes from any other source, and by Him all lights are effused according to their order.[30]

Al-Ghazzali is speaking here of the spiritual beings, of the "celestial lights," which must be understood as the intermediary agents in God's creative illumination. These orders may thus be called light; however, in the strictest sense they may be called light—creative light—only metaphorically, for they too do not possess light; they have only received it from the superior source, the only Light:

> The name of light attributed to any other than the first Light is a pure metaphor, since all others, if considered in themselves, have no light at all in themselves and by themselves.[31]

Al-Ghazzali's concept of the Cosmos is therefore one of a structure with an increasing luminosity based on the ontological proximity of the various orders of being to the primal source of Light :

> Thus the nearest one to the primal source is the worthiest of the name light for it is the highest in rank.[32]

In the terrestrial orders, this creative aspect of the divine illumination is no longer active. There we can only speak of Lamps which are lit, but not of lights in this sense, for they do not pass on the real aspect of the divine illumination, namely its creativity.

It is also within the frame of the above that we must understand the intellectual processes of man. They, too, are the product of the creative illumination of the Divine, as they partake of its most essential aspect, that of Being. They too proceed from the source of all, God, and they too must be considered as part of a structuring which goes from the lowest—the human—to the most superior of all which is God Himself.

> The whole world is filled with external lights of perception and internal ones of intelligence, . . . and the supernal ones are lit one from another;

---

[30] Afifi ed., p. 54; Gairdner, p. 101.
[31] Afifi ed., p. 54; Gairdner, p. 101.
[32] Afifi ed., p. 53; Gairdner, p. 99.

> . . . further all of them rise to the Light of Lights, their origin and primal source which is God alone.[33]

However, in the analysis of the intellectual processes, al-Ghazzali is considering the psychological problem from the point of view of its very existence, not of its mechanism alone. And thus God's illumination is also to be considered a creative one, similar to the illumination which created the World. This is the reason why all discussions of God as Light end with a reference to the ontological nature of God's illuminative action.

> Then they all rise to the Light of lights, their origin and primal fountainhead. This is God most high, the unique and only One, and all other lights are metaphorical. The Real is only His Light; everything is His Light. Nay, He is everything. Nothing beside Him has any essence (*huwīya*) save by metaphor. So therefore there is no light but His.[34]

In the normal intellectual process of man, the divine omnipresence resulting from His creative and preservative action is reflected in the paradox of mystical esoterism.

> Its obscureness (that of the knowledge of God) results from its very obviousness and its very elusiveness because of the splendor of its brightness. Thus glory be to Him who hides from His own creation through His very manifestation, and veils Himself from all through the splendor of His Light.[35]

The problem therefore is one of human perception of the divine reality, not the divine reality itself. Only God's gnostics, who rise "from the slopes of metaphors to the summit of the reality"[36] are able to perceive the ontological nature of the divine illumination:

> At the end of their ascent they see, as with the direct sight of eyewitnesses, that there is nothing in existence save God alone most high.[37]

---

[33] Afifi ed., p. 60; Gairdner, p. 111.
[34] Afifi ed., p. 60; Gairdner, p. 111.
[35] Afifi ed., p. 64; Gairdner, p. 120.
[36] Afifi ed., p. 55; Gairdner, p. 103.
[37] Afifi ed., p. 55; Gairdner, p. 104.

In this state of rapture, the mystics find themselves united to the very essence of God, through the ontological ties of light underlying their own existence :

> All (feeling for) plurality was driven away from them through (that of) the universality. They were drowned in the absolute unity.[38]

This is the reason why al-Ghazzali finds nothing objectionable *per se* in their mystical outbursts caused by their raptures: "I am the One Real," "Glory be to me! How great is my glory!" This is not a case of pantheistic religiosity:

> These mystics, after their ascent to the heaven of Reality confess that they have seen nothing in existence but the One Real.[39]

These mystics have only been granted the perception of the mystery of their own reality, without the usual veils imposed by the process of natural perception. In this sense, they are, as long as they exist, divine.

Al-Ghazzali's ontology of the Cosmos is in its fundamental form similar to other concepts also based on principles derived from emanational doctrines. It explains the divine supremacy and the World's dependence on God as essentially linked to the very concept of its existence. The World exists not only because of the primal divine act of creation, but because it constantly and essentially partakes of the divine existence, communicated to it through the act of creation and preserved by His continuous illumination. In this respect, the World was not made, it is eternally being made. On the other hand, the ontological nature of divine illumination on the intellectual processes of man introduces a new element into the doctrine of divine presence in the human, an element which is of the greatest importance for the mystical consciousness of the Divinity.

The possibilities of this doctrine for symbolic and allegorical applications are obvious. Al-Ghazzali himself could not resist the temptation to exploit them throughout his *Mishkāt*, and this, at times, makes it more difficult to reach fully the depth of his philosophical thought. Thus the *Mishkāt* is not a philosophical treatise in the usual sense. Symbolism and allegorical expressions

---

[38] Afifi ed., p. 57; Gairdner, p. 106.

[39] Afifi ed., p. 57; Gairdner, p. 106.

are too deeply imbedded in it. However, its doctrinal content and philosophical level of thought are an essential part of al-Ghazzali's speculation on Light. His doctrine of Light must be conceived in terms of the Divine and his doctrine of illumination as the creative action of the Divine and as the basis of the Cosmos' ontological dependence on God.

With this, al-Ghazzali stands in the same line of neoplatonic thought which contributed to the major change in Western medieval theology—the turn from the concept of the Cosmos as the result of God's creation only to that of the Cosmos as being a manifestation of God's most intimate life.

THE PROBLEMS OF THE *BOOK OF SONGS* IN THE LIGHT OF RECENT LINGUISTIC RESEARCH

W. A. C. H. Dobson
University of Toronto

SCHOLARLY opinion as to the nature, date and composition of the *Book of Songs* (詩 經) has altered radically since Legge addressed himself to these problems in the "Prolegomena" published with his translation in 1876.[1] This change has been mainly due to the work of Karlgren, Granet and Waley.[2] To Karlgren we owe a text and glosses, based on monumental phonetic researches in Archaic Chinese, so superior to the text available to Legge that Waley was led to conclude that "his translation [Legge's] serves no useful purpose".[3] To Granet we are indebted for what Waley has called a contribution that was "epoch-making",[4] that of seeing in the *Book of Songs* not the esoterically interpreted moralistic tracts of the Confucian tradition which Legge followed, but the folksongs and ballads which have familiar parallels in other cultures, parallels Granet saw in the light of the anthropology of his day. To Waley we owe the abandoning of the traditional arrangement and dating[5] of the *Book of Songs* and a translation which reveals their poetic rather than their didactic quality.

In any new look at the problems of the *Book of Songs*, certain facts, recently elucidated by research on its language,[6] which

[1] James Legge, *The Chinese Classics*, vol. IV, *The She King* (London, 1876; reprinted, Hong Kong University Press, 1960) pp. 1-182.

[2] See Bernhard Karlgren, *The Book of Odes* (Stockholm, The Museum of Far Eastern Antiquities, 1950), and "Glosses on the *Book of Odes*", *Bulletin of the Museum of Far Eastern Antiquities*, vols. XIV (1942), XVI (1944) and XVIII (1946); Marcel Granet, *Fêtes et chansons anciennes de la Chine* (Paris, 1911); and Arthur Waley, *The Book of Songs* (London, 1937).

[3] Waley, *op. cit.*, p. 337.

[4] *Ibid.*, p. 337.

[5] See, for example, his comments in *The Book of Songs* on the arrangement, p. 18, and on the dating, pp. 11 and 159.

[6] These researches are described in W.A.C.H. Dobson, "Linguistic evidence and the dating of the *Book of Songs*", *T'oung Pao*, vol. LI (1964), pp. 322-334; "Studies in the Grammar of Early Archaic Chinese: iii, the word *yan*", *T'oung Pao*, vol. LI (1964) pp. 295-321; and *The Language of the Book of Songs* (Toronto, 1968).

Granet and Waley have failed to take into account must, in the opinion of the writer, be given due weight.

The first fact is that the language of the four parts into which the *Book of Songs* is traditionally divided (the *Sung*, the two *Ya* and the *Kuo Feng*) is materially contrastive and that that contrast is clearly one of period. These periods can be roughly dated. The closest dating possible from the linguistic evidence is:

Chou Sung	11th-10th centuries B.C.
Ta Ya	10th- 9th centuries B.C.
Hsiao Ya	9th- 8th centuries B.C.
Kuo Feng	8th- 7th centuries B.C.

The second fact is that poems cite whole lines from other poems (215 pieces out of a total of 305 share identical lines).[7] Such citation is not promiscuous but follows a detectable pattern. The statistical trend is for *Ta Ya* to cite *Chou Sung*, *Hsiao Ya* to cite *Ta Ya*, and *Kuo Feng* to cite *Hsiao Ya*. If analysis is pressed beyond that of the citing of whole lines in identical form, the degree and patterning of borrowing becomes even more pronounced.[8]

The third fact is that, contrary to expectation, the four parts of the *Book of Songs* has a homogeneity of language, which, while preserving the peculiarities of periods, does not betray evidence of regional ("dialect") or social (for example, hieratic and demotic) differences.

From these facts certain inferences are possible. One is that the progression from the hymns of the *Chou Sung* to the love songs of the *Kuo Feng* is a chronological one. The temple hymns are in fact earlier than the love songs. Another is that the pattern of citation reveals lines of filiation and derivation and establishes a genetic connection between the earlier poems and the later poems. The love songs derive in some way from the temple hymns. A further inference is that the unity of the anthology, suggested by the homogeneity of its language, points to a central and common poetic tradition. The authors of the latest pieces are the self-conscious heirs of the earlier pieces.[9] If these inferences are

[7] A listing of these citations will be found in Appendix II, "The homogeneity of the poetic tradition in the *Book of Songs*", in *The Language of the Book of Songs*.

[8] For example, near-identical lines occur in such patterns as "The team of four so .... /Six reins so ....", where the changes are slight; or identical lines are re-arranged to secure a rhyme.

[9] "Self-conscious" in the sense that since they cite and echo whole lines from the earlier pieces, they were presumably familiar with them.

acceptable, the *Book of Songs* cannot be thought of as a miscellany of folk songs drawn from disparate sources mixed with liturgical pieces of uncertain date. The *Book of Songs* is the product of a unified tradition. Neither can the traditional division of the *Songs* into four parts be disregarded. These divisions each represent a period and a stage in the development of poetry; and this is attested by innovations and developments in genre, in prosody and in the range of authorship, so that the chronological arrangement of the *Songs* is not only attested by linguistic evidence, but supported by a recognizable development in poetics, in types and in techniques.

If, therefore, we assume that the pieces of the *Book of Songs* can be placed in historical and chronological sequence and that a generic connection can be shown to exist between them, it is possible to build a theory of the beginning and evolution of poetry in China from the eleventh to the seventh centuries B.C.

In such a view, the earliest poetry is in the *Chou Sung*. The *Chou Sung* are hymns of invocation and confession addressed to the royal ancestors and recitals to the gods of deeds of valor, present and past. Other pieces celebrate the presence of vassals and feudatories at the ceremonies, songs of welcome addressed to them, and songs of fealty addressed by them to the king. Much light is thrown on the nature of these pieces by a consideration of the religious and social context in which they were produced.

Kingship in early China was sacerdotal. The Son of Heaven—the vice-regent on earth of the deities, the dead kings—worshipped his ancestors, invoking their "virtue" for "all under Heaven". The *mana* of the gods ensured the harmonious succession of the year in its seasons and the fecundity of man and beast, and brought society into harmonious accord as one large family under its priest-king, the "father and mother" of his people. The priest-king was kept in a courtyard in the central position of which were the Royal Shrines.[10] To the rear was his palace and harem, and in the fore-court of the Royal Shrine he held court. In the court ceremonies, part worship, part levee, the king invoked his royal ancestors, received and rewarded his feudatories and vassals and governed his kingdom.

[10] See the plan of the palace, temple and courtyards of the kings of early Chou in W.A.C.H. Dobson, *Early Archaic Chinese* (Toronto, University of Toronto Press, 1962), p. 233.

An inscription[11] preserves a description of these sacred ceremonies. Before dawn, the Chief Ministers ceremonially prepare the king in his palace and lead him to the Ancestral Temple. Victorious generals appear at the Main Gate and are summoned to the Great Court and present their captives. The captives are sacrificed. The king receives reports of the campaign in the Center Court and then proceeds to the Ancestral Temple and sacrifices to his ancestors. A feast is given to the assembled vassals, and the generals are rewarded.

Poetry first appears in China in the liturgy of these rituals, in the invocations to the ancestors and recitals to the gods of deeds of valor intoned at the sacrificial part of the ceremony, and in the songs of fealty and welcome sung at the ritual feasts which followed them.

If, therefore, the *Sung* (頌)—Legge's "sacrificial odes"—are in fact the liturgy of the Chou royal court ceremonies, part "religious", part "secular", we can arrange that liturgy by the part it plays in the ceremony, both the intercessory and sacrificial part of the ceremony held in the temple, and the audiences and royal entertainment part of the ceremony, held in the fore- and rear courts. This enables us to divide the *Chou Sung* by genre as follows:

1) In the Ancestral Temple

a) Hymns of worship to the departed kings (*Chou Sung* nos. 266, 267, 268, 272, 285 and 292)[12]

b) Hymns of personal intercession (especially those of Kings Ch'eng and K'ang) (*Chou Sung* nos. 271, 286, 287, 288 and 289)

c) Hymns of the fertility rites (*Chou Sung* nos. 275, 276, 277, 279, 281, 290 and 291)

d) Hymns of dynastic prowess (*Chou Sung* nos. 270, 293, 294, 295 and 296)

---

[11] See "Inscription No. 14" in *Early Archaic Chinese*, pp. 226-233.

[12] The numbering of the songs follows that of the system used in the *Harvard-Yenching Institute Sinological Index Series*, Supplement No. 9, *A Concordance to Shih Ching* (Tokyo, 1962), and by Karlgren; that is, serially from 1 to 305, as in the Mao text.

2) In the Royal Courts
   a) Songs of welcome to vassals
   (*Chou Sung* nos. 278, 280, 282, 283 and 284)
   b) Songs of fealty addressed to the king
   (*Chou Sung* nos. 269, 273 and 274)

This liturgical poetry has certain poetic characteristics. It is rhythmical but either unrhymed or loosely rhymed. The hymns are for the most part short, rarely exceeding twenty or so lines. The use of simile or metaphor is rare and somewhat obvious.[13]

The language of this liturgical poetry is, from a linguistic point of view, of a piece with the language of the early Western Chou bronze inscriptions. The language, frequently the phrasing, and occasionally a rhyme scheme of the inscriptions are in fact so close to the *Sung* hymns that it is possible that they are of common authorship. The inscriptions are frequently signed by the "recorders" who composed them, and it is possible that these recorders composed the hymns of the temple liturgy. If this is so, China's first poets were the temple and court "recorders", the *tso-ts'ê* (作冊) "makers of writings".

In summary, the earliest poetry in China known to us is from the liturgy of the royal court and temple. It was probably the work of the *tso-ts'ê*, the recorders of the court. Compared with the poetry of the centuries which followed, it is crude in prosody and primitive in poetic device. But it is classic in the sense that the poetry of the *Ya* and *Kuo Feng* recognizably develops from it.

When we turn to the *Ta Ya* period, we find that its pieces have an affinity with those of *Chou Sung* and are recognizably poems developed on classic themes, but with certain innovations in language, prosody and genre.

In the matter of genre, the *Ta Ya* period, has:

1) Hymns of worship to the departed kings
   (*Ta Ya* nos. 235, 236, 240 and 244)
2) Hymns of dynastic and feudal prowess
   (*Ta Ya* nos. 237, 238, 241, 250, 259, 260, 261, 262 and 263)

---

[13] See, for example, *Chou Sung* no. 278, where the simile is explained : "Flocks of egrets in flight, / Over the west moat, / Guests arrive and take their place, / Giving a similar impression". The only other simile in *Chou Sung* is that of the free-flying warbler and the immobile king in no. 289.

3) Hymns of the fertility rites
(*Ta Ya* nos. 242 and 245)
4) Songs of fealty and welcome
(*Ta Ya* nos. 239, 243, 246, 248, 249, 251 and 252)
5) Songs of protest
(*Ta Ya* nos. 253, 254, 255, 256, 257
258, 264 and 265)

These genre are very close to those of the *Chou Sung* repertory; indeed, certain *Ta Ya* pieces might very aptly be called "variations on a *Chou Sung* theme", but there are important developments, the differences being almost as striking as the similarities.

The hymns of worship to the departed kings—the cult of Kings Wen and Wu—in the *Ta Ya* have a very close affinity with hymns of the same genre in the *Chou Sung*. They echo whole lines from them, and their themes are similar, but the poems are much longer and the treatment more full. The *Ta Ya* hymns introduce a new theme, the celebration of the queens of Wen and Wu and of their more remote ancestors. The tone becomes more heroic and less pietistic. There are no hymns of the personal intercession type, such as are found in the *Chou Sung*.

The hymns of dynastic prowess rehearsing feats of dynastic glory also have a close affinity with hymns in the *Chou Sung*—but they amplify the themes of the early hymns and introduce an epic and legendary element. Much is made now of the distaff side of the royal house, of its marriage connections with the late house of Shang, and of tracing the conferring of Heaven's mandate on earlier generations of the Chou house. Legendary elements begin to appear in the history of the royal house prior to its rule as Sons of Heaven. A note of justification creeps in for Chou's assumption of the mandate of Heaven. These later dynastic hymns treat early history in more detail than the earlier hymns do.[14]

Ta Ya no. 238, which praises the armies of Chou, is reminiscent of *Chou Sung* no. 293. But the *Ta Ya* introduces a new genre of glory celebrating—songs celebrating the conferring of charges upon Chou vassals as rewards for deeds of valor. These songs are but rhymed versions of the sort of dedicatory inscriptions that nobles, on receiving a charge from the king, had inscribed on

[14] This is also true of the later fertility hymns, see below. It recalls the dictum of the historian Ku Chieh-kang on the reconstruction of early history from early philosophical sources, "the earlier the historical projection, the later the source".

bronze sacral vessels. Such inscriptions describe the occasion of the charge, cite excerpts from its wording and list the royal gifts which accompanied it. *Ta Ya* nos. 259, 260, 261, 262 and 263 celebrate the conferring of charges upon vassals and follow quite closely the format of the inscriptions. Nos. 259 and 260 include the name of the composer. The *tso-ts'ê* who composed the dedicatory inscriptions usually appended their signatures to an inscription. The connection between the inscriptions and the early songs is so close here as to make it almost certain that they were of common authorship.

The hymns of the fertility rite in the *Ta Ya*, addressed, as are the earlier hymns, to the Prince of the Millet, show a tendency, noted in the later hymns to Kings Wen and Wu, to introduce legendary elements. Here the miraculous birth of Hou Chi first occurs, and the story of his founding the settlement at Pin, from where Liu the Stalwart was said to come. Thus, legend begins to develop a historical connection between the historical house of Chou and a culture hero, no hint of which is given in the early fertility hymns.

The songs of fealty in the *Ta Ya* celebrating the attendance of the vassals at court echo whole lines from their archetypes in the *Chou Sung* and recognizably stem from them, but their tone is increasingly secular, and their emphasis more on the pleasures of the moment than upon the solemn purposes which occasioned them and which is characteristic of the earlier songs.

In these songs of welcome, two new themes are introduced, the archery contests associated with the feasting, and the "impersonator", the medium who makes "lucky pronouncements". In the congratulatory songs addressed to the king, which are adulatory and flattering, a further clue to authorship occurs. In *Ta Ya* no. 252 the song ends with the line, "I have added these few verses,/To cap your song". It appears to be not a conventional song from a repertory but a song made for the occasion. These songs of fealty, wishing happiness to the king and calling down Heaven's blessing upon him, in both the *Sung* and *Ta Ya*, have much in common in sentiment and phrasing. But in the *Ta Ya* this form of song begins to include a note of admonition and complaint. *Ta Ya* no. 255 ostensibly a hymn extolling King Wen, is in reality a protest against present evil conditions put in the guise of an indictment pronounced by King Wen upon the Shang. *Ta Ya* nos. 253, 254, 256, 257, 264 and 265, clearly the work of courtiers, are more directly addressed to the king and in the place of conventional good wishes, contain admonition and complaint. *Ta Ya* no. 258 is a plaint addressed by the king to God on High. It is in these songs that the line "O the grief of the heart!" occurs, which later becomes a conventional line in the poetry of complaint of a more personal nature—the plaint of the anxious lover or the lonely soldier.[15]

Thus the songs of the *Ta Ya* adhere in genre and theme closely to the liturgy of the *Chou Sung* but introduce important innovations. The celebrating of deeds of prowess before the gods becomes more epic in form and begins to incorporate legendary material. A similar tendency is found in the fertility hymns. The feudal lords begin to celebrate their own prowess in the form earlier reserved for dynastic prowess. The congratulatory songs of king and guest begin to take on an admonitory and complaining tone and provide a form for protest.

These thematic developments are paralleled by developments in prosody. The early hymns are a single unity. There is no verse structure. They are quite short. In the *Ta Ya* the songs are very much longer, sometimes exceeding a hundred lines in length.[16] The songs tend to structuring in verse, shown by a change in the rhyme scheme, into verses of eight to twelve lines in length and by an architectonic sense shown in the occasional reiteration of a single line, as, for example, in *Ta Ya* no. 250, to mark the beginning of a new verse.

In the *Ta Ya* there is also an increased, but still sporadic, use of simile and metaphor. There are the vines of the gourd and the ramifications of the house of Chou in *Ta Ya* no. 237; the sturdiness of the oaks and the stateliness of the king in *Ta Ya* no. 238; reeds growing in profusion and a host of vassals ("brothers"), in *Ta Ya* no. 246; thickets of hazel and redthorn and profusion of blessing in *Ta Ya* no. 239; the stripped mulberry and a depleted people in *Ta Ya* no. 257; and the depth of a spring and the profundity of the heart's sorrow in *Ta Ya* no. 264. These are rather obvious and direct, but they are the forerunners of the ballad form, whose leading characteristic is the juxtaposition in very subtle ways of simile and reality.

[15] See, for example, *Hsiao Ya* nos. 183, 192, 197, 207, 233 and *Kuo Feng* nos. 26, 27, 63, 109 and 150.

[16] From the reign of King K'ang onwards, the bronze inscriptions also greatly increase in length. See Dobson, *Early Archaic Chinese*, pp. 129 ff.

The occurrence of the feudal charge in verse form, with its authorship acknowledged in the closing verse, suggests that the early poets were still the *tso-ts'ê;* but certain of the protest songs are of more personal authorship—or at least are represented as protestations by ministers of the court—and at least one is a poem written for the occasion, attesting the beginning of a tradition of "capping songs". The strictly liturgical function and priestly authorship of the *Chou Sung* begins to give way to court verse—though its forms and genre are still close to the original liturgy.

The *Ta Ya* poems are also characterized by formal shifts in the grammatical repertory. The *Ta Ya* has characteristic grammatical usages peculiar to itself. Linguistically, these shifts are historical in nature. This, taken together with the thematic and prosodic evidence, suggests a development of poetry, from the strictly liturgical to the use of liturgical forms by courtiers for other purposes.

If the *Ta Ya* can be thought of as songs in the classic manner, that is, in the manner of the *Chou Sung*, the songs of the *Hsiao Ya* period might be thought of as songs in the *Ta Ya* manner. Once again, the relationship in genre and the filiation by citation is close, but the *Hsiao Ya* songs betray evidence of further development and innovation. The principle innovation is the adaptation of a genre for the expression of more personal and private emotions.

In the *Hsiao Ya*, it is the genre of dynastic prowess and the songs of the sacrificial feast that are developed. There are no longer hymns to the departed kings. There are hymns of the fertility cult, though the cult itself takes on a new form. The *Hsiao Ya* might be divided by genre as follows:

1) Hymns of the fertility cult
(*Hsiao Ya* nos. 190, 209, 210, 211 and 212)
2) Songs of war
a) The Hsien Yün campaigns
(*Hsiao Ya* nos. 167, 168, 177 and 178)
b) Soldiers plaints.
(*Hsiao Ya* nos. 162, 169, 181, 204, 205, 206, 207, 208, 227, 230, 232 and 234)
c) The hunt
(*Hsiao Ya* nos. 179 and 180)
3) Songs of the sacrificial feast
a) General
(*Hsiao Ya* nos. 220 and 222)

b) Blessings on our lord and on our guests
(*Hsiao Ya* nos. 166, 170, 171, 172, 175,
213, 215, 216, 221 and 231)

c) Thanks to the lord
(*Hsiao Ya* nos. 173, 174, 176, 214 and 228)

d) Welcome
(*Hsiao Ya* nos. 161, 182 and 186)

e) The clan feast
(*Hsiao Ya* nos. 164 and 165)

4) Songs of complaint

a) of conditions generally
(*Hsiao Ya* nos. 183, 191, 192, 193, 194,
195, 196, 197, 198 and 224)

b) of particular people
(*Hsiao Ya* nos. 184, 185 and 223)

c) of personal anxieties
(*Hsiao Ya* nos. 163, 200, 202, 203, 219
and 233)

d) of unhappy women
(*Hsiao Ya* nos. 187, 188, 189, 199, 201,
218, 225, 226 and 229)

The hymns of the fertility cult in the *Hsiao Ya* bear many similarities to the hymns of this genre in the *Ta Ya* and *Chou Sung*. Certain of them, notably *Hsiao Ya* nos. 209, 210 and 211 are a veritable patchwork of citation and cliché from the earlier hymns. But the cult itself changes. The *Chou Sung* hymns are intercessions addressed to the Prince of the Millet or to the king. In the *Ta Ya* hymns, the epic of the Prince of the Millet is developed as of an epic celebration of an ancestor. In the *Hsiao Ya* hymns, the Prince of the Millet is no longer invoked. He is subsumed into the gods and ancestors generally and a deity called "the father of the fields". These hymns also invoke the "pious descendant", a kenning for the celebrant worshipping his ancestors.

The hymns of dynastic prowess of the *Chou Sung*, to which the *Ta Ya* adds hymns in a similar vein celebrating the deeds of feudal lords, are developed in the *Hsiao Ya* in a series of epic poems on the theme of the wars against the Hsien-yün. Two of these are in the heroic style (*Hsiao Ya* nos. 177 and 178) and celebrate the feats of individual generals, Chi-fu and Fang-shu, reminiscent of the manner of the dedicatory inscriptions of the feudal lords; but a third, *Hsiao Ya* no. 168, while celebrating the general Nanchung introduces a note of complaint, "In the king's business, there is much hardship"—a line reminiscent of "In the king's business, there is no reprieve" in *Hsiao Ya* 167 and often cited in the more personal poems which occur later.[17]

The fourth of the Hsien-yün songs (*Hsiao Ya* no. 167), though containing much citation and cliché from the epic hymns of prowess, is frankly one of complaint. Its emphasis is upon the price the armies are called upon to pay in the endless fighting with the Hsien-yün. This note on the hardships of campaigning becomes a theme of a whole cycle of poems on the soldiers' plaint.

In the songs of the sacrificial feast, the familiar clichés of welcome to guests and blessings on the lord recur, but the songs tend towards triteness and convention. Certain of them become mere drinking songs, and in *Hsiao Ya* no. 220 a note of admonition against the excesses and drunkenness at these feasts is found. This suggests that the feasts and the songs that accompanied them had degenerated very considerably from their original solemn purpose. In these songs of fealty, one theme, the antiphonal "Before I saw my Lord...", "Now that I have seen him..." is adapted to a new purpose. This is shown in *Hsiao Ya* no. 186, where the song of welcome to the guest, put into the mouth of a woman, introduces a note of erotic love. The "lucky guest" is no longer only a feudal lord paying court to an overlord, but one whose visit is welcomed by the ladies of the house. In the *Kuo Feng* this becomes a form of love song, and the lines "Before I saw my Lord...", "Now that I have seen him..." change from adulation to a feudal lord to the longings of a girl seeking the fulfillment of her love. The "lucky guest", originally the vassal partaking in religious ceremonial, becomes the lover of lovelorn women. The welcome song changes to a welcome of a more personal nature. Thus the songs of welcome and blessing of prince and feudal lord, of host and guest, turn into ballads of personal courting between lovers.

But the songs of the sacrificial feast, like the songs of prowess, provide too, a form for the airing of plaints, of conditions in general, of criticism of individuals, of complaints of a more personal nature and of personal sorrow. The clichés of joy, such as, "Happy be our prince", occur with complaints; in *Hsiao Ya* no. 219, "Happy be our prince,/May he not believe the slander". Finally, in the

[17] In soldiers' plaints, see *Hsiao Ya* nos. 162, 169 and 205; and in a more private plaint in *Kuo Feng* no. 121 (*Songs of the Court of T'ang*).

Hsiao Ya, complaint first appears in the voices of women, the deserted wife and neglected loved one.

In the *Hsiao Ya*, there is considerable development from the eight or twelve line verse of the *Ta Ya* epic form to the ballad form with its short verses, its opening simile, and the repetition of the opening simile with variations. For example, *Hsiao Ya* no. 181, "Wild geese in flight,/ Wings, a-rustling" (verse 1), "Wild geese in flight,/ Settling in the marsh" (verse 2), and "Wild geese in flight,/ Sad cries resounding" (verse 3). The simile, crudely stated in the *Ta Ya*, becomes a device for setting the entire mood of a poem and dominating its structure, as, for example, in *Hsiao Ya* no. 181 cited above, where the mood is that of a sense of desolation imposed by the separation of distance. In broad terms, the ballad form tends to develop as poetry becomes more personal. The gradual emergence of the strict ballad form, as, for example, *Hsiao Ya* nos. 181, 170, 221 and 186, anticipates the perfection of this form in the *Kuo Feng*.

Authorship in the *Hsiao Ya*, though unacknowledged (*Hsiao Ya* no. 177 attributed to "a friend of his father", is an exception), also shows certain changes. In the *Chou Sung* and *Ta Ya* the poets are the *tso-ts'ê* and intimate courtiers of the royal court. In the *Hsiao Ya*, there is much citation and drawing on forms from these earlier pieces, but the authorship is from a broader field—slighted courtiers, officers on campaign and the like, and (an innovation of the *Hsiao Ya*) the ladies of the courts.

The language of the pieces of the *Hsiao Ya* shows a historical progression in time from the *Ta Ya*. The linguistic evidence is given support by developments in genre, in poetic device, and in the range of authorship.

The *Kuo Feng* contains roughly one half of the poems of the entire anthology. The preponderant note is erotic. These are for the most part love songs far removed in theme and tone from the hymns and epics of the earlier tradition. The air is lyric—poetic conceit takes command over subject matter. Prosody is considerably more advanced in technique and device than in the earlier songs.[18]

[18] A matter noted by Karlgren, "The *Kuo Feng* is more advanced and perfected in its versification than the other three Shï king sections: it has fewer exceptions from the regular rhythmical pattern than they and a stricter riming, with fewer hedge rimes." "Tones in Archaic Chinese" *Bulletin of the Museum of Far Eastern Antiquities*, vol. XXXII (1960), pp. 113-142.

Most of the songs of the *Kuo Feng* are feminine in authorship, or at least are put into the mouths of women. They are songs which, in contrast to the hymns and songs of the *Chou Sung* which pertain to the royal temple and courts, belong more properly in the "rear apartments", the seraglios of the feudal courts. Yet despite this (or more probably because of it) echoes abound in cliché and theme, in citation and adaptation, from the earlier songs. The *Kuo Feng* authors were obviously familiar with, and built upon, the songs of the earlier tradition. Granet's theories to the contrary, most of the songs are aristocratic in theme and courtly in tone. They are almost certainly the work of the ladies of the courts, as tradition has always maintained them to be.[19]

Take, for example, the songs of welcome to royal brides, of the Princess Chi (*Kuo Feng* no. 24, *Songs of the Duke of Shao's Court*), of Lady Meng Chiang (*Kuo Feng* no. 83, *Songs of the Court of Cheng*), of the Lady of Ch'i (*Kuo Feng* nos. 104 and 105, *Songs of the Court of Ch'i*), of the Lady Jen of Chung and of Princess Chuang Chiang (*Kuo Feng* nos. 28 and 57, *Songs of the Court of Wei*).[20] These songs celebrate princely marriages by describing the splendors of the brides' cortege and equipage. In so doing they echo whole lines and clichés from the earlier heroic songs which delight in descriptions of nobles' chariots and accoutrements. Thus, "sash gems tinkling", in *Kuo Feng* no. 83 occurs also in *Kuo Feng* no. 130, a welcome song to a noble. The description of the sash gems is an echo from *Kuo Feng* no. 134; "The teams of four stallions so tall" in *Kuo Feng* no. 57 is a quotation from *Ta Ya* no. 259 with echoes in *Ta Ya* no. 260; "The teams of four blacks so stately/ Dangling reins in such profusion" and "Bamboo awning, scarlet leather" have echoes in *Hsiao Ya* nos. 163, 178 and 214 and in *Ta Ya* no. 261. These are common clichés in the early songs describing the corteges of the princes. These *Kuo Feng* songs are

[19] See, for example, the attributions in the Mao Prefaces, upon which much of the traditional view of the *Book of Songs* is based. The dating of the *Book of Songs* at which one arrives by modern linguistic criteria is also curiously close to the traditional dating suggested by the Prefaces. As to the courtly origin of the *Kuo Feng* pieces, Maspero has long held that "ce ne sont pas les pièces populaires elles-mêmes: le seul fait qu'elles sont toutes écrites dans le même dialecte, de quelque principauté qu'elles viennent, le prouve bien; mais elles les imitent de près"—*La Chine Antique* (reptd. Paris, 1955), p. 356.

[20] The *Songs of the Court of Wei*, include those of P'ei, Yung and Wei proper. The spelling "Wei" distinguishes this state from Wey, another state altogether, and from the court of which songs are also included in the *Kuo Feng*.

certainly not folk songs originating in the countryside, but the songs of court ladies, courtly both in theme and language, patterning and echoing earlier court songs of nobles and their prowess. Neither are such songs "regional" in any sense other than that the courts of the Dukes of Shao, Cheng, Ch'i and Wei are separated by geography. These courts produced similar songs on similar themes in similar language unaffected by local variation, and we must suppose them to be the products of a class—of the court ladies, who shared a common poetic tradition and language.

Kuo Feng no. 28 (*Songs of the Court of Wei*), has the line "This young lady [*tzu*] is going to be married", a line common to a number of these songs and of particular interest because of the peculiar usage of the collocation *chih-tzu*, "this young lady/lord". The use of *chih* as a demonstrative here is archaistic and in the *Book of Songs* occurs only in this collocation. The earliest occurrence of *chih tzu* is in "This young lord is going on a campaign" (*Hsiao Ya* no. 179), and "These young lords are going afar off" (*Hsiao Ya* no. 229). "This young lady is going to be married" is clearly an adaptation from this line. The songs celebrating a noble bridal cortege which have this line are *Kuo Feng* nos. 6 and 9 (*Songs of the Duke of Chou's Court*), *Kuo Feng* no. 12 (*Songs of the Duke of Shao's Court*), which also echoes the line "a hundred carriages, rumbling" from *Ta Ya* no. 261 (in *Kuo Feng* no. 22, the line evokes the image of the royal marriage in a song bemoaning neglect by the ladies of the seraglio); and in *Kuo Feng* no. 156 (*Songs of the Court of Pin*). Thus, songs from several different centers cite an identical line, a line which is but the echo of a line from earlier court poetry.

The complementary lines "Before I had seen my lord...", "But now that I have seen him..." first appear in a conventional form of a song of fealty from a vassal to an overlord, and describe the subject's trepidation and fear before, and reassurance after, seeing his lord (see for example *Hsiao Ya* nos. 168, 173, 176, 217 and 228).[21] These lines occur in the *Kuo Feng*, adapted to love songs

[21] Waley, introducing his translation to *Kuo Feng* no. 176, says, "The next piece is a marriage song adapted to celebrate not the meeting between bride and bridegroom but an audience given by a feudal superior to his vassal. No doubt most of the other marriage songs in this book were often used in the same way; but this is the only one in which the wording *has manifestly been altered to fit the new purpose.*" *The Book of Songs*, p. 104 (The italics are mine). All the evidence points to the conclusion that the "adaptation" was quite the other way around. Similarly,

which describe a lady's doubts and hesitations before meeting her loved one, and reassurance and joy on meeting him, as, for example, in *Kuo Feng* no. 10 (*Songs of the Duke of Chou's Court*); *Kuo Feng* no. 4 (*Songs of the Duke of Shao's Court*); *Kuo Feng* no. 90 (*Songs of the Court of Cheng*); *Kuo Feng* no. 116 (*Songs of the Court of T'ang*); and *Kuo Feng* nos. 126 and 132 (*Songs of the Court of Ch'in*). It will be observed that this theme as with other *Kuo Feng* themes is geographically very widely distributed.

Further examples of derivation for the songs of the *Kuo Feng*, of the adaptation of earlier modes for later purposes, of the citation of and echoes from earlier genre, in short of the evolution of the love ballad from earlier court songs, could be pursued at great length. Suffice it here to draw attention briefly to the language of those love songs praising noble lovers by describing their court dress and regalia, which echoes the phrases of, and evinces the same delight in, such description in the earlier epics of prowess of the nobles; and to draw attention to the plaints of lovers, which echo the line "O! the sorrows of the heart"—a line which derives from the early hymns of admonition.

In general it can be said that for the most part the love songs of the *Kuo Feng* are not really intelligible except in the light of the songs and hymns of the *Sung* and *Ya*, which provide their vocabulary and motifs, and upon which, quite clearly, they are modelled. In a division of the *Kuo Feng* by genre, very few pieces are not referable by adaptation and citation to earlier pieces.

The multiplicity of borrowing and citation, and the process by which later poems are built upon earlier ones in the *Book of Songs* is reminiscent of the practice in Medieval Chinese poetry of *tai* (代) "substitution", whereby a poet retains the structure, rhyme scheme or even a whole line of a poem of an admired master, but by deft substitutions in the rest of the poem creates a new one.

From first to last, the *Songs* were composed to be sung. We may suppose a very considerable development in music from the eleventh to the seventh centuries B.C.; from the intoning of the solemn liturgy of the temple in the early hymns, to the more

commenting on *Ta Ya* no. 236, Waley says, "The narrative songs developed out of lyric poems in which each verse deliberately echoes the last, and there are considerable survivals of this structure in the long ballads" (*op. cit.*, p. 333). Again, all the evidence is that the reverse is true. The "long ballads" (in the instance cited by Waley—an early dynastic hymn) preceded the lyrics. The ballads, in fact, derive from the hymns.

personal lyric music for the expression of individual sorrow and happiness in the later ballads. At all events, the song structure, while maintaining a four beat measure throughout, changes considerably, and this suggests a change in the form of its musical accompaniment. Writing of a later period, Professor David Hawkes has said, "It would be no exaggeration to say that every new verse-form which emerged derived its existence from the evolution of some new song-form, and that this in turn was the result of some new musical development".[22]

In the *Book of Songs*, it is in the *Kuo Feng* that the ballad form, with its repetitions and artifices, its sophisticated diction and rhyming, its skillful use of simile to set a mood, is developed to a fine art. The transition is one from the general to the personal. The evolution of this form is clearly traceable from the earlier songs and pieces, but in sophistication the *Kuo Feng* greatly surpasses them.

The traditional division of the *Kuo Feng* by regions of provenance is not supported by linguistic evidence of regional differences in language. The *Kuo Feng* language, though recognizably later than the language of the rest of the anthology, has a homogeneity in itself, and, as studies of genre and citation show, the songs of the *Kuo Feng* have a genetic connection with the earlier songs and hymns. This is not to say that the regional differences of the traditional division of the *Kuo Feng* is meaningless. The *Kuo Feng* may well be love ballads sung in and gathered from regional courts, but their composers—the ladies of the royal courts—despite the broad geographical distribution of the courts, evidently shared a common language and a common tradition of song making—just as they shared common kinship and custom as a class, as the women of the aristocracy.

It is not necessary to suppose that the ladies of the courts of the 7th century B.C., intricately related to each other as they were by aristocratic marriage alliances, had any deep roots in local ethnic groups or composed their songs in a local dialect. More in keeping with the evidence is the homogeneity of the ballad tradition, passed among the women from court to court. It is true that certain songs contain topical references, but this is not unnatural. Regional references are not evidence of regional dialect.

Two problems should be briefly commented upon here. The first

[22] See David Hawkes, *Ch'u Tz'ü: Songs of the South* (Oxford, 1959), p. 5.

is the suggestion by Granet that the *Kuo Feng* songs are the folk libretti of the mating ceremonials of the countryside, that is, are folk and local in origin, an interpretation which has influenced Waley considerably in his translations.[23] It is difficult, in view of the linguistic evidence, to see that this suggestion has any foundation. Apart from the clearly courtly and aristocratic themes of noble marriages and their attendant ceremonies, the songs of illicit love, with the fear of disclosure, paternal displeasure, scandal and reprimand which they betray are hardly consonant with the mass-mating rites of spring and autumn of the common folk. It is true that references are made in the *Kuo Feng* to such ceremonies, to the accessibility of village women and the like (though such references are not common), these may just as well originate in seraglio gossip as in the countryside. The most forceful evidence against folk origin, however, is not theme but language. Here it is quite clear; the language of the love songs of the *Kuo Feng* is of the court, and has demonstrable lines of filiation with other and earlier court poetry.

The second is the problem of the moralistic and allegorical interpretation of the *Book of Songs*. The use by the early Confucians of the *Book of Songs* as an exemplar of Confucian morals began very soon after the completion of the anthology. This tradition is a very early one. It is easy to see how the piety of the hymns, exemplifying the spirit of the kings of early Chou—already a utopian age in Confucian eyes—could be turned to moral advantage. It is not difficult to see how, for the tutors of the sons of the aristocracy, the songs of admonition and reproach of a slightly later date might serve a cautionary purpose. But it is not at all clear how the later love ballads could be thought to contain moral precepts or form part of a scripture for puritanical Confucians. Indeed, certain of the esoteric interpretations of such songs by Han scholiasts strike us as ludicrous. But did this strike the early Confucians as ludicrous? Scholars, so close in time to the compilation of the anthology, may well have seen, more clearly than we, the genetic connection of the late ballads and the early hymns, and, indeed, once the connection is pointed out, it is difficult to

[23] See footnotes 3, 4 and 21. Waley does, however, say, "I think that too many of the songs have been explained by M. Granet as being connected with a festival of courtship in which the girls and boys lined up on opposite sides of a stream—a type of festival well-known in Indo-China" (*op. cit.*, p. 29).

read the late ballads without seeing underlying them, as though in a palimpsest, vestiges of the early hymns. And might this not have given rise to a theory of esoteric interpretation?

Thus, it is possible to view the *Book of Songs* as a chapter in literary history, the first chapter, providing exemplars of the first five centuries of poetic writing. And if the conclusions drawn from the linguistic evidence set out in the body of this article are valid, then we can trace, in the evolution of language, diction, theme and genre, the development of Chinese poetry from the simple and primitive pieces of the temple and court liturgy, by way of the courtly verse of the nobles, to the sophisticated love songs of their ladies. A transition from hymn to song, from priestly to popular authorship, from the expression of religious feeling to the release of more secular passions, from the sacred to the profane, from the epic to the lyric.

STORY AND HISTORY: OBSERVATIONS ON GRECO-ROMAN RHETORIC AND PHARISAISM*

by Henry A. Fischel
Indiana University

TEXTS CITED

AdRN: Aboth de Rabbi Nathan, ed. S. Schechter; reprinted, N.Y. 1944

BT: Babylonian Talmud (any edition)

"Cynicism": H. A. Fischel, *Cynicism and the Ancient Near East*, American Academy For Jewish Research, New York–Jerusalem, forthcoming

D.L.: Diogenes Laertius, *Vitae Philosophorum*, 2 vols., ed. H. S. Long, Oxford 1964

P.A.: Pirqe Aboth, as in Mishna (any edition)
In parentheses: Chas. Taylor, *Sayings of the Jewish Fathers*,[2] 2nd ed., Cambridge 1897

P.T.: Palestinian (Jerusalem) Talmud (Vilna or Krotoshin, as indicated)

P.W.: Pauly, Wissowa (Kroll, Mittelhaus, Ziegler), *Realencyclopaedie der classischen Altertumswissenschaft*, Stuttgart, 1894— (in progress)

R.: (Midrash) Rabba (any edition); for Leviticus Rabba: ed. M. Margulies, 5 vols., Jerusalem 1953–1960 (Gen. R., Deut. R., not quoted)

Tos.: Tosefta, ed. M. S. Zuckermandel; reprinted, Jerusalem 1962

W.H.: C. Wachsmuth, O. Hense, *Joannes Stobaeus, Anthologium*, 5 vols.; reprinted, Berlin 1958

Arrian-Epictetus, Aristotle, Athenaeus, Cicero (and *Auctor ad Herrenium*), Dio of Prusa, Hippocrates, Julian, Juvenal, Ovid (and *Ad Liviam*), Philo, Plato, Plutarch (and *Ad Apollonium*), Quintilian, *Scriptores Historiae Augustae*, Seneca, Varro, Xenophon: the texts as in *The Loeb Classical Library*, London, are sufficient for the purposes of this essay.

THE historian who wishes to utilize ancient literature for the reconstruction of Greco-Roman and Hellenistic Near Eastern history faces formidable difficulties indeed, for in any inquiry of

* This is the complete text of a paper the major parts of which were read at the Eighty-first Meeting of the American Historical Association in New York, December 29, 1966, at a Symposium on "The Impact of Hellenistic Civilization on the Pharisees." The terms Hellenistic and Greco-Roman are synonymous in this essay.

this sort the wide diffusion of Greco-Roman rhetoric in ancient sources must be recognized and accounted for. Rhetoric, whether in its oral or written crystallization, was apt to color historical reports and even to create, in its own way, non-history.

The classical and Hellenistic periods of both Greece and Rome witnessed a number of vital functions carried on in this medium. Thus, in his work on *The "Art" of Rhetoric*, Aristotle—who functions here as a summarizer rather than an innovator—distinguishes rhetoric in its use for literature, . . . *graphikē* . . ., and for debate, . . . *agōnistikē* . . ., and, apparently subdividing the latter, for public use, . . . *dēmēgorikē* . . ., i.e., politics, and in court, . . . *dikanikē* . . ..[1] Philosophical and religious argument from the Sophists on was increasingly expressed in this medium. The propagation of new ideas and the preservation of proven traditional values were equally the task of rhetoric. It drew disciplines such as literary criticism, grammar, and exegesis, both critical and uncritical, both new and old, into its orbit. Precisely the same situation again prevailed in Roman culture. The writer, the teacher-philosopher, the critic-grammarian, the politician, and the lawyer-administrator—amazingly often combined in the same person—expressed themselves in this literary medium. Precisely the authors in whose works the great majority of parallels to Pharisaic stances are found, are prominent examples: Cicero (106–43), Seneca (5 B.C.–65), Dio of Prusa (Chrysostom, 40–after 112), Plutarch (c.46–after 120), and Aelianus (c.170–235)—the latter two are also priests[2]—but similarly also Philo (30 or 22 B.C.–c.45) and Paul (8–68 ?).

Apart from its style and technique, Greco-Roman rhetoric[3]

---

[1] III.xii.1, 1413b. In I.ii.7, 1356a, Aristotle discusses the close relationship between rhetoric and the disciplines of dialectic and ethics.

[2] For a brief survey of their political and administrational functions see *The Oxford Classical Dictionary*, 1964. Epictetus (c. 55–135), who should be on this list, was the slave of a secretary (*a libellis*) of Nero and Domitian, Epaphroditus, but in his later life he merely taught philosophy. Cf. further E.P. Parks, *The Roman Rhetorical School as a Preparation for the Courts under the Early Empire* (Johns Hopkins University Studies in History and Political Science, 63), Baltimore 1945.

[3] The modern literature on this subject is very large. Apart from P.W., "Rhetorik," Suppl. VII, 1940, 1039–1138, and standard histories of literature, such as W.v. Christ, W. Schmid, and O. Staehlin, *Geschichte der griechischen Literatur...*, 7 vols., Munich 1920—; H.J. Rose, *A Handbook of Greek Literature...*[4], London 1951; M. Schanz, C. Hosius and G. Krueger, *Geschichte der roemischen Literatur*, 5 vols., Munich 1914–35, under revision; J. Wight Duff, *A Literary History of Rome...*[3], 2 vols., New York 1960-64; these are among the more important titles

is characterized by its use of a great variety of larger literary forms, such as oration, diatribe,[4] essay, symposium, epistle, biography and others. These literary forms are composite and consist of a combination of a great many smaller independent literary (or oratorical) genres and a great many social concepts, values, and ideas. Moreover, rhetorical stances heavily penetrated other literary forms, such as aretalogy, martyrology, history, and romance, even poetic (metered) forms, such as comedy and satire.

In the Roman Age the rhetor-writer less frequently consulted original works and was no longer an adherent of any particular philosophical school—though he might choose one as the preferred target of his attacks.[5] He used ready-made handbooks, anthologies and collections of various kinds, including works on the lives and opinions of the philosophers (*bioi*, *vitae*, *memorabilia*, *apomnēmoneumata*), gnomologies, and even school exercises, many of which were created for the specific purpose of aiding the rhetor.[6] In all probability he did not neglect to consult the rhetorical production of others.[7] It is this entire immense phenomenon which is here

---

(that also will open up the entire field): E. Norden, *Die Antike Kunstprosa*[5], Darmstadt, reprinted 1958; G.M.A. Grube, *The Greek and Roman Critics*, Toronto 1965; J.F. Dobson, *The Greek Orators*, London 1919; B.A. van Groningen, *La composition littéraire archaïque grecque...*, Amsterdam 1958; W.R. Roberts, *Greek Rhetoric and Literary Criticism*, New York 1928; M.L. Clarke, *Rhetoric At Rome*, London 1953.

[4] In modern literature this term is occasionally used for rhetoric in general but actually signifies a Cynico-Stoic treatment of a theme by means of harangue, dialogue, wit, and continued argument, later used by all popular moralists as well as by Philo, Paul and Tertullian; see P. Wendland, *Die hellenistisch-roemische Kultur in ihren Beziehungen zu Judentum und Christentum*[2,3], Tuebingen 1912; A. Oltramare, *Les origines de la diatribe romaine*, Lausanne 1926 (defines this term too narrowly); Rudolf Bultmann, *Der Stil der paulinischen Predigt und die kynisch-stoische Diatribe*, Goettingen 1910.

[5] This accounts for the divergence in ancient as well as modern opinions on rhetorically inclined writers as to their adherence to a particular philosophical school, as, for example, on Cicero, Musonius, Demetrius, Dio, Epictetus and others. Cf. the differing classifications of the same authors with D.L., D.R. Dudley, *A History of Cynicism*, London 1937, and Max Pohlenz, *Die Stoa*[2], 2 vols., Goettingen 1955–59.

[6] Cf. E. Ziebarth, *Aus dem griechischen Schulwesen*[2], Leipzig 1914, and *Aus der antiken Schule*[2], *Kleine Texte...* 65, Bonn 1913. D. Clark, *Rhetoric in Graeco-Roman Education*, New York 1957.

[7] This general condition of prose literature makes it rather incongruous to demand from Near Eastern writers more than from their Greco-Roman counterparts, and to accuse Aristeas, Philo, Paul or Clement of philosophical eclecticism.

called rhetoric—a use of the term in the widest of all its possible meanings.

In the rhetorical creations of the Hellenistic and Roman worlds, the figure and concept of the ideal Sage, the *sophos* or *sapiens*, plays a prominent part. He is most often a founder of a philosophical school or of a scientific discipline, or a lawgiver or creative statesman. Through his actions and words, wisdom—i.e., virtue, the use of reason, and closeness to nature—is taught in an exemplary manner. His courage, presence of mind, wit, and incisiveness are proverbial, and his personality attracts disciples and converts them to his way of life. Socrates is often expressly named as the principal model for this type of Sage, and in his image many other ancient founder-sages make their appearance in rhetoric:[8] thus Antisthenes, Diogenes, Crates, the youthful Zeno (all supposedly founders of different shades of Cynicism); Cleanthes, Chrysippus and Aristippus (all frequently treated as Cynics);[9] to a lesser degree and, probably later, Thales or all the Seven Sages;[10] further, Pythagoras, Democritus, Heraclitus, Aesopus,[11] Theodorus the Cyrenaic, Pericles, and some others.[12] Finally, even for Aristotle and some of Plato's successors, especially Xenocrates, a similar tradition began to develop.[13]

[8] The impact of Socrates seems to have reshaped Greek biography, according to A. Dihle, a recent contributor in a long list of predecessors: *Studien zur griechischen Biographie*, Goettingen 1956 (against F. Leo, *Die griechisch-roemische Biographie nach ihrer literarischen Form*, Leipzig 1901). Rhetorization is indicated in invented dialogues, as, for example, Satyrus' Euripides *vitae* (*Pap. Ox.* 1176, ed. F. Leo, *Nachrichten Goettinger gel. Ges.* 1912, 273ff.). Since Antigonus of Carystus (*fl.* 240 B.C.), portrayal of the person and personality became more important than technical concerns. The *ēthē* of the hero is illustrated by his *praxeis.*, see U.v. Wilamowitz-Moellendorff, *Antigonos von Karystos, Philol. Untersuch.* VI, Berlin 1881. Cf. also D.R. Stuart, *Epochs of Greek and Roman Biography*, Berkeley 1928.

[9] See "Cynicism" 5.5. Zeno is the founder of Stoicism, Aristippus, of the Cyrenaic school of philosophy.

[10] Bruno Snell, *Leben und Meinungen der Sieben Weisen*[3], Tuebingen 1952.

[11] The Aesopus Romance, ed. Ben Edwin Perry, *Aesopica I*, Urbana 1952, is almost entirely rhetorical *sophos* material, set in the merest pretext of an aretalogical framework.

[12] See "Cynicism" 5.5f.

[13] I. Duering, *Aristotle In the Ancient Biographical Tradition*, Goeteborg 1957. Olof A. Gigon, "Interpretationen zu den antiken Aristotelesviten," *Museum Helveticum* 15, 1958, 146–193. In the Greek anecdote on the Sage (to be discussed below) Plato is a negative figure who, in syncrisis with Diogenes, usually loses the battle of wits and herein resembles Shammai of the Hebrew anecdote: D.L. VI. 24–26; 40 (but cf. 41); 58. Similarly in the Aristippus cycle: II.69; 78; 81.

This concept of the *sophos* finally encompassed not only reason, closeness to nature, and virtue, but also a certain type of cosmopolitanism (or, rather, universalism),[14] *philanthropia*, and even a strong approximation of monotheism,[15] contributed mainly by the Cynics and Stoics. Platonic and Pythagorean elements in rhetoric provided ideas of immortality. This new synthesis was characterized by the centrality of ethics, and in it the original contributions of the schools lost their technical character and even their identity (except when they were expressly quoted as the opinion of a specific school). This synthesis included the ennoblement and refinement of the ancient customs and myths through reinterpretation, and in spite of its cosmopolitanism, it was not hostile to a glorification of *patria*. With few exceptions, it was non-dualistic, i.e., it neither condemned matter as such nor apotheosized spirit or soul *per se*. This rhetorical "system" seems thus superficially to resemble the system connected with the name of the Pharisees and their Tannaitic successors.

The Pharisaic movement (c. 165 or 135–70 A.D.)[16] and its continuation in the culture of the Tannaim (70–200)—contrary to frequent claims of their isolation and autarky—apparently have been in close contact with Greco-Roman culture. The latter

---

[14] Cynic cosmopolitanism is not more than the feeling that the Sage belongs anywhere or nowhere. The Stoic variant is the claim that man is the citizen of a world state. Rhetorical cosmopolitanism often goes farther: it stresses that human nature and fate are one everywhere and that all men are equal before the tribunal of reason.

[15] Karl Joel, *Geschichte der antiken Philosophie*, I, Tuebingen 1921, has the most complete list of the positive achievements of the philosophical schools (especially Cynicism). Some of his overstatements have been corrected by subsequent scholarship.

[16] The vast literature is accessible through Salo W. Baron, *A Social and Religious History of the Jews*[2], 10 vols. (in progress), New York or Philadelphia 1952—(via *Index Volume* for vols. I-VIII) 1960. Cf. Sidney B. Hoenig's recent review, "Pharisaism Revisited," *Jew. Quart. Rev.* 61, 1966, 337–353, of L. Finkelstein, *The Pharisees*[3], 2 vols. Philadelphia 1962.
Many of the observations in this paper are made on the Tannaitic successors of the actual Pharisees. Although there is a considerable difference between Pharisees and Tannaim, it is usually assumed that in some aspects of their function and teaching continuity prevailed. The formation of the literary genres described in this article may have occurred as early as a generation after the death of a hero, if not in his very lifetime after the achievement of fame. Although the sources at our disposal are Tannaitic, i.e., post-Pharisaic, some of the material may thus go back to Pharisaic times. Cp. Socrates' lifetime (469–399) and the formation of his legend with his younger contemporary Xenophon (c. 430–c. 354).

seems to have been the source for a significant number of early Pharisaic-Rabbinic parallels to Hellenistic materials, discovered and discussed by, among others, Saul Lieberman,[17] Yitshak F. Baer,[18] Leo Baeck,[19] David Daube,[20] Siegfried Stein,[21] Hans (Johanan) Lewy,[22] Edmund (Menahem) Stein,[23] Elias J. Bickerman,[24] Morton Smith,[25] Rudolf Meyer,[26] A.A. (Elimelech Epstein) Hallewy,[27] and, in the field of jurisprudence, Boas Cohen.[28] Unlike earlier writers, such as Judah Bergmann[29] and Arnold Kaminka,[30]

[17] *Greek in Jewish Palestine*; *Hellenism in Jewish Palestine*, New York 1942 and 1950.

[18] *Yisra'el ba-'amim*, Jerusalem 1955.

[19] *The Pharisees and Other Essays*, New York 1947.

[20] "Rabbinic Methods of Interpretation and Hellenistic Rhetoric," *Hebrew Union College Annual* 22, 1949, 239–264; "Alexandrinian Methods of Interpretation and the Rabbis," *Festschrift Hans Lewald*, Basel 1953, 21–44, etc.

[21] "The Influence of Symposia Literature and the Literary Form of the Pesach Haggadah," *Journal of Jew. Studies* 8, 1957, 13-44.

[22] "Ein Rechtsstreit um den Boden Palaestinas im Altertum," *Monatsschr. fuer Geschichte und Wissensch. des Judentums* 77, 1933, 84-99, 172-180; *'Olamoth nifgashim*, Jerusalem 1960.

[23] "Die homiletische Peroratio im Midrasch," *Hebrew Union College Annual* 8–9, 1931–32, 353–371.

[24] "The Civil Prayer For Jerusalem," *Harvard Theol. Rev.* 60, 1962, 163–186; "The Maxim of Antigonus of Socho," *ibid.* 64, 1951, 153–165.

[25] "The Image of God," *Bull. of the John Rylands Libr.* 40, 1958, 473-512; "Palestinian Judaism in the First Century," in Moshe Davis, ed., *Israel: Its Role in Civilization*, New York 1956.

[26] *Hellenistisches in der rabbinischen Anthropologie*, BWANT 74, Stuttgart 1937.

[27] *Sha'are ha'aggadah*, Tel-Aviv 1963, and a number of articles in *Tarbits* (*Tarbiz*), Jerusalem (29, 1959; 31, 1961) and *Me'assef*, Tel-Aviv (5–6, 1965) on the "Aggadists and the Greek Grammarians," "Aggadic Exegesis and Homeric Exegesis," and "On Prophecy" (Heb.).

[28] *Jewish and Roman Law*, 2 vols., New York 1966. Cf. I. Sonne, "The Schools of Shammai and Hillel Seen From Within," *Louis Ginzberg Jubilee* Vol. I, New York 1945, 275–291.

The series of preceding items does not account for a host of contributions in the field of architecture, art, music, epigraphy, and political and material history by many other scholars, nor for earlier contributors whose works are still important, such as Heinrich Graetz, Emil Schuerer, Manuel Joel, I.N. Weinstein, Israel Lévy, Wilhelm Bousset, Isaak Heinemann, Samuel Krauss and many others. On A. Marmorstein below.

[29] "Die Stoische Philosophie und die juedische Froemmigkeit," *Judaica* (Festschrift Hermann Cohen), Berlin 1913, 143–166 (denies interdependence in spite of acknowledged resemblance).

[30] Among others "Les rapports entre le rabbinisme et la philosophie stoïcienne," *Rev. des Études Juives* 82, 1926, 232–252. A number of essays of this type are included in vol. 2 of his *Meḥḳarim*, Tel-Aviv 1951. It is obvious that by then this important scholar had become more cautious.

these scholars have been cautious enough not to ascribe all of the parallel material to any one Greek philosophical school. Popular Greco-Roman rhetoric (rhetoric in its widest sense) in this attempted synthesis as the actual source of such Pharisaic parallels, however, has not yet been seriously suggested in any of the previous enterprises.[31]

If such a hypothesis has any merit, a few preliminary methodological questions are in order. Before any effort is made to utilize materials of rhetorical coloration, whether Greco-Roman or Near Eastern,[32] for historiography or biography, the question of the literary genre of the material involved must be clarified.

If we find, for example, that the political fable plays a role in both cultures, we are fully aware of the fact that the animals never actually did what they are said to have done in the narrative—although the use of this particular genre and its lessons does presuppose a certain historical reality. If, however, this genre is transformed into a type of anecdote in which the clever or good animal is replaced by a Sage and the dumb or wicked animal by his antagonist (be it a member of an opposed school, or a fool, debauchee or tyrant),[33] the modern scholar has too often been

---

[31] A number of the attempts mentioned above rightly compare, for example, talmudic-midrashic exegesis or Pharisaic exercise-practice (*askēsis*) with appropriate Hellenistic sources and admit various kinds of interrelation. The question of the immediate and specific source of this adoption is, however, left open (and is, in any case, not the subject of these essays). The working hypothesis of this essay is that the Aggadists (and to some extent the Halachists) did not have to consult difficult works on the "art of rhetoric" but could gain their insight into Hellenism from the popularized form of rhetoric (which was the usual medium of the Greco-Roman writer-scholar-administrator class, too). They may have encountered this medium in its oral crystallization, since oral communication was ubiquitous in Palestine (occupational forces, Roman administration, wandering preachers, Greek colonists, Hellenistic-Jewish pilgrims, Herod's Court, Jewish evacuees from Greek cities in the Hasmonean period, etc.). But with their certain knowledge of Greek (cf. Greek marriage documents among recent finds) the availability of even one copy of a rhetorical work could go a long way.

[32] Of course, other Near Eastern literary cultures, such as the Samaritan, Phoenician-Punic, pre-Koranic Arab, (Hellenistic-) Babylonian, native Egyptian (in Greek garb), and early Christian, must have encountered Greco-Roman rhetoric, too.

[33] Reference is to the *chria*, to be discussed forthwith. The possibility of the derivation of this genre from the fable is occasionally mentioned: C.v. Wartensleben, *Begriff der griechischen Chreia und Beitraege zur Geschichte ihrer Form* (Diss.), Heidelberg 1901; W. Gemoll, *Das Apophthegm*, Wien 1924; G.A. Gerhard, *Phoinix von Kolophon*, Leipzig 1909; Sophie Trenkner, *The Greek Novella In the Classical*

tempted to consider every detail as true history. Here a habit of classical scholarship has perhaps reinforced this error, i.e., the inclusion of an anecdote of this type among the genuine works of the philosophers by the editors of sources and fragments.[34] The question as to precisely where and when Alexander the Great met Diogenes the Cynic has been discussed by serious historians on the grounds of information supplied by anecdotal literature[35] —although no one has as yet attempted to compute the strength of the sun in which Diogenes basked when Alexander offered him the fulfillment of any wish and received the now famous request to stay out of the sun.[36] When it comes to the question of what really transpired at this supposed meeting, we find quite a number of widely different witticisms in these stories, all indicative of non-historicity.[37]

In a recent study[38] the present writer has dealt with this type of anecdote, called most often *chreia* by the Greeks and *chria* by the

---

Period, Cambridge 1958; Ben Edwin Perry, "Fable" [*sic*], *Studium Generale* 12, Berlin 1959, 17–37.

[34] e.g., J.v. Arnim, *Stoicorum veterum fragmenta,* 4 vols., Leipzig 1921–24; H. Diels, *Doxographi Graeci,* Berlin 1879 (reprinted 1958); H. Diels, W. Kranz, *Die Fragmente der Vorsokratiker*⁷, Berlin 1954. More cautious, A.C. Pearson, in his *The Fragments of Zeno and Cleanthes,* London 1891, listed obvious anecdotes separately. To be sure, some of the aforementioned knew of this pitfall and even warned of it in their introductions, but the factual inclusion of anecdotes proved a strong temptation to the user.

[35] E.g., W.W. Tarn, "Alexander, Cynics and Stoics," *Amer. Journal of Philol.* 60, 1939, 41–70.

[36] Plutarch, *Alex.* XIV.2: "stand a little out of the sun"; D.L. VI.38: "get out of my light." On the problem of the verb in the latter see Liddell-Scott, *Greek-English Lexicon*[9], Oxford 1940, *s.v. aposkotizō* II.

[37] Alexander, who neither entirely nor wholeheartedly followed Aristotle, would hardly have been attracted by a less sophisticated philosopher (his "meeting" with the Indian Gymnosophists notwithstanding, since the latter seems to represent the same apocryphal cynicizing tradition. See in detail "Cynicism" 16.6). Cf. also Luitpold Wallach, "Indian Gymnosophists in Hebrew Tradition," *Proc. of the Amer. Acad. for Jew. Research* 11, 47–83.

The obviousness of the stereotype of the clash between the (Founder-) Sage representing virtue, freedom, and simplicity and the Ruler as a representative of tyranny or *typhos* (vain luxury) in the cynicizing *chria* and related genres is, of course, a decisive factor in judging on the historicity of a story. Practically all conspicuous rulers have thus been affected (Xerxes, Sardanapalus, Croisus, Midas, Archelaus, Cleomenes III, Mausolus, Dionysius of Syracuse the Younger, etc.). A new set of such anti-heroes in the persons of oppressive Roman emperors appears in Near Eastern and Alexandrinian literature from the time of the Principate on.

[38] "Cynicism."

Romans.[39] In this literary genre the Sage appears in an encounter or demonstration which is most often odd and witty, if not bizarre. The most extreme form, the burlesque *chria*, is usually told of the Sages of the Cynics, and of their associates, predecessors or descendents, and the ethic involved is strongly cynicizing. Stressing the rational in man and the simple life in conformity with nature, these terse stories are entirely free of the miraculous and the supernatural.

The cynicizing *chria* with many of its major motifs, forms, and elements is found also in Tannaitic literature. Without exception, all the stories on Hillel the Elder[40]—as distinct from brief historical notes and the actual halachic-technical materials—prove to be Greek-chriic, representing either (a) a complete Greek *chria*; (b) a composite of several chriic parts; or (c) an aggregate of the smallest meaningful chriic elements (henceforth called motemes) which, in these stories, achieve narrative unity precisely in the manner of the Greek *chria*.[41] Furthermore, some Hillel *chriae* are joined to one another within a narrative framework precisely as in Hellenistic sources.[42]

---

[39] Thus in ancient headings or expressly by ancient literary critics, such as (Pseudo-?) Demetrius of Phaleron, Bassus, Quintilian, Hermogenes and Theon. A somewhat different use of the term is reflected in Harry Caplan's modern use in his edition and translation of *Rhetorica* (*Auctor*) *ad* (*C.*) *Herrenium.* There are a number of parallel terms in ancient literature for our *chriae*: *apophthegmata, apomnēmoneumata, exempla,* etc., see in detail "Cynicism" 8.2-3.

[40] The great Pharisaic leader, an approximate contemporary of Herod the Great (41–4 B.C.).

[41] Treated in detail in "Cynicism" V (on the atomistic structure of the *chria*). The talmudic use of the *chria* and its narrative techniques does not exclude ingenuity if not creativity in the recombination of elements and the synthesis of the new story.

[42] One of the largest collections outside the gnomologies and Stobaeus is D.L.'s account of Diogenes of Sinope (the Cynic, VI.20–81) in which he used several independent sources, among others probably a collection called *Diogenis Prasis* (The Sale of Diogenes), which was used also by Philo (four items in *Quod omn.*, 121ff.). Other such accumulations, with or without a special framework, occur throughout D.L.'s work as well as that of Plutarch (especially in his *Laconica*, in sections on Pericles and Alcibiades—both associates of Socrates—in *Mor.* 461 D, i.e., *de cohib. ira*, etc.); all of Papyrus Vienna, in W. Croenert, *Kolotes und Menedemus,* Leipzig 1906, 50–52; part of Papyrus Bouriant (ff. VI–VIII, Ziebarth, "Schule," No. 46); Cicero's *Tusculan Disputations* (e.g., I.xliii.102ff.); the bawdy Machon collection in Athenaeus' *Deipnosophistae*, cf. now A.S.F. Gow, *Machon, the Fragments*, Cambridge 1965; and all of Lucian's moving accounts of *Demonax.* An early non-burlesque accumulation is found in Xenophon's *Memorabilia* III.xiii

Others affected by chriization are Eliezer ben Hyrcanus (*fl.* 70–100; his opponent Joshua only in syncrisis with him), to a lesser degree R. Meir (second century), and, still less, his teacher Akiba (c.50–135), whose portrait, however, is affected by actual folklore.[43]

To be sure, a Pharisaic Sage could have consciously followed the example of a Greek chriic Sage. However, a considerable number of the events reported in the Pharisaic *chriae* happen *to* the Sage. The beginning of the career of the *sophos* is encouraged by ambiguous or opaque oracles (Socrates, Diogenes, Zeno, Hillel)[44] and his life's work is endorsed by an oracular encomium (Thales, Socrates, Hillel).[45] In the famous episode on Passover[46] the following Greek chriic motifs are involved, in almost all of which the Sage is passive:

(1) The Sage is a foreigner.[47]
(2) The Sage encounters natives who perform a clever trick with sheep.[48]
(3) The Sage utters what later will be (or already was) a proverb regarding the natives and their sons.[48]

---

and xiv, beginnings. The most famous talmudic series occurs in BT Shabbat 30b, partially paralleled in AdRN A, ch. 15; B, ch. 29. All accumulations, whether Greco-Roman or Tannaitic, have similar key-words or key-situations: "seeing," guests, proselytes, burials, Spartans, disturbances, the Sage-slave, etc.

[43] See Dan Ben-Amos, *Narrative Forms in the Haggadah; A Structural Analysis* (Diss.) Bloomington, Ind., 1966; the *chria* is not treated in this dissertation.

[44] Usually in the beginnings of the reports of D.L. on the individual philosophers. For Hillel: BT Sotah 21a.

[45] D.L. I.28–33; II.37. For Hillel: BT Sotah 48b and parallels; PT Sotah IX.16 (24c end, Vilna; 24b middle, Krotoshin). On this and the preceding note cf. "Cynicism" 29.1-30.3.

[46] Longest version: PT Pes. VI.1 (33a Krotoshin); medium: BT Pes. 66a; shortest: Tos. Pes. IV.1-3. Motemes (1)–(5) are found in all three in slightly different combinations and with some variants.

[47] This moteme further frustrates Kaminka's repeated attempt to identify the historical Hillel as a native of Alexandria. The *sophos* in the *chria* and the *thaumaston* (more on this below) is a "foreigner," because this stance gives him greater scope to marvel at the "outlandish" customs of the "civilized" nations and to criticize them more freely. A similar misuse of chriic material is Kaminka's identification of the floating skull of P.A. 2.7 (*ibid.*), a rhetorical item amply paralleled with that of Pompey in Egypt! Cf. A. Kaminka, "Hillel's Life and Work," *Jew. Quart. Rev.* 30, 1939-40, 107-122 and a criticism of several similar attempts in "Cynicism" 24.9.

[48] Motemes (1)–(3): D.L. VI.41. An early date for this Greek *chria* seems to be certain on the grounds of Augustus' witty allusion to D.L.'s "punchline" ("it is better to be a Megarian's ram than his son") when commenting on Herod's

(4) The Sage forgets essentials of his teaching.[49]

(5) The Sage becomes suddenly and unexpectedly the head of the academy.[50]

It would be difficult, even for a Sage, to arrange for all this, and the story must be counted as unhistorical in view of the parallel material in Greek, partly told of Thales, partly of Cleanthes and Xenocrates, and, motifs (1)–(3) as a complete *chria*, of Diogenes at Megara.

Another important branch of classical culture, consolation literature,[51] had from its very (Sophist) beginning and owing to its very purpose, strong affinities to rhetoric, presenting, as it does, a continuous argument of urgency and persuasion. Most major ancient prose writers made a contribution to it, whether in Greek or in Latin.[52] After having absorbed actual rhetorical materials,

---

treatment of his son ("I would rather be Herod's pig than his son"), preserved in Macrobius, *Saturnalia* II.iv.11 (erroneously attached to the Slaughter of the Innocents by Macrobius).

[49] E.g., Thales, D.L. I.34.

[50] Cleanthes, D.L. VII.174. Xenocrates in the later Aristotle tradition, cf. n. 13. Sudden luck in court for both: D.L. VII.169; IV.8ff.

In a completely different study, employing different methods, Professor E.E. Urbach arrives at the result that Hillel was not the Patriarch of Israel and not the permanent president of the Sanhedrium. His study is based on the inner evidence of factual bits in the talmudic sources regarding status, title and function of the Palestinian Sages, without resort to Greco-Roman literature. Cf. "Class-Status and Leadership in the World of the Palestinian Sages," *The Israel Academy of Sciences and Humanities, Proceedings* II, no. 4, Jerusalem 1966 (separate edition).

[51] Among modern treatments: Rudolf Kassel, *Untersuchungen zur griechischen und roemischen Konsolationsliteratur*, Munich 1958. Constant Martha (*sic*), *Études morales sur l'antiquité*[3], Paris 1896, 135–189; Chas. Favez, *La Consolation Latine Chrétienne*, Paris 1937; *idem*, introductions to his editions of Seneca's *Ad Marciam de consolatione*, Paris 1928 and *Ad Helviam matrem de consolatione*, Paris 1918. Mary E. Fern, *The Latin Consolation As Literary Type*, St. Louis 1941; Mary Evaristus (Moran), *The Consolations of Death In Ancient Greek Literature* (Diss.), Washington, D.C., 1917. Still important: Car(o)l(us) Buresch, *Consulationum a Graecis Romanisque scriptarum historia critica*, Leipzig 1886.

[52] Crantor (360–268) with his exemplary *Peri penthous pros Hippoklea* (now lost, Jerome still remembered it)—the "Golden Book" (Cicero)—ushered in the post-Sophistic development. The most famous examples come from works and writers that also otherwise proved close to Pharisaic-Tannaitic items in the earlier study ("Cynicism"), such as Cicero (*Tusc. Disp.* I and III, *Ep. ad Fam.* (to or from him) IV.5; V.16, 18; VI. 3. *Brut.* I.9, etc.); Seneca, *Ad Marciam* (*Dial.* VI), *ad Helviam* (*Dial.* XII), as in n.51; *ad Polybiam* (*Dial.* XI); Ep. 63, 81, 93, 99, 107; (Pseudo-) Plutarch, *Ad Apollonium*; poetic: (Pseudo-) Ovid, *Ad Liviam.* The Church Fathers adopted the classical *consolatio* almost intact.

the *consolatio* entered the mainstream of rhetoric through a wide diffusion of its stories, arguments, and motemes, many of which became attached to the Sage.[53] Thus, on the occasion of a tragic event, usually death but also exile,[54] the Sage comforts or is comforted himself. A whole series of stories tells us that two children of the same hero died on the same day: so with Pericles, Anaxagoras, L. Paullus, Lucius Bibulus, a priestess of Juno, and others; so with R. Meir,[55] R. Ishmael,[56] and, according to one version, R. Akiba.[57] Not only this framework but also the arguments of comfort and the similes involved in a number of Tannaitic parallels suggest a common rhetorical background for this genre also.[58]

A third area of rhetorical literature suggests still another *sophos* genre, as yet little explored and little understood.[59] In rhetoric, especially in the popular doxographic works and their Tannaitic counterparts, a body of legends on the schools seems to have been current. It consists of stories or statements on the following subjects:

(1) The number of the Sage's pupils, whether few or many, and whether received with a "smiling face" or driven away with a stick—both motemes being claimed for Shammai, Hillel's contemporary and opponent in chriic (and halachic) syncrisis![60]

(2) A typology of learning, i.e., different characteristics found in teachers or disciples, the final sources of which seem to be Plato's

[53] The present writer has begun to trace these in Tannaitic literature.

[54] Ironical, on a monetary loss: Juvenal, *Satires* XIII. In the aretalogy: in prison, Apollonius consoles the inmates, Philostratus, *Life of A. of Tyana* VII.26. According to Seneca (after Posidonius) *Ep.* 95.65, the Sage-Philosopher needs, for the teaching of "average" practical virtue, not only "praeceptio" (principles) but also "suasio," "consolatio" (*logos paramythētikos*) and "exhortatio."

[55] Midrash Mishle 31; AdRN A, ch. 24.

[56] BT Mo'ed Katan 28b.

[57] BT Mo'ed Katan 21b. In (post-BT) Semahoth 8, however, only one son is mentioned. W. Bacher, *Die Agada der Tannaiten*[1], Strasbourg 1884, p. 305, n.3, tries to dissolve this discrepancy as a misreading of Akiba's speech, in which he mentions several sons in a simile. However, the gradual penetration (or the memory) of rhetoric stances creates precisely such discrepancies ("Cynicism," *passim*). The death of two sons as a simile occurs in Lam.R. (Proems) II; as a memory of Aharon's two sons in Lam. R. 20.1.

[58] The story of R. Meir's marriage to Beruria, the comforting she-Sage of one story, seems to be a variant of the purported quasi-experimental marriages of the Cynic philosophers to similar spouses, among them Hipparchia and Arete, D.L. VI.96–98; II.86.

[59] Dealt with in "Cynicism" 32.1–33.2.

[60] BT Shabbat, *loc. cit.*, versus P.A. 1.15 (1.16). On syncrisis see F. Focke, "Synkrisis," *Hermes* 58, 1923, 327-368.

Theaetetus and Hesiod's Ages of Mankind, as applied by the Cynic Bion (c. 325–255).[61]

(3) The *diadochē* of the school leaders, usually seven following each other, i.e., a rhetorical-doxographic pattern.[62]

(4) The two simultaneous leaders who are supposed to have headed the academies.[63]

(5) Difficult questions, *akousmata* or *erōtēmata* (*problēmata*) and their answers, usually of an ethical nature, requiring the definition of the *summum bonum*. Iamblichus distinguishes three different forms in his *Life of Pythagoras*, 18.81-82 (Deubner).

(6) Near-"unanswerable" questions, *apora*, or *aporiai* (*aporiae*), and their final answers ("Of what are there more, of the living or of the dead?").[64]

(7) The *sophos*, as a "hero" of virtue, possessing immense, encyclopedic knowledge, including the ability to write fables.[65]

---

[61] *Theaetetus* 191-195; Stobaeus XXXI.97 (vol.II, p. 218 W.-H.); D.L. VII.37; Cicero, *Part. orat.* VI.21, *de orat.* II.88.360; *Auctor ad Herren.* III.17.30 (Shakespeare, Hamlet I.5.98); AdRN B, ch. 28 and many parallels; P.A. 2.8 (2.10f.); AdRN B, ch. 29, 58f.; P.A. 5.15 (5.18) ff; 5.12 (5.15). Cf. Plutarch, *Mor.* 78 E.

Judah Goldin has recently commented on the passage AdRN B, ch. 29, and several other passages referring to Johanan ben Zakkai's academy, *Traditio* 21, 1965, 1-21, "A Philosophical Session in a Tannaitic Academy"; similarly, *Harry Austryn Wolfson Jubilee Volume*, Heb. Section, Jerusalem 1965, 69-92, "*Mashehu ʿal beth midrasho shel Rabban Yohanan ben Zakkai.*" The atmosphere of Pharisaic-Tannaitic teaching becomes alive in these articles. The historical assertions, however, that, for example, an actual session on the particular subject took place and that the teachings are actually authored by the teachers mentioned, are, owing to the rhetorical-legendary nature of this material, highly improbable. Cf. n. 83.

[62] Cf. D.L.'s seven "Cynics." That there is an affinity to Hellenistic sources in similar structurings, for example in P.A. ch.1 (the sevenfold pattern as such has been described by L. Finkelstein in his *Mabo' le-masichtoth Aboth ve-AdRN*, New York 1950), has been effectively asserted by Élie (Elias J.) Bickerman, "La chaîne de la tradition pharisienne," *Revue Biblique* 59, 1952, 44-54 (a comparison with doxographic-diadochic patterns) and by Boas Cohen, "Peculium in Jewish and Roman Law," *op. cit.*, vol. I, 275ff. (comparison with the legal-historical Encheiridion of Pomponius, 129 A.D.). It is possible that both patterns may have merged in the consciousness of the rhetoricians when both jurisprudence and philosophy became aspects of the *sophos* concept.

[63] Cf. titles in n. 13, above.

[64] See "Cynicism" 11.16; related material in L.W. Daly and W. Suchier, "Altercatio Hadriani Augusti et Epicteti Philosophi," *Ill. Studies in Language and Literature*, 24, Nos. 1-2, Urbana, 1939, pp. 12, 17, 26.

[65] Although true for some of the Greek philosophers, the assertion of encyclopedic knowledge becomes a literary stereotype. Its Tannaitic equivalent, for example, the assertion that a Sage knew Halacha, Aggada, Mishna, Midrash, etc., down to the language of animals and plants, should therefore not be used as an unchecked

Almost all of these themes may occur as *chriae*, or brief dialogues (eristic form), or as factual statements.[66]

Similarly, another startling phenomenon is found in both cultures. The same gnome (aphorism, *sententia*, saying) may be quoted in the name of several different Sages, thus making for contradictory features in the overall portrait of a particular Sage. Further, and more important, the same gnome may occur:

(1) As the "punchline" of a *chria*,
(2) As an independent unit, without a story,
(3) Anonymously, often as a popular proverb,
(4) Occasionally as the moral of a fable.

It thus seems that the ascription of a *sententia* to a Sage might merely have been another means of stressing his importance and does not reflect an actual teaching of his. The Golden Rule, in a number of slightly different patterns, appears thus in connection with an impressive number of Greek and Roman rhetorical writers, put in the mouth of a Sage within a *chria*, or in a dialogue, or as an independent item in a gnomology.[67] It also appears in Hellenistic-Jewish rhetoric, in the Gospels and the Didache, and in chriic form attached to Hillel and Akiba. In all these cultures it is frequently accompanied by the same test case or by the assertion that the Golden Rule is a *kephalaion*, a basic and all-embracing rule, i.e., the "whole Torah" of the Midrash, and the "Law and the Prophets" of the Gospels, the Greek formulation preceding its Near Eastern parallels by centuries. To be sure, various forms of the Golden Rule had been current earlier in the Near East in general (Ahikar) and in Judaism in particular (Tobit, Sirah), as they were in other probably unrelated cultures (China, India).[68]

claim for the emergence of mysticism but can be regarded as an indication that "arcane" knowledge was important at the time of the creation of the legend.

The claim of having written fables is already doubtful for Socrates, Plutarch, *Mor.* 16 C after *Phaedo* 60 d. Fables recommended in Aristotle's *Rhetoric* II.xx.5-8, 1393 b-1394 a. Thus also for Solon, Antisthenes, Hillel, Meir and Akiba. Legendary fable tellers may become rhetorical (or "Cynic-Stoic") heroes: Odysseus, Aesopus. In detail in "Cynicism," 32.5.2.

[66] See "Cynicism" 11.16ff. for discussion and sources.

[67] For detailed references and discussion of the entire subject see "Cynicism" 19.16-20.

[68] Cf. L. Philippides, *Die Goldene Regel* (Diss.), Leipzig 1929; H.H. Rowley, "The Chinese Sages and the Golden Rule," *Bull. John Rylands Libr.* 1940, 321-352; A. Dihle, *Die Goldene Regel*, Goettingen 1962.

The point here made is that Greco-Roman rhetoric reactivated and reformulated older original materials in the Near East.[69] A common historical fate, first under Alexander the Great, and then under the Roman Empire, must have favored this process.

However this may be, the genres used by both Greco-Roman rhetoric and Tannaitic literature must be recognized and evaluated. For Greco-Roman literature in general some of this task has been undertaken by classicists,[70] by New Testament scholars,[17] and more recently by folklorists.[72] The field is still wide open, however, for the same task in Tannaitic literature, in spite of the pleadings of the late Arthur Marmorstein[73] and recently of Jacob Neusner.[74] Apart from preliminary attempts, mostly in the form of prolegomena, some serious beginnings have been made,[75] especially in

---

[69] Lev. 19.18 may thus have been the original form of the Golden Rule in earlier Jewish culture, cf. Targum Lev. 19.18. Lev. and the rhetorical echoes together in the Akiba story.

[70] Among others, by Norden, *op. cit.*, Gerhard, *op. cit.*, Perry, *op. cit.*, R. Hirzel, *Der Dialog* I, Leipzig 1895; R. Reitzenstein, *Hellenistische Wundererzaehlungen*², Leipzig, reprinted 1963; Eliz. Haight, *The Roman Use of Anecdotes In Cicero, Livy and the Satirists*, New York 1940; John Barns, "A New Gnomologium...," *Class. Quart.* 44 and 45, 1950 and 1951, 126-137 and 1-19. Scattered items in P.W. (cf. Index in vol. 23; 9 of 1959—which is exclusive of vol. 24;9A1 and Supplements IX-X) and v. Christ, Schmid, Staehlin, *op. cit.*, index.

[71] G. Rudberg's articles in *Symbolae Osloenses* 14 and 15, *Theol. Studien und Kritiken* C11; *Coniectanea Neotestamentica* II, etc., and the movement of Formgeschichte, especially the work of Rudolf Bultmann and Martin Dibelius.

[72] André Jolles, *Einfache Formen*², Darmstadt 1930 (reprinted 1958); Trenkner, *op. cit.*; C.W.v. Sydow, "*Kategorien der Prosa-Volksdichtung*," in *Selected Papers On Folklore*, Copenhagen 1948, 60-88; Kurt Ranke, "Einfache Formen," in *Suppl. Fabula*, Berlin 1961, 1-11.

[73] "The Background of the Haggadah," *Hebrew Union College Annual* 6, 1929, 184. He was aware of the relationship between "diatribe" and Midrash, but preferred a mixture of literary and theological analysis to a technical one. (His essays are reprinted in *Studies in Jewish Theology*, Memorial Vol., ed. J. Rabbinowitz and M.S. Lew, Oxford 1950).

[74] *A Life of Rabbi Yohanan ben Zakkai...*, Leiden 1962, p. 3.

[75] E.g., in Birger Gerhardsson's *Memory and Manuscript*, Uppsala 1961 (criticized in W.D. Davies, *The Setting of the Sermon on the Mount*, Cambridge 1964, Appendix XV); E. Stein, *op. cit.*; Dov Noy's extensive writings: Diss., an analysis of Hebrew material— yet unpublished—as an addition to Stith Thompson, *Motif Index of Folk Literature*, 6 vols., Bloomington, Ind., 1955–58; *ha-sippur ha-ʿamami...*, Jerusalem 1960 (mimeographed); *mabo' le-sifrut ha-aggada, ibid.*, 1961 (mimeographed.) Benjamin de Vries' "The Literary Nature of the Haggada," (Heb.), *Niger Jubilee Vol.*, ed. Arthur Biram *et. al.*, Soc. for Bibl. Research, Jeru-

the pioneering work of Siegfried Stein on symposia literature,[76] that branch of ancient literature which described a banquet as "a fellowship of seriousness and gaiety, and of discourse and activity," as Plutarch has it,[77] and finally began to include the treatment of food and eating habits as part of the conversation, culminating in Athenaeus' 15-"volume" *Deipnosophistae*. Sympotic literature of the Roman period leans heavily on rhetorical genres and devices, and rhetoric, in turn, has made heavy use of it.

Systematic treatment is overdue also for the smallest literary elements of rhetoric,[78] for motemes, as we called the minimal motif-like independent element, and for similemes, as one could call the minimal basis in literary comparison, such as in parable, metaphor, simile, and others. Such similemes are: the soul as a guest; life as a deposit; the choice of two ways at the crossroads;[79] the athlete; the craftsman; the statue; the theatre and the circus; all common in Hellenistic rhetoric as well as Tannaitic and Amoraic (200–500) Midrash.[80] Another such elementary unit is the numerical saying, i.e., items stating summarily the number of various phenomena, such as Anacharsis' three grapes of the vine—pleasure, drunkenness, disgust—and Thales' (or Socrates' or Plato's) three reasons for gratitude—to be a human, and not a beast; a man, and

salem 1959, 303-309, is a precarious attempt to prove that Gunkel's biblical categories are applicable to the Midrash. Cf. also Ben-Amos, *op. cit.* Mostly concerned with later periods is Bernard Heller, "Das hebraeische und arabische Maerchen," in J. Bolte, G. Polívka, *Anmerkungen zu den Kinder- und Hausmaerchen der Brueder Grimm*, 5 vols., Leipzig 1913–32, vol. IV, 315-418. For earlier articles on fable and *mashal* see Ben-Amos and Emanuel bin Gorion, *Shevile ha-aggada*, Jerusalem 1949.

[76] *Op. cit.*, n. 21.

[77] *Mor.* 708 D, *Quaestiones conviviales.*

[78] As distinct from genre research. The motemes of the *chria*, as far as they are pertinent for Tannaitic literature, have been treated in "Cynicism" IV, "The Atomistic Structure of the Chria."

[79] That is, the famous "Choice of Heracles," also called "Heracles at the Crossroads" or Prodicus' Fable, as in, for example, Xenophon's *Memorabilia* II.i.21ff. Its use and role in Greco-Roman literature, especially in Cynicism, are amply treated in Karl Joel's *Der echte und der xenophontische Sokrates*, 3 vols., Berlin 1893-1901.

[80] Parallels usually concern a single item but a sequence of similes attached to a *chria* on Hillel in *Lev.R.* 34.3, 776f., is paralleled by a similar sequence in Seneca, *Ep.* 64.9-10, see "Cynicism" 15.10f. This practically eliminates the possibility of coincidence.

not a women; a Greek, and not a barbarian,[81] the latter being paralleled in the Tannaitic daily morning prayer[82]—Zeno's seven sophisms, D.L. VII.25, the seven treatments of a theme (among them hermeneutics) in *Auctor ad Herrenium* IV.iv. 57ff. (written c.85 B.C.), and Hillel's seven (occasionally three) hermeneutic rules, Tos. Sanhedrin 7 end. Proverbs; catalogues of vices and virtues;[83] and *thaumasta*, i.e., terse narratives expressing the

---

[81] D.L. I.103; I.33; Lactantius, *Div. Instit.* III.19 (Plato) cf. Plutarch, *Marius* 46.1 (third blessing: to be a contemporary of Socrates). On the parallels to the three (or four) stages of drunkenness of the Anacharsis item in midrashic and other cultures, see Max Gruenbaum, *Gesammelte Aufsaetze zur Sprach- und Sagenkunde*, ed. Felix Perles, Berlin 1901: "Die verschiedenen Stufen der Trunkenheit in der Sage dargestellt," pp. 435-441. Another example of the basic genre: Plato's three *archai*: God, matter, idea, as in (Pseudo-)Plutarch's (Aetius') *De placit. philos.* (quoted as Plutarch in Diels, *Doxographi*, p.1) and the three Tannaitic "things on which the world rests," i.e., *archai*, in P.A.1.2. and 1.18 (1.19): Torah, (Temple-) cult, active loving-kindness, etc.

[82] Initial blessings: "...not a barbarian; ...not a slave; ...not a woman," S. Baer, *Seder 'Avodath Yisra'el*, rev. ed., New York 1937. Cf. Tos. Berakhoth 7.18, p. 16, 1.22, BT Menahoth 43b; PT Ber. IX.2, 13b (Judah b. Ilai or R. Meir!); cf. Paul in Gal. 3.28. Cf. Ismar Elbogen, *Der juedische Gottesdienst*³, Frankfurt 1931, p. 90.

[83] J. Goldin, *Traditio*, p. 12, failing to recognize the genre, considers (the five-fold catalogue of virtues and vices of) P.A. 2.9f. (2.12f.) as philosophical material once discussed at an actual session. Actually, it is closer to folklore, as are so many numerical sayings and "catalogues" in rhetoric, or, at best, popular-rhetorical ethics, and this is also the reason for the missing mention of Torah in the passage. Such catalogues are frequent, too, in early Christian non-philosophical works such as the Didache. To be sure, ethical propositions were prominently discussed in the Hellenistic philosophical schools but, as it seems, in a more technical and systematic manner. Johannes Straub, in his *Heidnische Geschichtsapologetik in der christlichen Spaetantike*, Bonn 1963, p. 113, represents a minority opinion in his assumption that for practical purposes the philosophical schools taught *Vulgaerethik* (under the term of *hypothētikos logos* and other terms) as a permissible popular summarization of the usual formal and technical (analytical, argumentative and decisory) ethics. Assertions that seem to confirm this opinion in Seneca's *Epistles* 94 and 95 are, however, already rhetorical rationalizations for the preponderance of popular ethics in rhetoric. On the other hand, Cynical ethics must have been of the popular variety to begin with (though perhaps not with Antisthenes), but then it was ethics of the street and not of the academy.

The pattern for Goldin's passage seems to have been a rhetorical catalogue of vice and virtue. The session is probably apocryphal, and the item glorifies the *sophos* and his world. Concerning these catalogues cf. Siegfried Wibbing, *Die Tugend- und Lasterkataloge im NT und ihre Traditionsgeschichte*, BZNT 25, Berlin 1959.

Sage's amazement at the contradictions inherent in any culture, are other such brief items.[84]

Sound method requires further the tracing of the dimensions of a literary phenomenon, i.e., its statistical properties. In the case of the cynizing *chria*, for example, there are 30-35 different examples in all of talmudic literature, whereas there are probably more than 1,000 in Hellenistic literature and the papyri, among them some 20 different items on the use of the Sage's stick alone.[85] There are probably over 5,000 different aphorisms in Hellenistic rhetorical and gnomological literature. There are hundreds of pseudo-rational explanations of "natural phenomena," such as answers to the question why Babylonians have elongated heads, which turns up in the widely distributed pseudo-Hippocratic collections as well as the first *chria* on Hillel of BT Shabbat 31a. Some of this material is contributed by Euhemerus and Euhemerism, e.g., the attempt to explain the origin of the gods by a historical-psychological theory, which made so profound an impression on the ancient world. The massiveness of these examples in Greco-Roman rhetoric puts a number of phenomena into proper perspective. It is, for example, of invaluable help in understanding the total literary pattern as well as the total content and value system of the genres. It becomes thus clear that in the *chria* all Sages were once slaves, all were abjectly poor, and almost all once did menial work. Only on these grounds can the interdependence of Cleanthes items and Hillel anecdotes be fully established and their probable non-historicity be suggested. To be sure, an entire profession may have occupied a certain rung on the economic scale—all monks are poor and in some countries all university professors—but, then, the *chria* speaks of the self-same Sage-Heroes as being wealthy,

---

[84] Examples of *thaumasta* below, p. 84.

The problem of rhetorical components of larger non-rhetorical genres, such as romance, aretalogy, martyrology, satire, mime, comedy, etc., is not mentioned here, since Tannaitic parallels to these genres are rare and mostly extra-rabbinical; e.g., the romance included in the Testament of Joseph (Phaedra and Hippolytus motif, cf. Martin Braun, *History and Romance in Graeco-Oriental Literature*, Oxford 1938). Theodore Burgess' *Epideictic Literature*, Chicago 1903, reconstructs a literary mood or aspect of much of rhetoric rather than a true genre.

[85] Cf. "Cynicism" 10.3. They are the pattern for Shammai's often misdiagnosed building ruler, *'ammath habinyan*, BT Shabbat 31a. This strange term seems to be merely a variant of this moteme, introduced owing to the use of the regular keyword "stick," *maqqel*, in the item immediately before, *ibid.*

so Diogenes, so Crates,[86] so Cleanthes, and so Hillel.[87] Attempts to harmonize such contradictions are as fruitful as the simple solution that was once offered when the "original" skull of a saint was shown at two different places: one skull was said to represent the saint in his younger years, the other in his ripe old age. Rather, the *chriae* are aimed at teaching incisive social ideals: *ataraxia*, self-knowledge,[88] the simple life, absolute freedom (*parrhesia*),[89] non-conformity, the acquisition of virtue through knowledge. Whereas the stress on these values does mirror a historical situation, the mention of the Sage may only indicate the esteem in which he was held as well as the esteem of the social value in question. "De personis indicatur, sed de rebus contenditur," says Quintilian rightly.

The concept of the great individual in later rhetorical culture is thus determined not by his actual achievement—which may have been merely the catalyst—and not by his actual teachings—which were frequently unknown—but by an *a priori* concept of the Sage, and it is this concept which seems to have determined the use of *chriae* and aphorisms in the description of his wisdom and career. In other words, the so-called problem of the "historical Socrates,"—as realistically recognized by Gigon and Chroust;[90]— of the "historical Thales" or Democritus, to whom cynicizing gnomic material was ascribed posthumously,—as rightly asserted by Classen, Snell and Stewart;[91]—the "historical Diogenes," —as critically analyzed by Gerhard, v. Fritz, Rudberg and

---

[86] Cf. D.L. VI.87 with Teles' item in Stobaeus III.1.98 (p. 44 W.H.). On Diogenes cf. Plutarch *Mor.* 499 D (*An vitiositas*); Suidas △ 1143, ed. Adler, II, p. 101; Musonius, ed. Hense, 87 A, p. 43.

[87] D.L. VII.170; BT Ketuboth 67b cf. BT Sotah 21a. Fully documented in "Cynicism" 27.3 and 30.5ff. The motif that a *sophos* gives his entire fortune away, is another matter again.

[88] Even the Delphic "know thyself" occurs in the mouths of several Greek Sages.

[89] Preserved in the Hebrew-Aramaic cognate *parhesia*, which seems to occur occasionally in the original chriic sense.

[90] Olof A. Gigon, *Sokrates*, Bern 1947; Anton-Hermann Chroust, *Socrates, Man and Myth*, London 1957.

[91] C.J. Classen, in P.W. Suppl.X., 1965, *s.v.* "Thales," especially 931-935; Snell, *op. cit.*; Zeph Stewart, "Democritus and the Cynics," *Harv. Stud. in Class. Philol.* 63, 1958, 179-191.

Sayre;[92]—the "historical Jesus,"[93] as well as the "historical Hillel,"[94] reflects the general historical problem of all who were at one time or another considered *sophoi*.[95]

Among the statistical properties of a genre its distribution, i.e.,

---

[92] Gerhard, *op. cit.*; Rudberg, *op. cit.*; F. Sayre, *Diogenes of Synope*, Baltimore 1938; *The Greek Cynics*, Baltimore 1948. K.v. Fritz, *Quellenuntersuchungen zu Leben und Philosophie des Diogenes von Sinope*, *Philologus* Suppl. 18.II, Leipzig 1926.

[93] A huge field of endeavor, accessible through the Subject (Title) Index of Libraries, Introductions to the NT, surveys on recent NT research, or pertinent encyclopedias (Hastings, *Religion in Geschichte und Gegenwart*; etc.). Quite frequently the problem is seen in "reverse": apocalyptic, soteriological, proto-"gnostic," and Sonship portrayals are rejected as unhistorical, whereas the portrayal as *sophos* is taken at face value.

[94] In the light of the approach suggested here, the 19th century struggles between Abraham Geiger, Delitzsch and Renan as to the question of influences (Jesus/Hillel) are somewhat quixotic. If at least they had discussed the influences of the respective idealizations! Even recent biographies of Hillel use the talmudic material uncritically, except Kaminka, *op. cit.*, and Hallewy, *Sha'are*. They, in turn, rely frequently on haphazard and unsystematic comparisons.

[95] Here the difficult problem arises as to what made a Sage important enough to deserve such posthumous recognition. As indicated before, this may be his creations and activities as a Founder. (The Founder and Inventor appears in myth as the Culture-Hero, e.g., Anacharsis as the inventor of the anchor and the potter's wheel, D.L. I.105.)

Intriguing is the further question whether the *sophos* features acquired in legendarization and rhetoric are in any intrinsic way related to the original contribution of the Sage. The answer, if any can be given with any certainty, will depend on the availability of other sources, especially genuine fragments, or on particular features within the rhetorical portrait that are not in line with the stereotype. It is thus certain from non-rhetorical sources that Thales is indeed the author of important mathematical insights, see Classen, *op. cit.*, Diels, *Vorsokratiker*, and G.S. Kirk and J.E. Raven, *The Presocratic Philosophers*, Chicago 1964. Thales' mathematical pioneering apparently became the catalyst in the formation of his chriic and gnomic features as a Founder-Sage. These features, however, have little or nothing to do with mathematics. Similarly, Democritus' aphorisms (and his eternal smile) have little to do with his atomic philosophy or his equally important mathematics.

To be sure, many creative minds of the Western orbit have indeed excelled in science *and* philosophy. Thus Plato, Leibniz, Pascal and Bertrand Russell are known for both. If we would encounter, however, a popular-rhetorical report which would describe the philosophy of all these four as essentially one, as non-technical, and, above all, as identical with the philosophy of the era of the report, a serious historical problem would present itself to the critic.

Hillel's main historical achievement (it may have been multiple) could have been a legal reform or measures of timely "emergency" halachah, probably historical if one compares similar emergency measures in the Rome of the Principate. For preliminary orientation see *Oxford Class. Dict.*, "Law and Procedure," 5.

the frequency of its use, its whereabouts and accessibility, are of significance. The Near East would hardly reproduce a *hapax legomenon* but would have a far better opportunity to get hold of an item that is quoted frequently. Once the "scope" of a genre has thus been established, its history has to be traced. The Greek *chria*, for example, is centuries older than the Pharisaic-Tannaitic examples, and developed from a static form, centering around the mere utterances of wisdom or bon mots, to the burlesque form of the Cynics Teles and Bion in the 3rd century.[96] Its great Roman revival slightly precedes Hillel's lifetime, as, for example, in the *Tusculan Disputations*, c. 45 B.C., or coincides with it, and is thus a *terminus a quo*. But one must not omit the fact that the Hillelite *chriae* occur for the first time in the codifications of c.200–250 A.D. This date coincides with the heavy *chria* users Aelianus, Athenaeus, Diogenes Laertius and the authors of the pseudo-Cynic letters,[97] as a *terminus ad quem* for the rise of the Tannaitic *chria*.

Another methodological desideratum is the determination of the social function of the genres. Undoubtedly rhetoric did not only provide a useful mode of expression and operation for the speaker, writer, jurist, and politician. It had become strongly ethicizing, propagating the way to virtue as ennobling or redemptory for a society in rapid change and under stress.[98] Rhetoric would thus also view the nature of man and the dimensions of the gods or even of God, using a fervent, pleading or sentimental tone, quite unlike the detached, objective, and systematic way of formal philosophy. And yet, a practical popular quasi-rational ethics that would weather the vicissitudes of life and encourage simplicity and ataraxy was central in rhetoric. It is perhaps owing to the usefulness of this rhetorical *sophos*-ethics that it could finally approximate an inter-cultural "currency" as much as Greek art or Greek burial custom; that the "pagan" and Christian versions

---

[96] See "Cynicism" ch.3.

[97] Ed. R. Hercher, *Epistolographi Graeci*, Paris 1873.

[98] The factors usually given for this historical situation are the "decline" of the polis and the rise of empire, the emergence of new social classes, the expansion of slavery, the continuous economic crisis (of Rome), earlier Greek particularism and later Roman civil wars, foreign invasions, the increasing number of competing cults and ways of life—all encouraging a flight into the self. Generalizations of this kind can be variously applied for the period of 400 B.C. (the proliferation of the Greek philosophical schools) to 400 A.D. (the establishment of Christianity). These are also the centuries of the domination of rhetorical culture.

of the *Sentences of Sextus* could largely overlap;[99] that "Pagan," Jew and Christian alike could view their lifelong struggle for virtue as an "athletic" and "ascetic" contest—i.e., as requiring continuous practice and strenuous effort;[100] and that Origen could claim that Christianity was a popular version of the same ethics of which Plato was a learned version.[101]

Rhetoric had also to provide the necessary legitimization and glorification of its own spokesmen, of the scholar-teacher-jurist-administrator class. To a certain extent, it is thus self-glorification. Chrysippus, according to D. L. VII.122, thus reformulated Plato's rule that the philosophers should be kings, quite realistically, when he recommended that the wise alone are fit to administrate, judge, and orate. Philodemus of Gadara, c.110–40/35 B.C., claimed that "rhetoric alone makes laws" and that the true rhetors were righteous.[102]

Since the belief in life after death had become quite common, we would expect that a class aspiring to *sophos*-status and propagating it as the true way of life would project this ideal into their concept of the Hereafter, most likely in the form of an academy or, at least, as a learning experience. This is, indeed, the case. Plutarch, c. 46–after 120, using ample Platonic precedents,[103] tells

---

[99] Cf. the recent edition of Henry Chadwick, *Texts and Studies*, Cambridge 1959, 2nd ser.

[100] W. Jaeger, *Early Christianity and Greek Paideia*, Cambridge, Mass. 1961, *passim*; F.C. Grant, *Roman Hellenism and the New Testament*, Edinburgh 1962, p. 164; Joh. Leipoldt, "Griechische Philosophie und fruehchristliche Askese," *Berichte ueber die Verhandlungen d. saechs. Akad. d. Wiss. z. Leipzig*, Philol.-Hist. Klasse, v.106, Heft 4, Berlin 1961, 1-67, *passim*; Y. F. Baer, *Yisra'el ba-'amim*, Jerusalem 1955, *passim*. The two latter fail to distinguish clearly between the rhetorical varieties of *askēsis* which are non-dualistic—i.e., not based on a dichotomy of body and spirit but practice-achievement directed and strongly Cynico-Stoic—and Pythagorean, Platonic, Neoplatonic and quasi-Gnostic varieties which presuppose the superiority of the "Spiritual" over the Physical; cp. especially the *non sequitur* in Leipoldt, *op. cit.*, p. 4. In most "pagan" and Jewish (-Palestinian) sources and in some (non-Pauline) Christian rhetoric the former type of *askēsis* prevails.

[101] *Contra Celsum* VI.1-2; VII.61.

[102] Cf. H.M. Hubbell, "*The Rhetorics of Philodemus*," *Transactions of the Conn. Acad. of A. and S.*, vol. 23, 242-382, p. 343 (*Fragm. inc.* Sudhaus II, 179, fr.III), cp. p. 360 (*Fragm. hypomn.* II, 275, fr. X) and *ibid.* (II, 279, fr. XXII). Some criticism of rhetoric, however, is proffered in Philodemus' treatise.

[103] Cp. *Timaeus* 30 B, 41-42, 90 A; *Phaedo* 81 B-C; *Phaedrus* 256 B, *Republic* 621 C-D; *Timaeus* 58 D, *Phaedo* 109 B, 111 B; *Phaedrus* 248 A-B; etc.

the tale of the gradual liberation and improvement of the mind-element after death of those who had made righteousness and reason dominant in their lives. Although this experience resembles more a mystical astral ascent and an initiation rite than an academic session, the developing "Spirits," nevertheless, see and learn a great deal.[104] Much clearer is Origen's case (c. 185–253). In Paradise God will organize a school for souls with angelic instructors, and syllabus, examinations and promotions to higher spheres are not missing.[105] In the Amoraic sources the concept of the Academy On High, *yeshivah shel ma'alah* (heb.) or *methibhta de reqiy'a* (aram.) emerges in Palestine c. 250, in Babylonia c. 300. Details include talmudic discussion, God as teacher, the depth and esoteric character of the instruction—which is superior to angelic lore—and even a seating order.[106]

The intriguing question can now be asked whether the Tannaim and their Pharisaic predecessors, using rhetorical techniques and the ideology of the Sage in a similar fashion, represent in Judean culture the identical class, similarly entrusted with the practical tasks of law, administration and cult, similarly under the threat of a still more powerful ruler,[107] similarly concerned with the preservation of the ancient heritage by new techniques, and similarly clashing with the *hoi polloi*, i.e., the *'Am ha-'arets*. Indeed, its attractiveness as an ideology for an elite scholar-bureaucracy may have been among the reasons for the adoption of this rhetorical system in the first place.

---

[104] *Mor.* 943ff. (*de facie*). Cp. the use of the notions of joy (943 C), crowned victors, ray of light (D), and nourishment by exhalation (E) with the similar syndrome in BT Berakhot 17a (Rab, 160/175-247, Palestine and Babylonia) and AdRN, Version A, 3a, p.4 (anon.): "...the righteous sit (with) their crowns on their heads and are nourished by (Ber.: enjoy) the radiance of the Shekhinah..."

[105] *De principiis* (Rufinus), ed. P. Koetschau, II.2.4ff. (*Die Griech. Christl. Schriftsteller d. Ersten Drei Jahrh.*, Origenes Werke I), Leipzig 1913. Cf. E.R. Dodds, *Pagan and Christian in an Age of Anxiety*, Cambridge 1965, p. 129, who remarks that for Origen "Heaven is an endless university." The idea of the heavenly academy is here combined with concepts of purgation and sublimation that strongly resemble the situation in the Platonic item of Plutarch, above, whereas the details to be learned and their esoteric nature resemble the talmudic material quoted below.

[106] BT Pes. (Johanan, died 279, Palestinian); BT Baba Metsi'a 85b (Pal.); 86a (Bab.); Pesikta de R. Kahana, ed. S. Buber, 107a; PT Shabbat VI, end, 8d (Krot.).

[107] A native tyrant or Rome. Exile or martyrdom was more often than not the fate of the major figures of both cultures.

While in this present study the existence of such a scholar-bureaucrat class in Palestine is proposed on the grounds of their *sophos*-ideology and their use of Greco-Roman rhetorical forms and stances, Prof. Urbach, in his aforementioned study and Prof. Neusner, in a recent essay[108] use historical and legal talmudic material to suggest the existence of such a judicial-administrative-instructional class. Prof. Neusner deals with the Babylonian Amoraim and is able to demonstrate that their influence on synagogue, piety and custom was only through their expository skill, while their official activities consisted of the adjudication of property transactions, family status and market supervision as well as other doings in the interest of the Exilarchate.[109]

The entire situtation evokes further the suspicion that the Pharisees may have been the most Hellenized group in Judea and may have offered a desirable alternative to the creation of a foreign court bureaucracy, or native bureaucracy of their own, for the later Hasmoneans and the Herodians.[110] The strongly Israel-centered and devout makeup of the Pharisees and Tannaim does not preclude Hellenization. A revealing instance is the great Roman conservative and patriot Cato Major (M. Porcius, 234-149), who counts among the most brilliant Hellenists of the Romans.[111] Toynbee felt inclined to call his anti-Hellenism a pose, following herein Plutarch's evaluation.[112]

The inner dynamics of a bureaucracy of this type has recently been the subject of some special studies, such as those of Fred N. Riggs at Indiana, and Shmuel Noah Eisenstadt at Jerusalem.[113]

---

[108] Jacob Neusner, "The Rabbi and the Community in Talmudic Times," *C(entral) C(onference of) A(merican) R(abbis) Journal* 14, 1967, 65-76, cf. his *A History of the Jews in Babylonia* II, Leiden 1966.

[109] The essays by Urbach and Neusner were published after the conclusion of the present study and are otherwise not used in it. It is gratifying to observe that a cross-cultural and literary study as this one would arrive at a similar result. The Urbach and Neusner essays do not discuss literary genres nor the relation of talmudic materials to Greco-Roman situations.

[110] Cf. their periods of collaboration with the Pharisees. No clash between Hillel and the Judean court or Rome is reported.

[111] He was able to orate in vernacular Greek and to use the classics effectively. Plutarch, *Cato Major*, ch. 12; E.V. Marmorale, *Cato Major*^{2}, Bari 1949.

[112] A.J. Toynbee, *Hannibal's Legacy* II, London 1965, 414-428.

[113] Riggs: *Comparative Bureaucracy: The Politics of Officialdom*, Bloomington, Ind., 1962; *Administration in Developing Countries* (The Theory of Prismatic Society), Boston 1964. Eisenstadt: *Comparative Institutions*, New York 1964, Section III, "Bureaucracy and Bureaucratization."

Their observations, made on other bureacracies of this type, seem, at first glance, to throw a great deal of light also on Pharisaic moves, maneuverings, and attitudes. The Hellenist skills of Judean Pharisaism may quite well have developed with historical predecessors of theirs under the Ptolemaic regime, which was apparently a period of fruitful symbiosis.[114] Newly acquired political independence will sooner or later bring the most skillful class to the fore, unless their members have compromised themselves entirely through allegiance to their former oppressor.

An additional shortcoming of previous scholarship is the habit of juxtaposing in parallel columns talmudic materials with similar items of the New Testament. The largest attempt of this sort was Strack-Billerbeck's monumental commentary on the New Testament from Talmud and Midrash.[115] To be sure, this is in some respects a useful undertaking, but more often it leads to erroneous conclusions about relationships and sources. When passages seem to indicate rhetorical coloration, comparison should include the Greco-Roman parallels; i.e., a triple column is a must.[116] Thus, the Sermon on the Mount, Matt. V–VIII, Luke VI: 20–37, should be compared not only to a midrashic homily, or considered to be an echo of the Decalogue or a reaction to the Tannaitic legislation at Jabneh (Jamnia),[117] but also be explored in its relation to Greco-Roman rhetoric,[118] since it shows traces of rhetorical style and

[114] Cf. the Ptolemaic use of Jewish mercenaries and of Alexandrinian Jewish officials of many types, and Ptolemaic ties with the Tobiads. Cf. V.A. Tcherikover, *Hellenistic Civilization and the Jews*, Philadelphia 1959; and (with A. Fuks), *Corpus Papyrorum Judaicarum*, 3 vols., Cambridge, Mass. 1957-64. Cf. also the subsequent rapid Hellenization of the Hasmoneans. The latter must have fought for independence rather than for de-Hellenization.

[115] *Kommentar zum Neuen Testament aus Talmud und Midrasch*³, 7 vols., Munich 1926 (partial reprint 1961).

[116] Gerhard Kittel's (ed.) equally monumental *Theological Dictionary of the NT*, tr. G.W. Bromiley, 3 vols. (in progress), Grand Rapids 1964— is virtually a three column study (German: 6 vols., reprinted Stuttgart 1957. The usefulness of this work is lowered in many places by an artificial differentiation between Christian and non-Christian phenomena and an *a priori* devaluation of the latter). In a fourth "column" OT precedents are given. Still valuable is J.J. Wet(t)stein's *Hē Kainē Diathēkē*, 2 vols., Amsterdam 1751-52 (reprinted Graz 1962).

[117] So variously Asher Finkel, *The Pharisees and the Teacher of Nazareth*, Leiden 1964; W.D. Davies, *The Setting of the Sermon on the Mount*, Cambridge 1964.

[118] Illumination through Hellenistic materials: K.F.G. (also D.C.F.G.) Heinrici, *Die Bergpredigt*, BGENT III.1, Leipzig 1905 (biased). On early Christianity generally: Carl Schneider, *Geistesgeschichte des antiken Christentums*, 2 vols.,

sophos ideology. Public temple scenes in which Hillel or Jesus castigate popular piety must not be juxtaposed without relation to Diogenes' or Antisthenes' many similar actions.[119] When in Matthew's attempt at a *sophos* portrayal the central Sage attacks the hypocrisy of Pharisaism, no excess on the part of actual Pharisees living or dead may have been the cause, but rather the temptation to use the Greek cynicizing *thaumaston* in the style of Anacharsis, a Scythian Sage, who "uncovers" the hypocrisies of Greek culture: "He said he wondered (*thaumazein ... elege*) how the Greeks should legislate concerning violence while they honor athletes for wounding each other," D.L. I.103, and a host of others. Only the representatives of Formgeschichte and Rudberg have moved in this direction, without committing themselves, however, in regard to questions of historicity.

The claim of such an adoption of rhetorical content by an otherwise apparently exclusive culture would be more plausible if parallels to it existed elsewhere. This is indeed the case. The early Church, for example, was so impressed with the rhetorical mold that, among others, Arrian-Epictetus' *Encheiridion* was more than once edited in the form of a Christian paraphrase, and Minutius Felix reworked Cicero's *De natura deorum* into his dialogue Octavius, all without mention of the original author.[120] Of course, in the Near East, the adoption of short rhetorical items was probably made "subconsciously," i.e., on the supposition that it was unthinkable that a true teacher would not have embodied in himself all known features of any positive ideal or happening. The Romans, hardly a spineless people, had made such adoptions from Greek rhetoric on a small scale. On a large scale, they preferred to

---

Munich 1954. Papyri: Adolf Deissmann, *Licht vom Osten*[4], Tuebingen 1923 (*Light From the East*, tr. L.R.M. Strachan, London 1911). Chas. Norris Cochrane, *Christianity and Classical Culture*, New York 1941, 1944 (reprinted 1957) and the writings of Henry Chadwick, Adolf Bonhoeffer, F. Pfister, W.L. Knox, C.H. Dodd, F.J. Doelger, F.C. and R.M. Grant and R. Bultmann.

[119] Derivation of these scenes from Greco-Roman rhetoric (and the suspicion of their non-historicity) does not preclude the possibility that these items counter the influence of another Teacher-Sage or movement, i.e., that Hillel items attempt to counter Jesus' portrayal, or vice-versa, or that Hillel's portrayal counters that of Nicolaus of Damascus (the latter idea briefly suggested by B. Wacholder, *Nicolaus of Damascus*, Berkeley 1962). For this reason, the attempts of Finkel and Davies (see n. 117, above) are of value.

[120] J. Stelzenberger, *Die Beziehungen der fruehchristlichen Sittenlehre zur Ethik der Stoa*, Munich 1937, ch. 14: *Paraphrasis Christiana* and Pseudo-Nilus.

identify themselves openly with the heroes of the Greeks and could thus leave the original names intact. This happened, too, in later patristic tradition, as, for example, with Maximus Confessor, c. 580-662, in his valuable collection *Loci communes*,[121] and in medieval Islam where scholarly habits were quite advanced.[122]

A final requirement of scholarship is a greater appreciation of what adoption actually means. Adoption is very rarely slavish. As a rule it signifies the recognition that a kindred spirit prevails in the other culture, or that an urgent common problem has been successfully solved there. When it comes to the means of survival, there is often little choice. But only vital and living cultures borrow; rigid and stationary societies do not. Moreover, the rhetorical world, in its stress on practical ethics and the ideal of the Sage, resembled ancient Oriental Wisdom Literature (c. 2500-700), which had been acceptable to the earlier Hebrew culture of the biblical period.[123] Indeed, philosophy, as Seneca understands it, is actually called "sapientia" in his 94th Epistle, 15f. and *passim*. Philosophy, rhetorically hypostasized, can "speak"—"inquit," 95.10—just as *hokhmah* in biblical and midrashic texts. Considerable sections of both Oriental Wisdom and Greco-Roman rhetoric were religiously neutral or inoffensive. Both seem to have been the product and tool of bureacracies.[124] Rhetorical-Cynical non-conformism, especially the odd demonstrative act and the critique of the public by the Sages, resembled earlier Hebrew prophetic stances.

Adoption, furthermore, means adaptation. The latter was manifold and complex in early talmudic culture: the Greek *chria*, for example, was: (1) "naturalized," i.e., told of Pharisaic and Tannaitic heroes; (2) transcendentalized, i.e., used for the propagation of revealed Torah and the acquisition of immortality; (3) most often "legitimized" or "testimonialized" by the addition of a more or

---

[121] In *Opera Omnia*, J.P. Migne, *Patrologia Graeca*, vol. 91, Paris 1865.

[122] See Franz Rosenthal, *Das Fortleben der Antike im Islam*, Zurich 1965.

[123] All introductions to the OT. Further : J.C. Rylaarsdam, *Revelation in Jewish Wisdom Literature*, Chicago 1946 (he continues the work of Gressmann, Baumgartner and Fichtner); Robert Gordis, *The Book of God and Man*, Chicago 1965; James B. Pritchard, *Ancient Near Eastern Texts...*², Princeton 1955; ed. M. Noth, D. Winton Thomas, *Wisdom in Israel and in the Ancient Near East*, Leiden 1955. H. Schmoekel, *Kulturgeschichte des Alten Orient*, Stuttgart 1961.

[124] In the widest sense of the term. Robert Gordis speaks of a responsible middle class, "The Social Background of Wisdom Literature," *Hebrew Union College Annual* 18, 1943-44, 78-118.

less fitting confirmative biblical quotation, *a testimonium* or *martyrion* as it is sometimes called in Greco-Roman rhetoric where it is similarly used;[125] (4) "humanized," i.e., the Sages were made to be less mordant with the "victims" of their wit and, consequently, less witty. At a later stage, when the true chriic nature of the stories was perhaps no longer fully understood or no longer admissable, the *chria*, and with it the fictional debate and other genres, were (5) halachized, i.e., considered an actual event and legal precedent from which further law could be derived.[126] Adaptation of this sort, however, signifies a partial rejection of the original material, and its elevation from a popular level to serious legal use.[127] (6) Rhetorical material was, of course, only selectively adopted; and, finally, (7) its narrative technique was used creatively in the (still rhetorical) combination of chriic and other motemes into a new unit, as, for example, in the story of Hillel in the Snow, BT Yoma 35b, which is totally made up of chriic elements.

Many additional circumstances point to such an adoption of Greco-Roman rhetoric in early talmudic culture. The express distinction between oral and written lore and the consciousness of their problematic relationship is found in both cultures[128] and finally ended in a general wave of codifications of cultural materials of all types in both cultures from 150 to 250.[129] We find

[125] Definition in Cicero's *Topica* 73; see "Cynicism" 41.1.

[126] For example, the rather bawdy and witty report, totally composed of similar Greco-Roman elements, of Hillel's exhibiting a bull as a cow in the Temple, TB Betsah 20af. *Chriae* are also used to illustrate already existing law. Cf. "The Transformation of a *Chria*," *Erwin R. Goodenough Memorial Volume*, Suppl. *Numen*, XIV, *Religions in Antiquity*, Leiden 1968, 372-411, IV.2.

[127] The Hebrew *chria* is non-political; its Hellenistic counterpart is often aggressively political. In Judaic culture, however, opposition against Rome, empire and tyranny found expression in other literary media, such as the martyrology, the apocalypse, even the romance, halachah, and various midrashic forms. The political fable, however, exists in both cultures.

[128] Aristotle, *Rhet.* I.x.6, 1368 b; I.xiii.2, 1373b. Cf. Diogenes in D.L. VI.48 (oral transmission superior) with Hillel in Shabbat 31a (reliance on oral transmission necessary). Cf. Ben-Amos, *op. cit.*, pp. 19-29. Gerhardsson's work, throughout, is devoted to this subject : Rabbinic Judaism: 19-181; early Christianity: 182-335.

[129] West: grammar and criticism, curiosa, symposia, gnomes, philosophical *vitae* and, above all, law. Judea: earlier attempts and final Mishna, Tosefta, halachic Midrashim, AdRN, possibly Gen.R. and Lev. R., Megillath Ta'anith, earliest form of Seder Olam. Our contention is that some historical necessity (possibly a mere receding of creativity) in both cultures brought about practically simultaneous codifications of both Roman and Judean material by the representatives of similar bureaucracies.

the same singling out of Epicurus and Oenomaus as the *bêtes noires* of later rhetoric,[130] and the same diffusion and proportional distribution of echoes of popular Hellenistic philosophies, such as Pythagorean bits, some Platonic material, a fair amount of Stoicism (all twice if not thrice removed from their origin) and, above all, the all-pervading coloration of Cynicism, partly in the sense in which rhetors and even Stoics asserted "that the Sage cynicizes, Cynicism being a short-cut to virtue."[131]

If Pharisees and Tannaim—and similarly the Fathers of the Church—indeed have acquired and developed farther the literary tools of another bureaucracy, the possibility exists that Roman administrators may have borrowed from their Near Eastern counterparts. Indeed, the *Scriptores Historiae Augustae*, XLV. 6f., i.e., Lampridius, thus claims that the Emperor Alexander Severus recommended the ordination procedures used for Christian and Jewish "priests" (i.e., in the case of the latter: rabbis) to Roman officials for the installation of provincial governors, revenue officials and army officers! In LI. 5 Alexander Severus is shown to have made the Golden Rule, as received from Christians and Jews (thus expressly the text), an official imperial slogan, being used even in military law.[132]

A final example from the Christian hierarchy reflects the blurred borderlines between bureaucratic-rhetorical terminology, popular philosophy, and religious doctrine. Augustine calls the Golden Rule, as it appears in different formulations, "vulgare proverbium"

[130] Thus in *Orations* VI and VII of Emperor Julian. On a positive use of Epicurean materials in Rabbinic literature cf. *Encyclopaedia Judaica* (Engl.) Jerusalem-New York, 1969-70, *s.v.*, "Epicureans and Epicureanism."

[131] D.L. VII.121 (Apollodorus). Rhetorical nostalgia for Cynicism (often hand in hand with criticism of its abuses) with Philo, Seneca, Musonius Rufus, Epictetus, Dio, Favorinus, Lucian, Plutarch, Maximus of Tyre and Julian, also with a number of Church Fathers. Last but not least with Diogenes Laertius. On Philo's "Cynical source," reflected in a description of the festival cycle in Cynic-nostalgic terms, see Isaak Heinemann, *Philo's griechische und juedische Bildung*, Darmstadt 1929-32 (reprinted 1962), 142-145.

[132] The test cases supplied in this passage may have been older valid military law to which the Golden Rule became secondarily appended. On the other hand, similar test cases combined with the Golden Rule are already found in the Akiba passage, Philo, Luke, and some others, cf. n. 67.

Whether Lampridius' incidents are historically true or only express a certain tendentiousness of his work is not decisive for our argument. In either case, the existence of such a rhetorical-bureaucratic-ethicizing ideology is evident, either with the emperor or with his historian.

in *De ordine* II.8.25; he counts it among the "praecepta sapientium" and as part of Natural Law in *De quantitate animae* 73; he stresses its absolute validity in *De doctrina Christiana* III.14 but establishes closer ties with revelationary doctrine mainly in *Enarrationes in Psalmos*.[133]

A critical reflection on Greco-Roman rhetoric and its techniques and genres, as it was in fact undertaken in Greco-Roman antiquity in a highly sophisticated attempt, must be continued in modern scholarship and followed by an exploration of the Near Eastern genres. Only then can their significance for history, biography, and intercultural relations be determined. The historian, meanwhile, has to use this material only with the greatest of caution and the greatest of ingenuity.

[133] Migne, *Patrologia Latina* 32, p. 1006; 32, p. 1075; 34, p. 74. *Enarr*. Ps. 35 (sermo 1.34); Ps. 51 (sermo 10.23); Ps. 57 (sermo 1.8).

NOTES ON THE POPULATION OF THE JAZĪRAH IN EARLY ISLAMIC TIMES

by Oleg Grabar
University of Michigan

SINCE 1964 the Kelsey Museum of Archaeology at the University of Michigan—with additional support from the Center for Near Eastern and North African Studies and from the Horace H. Rackham School for Graduate Studies—has sponsored the excavation of Qaṣr al-Ḥayr al Sharqi in the arid steppe of Syria, halfway between Palmyra and the Euphrates. Two seasons of work have already taken place, in 1964 and 1966, and the next expedition is planned for 1968. Whatever had been known about the site until the beginning of our work can be found in K. A. C. Creswell's works on early Islamic architecture, and J. Sauvaget formulated about Qaṣr al-Ḥayr a series of brilliant hypotheses which may not be accepted as a whole but which did bring to light some very important new information.[1] Preliminary results of our first expeditions have been or are about to be published in the journal of the Service des Antiquités of Syria.[2]

Even though we are not yet in a position to explain satisfactorily why, when, and how a huge enterprise of monumental proportions (fig. 1) was created in a waterless area of the Syrian steppe, certain preliminary results have begun to emerge. These in turn have compelled us to raise a few questions which extend beyond the purely archaeological problems of Qaṣr al-Ḥayr al-Sharqi (its ancient or mediaeval names are still uncertain) and it is on one of these that I should like to make a few comments. For archaeological activities are indeed of little value if they cannot contribute to the solution of old problems or if they do not create new questions for scholars in may different disciplines.

Thanks to a celebrated inscription seen first and last by the

---

[1] K.A.C. Creswell, *Early Muslim Architecture*, vol. I (Oxford, 1932), pp. 330ff.; J. Sauvaget, "Remarques sur les Monuments Omeyyades," *Journal Asiatique*, vol. CCXXXI (1939).

[2] O. Grabar, "Qasr al-Hayr al-Sharqi," *Annales Archéologiques de Syrie*, vol. XV (1965); further instalments in forthcoming volumes.

French consul Rousseau in 1808[3] it has been known that the Umayyads were responsible for major constructions on the site, and the existing working hypothesis with which we began our work was that the two existing large enclosures and the walled area surrounding them were an Umayyad palace and city, comparable to many sites in Syria, Palestine, and Transjordan.[4] Most of these had a pre-Islamic history, and the existence of a pre-Islamic past at Qaṣr al-Ḥayr is suggested by a large and still unpublished Palmyrene inscription on the reused stones of the mosque. But most of these Umayyad sites also dwindled in importance after the first Islamic dynasty, and some even disappeared from existence, especially the ones which are in semi-desertic regions. One of the most surprising facts learned as a result of our excavations so far has been that Qaṣr al-Ḥayr remained a major and active center until the thirteenth century, if not even the fourteenth. This point may be considered as proved by evidence provided by ceramics, coins, inscriptions, and numerous architectural and archaeological details. There is, of course, no certainty that it maintained throughout several centuries the same purposes and the same functions, and, indeed, one of our eventual tasks is to disentangle what appears to be a particularly complex history. It is clearly premature at this stage to do more than hypothesize on the specific nature and development of Qaṣr al-Ḥayr over almost 1000 years of archaeologically documented history. But it is also clear that an eventual understanding of the site's problems must take into consideration wider questions on the nature of the area in which Qaṣr al-Ḥayr is found.

On this point, however, scholarship so far has been very reticent. It is known, of course, that today the triangular area which extends from Palmyra to the north and to the east as far as the Euprates (reached around the present towns of Raqqah and Abu Kemal) is a vast desert with only four permanently settled places (fig. 2): Erek, Sukhneh, Tayyibe, Qawm. The consistent presence of ruins, be it Qaṣr al-Ḥayr or the more celebrated Ruṣāfah or the large

[3] First published by Ch. Clermont-Ganneau, *Recueil d'Archéologie Orientale*, vol. III (Paris, 1900), pp. 285ff.

[4] No full list of these sites exists; cf. bibliography and statement of problems in O. Grabar, "Umayyad palace and the Abbasid revolution," *Studia Islamica*, vol. XVIII (1963); the most important addition since then is that of the excavations at Jabal Says, K. Brisch, "Das omayyadische Schloss in Usais," *Mitteilungen des Deutschen Archéologischen Instituts Abteilung Kairo*, vols. 19 and 20 (1963, 1965).

FIG. 1

mounds surrounding Tayyibe or Qawm, does indicate, however, that the area may have been more fully settled in the past, not necessarily in terms of total population as in terms of numbers of locations used for permanent living. In this sense this region appears to be somewhat related to the vast group of "dead cities" or of *tells* which define the archaeological landscape of western Syria,

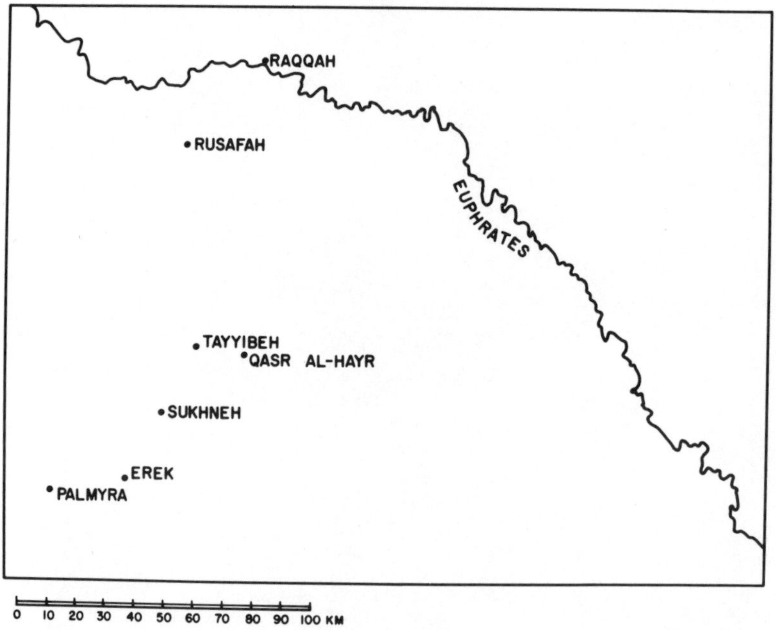

FIG. 2

of the Euphrates valley, and of the valleys of the Euphrates' tributaries in the Jazīrah. Except for G. Tchalenko's magnificent volumes on a small region of northern Syria,[5] scholarly consideration of these sites has tended to be limited to attempts at identifying the ancient and mediaeval names of these sites or, alternately, to set on maps the information provided by written sources. Such was the main concern of Dussaud's great work on

[5] G. Tchalenko, *Villages Antiques de la Syrie du Nord* (Paris, 1953-8).

the topography of Syria[6] and such was the primary, but not sole, interest of Musil's surveys.[7] Yet, however important it is to know the exact nomenclature of all these sites over the centuries, it is equally important to understand what was done in these places and who lived there. On this point few significant hypotheses outside of that of the *limes*[8] have so far been put forward.

The need for such hypotheses occurs with particular acuity when one considers the early Islamic period, for three closely related phenomena affected Syria and the Jazīrah in the seventh, eighth, and ninth centuries. First, the valleys of the Euphrates, of the Balikh, and of the Khabur changed radically in character. Instead of being part of a frontier area between Rome or Byzantium and the Parthian or Sasanian empires, studded with fortresses whose rebuilding in the sixth century is described by Procopius,[9] the western Jazīrah—the Diyār Rabīʿah of mediaeval geographers—became a central part of the new Muslim empire, a critical *charnière* between Iraq and the newly conquered Iran on the one hand and, on the other, the traditional western Semitic world of Syria and Palestine on the way to Egypt and the Maghrib or to the *thughūr* of Cilicia. The frontier was then in the Amanus mountains and farther north in the Diyār Bakr and in Armenia, and it is only after the conquest of Anatolia in the late eleventh century that this frontier area will also, at least for a few centuries, change in character. All sources make it very clear that Umayyad and ʿAbbāsid rulers alike were conscious of the new position of western Jazīrah, since from the time of al-Walīd I considerable efforts were expanded into digging canals, clearing swamps, and transforming the river valleys into fertile agricultural lands,[10] which they had not been on any scale at all since Hellenistic times.

The second phenomenon is perhaps less revolutionary from an ecological point of view. While agriculture became in Islamic times

[6] R. Dussaud, *Typographie Historique de la Syrie Antique et Médiévale* (Paris, 1927).

[7] Primarily A. Musil, *Palmyrena* (New York, 1928).

[8] V. Chapot, *La Frontière de l'Euphrate* (Paris, 1907); Poidebard, *La Trace de Rome dans le Désert de Syrie* (Paris, 1938); and articles on *limes* in various classical encyclopedias; the whole subject probably needs considerable revision and re-interpretation; cf. L. Dilleman, *Haute Mésopotamie Orientale et Pays Adjacents* (Paris, 1962).

[9] Procopius, *De Aedificiis* (Loeb ed., London, 1940), Book II.

[10] See evidence and bibliography in *Studia Islamica*, p. 15.

an important activity in the Euphrates valley, the valley's use as a means of communication was intensified rather than created anew. Communications were both strategic in allowing for large military movements and economic in providing for the easy flow of goods. The complex urban organism which goes by the name of Raqqah—and which has never been properly studied either through texts or through excavations[11]—included barracks for soldiers (both permanently settled units and passing ones), storage areas for transit goods and caravans, and markets for local products. Obviously we have to assume the existence of a whole range of locally provided services for all these activities. These transformations of the Jazīrah had yet another significant aspect. They corresponded to a decline of the properly Syrian axis in the areas of Damascus, Homs, and Aleppo,[12] at least after the fall of the Umayyads. The archaeological evidence from Qaṣr al-Ḥayr would confirm this well-known fact in showing, for instance, the predominance of Mesopotamian ceramic wares over western Syrian ones, known, for instance, through the Danish excavations at Hama,[13] at least from the early ninth century on. It would appear thus that the desert area north of Palmyra tended to belong to the orbit of Raqqah and of the Euphrates valley rather than to that of Homs or Damascus. This is quite clearly a reverse of the pre-Islamic pattern, when the bishop of Palmyra was subservient to the metropolitan of Damascus,[14] and of the Umayyad pattern, since the lost inscription refers to the people of Homs, and of the contemporary pattern when Palmyra appears as an outpost in the desert of western Syria rather than of the newly developed Jazīrah.

While many details of these two phenomena are still far from being assured, their general lines are fairly clear and can be documented with literary as well as archaeological sources. This is far from being as true of the third characteristic of early Islamic

[11] Convenient summary in J. Sauvaget, "Tessons de Rakka," *Ars Islamica*, vols. XIII-XIV (1948); see also recent Syrian excavations, mostly unpublished.

[12] Clearly documented archaeologically through the very fact of the "dead cities" (Tchalenko, pp. 422ff.), the phenomenon was probably equally true in the large urban centers; J. Sauvaget, *Alep* (Paris, 1941), *passim*; N. Elisséev, "Dimashḳ," *Encycl. of Islam*, 2nd ed.

[13] P. J. Riis and others, *Hama, Les Verreries et Poteries Médiévales* (Copenhagen, 1957).

[14] R. Devreesse, *Le Patriarcat d'Antioche* (Paris, 1945), p. 305.

times. The economic and ecological changes which can be defined imply a major increase in population, but from where did this population come? One source consisted certainly in newly settled Arab tribesmen from the south, probably continuing in ways which are not yet totally explored[15] earlier patterns of settlements. A thorough study of sources such as the as yet not totally published *Anṣāb al-Ashrāf* of Balādhuri should provide important information concerning the ways in which these settlements actually did take place in early Islamic times. Yet, even if much of the urban or semi-urban population may indeed have consisted of immigrants, nomads or not, from Arabia, there is some doubt as to whether many of them could have easily become the farmers of the newly irrigated Euphrates valley. An eventual comparison with the social and psychological problems posed in the contemporary sedentarization of eastern Syria may prove quite useful to develop further this particular point.

But there may also have been another possible source of people for the Jazīrah. It is fairly well established by now that the Muslim conquest of Syria coincided with the depopulation of agricultural northern Syria,[16] but no clear hypothesis seems to exist as to what happened to the Christian population. Some families certainly left Syria for Anatolia or for other parts of the Christian empire. Others were fairly soon converted to Islam. But it may also be suggested that a number, especially among the farmers, may have formed the core of the new inhabitants of the Jazīrah.

It may be noted first of all that many of our most important sources about the history of the Jazīrah consist in the Syriac writings of heterodox churchmen. Dionysius of Tell Mahre, Agapius of Manbij, Michael the Syrian and a number of anonymous chroniclers all seem to represent an intellectual group of ecclesiastics largely freed from what seemed to them to be the yoke of Chalcedonian orthodoxy, who were certainly unwilling to be involved in the affairs of Byzantium like their Melkite brethren, even though themselves riddled with internal intrigues and disturbances for which the Muslim power was often called to be the arbiter.

---

[15] R. Dussaud, *La Pénétration des Arabes en Syrie* (Paris, 1955); F. Altheim, *Die Araber in der alten Welt* (Berlin, 1965); neither of these works can be considered to be definitive studies on the subject, but they may serve as introductions to the problems and to the documents.

[16] Tchalenko, pp. 422ff. and *passim*.

Limiting ourselves to western Jazīrah, the information provided by these writers suggests an extraordinary activity which can only be understood if there was a large heterodox population in the area. Thus, at one point around 812, a patriarch and a bishop find themselves blocked in Rāfiqah by bandits.[17] In 818 a meeting of forty-five bishops took place in Kallinicos, which was the pre-Islamic part of the Raqqah complex.[18] Christian women and children were used by some rebels as protection against the machines of ʿAbdallāh ibn Ṭāhir,[19] and many instances exist which suggest that life often seemed quite hard to the heterodox Christian populations of the Jazīrah. Michael the Syrian provides a striking description of the growth of an official bureaucracy in early Islamic times which, in the eyes of the Christians, was but a rapid multiplication of petty tyrants. "More than at any other time of Arab domination, calamities have been accumulating on the men of to-day because of the cupidity of prefects; for each one of them used to take for himself what he added on to taxes and he could add and increase as much as he wanted. They [the prefects] appointed and established special officials for each kind [of activity] and thus ate up and devoured the poor. In Kallinicos they put up a judge called *qāḍi*, and a governer for taxes, and a prefect to supervise crimes, and another one in charge of correspondence with the king about the state of the land, and another one in charge of the revenues from wool, and another one to suppress injustice toward men, even though he was the most unjust of all. And they set up similar officials in all cities."[20] It is mostly Christian sources which reflect complaints about excessive taxation under Hishām.[21] Churches and monasteries were often destroyed but also rebuilt in a matter of days, which suggests at the same time that the destructions were more symbolic than real and that the buildings were rather primitive and new.[22] The countryside was not always secure, especially during the civil war in the latter years of Umayyad rule,[23] and banditry seems to have been endemic. And yet these Christian

---

[17] Michel le Syrien, *Chronique*, tr. J.-B. Chabot (Paris, 1905), vol. III, p. 30.
[18] Ibid., p. 31.
[19] Ibid., p. 51.
[20] Ibid., pp. 104-5.
[21] Ibid., vol. II, p. 490.
[22] Ibid., vol. III, pp. 47-8.
[23] Agapius of Manbij, *K. al-'Unvān*, ed. and tr. A.A. Vasiliev, in *Patrologia Orientalis*, vol. VIII (Paris, 1912), p. 517.

communities survived and probably flourished at times, especially until the twelfth or the thirteenth centuries, and the endless complaints seem at times to reflect conditioned reflexes to authority rather than fully ascertained abuses of power and persecutions; for most of this Christian population was quite conscious of what was happening in the Muslim world, and it is interesting to note that around 500 A. H. Michael the Syrian begins to count the years in terms of "Turkish" rule.[24]

The examples we have brought together have come mostly from one source only. They can easily be multiplied and thus permit the hypothesis that a fairly large proportion of the newly settled inhabitants of the Jazīrah were heterodox Christians. This hypothesis may also help in explaining where the Christian population of western Syria went after the Muslim conquest. For it has perhaps not been sufficiently noted that not all of the pre-Islamic Christian population of Syria was Melkite or Chalcedonian. In the area surveyed by Tchalenko, over 80 religious buildings were found to have been primarily Monophysite.[25] Numerous inscriptions testify to their importance and it is particularly likely that the simpler farmers shifted allegiances quite easily.[26] After the conquest the lessening of the authority of Byzantium and of the orthodox church certainly led to a growth of the power of various heterodox sects.

But our hypothesis, if acceptable, may lead to a point of somewhat wider significance. It would point to a fairly obvious fact, which is often overlooked in general histories, that for an undetermined period of time much of the population of the Near East remained non-Muslim under Muslim rule. Muqaddasi had observed that in his native Jerusalem Christians and Jews still had the upper hand in the tenth century.[27] The case of Jerusalem may have been exceptional for obvious reasons, but it is likely indeed that much of the population of Iranian cities remained Zoroastrian for several centuries and that the formerly Christian lands had a predominantly Christian population, particularly among the farmers, small artisans, and merchants. It is through the maintenance over the early centuries of Islam of these mostly heterodox communities

---

[24] Michel le Syrien, vol. III, pp. 215, 219.

[25] Tchalenko, pp. 128, 135, 145ff.

[26] Devreesse, pp. 163ff. for examples.

[27] Al-Muqaddasi, in *Bibl. Geogr. Arab.*, vol. III (Leyden, 1906), p. 165.

that one can perhaps explain the development in the twelfth and thirteenth centuries of an art with Christian themes in the midst of the general explosion of the arts which characterizes the Near East just before the Mongol invasion.[28] The phenomenon of Christian populations in the Jazīrah, aside from suggesting a solution to the problem of the disappearing Christians from western Syria, serves also to illustrate the remarkable openness of the early Islamic cultural structure, which could include the most diverse communities.

[28] This is still a very little studied subject; for some very important information in a limited area, see P. J. Fiey, *Assyrie Chrétienne* (Beyrouth, 1965); for manuscripts, R. Ettinghausen, *Arab Painting* (Geneva, 1962), p. 96; none of the pertinent objects has ever been fully published.

AN INITIATION RITE FOR A HITTITE PRINCE

by Hans G. Güterbock
University of Chicago

AMONG the many Hittite texts in which the ritual for so-called festivals, Sumerian *ezen*, Akkadian *isinnu*, is laid down in great detail, there is one that is unusual with regard to both its name and its contents. The tablet Bo 2017, published in cuneiform by the present author as *IBoT* I No. 29[1], is, according to its colophon (reverse, line 57) "[The first tablet], text not complete, of the EZEN *ḫaššumaš* in [. . .]." The tablet number, though broken, can be restored as "first" because the fragmentary beginning of the tablet (obverse 1-5) looks like the beginning of the whole text, giving in line 1 the name of the festival and in line 2 the place where it is performed, [*Ḫa*]*ttuši*, "in Hattusa." The word *ḫaššumaš* is the genitive of the gerund of the verb *ḫaš*- "to procreate, beget, give birth." In order to find out which of these shadings, if indeed any of them, is applicable, we have to look at the contents of the text.

The main figure in the ritual is a prince, DUMU.LUGAL, "son of the king;" the king himself appears only in the first paragraph (obverse 4), never thereafter, whereas the prince, who may have been first introduced in line 5 (restored), is mentioned all through the text from there on.

The rites continue for several days: four days are covered by the extant tablet, and more days must have been contained in the lost continuation.

A great number of priests and representatives of various professions participate in the performances. There are several lists of such officials in the text, none of them completely preserved; the lists vary, but some of the officials recur.

Most important are the localities at which the rites are performed and the nature of these performances. One striking feature is that

[1] H. Bozkurt, M. Çiğ, H. G. Güterbock, *Istanbul Arkeoloji Müzelerinde bulunan Boğazköy Tabletlerinden seçme metinler* (Istanbul, Maarif Matbaasi, 1944), text No. 29. The fragment 141/s, found in 1960, is a duplicate (hitherto unpublished).

This paper was read at the meeting of the Middle West Branch of 1960. A full edition of the text with transliteration and translation must await another occasion. The passages discussed in this paper are given in transliteration at the end.

eating and feasting are predominant throughout the text, and in accordance with this the places most often mentioned are the É [lú]MUḪALDIM, "house of the cook," i.e., the kitchen, and the *arzanaš parna-*, a building which has been explained as "inn" or "dining room." Thus we read (obverse 18 f.):

> When the prince asks for food in the kitchen, then twelve priests sit down in front of him.

After an enumeration of the twelve different priests, the text goes on (25 f.):

> Before they sit down to eat, the "anointed one" and the priests perform purification rites at the kitchen door.

Similarly (obverse 50): "The prince goes into the *arzana* house and asks for food." Then, after an enumeration of foods and beverages, (53) "all the priests sit down in front of the prince. But for eating they are called into the kitchen." Thereafter bread is put on the tables of the prince and the various priests.

Similar scenes recur several times. In outline, the performances in the various localities run as follows:

The beginning of the rites taking place in the morning of the second day (obverse 6 ff.) is badly damaged, but eating is repeatedly mentioned.

The prince asks for food in the kitchen (obverse 18); purification rites at the kitchen door (26, see above).

The prince goes into the *arzana* house; food and offerings (29 ff.).

He goes into the temple of the goddess Kataḫḫa and asks for food (35 ff.).

Third day: Ceremonies for the goddess Ariniddu in the kitchen (39 ff.).

The prince goes into the *arzana* house; eating in the kitchen; listing of tables set up for the various priests and of offerings (50 ff.).

Gap between obverse and reverse.

After some mutilated lines at the beginning of the reverse, tables, food, and offerings are listed again (rev. 10 ff.).

Meat is carried into the inner chamber of the bath house (23 f.).

The prince goes into the *arzana* house; eating (28 ff.).

Fourth day: Breakfast (33), followed by special rites to be discussed presently.

The prince leaves (probably the *arzana* house) and goes back to the temple of Kattaḫḫa; eating (41 ff.).

He then goes to the *arzana* house (again), where the following ceremony takes place (last paragraph of our first tablet, rev. 46-56):

> He goes into the *arzana* house and there, too, asks for food. Three hot breads, 10 moist breads, 10 barley breads, 10 sweet breads, 3 handfuls of groats, 2 *wakšur* measures of milk, 2 *ḫuppar* vessels of beer. And twelve prostitutes sit down before him. They eat and drink. And on that night they purify the prince again and make him lie down. At either side of his head they put two thick breads, and at either side of his feet they put two thick breads, and around him they make a drawing out of beer. When [. . . .], then they bring in the prostitutes.

Thus ends the extant part of the text. It takes little imagination to guess what this ceremony means. It seems that this passage gives the clue to the nature of the text and thereby to the meaning of its title: it is the "festival of procreating" by which these women, written with the logogram $^{\text{sal.meš}}$ KAR.KID, Akkadian *ḫarimāti*, "prostitutes," initiate the prince into adult life.

The preparations for this include, apart from the purification before going to bed and the extensive feasting mentioned earlier, some other ceremonies that may now be considered. At the end of the second day we read (obverse 35-38):

> Then he goes into the temple of Kattaḫḫa and asks for food. Twelve plowmen sit down before him. Then he provides the gods (with offerings). The plowmen lift yokes from in front of the deity and harness one team of purified oxen and drive them to the fallow. End of second day.

Or take another scene (rev. 17-19):

> A handmill is put in front of the fireplace. The prince, the "anointed" priest, the chamberlain, the barber, and the brick moulders turn the mill.

These two scenes may very well symbolize the food-providing aspects of kingship and serve to initiate the prince into the duties of plowing and flour making. In this connection it may be mentioned that one of the deities named in the text is ^{d}LAMA.LUGAL, "the Protective Deity of the King."

Finally, at the beginning of the fourth day we read (rev. 33-41):

> On the fourth day for breakfast: three hot breads (etc., an enumeration

of food and beverages follows; then in line 35) The "anointed" priest goes to the House of the Dead. (More breads listed; libation for the gods). They lead a he-goat outside, slaughter it and eat it, and take the hide of the he-goat. They strip a blind man, beat him, and lead him to the House of the Dead. Then they eat and drink.

This rite, which is difficult to understand in all its implications, may have something to do with putting the old ego to rest now that the prince enters a new phase of his life.[2]

While many problems raised by this unique text remain unsolved, and although features known from ethnology as characteristic of initiation rites are lacking here, it seems that the references to such basic duties as plowing and grinding fit the pattern, just as the last paragraph describes the prince's initiation into adult life.

TRANSLITERATION OF SELECTED PASSAGES

OBVERSE

1 . . . .]-*ḫa* EZEN *ḫa-a*[*š-šu-ma-aš* . . . .

2 . . . . ^{uru}*Ḫa-a*]*t-tu-ši A-NA* [. . . . .

3 . . . .]x *3 UP-NU ḫa*-x[. . . . .

4 . . . .] NINDA.KUR$_4$.RA.ḪI.A LUGAL-*uš p*[*ár-ši-ia*

5 . . . . DUMU.LU]GAL *a-še*[*-e*]*-ša-an-zi n*[*u* . . . .

. . . .

18 *nu* DUMU.LUGAL *ku-wa-pí I-NA* É ^{lú}MUḪALDIM *a-da-an-na ú*[*-e-ek-zi nu-uš-ši pí-r*]*a-an* (19) *12* ^{lú}SANGA *e-ša-an-da*

. . . .

25 . . . *nu-uš-ša-an ku-it-ma-an a-da-an-na n*[*a-a-ú-i e-ša-an-t*]*a-ri*

26 *a-aš-ga A-NA* KÁ É.MUḪALDIM ^{lú}*ta-zi-li-iš* $^{lú.meš}$SANGA *šu-up*[*-pí-ia*]*-aḫ-ḫ*[*a-an-z*]*i*

. . . .

35 . . . *ta-aš I-NA* É ^{d}*Ka-taḫ-ḫa pa-iz-zi nu a-da-an-na ú-e-ek-zi*

36 [*nu*]*-uš-ši 12* $^{lú.meš}$APIN.LAL *pí-ra-an e-ša-an-ta-ri na-aš-ta* DINGIR.MEŠ *aš-nu-zi*

---

37 $^{lú.meš}$APIN.LAL ^{giš}ŠUDUN.ḪI.A *IŠ-TU PA-NI* DINGIR-*LIM kar-pa-an-zi nu 1 ḫa-ap-ki-ri* GUD

38 *šu-up-pí-ia-aḫ-ḫa-an-da-an tu*[*-u-r*]*i-ia-an-zi nu wa-ar-ḫu-uš-šu-i pé-en-na-an-zi* UD.2.KAM *QA-TI*

---

[2] This interpretation was suggested by Thorkild Jacobsen in the discussion of the paper.

. . . .

50 [*nu*] DUMU.LUGAL *ar-za-na pár-na pa-iz-zi nu* DUMU.LUGAL *a-da-an-na ú-e-ek-zi*

. . . .

53 *nu A-NA* DUMU.LUGAL $^{\text{lú.meš}}$SANGA *ḫu-u-ma-an-te-eš pí-ra-an-še-et e-ša-an-da-ri*

---

54 *a-da-an-na-ma I-NA* É ^{lú}MUḪALDIM *ḫal-zi-ia-at-ta-ri* . . .

REVERSE

17 . . . *1* $^{\text{na4}}$ARÀ *ḫa-aš*[*-ši-i pí-ra*]*-an* (18) *ti-an-zi ta* $^{\text{na4}}$ARÀ DUMU.LUGAL *1 ta-zi-el-li-iš* ^{lú}ŠÀ[.TAM] (19) ^{lú}ŠU.I $^{\text{lú-meš}}$SIG$_4$*-na-al-le-e-eš ma-al-la-an-zi* . . .

. . . .

33 *I-NA* UD.4.KAM *wa-ga-an-na 3* NINDA *a-a-an* . . .

35 . . . *ta ta-zi-el-li-iš I-NA* ^{é}*ḫé-eš-ta-a pa-iz-zi*

. . . .

37 . . . MÁŠ.GAL*-ma a-ra-aḫ-za pé-e-ḫu-da-an-zi*

38 *nu-kán* MÁŠ.GAL*-an ar-kán-zi na-an ar-ḫa a-da-an-zi*

39 KUŠ.MÁŠ.GAL*-ma da-an-zi 1* LÚ.IGI.NU.GÁL *ni-ku-ma-an-da-ri-an-zi*

40 *na-an wa-al-ḫa-an-ni-an-zi na-an* ^{é}*ḫé-eš-ta-a pé-e-ḫu-da-an-zi*

41 *nu a-da-an-zi a-ku-wa-an-zi na-aš-ta* DUMU.LUGAL *pa-ra-a ú-iz-zi*

42 *nu* EGIR*-pa I-NA* É ^{d}*Ka-taḫ-ḫa pa-iz-zi ta a-da-an-na*

43 *ú-e-ek-zi* . . .

. . . .

46 *I-NA* É *ar-za-na pa-iz-zi nu a-pí-ia-ia a-da-an-na ú-e-ek-zi* (47) *3* NINDA *a-a-an 10* NINDA *LA-AB-KU 10* NINDA.ŠE *10* NINDA.KU$_7$ *3 UP-NU AR-ZA-AN-NU* (48) *2 wa-ak-šur* GA *2* ^{dug}*ḫu-u-up-pár* KAŠ *nu-uš-ši 12* $^{\text{sal.meš}}$KAR.KID (49) [*pí-r*]*a-an e-ša-an-ta nu a-da-an-zi a-ku-wa-an-zi* (50) [*nu a-p*]*é-e-da-ni* MI*-ti* DUMU.LUGAL *QA-TAM-MA šu-up-pí-aḫ-ḫa-an-zi* (51) [*nam-ma*]*-an ša-aš-ša-nu-an-zi nu-uš-ši IŠ-TU* SAG.DU*-ŠU* [*ke-e-ez-za*] (52) [*2* NINDA.KUR$_4$.R]A *ke-ez-zi-ia-aš-ši 2* NINDA.KUR$_4$.RA *ti-an-zi* (53) [*IŠ-TU*] GÌR.MEŠ*-ŠU-ia-aš-ši ke-e-ez-za 2* NINDA.KUR$_4$.RA *ke-e-ez*[*-zi-ia*] (54) [*2* NINDA.KUR$_4$.RA] *ti-an-zi nam-ma-aš-kán ši-eš-ša-ni-it* (55) [*a-ra-aḫ-za-a*]*n-da gul-ša-an-zi ma-aḫ-ḫa-an-ma ku*[*-. . . . .*] (56) [*nu-kán an-da* ^{sa}]$^{\text{l.meš}}$ KAR.KID *ar-nu-wa-an-zi*

---

57 [DUB.*1*.KAM] NU TIL EZEN *ḫa-aš-šu-ma-aš I-NA* x[. . . .]

EGYPTIAN Ǧ AMID AFROASIATIC LANGUAGES

by Carleton T. Hodge
Indiana University

THE relationship of the Egyptian *ǧ* (I 10 in Gardiner's Sign List) to the sounds of other Afroasiatic languages has concerned scholars for many years. By far the greatest effort has been directed to studying the possible correspondences of Egyptian with Semitic. This is natural, and the results, carefully considered, may be used in working on a broader scale. The effort here is to investigate possible correspondences not only in these two branches but also in Cushitic, Chadic and Berber. The results are tentative, deictic rather than definitive, but they are at least encouraging.

Some notes on previous work will indicate the state of the art.[1] While earlier useful work was done, Adolf Erman's article (1892) comparing Egyptian with Semitic may be cited as a comprehensive, careful and still useful statement.[2] He lists *ǧ* as corresponding to Semitic *ṣ ṭ ẓ g ʿ*.[3] Albright in 1934 considers it "quite certain, from many precise equivalences, that Eg. *ḏ* goes back to Sem. *g* on the one hand and *ṣ*, *ḍ*, *ẓ* on the other."[4] Vergote (1945) lists correspondences of Egyptian *ǧ* with Semitic *g*, *ʿ*, *ṣ*, *ḍ*, *ẓ* (?).[5] Cohen (1947) says of Egyptian *ǧ*: "On peut se demander s'il n'y avait pas deux prononciations en face de la graphie unique; il est plus probable que *ǧ* remplaçant des emphatiques non existantes en égyptien."[6] He is concerned with its correspondence to *g* on the one hand and the emphatics on the other. His list includes correspondences with *ʿ* (p. 93), *g* (p. 118), *ṣ* (p. 146), *θ̣* (Ar. *ẓ*) (p. 160), *ḍ* (p. 162).

Relations to the western branches of the family have been less

[1] For an overall survey of the literature see Marcel Cohen, *Essai comparatif sur le vocabulaire et la phonétique du chamito-sémitique* (Bibliothèque de l'École des Hautes Études, No. 291; Paris, 1947), pp. 3–42.

[2] Adolf Erman, "Das Verhältniss des Aegyptischen zu den semitischen Sprachen", *ZDMG*, XLVI (1892), pp. 93-129.

[3] Ibid., p. 125; examples, p. 123.

[4] W.F. Albright, review of Worrell, *Coptic Sounds*, *Lg*, X (1934), p. 221.

[5] J. Vergote, *Phonétique historique de l'égyptien* (Louvain, 1945), pp. 146-148.

[6] Cohen, op. cit., p. 145.

well studied. Vycichl (1934) believes *ǧ* to be from**g* (Semitic and Hausa *g*)[7] and *γ (Semitic ʿ, Hausa *g*).[8] In a later (1950) article he equates *ǧ* with Semitic *g* and *ṣ*.[9] Zyhlarz (1933) argues that *g* is of multiple origin, including *g*, *q*, *ṣ*, *ẓ*, etc.[10] In the same monograph he equates *ǧ* with Bedauye *d*, *r*, *g*[11] and with Berber *r*.[12]

The latest survey of the field is that of Diakonoff (1965).[13] As his is the most complete, I give here a selection of his correspondences for *ǧ* and also for Semitic *ṭ*, which will be relevant to the discussion below.[14]

SEMITIC	BERBER	EGYPTIAN	CUSHITIC	CHADIC
ARABIC			SOMALI	HAUSA
ṭ	ḍ/ṭ	d (and t ?)	ḍ ?	d' ?; d ?
ṣ	ẓ	ǧ ?	ṣ ?	?
ẓ	t ?	ǧ (and t ?)	s ?	c'
ḍ	d ? ?	t (and ǧ ?)	?	? ?
ǰ	g	g; ǧ	g	g ?

The uncertainties of the situation are clear, but it is hoped that the present article will remove at least some of the question marks.

I have pointed out in another article that Egyptian *ǧ* corresponds to Hausa *s'*.[15] The question to be resolved here is whether any pattern can be made of the correspondences of the emphatic and glottalized consonants of the other languages with Egyptian *ǧ*.

---

[7] Werner Vycichl, "Hausa und Ägyptisch", *MSOS*, XXXVII No. 3 (1934), pp. 36-116.

[8] Ibid., p. 56.

[9] Werner Vycichl, "Grundlagen der ägyptisch-semitischen Wortvergleichung", *MDAI* XVI (1950), pp. 367-405. In the list given, Eg. *ǧ* is equated with Sem. *g* in Nos. 22, 24, 57 and with Sem. *ṣ* in Nos. 3, 23.

[10] E. Zyhlarz, *Ursprung und Sprachcharakter des Altägyptischen*, (Berlin, 1933, reprinted with independent pagination from *ZES*, XXIII, 1932/33), p. 89.

[11] Ibid., p. 66.

[12] Ibid., pp. 45-46. His example, the word for "ten", is to be found in Carl Meinhof, *Die Sprachen der Hamiten* (Hamburg, 1912), p. 240. Cohen omits it.

[13] I.M. Diakonoff, *Semito-Hamitic languages* (Moscow, 1965).

[14] Ibid., pp. 26, 27.

[15] Carleton T. Hodge, "Hausa-Egyptian Establishment", *Anthropological Linguistics*, VIII, No. 1 (1966), pp. 40-57. This was written before Diakonoff's book came to hand, so that I was unaware of the fact that he had equated Hausa *c'* (an alternate of *s'*) and Eg. *ǧ*, though I find no examples cited to support the equation.

Hausa *d'* must also be taken into account. No neat pattern has emerged to date, but a larger number of possible etymologies has been uncovered than has previously been published. The possible correspondences of *ǧ* with other consonants (especially *g*) is not here investigated.

It is possible to question the unity of the emphatic or glottalized phonemes, both in the proto-language and many of the extant ones. The present purpose is to list possible cognates in the various languages, without attempting a reconstruction of the proto-form. Much more work must be done before such reconstructions may be made, at which time the issue of the unity of the emphatic phonemes must be dealt with.

The traditional reconstruction of proto-Semitic lists four consonants believed relevant to the discussion of *ǧ*: **ṣ*, **ṭ*, **θ̣*, *ð̣.[16] The postulation of four such proto-phonemes is based directly on the Arabic evidence (North Arabic and Epigraphic South Arabic). This evidence is, however, open to reexamination. Contrasts may readily be found for all four, as North Arabic *ṣalla* "rattle", *ṭalla* "besprinkle", *ẓalla* "become" (*ẓ* from **θ̣*), *ḍalla* "go astray" (*ḍ* from *ð̣). At the same time, the occurrence in Arabic of numerous doublets or near doublets, differing only or primarily by which emphatic consonant they use, is an indication that all four may not go back to proto-Semitic. Compare (North) Arabic: *ṣabara* "bind", *ḍabara* "gather"; *ṣaḥā* "be clear", *ḍaḥā* "become visible"; *ṣadda* "alienate", *ḍ d* III "be contrary", *ṭarra* "sharpen", *ẓirrun* "sharp stone", *ṣaraʿa* "throw down", *ṭaraḥa* "throw"; *ṣuffatun* "ledge" *ḍaffatun* "bank, shore". These present complications to the would-be comparativist, and one is inclined to seek the solution within Arabic. It is possible that they represent internal dialect borrowing.

Despite the doubt just cast upon them in the following list the four proto-Semitic phonemes are used as a point of departure. The list gives suggested etymologies, numbered consecutively for convenience. The languages cited are Semitic (Akk.: Akkadian, Ar.: Arabic, Eth.: Geez, Heb.: Hebrew, Phon.: Phoenician), Egyptian (Eg.: Old/Middle Egyptian, C.: Coptic), Cushitic (Som.:

[16] See, for example, Heinrich Zimmern, *Vergleichende Grammatik der Semitischen Sprachen*, (Berlin, 1898), pp. 8-10; Sabatino Moscati, ed., *An Introduction to the Comparative Grammar of the Semitic Languages* (Wiesbaden, 1964), pp. 24, 27-31, 43-45. The consonants of proto-Semitic are the same in the two. Diakonoff differs somewhat (op. cit., table, p. 24), but his additions are doubtful.

Somali, Ga.: Galla, Sid.: Sidamo), Chadic (Ha.: Hausa), Berber (T.: Touareg, Z.: Zenaga, Sh.: Shilh). Most of the examples are from Arabic, Egyptian, Somali, Hausa and Touareg.[17]

Group A: Sem. **ṣ*, Eg. *ǧ*, Som. *d'*, Ha. *d'/s'*, T. *ḍ/ẓ*.

1. Akk. *waṣābum* "double", Eg. *w ǧ b* "fold over", Ha. *s'ibàà* "piled up". Cf. Ar. *ʿaṣaba* "wind, fold", T. *eẓabi* "conical sea shell".

2. Ar. *waṣala* "connect, unite", Eg. *w ǧ ꜣ* "whole, sound". Cf. Ha. *wad'àrii* "arranging thread in required length for weaving".

3. Ar. *naṣṣa* "appoint", Eg. *n ǧ* "appoint", Ha. *nad'àà* "appointed", T. *neheḍ* "decide", *tanaṭ* "decision". Cf. Ar. *naṣaba* "appoint".

4. Ar. *ṣabba* "pour, cast", Eg. *ǧ b t* "brick". Cohen does not have this set but plausibly compares Ha. *tàb'oo* "mud" (there is an alternate form *càb'oo*), *càab'ii* "slush".[18] The glottalization is on the second consonant, but this does not invalidate the comparison. It may rather point to the "prosodic feature" nature of this element.

5. Ar. *ṣabara* "to bind, tie", Eg. *ǧ b ꜣ* "garment (worn by god)", Ha. *d'awràà* "fastened (one thing on another)". Note that *-br-* alternates with *-wr-* in Hausa.

6. Akk. *eṣēru* "draw", Heb. *yāṣar* "make", *yōṣēr* "potter", Eg. *ǧ ꜣ ǧ ꜣ w* "pot", *ʾ ǧ r t* "container for oil", Som. *d'éri* "cooking pot of clay", Ha. *d'òòree* "building with clay".

---

[17] The primary sources for the data were : Akkadian—Carl Bezold, *Babylonisch-Assyrisches Glossar* (Heidelberg, 1926). I.J. Gelb and others, eds., *The Assyrian Dictionary* (Chicago, 1956—), I-VII, XVI, XXI. Wolfram von Soden, *Akkadisches Handwörterbuch* (Wiesbaden, 1965), I, A-L. Arabic—Hans Wehr, *A Dictionary of Modern Written Arabic*, ed. J Milton Cowan (Ithaca, 1961). J. G. Hava, *Arabic—English Dictionary* (Beirut, 1915). Egyptian—Adolf Erman and Hermann Grapow, *Wörterbuch der aegyptischen Sprache* (Berlin, 1957—) I-VI. R. O. Faulkner, *A Concise Dictionary of Middle Egyptian* (Oxford, 1962). W. E. Crum, *A Coptic Dictionary* (Oxford, 1939). Somali—R. C. Abraham, *Somali-English Dictionary* (London, 1964). Hausa—R. C. Abraham, *Dictionary of the Hausa Language* (n.p., 1949). Berber—Charles de Foucauld, *Dictionnaire touareg-français* (Imprimerie Nationale de France, 1951–52), I-IV. F. Nicolas, *La langue berbère de Mauretanie* (Dakar, 1953). Joseph R. Applegate, *An Outline of the Structure of Shilḥa* (New York, 1958). Applegate analyzes an emphatic component, indicated by *.

[18] Cohen, op. cit., No. 253.

Group B: Sem. *ṭ, Eg. ǧ, Som. d', Ha. d'/s', T. ḍ.[19]

7. Ar. *ṭalla* "besprinkle", C. *ǧol* BF "wave", Som. *d'aláalayya* "melt (intr.)", Ha. *s'uulàà* "poured out".

8. Ar. *naṭaḥa* "to butt", Eg. *n ǧ ḥ y t* "tusk", Som. *d'ùuḥ* "marrow".

9. Ar. *sāṭa* "whip", Eg. *s ǧ* "break", Ha. *šawd'àà* "whipped" (loan ?).

10. Ar. *ṭanṭana* "hum, buzz (of insects)", Eg. *ǧ n ǧ n* (a kind of bird), Ha. *s'uns'uu* "bird". It is interesting to note that reduplication is a frequent feature in the names of birds in Arabic.

11. Ar. *ṭāfa* "go about", Eg. *ǧ f n* (a verb of motion), C. *ǧōfe* "pass by", Som. *d'áafayya* "pass by", *d'óofayya* "travel in a vehicle", Ga. *ḍuf-* "come". Cf. Ha. *tàfi* "went". The possibility of Eg. *ǧ f y* "penetrate" being related should also be kept in mind (see below, No. 26).

12. Akk. *xaṭṭu* "scepter", Ar. *xaṭara* "brandish", Eg. *ḥ ǧ* "mace". The correspondence x:ḥ is very possibly invalid, but the probability of connection, whether etymologically or by loan, seems extremely high. Cf. Phon. *ḥ ṭ r* "scepter" and Ha. *fad'àà* "quarrel".[20]

13. Ar. *ṭarratun* "flank", *ṭurratun* "bank, side, edge", Eg. *ǧ r w* "side, flank", Ha. *s'araa* "middle of back", T. *aḍer* "leg". A strong claimant to a position here is Ar. *ẓahr* "back". There is also Eg. *ǧ r w* "boundary", as well as words such as *ǧ ȝ* "cross over" which could easily be connected both formally and semantically. The overlapping seen in such a group may be due to either merger or split. At this stage of investigation it is safest to keep as many items separate as possible. Eg. *ǧ r w* "boundary" has been connected with Semitic forms with ṣ: Ar. *ṣarra* "tie up", Heb. *māṣōr* "fortress", Akk. *miṣru* "boundary", etc.[21] One may add Cushitic and Chad parallels: Som. *d'aróorayya* "bank up (edge of water hole)", Ha. *s'aaràà* "aligned, arranged", *s'àrnuu* "fencing post". Ar. *ḥaṣara* "limit, encompass" is probably also related.

Group C: Sem. *θ, Eg. ǧ, Som. d', Ha. d'/s', Sh. d*/ž*.

14. Ar. *ẓillun* "shade", *ẓulmatun* "darkness", Eg. *ǧ ȝ w* "night", C. *ǧōr* "be black", Sid. *č̣ālé* "shade". Cf. Som. *had'áynayya* "to

[19] The examples of Sem. *ṭ* corresponding to Eg. *t* and *d* in Cohen (op. cit., pp. 155-156) are not very convincing.

[20] Compare Cohen, op. cit., No. 146.

[21] Vergote, op. cit., p. 147, Cohen, op. cit., No. 311.

shade", Ha. *d'inyaa* "wearing black". The Semitic relexes of *θ *l l* are connected with Cushitic (Agau and Bilin *č̣alal* "shade") by Cohen.[22]

15. Ar. *ẓanna* "think", Eg. *ǧ n ǧ n* "be angry", Ha. *s'àmmaanìì* "thinking", Sh. *dnu** "think". Semantically one may compare Skt. *manyate* "thinks" and Gk. *maínetai* "is mad". It is possible that Ha. *s'àmmaanìì* is an Arabic loan and that Ha. *d'and'ànaa* "tasted, experienced" offers the proper correspondence. Cohen connects the latter with other roots.[23]

16. Akk. *ṣurru* "flint", *ṣurtu* "flint blade", Ar. *ẓarra* "sharpen", *ẓirrun* "sharp stone", *miẓarratun* "flint", Eg. *ǧ* ꜣ "fire drill", *w ǧ* ꜣ *t* "knife", *m ǧ* ꜣ *t* "knife", C. *ǧōr* "sharpen", Ha. *s'uuràà* "pierced", *s'uuraa* "knife without a handle".

17. Ar. *ẓiyatun* "putrefying corpse", Eg. *ǧ t* "body", Som. *d'ùù* "garment made of skin", Ha. *d'òòyii* "stench", Sh. *ža** "stink". This runs counter to the more familiar combination of Eg. *ǧ t* with Heb. *gēw* "interior", Ha. *gaawaa* "corpse".[24] It is suggested in order to test all reasonable connections of *ǧ* with the emphatic/glottalized series.

Group D: Sem. *ð̣, Eg. *ǧ*, Som. *d'*, Ha. *d'/s'*, T. *ẓ/ṭ/ḍ*.

18. Akk. *ṣerru* "adversary", Ar. *ḍarra* "harm", Eg. *m ǧ* ꜣ *w* "opponent", Sh. *du*ru** "harm".

19. Ar. *waḍaʿa* "put down", Eg. *w ǧ* ʿ "assign". Cf. Som. *fad'íyyayya* "to be seated", Ha. *faad'ìì* "fell down".

20. Akk. *peṣū* "break, crush", Ar. *faḍḍa* "break open, pierce", Eg. *p ǧ* ꜣ "sharpen (knife)", Som. *fád'ayya* "scrape away", Ha. *feed'àà* "flay", T. *feḍei* "be pierced".

21. Akk. *ṣabātu* "seize", Ar. *ḍabba* "take hold of", *ḍabara* "gather", Eg. *w ǧ b* "gather", *ǧ b w* "revenue", Ha. *d'iibàà* "gathered", T. *ṭoubet* "be gathered together". Cf. Ha. *d'ibìì* "thing placed on another" and the set given in No. 1 above. There is also a Hausa word *s'ibìì* "pile".

22. Ar. *ḍadda* "overcome", Eg. *m ǧ d* "press hard on", T. *eẓed* "reduce to powder". This assumes Eg. *m ǧ d* is *ǧ d* with a prefix *m-*, rather than *m ǧ* with an extension *-d*.[25]

---

[22] Cohen, op. cit., No. 352.

[23] Cohen, op. cit., No. 337, with query.

[24] Cohen, op. cit., No. 220 and Joseph H. Greenberg, *The Languages of Africa* (Bloomington, Ind., 1963), p. 53.

[25] Contrary to its inclusion with *m ǧ* in Hodge, op. cit., p. 45.

23. Akk. *iṣu* "tree, wood", Ar. *ʿiḍatun* "any thorny tree", Eg. *ʿ ǧ* "spool, reel",[26] Z. *teiðuð̣* "big stick". Cf. Ar. *ʿaṣātun* "staff, rod".

24. Ar. *ġuḍḍatun* "fault", Eg. *ʿ ǧ t* "offence", Ha. *gàs'ee* "sarcasm", T. *ăġaḍ* "noisy quarrel". It is tempting to see a connection with Eg. *ʿ ǧ* "destroy", Ha. *gàwd'aa* "give a severe blow". However, there are a number of reasonable Arabic correspondences to *ʿ ǧ*: *ġaḍḍa*, *ġāḍa* "diminish", *ġāẓa* "distress, enrage", *ʿaṭiba* "be destroyed", *ʿaẓā* "harm", *ʿaẓẓa* "fell to the ground", possibly even *ʿaḍḍa* "bite", "torment".

25. Eth. *waḍ'a* "go out", Eg. *w ǧ ʾ* "send out", Ha. *waas'àà* "scattered", T. *aouḍ* "reach".[27] Cf. Som. *wadayya* "drive forward".

26. Ar. *ḍafara* "intertwine", Eg. *ǧ f ʾ* "penetrate", Som. *d'áfayya* "mix", Ha. *s'aafàà* "squeezed through", *s'eefèè* "combed".

27. Ar. *ruḍaabun* "saliva", *raḍḍa* "to bruise" IV "make sweat to flow", Eg. *r ǧ w* "efflux" (of body), Ha. *raas'ìì* "human excrement", T. *ereḍ* "produce wind".

28. Ar. *ḍabaḥa* "blacken", Eg. *ǧ ʿ b* "coal-black", T. *ouẓẓaf* "be black".

29. Ar. *ḍamma* "unite", Eg. *d m ǧ* "unite" (for **ǧ m ǧ* with dissimilation ?), Ha. *d'aamàà* "attached".[28]

30. Ar. *faḥaḍa* "split open", Eg. *p ḥ ǧ* "cut open", Som. *féed'ayya* "comb".

31. Ar. *ḍahrun* "summit, high", Eg. *ǧ ȝ t* "remainder", *w ǧ ȝ* "remain over", Som. *d'eer* "tall, deep", *d'éeràad* "surplus", Ha. *d'aràà* "exceed slightly".

32. Ar. *ḍaraba* "beat, throw overboard", Eg. *m ǧ ȝ b t* "bailer (of boat)", *m ǧ ȝ b t* "drainer (for bilge) ?", Som. *d'úrayya* "scoop up", *d'aruur* "filter, strain", Ha. *d'uuràà* "poured liquid through narrow opening", *d'urààree* "trickled out", *d'àwrayàà* "plated, rinsed".

It is hoped that, despite the obvious uncertainties, these examples will strengthen the thesis that the primary correspondences of Eg. *ǧ* are to be found among the emphatic and glottalized series of the other languages.

---

[26] Cf. Erman-Grapow, op. cit., I, p. 237, "der Gegenstand, den die Hieroglyphe darstellt (das Holz, worauf das Seil gewickelt wird)".

[27] The Sem. and Eg. are given in Vergote, op. cit., p. 148.

[28] See Vergote, op. cit., pp. 145, 148 for other Semitic (Akk. *ṣamādu*, etc.).

PERSIAN VERBS
DERIVABLE FROM OTHER PART OF SPEECH

by Mohammad Ali Jazayery
University of Texas

1. In some languages verbs can be derived from other parts of speech. This may be done in several ways: (1) by using verbalizing affixes, as in English whiten, endear, naturalize, decode, disbelieve, befriend, etc., (2) by phonological modification, as in house: to house; use: to use; advice: to advise; breath: to breathe; food: to feed; blood: to bleed; etc., as well as pairs differentiated by stress, such as súspèct: suspéct, etc., (3) by simple transfer, without any addition or other modification. This last variety is extremely common in English, where almost any word, of whatever part of speech, can be made into a verb at will; e.g., to up the price or to lower it, to water the lawn, to better one's lot, to best an opponent, to busy oneself, to shoulder responsibility. In these and similar cases, the noun, adjective, etc., do not undergo any modification. They are "transferred" to the class of "verb" by virtue of the change in their syntactic function. (As verbs, they of course take the verbal inflectional affixes when these are needed: she is watering the lawn, he ups the price every so often, she bested her opponent, they have lowered the lid, etc.) The number of such English verbs has increased in the course of history, especially in American English, and particularly in recent decades[1]. Other languages may show a complete lack of such a tendency, or they may show it on a smaller scale. In what follows we shall examine the Modern Persian language of Iran with reference to this grammatical process.

[1] On the transfer of words from various parts of speech to the class of verbs in English, see Otto Jespersen, *A Modern English Grammar on Historical Principles*, I-VII (Copenhagen, 1909–1949), VI, ch. vi. The phenomenon is often referred to as "conversion", according to Jespersen. Jespersen himself would rather interpret the verbs as forming from other parts of speech with a suffix zero (p. 85). Elsewhere, referring to this phenomenon in English, as applied to all parts of speech, he says that this is "one of the most characteristic traits of English, and is found to a similar extent in no other European language". See *Essentials of English Grammar* (New York, 1933), p. 73.

2.1. Each Persian verb has two stems, known as the /t-/ (or past) stem, and the present (or imperative) stem. All tenses and aspects are formed on one or the other of these, which take an identical set of person-and-number endings (with one exception), and (with certain limitations) an identical set of prefixes. The addition of the suffix /-ǽn/ to the past stem results in the *maṣdar* "infinitive", which functions as a noun (rather than verb).[2] The infinitive is the form generally used, in grammars for example, to refer to the verb as a whole; e.g., /ræftǽn/ "to go", /ʔazmudǽn/ "to examine", /busidǽn/ "to kiss", etc.[3]

2.2 Native Persian grammatical tradition usually recognizes four types of infinitives: (1) A "real" (*aṣlī*) infinitive is one which is an "infinitive in its origin" (i.e., historically). (2) A "false" (*ja'lī*) or "invented" (*mowẓu'*) infinitive was not an infinitive originally but has been formed by the addition of the infinitive suffix /-idǽn/ (actually a suffix complex) to a Persian or Arabic word other than an infinitive (a restriction not usually stipulated by grammarians). The examples given are usually nouns.[4] (3) A "simple" (*basiṭ*)

[2] Persian names, titles of publications, and grammatical terms are transliterated. Otherwise, the Persian forms cited are given in a phonemic transcription, in which the following values are attached to the symbols used: /c q š x ž ʔ/ represent the sounds usually transliterated as *ch, gh* and *q, sh, kh, zh,* '('ayn) and '(hamza), respectively. /i e æ/ are the high, mid, low front vowels, respectively, and /u o a/ their back counterparts. The other letters have values similar to their values in English. /´ `/ are the primary (strong) and secondary degrees of stress, with the weak stress left unmarked. Slash lines are used to enclose phonemic transcriptions. Where a form has more than one pronunciation or meaning, only one pronunciation variant and (with few exceptions) only one meaning are given.

[3] Sometimes, we find, in grammars and dictionaries, infinitives formed on the present stem, by the addition of /-idǽn/; e.g., /rævidǽn/, /ʔazmaʔidǽn/, etc., by the side of the expected /ræftǽn/, /ʔazmudǽn/, etc. Such forms, however, are often theoretical, and merely provide forms to be used in speaking about the present stem. That they are theoretical is seen in the fact that only the past-stem-based infinitive is used in all situations where the noun (to which class the infinitives belong) is needed. On verb stems in Persian, see, among others, Gilbert Lazard, *Grammaire du persan contemporain* (Paris, 1957), pp. 125-130, and Carleton T. Hodge's review of that book in *Language,* XXXIV, pp. 111-121 (1958).

[4] At least one writer uses the term *ja'li* to refer to words in Persian formed by the addition of the Arabic borrowed suffix complex /-iyyǽt/ to other words (usually Arabic loans); e.g., /vǽzʔ/: /væzʔiyyǽt/ "situation", /mowqéʔ/: /mowqeʔiyyǽt/ "occasion, situation". See Ḥ. Āmuzgār, *Farhang-e Āmuzgār*, 3rd ed., (Tehran, 1933/1954), p. 22.

Among the European grammarians of Persian, D. C. Phillott, in *Higher Persian Grammar* (Calcutta, 1919), p. 248, discusses the real-false contrast. However,

infinitive is one consisting of a single word. (4) A "compound" (*morakkab*) infinitive is composed of two or more words, including a simple infinitive, with the other word or words coming from the parts of speech of nouns, adjectives, adverbs, or prepositions; or from a number of prefixes.[5]

Persian grammars often list the preceding as parallel categories. They actually represent two levels. "Simple" and "compound" represent one level; "real" and "false" another. The latter two each consists of a single-word infinitive, and so they are both sub-types of the "simple" infinitive.[6] The relevance of the real-false contrast is almost purely historical-etymological; synchronically, they are both "simple". The simple-compound distinction, on the other hand, is relevant synchronically.

2.3. An examination of the developments in Modern (i.e., Islamic) Persian, as far as the verb is concerned, brings out two opposing tendencies. On the one hand, there has been an increase in the number of compound verbs, replacing already existing simple verbs or at least rendering them less frequent. On the other hand, new verbs have been formed from other parts of speech.

2.4. The increase in the number of compound verbs during the Modern Persian period is usually said to have been a result of the large number of Arabic loanwords in Persian. Arabic substantives, often verbal nouns, were combined with Persian simple verbs to form compounds expressing, in verbal function, the contents of those substantives. The very large number of borrowed Arabic

---

he states that the real infinitives are pure Persian, and the false ones are those formed on Arabic (and in one case Urdu) words; for this reason, he renders *ja'li* as "hybrid". His assumption is erroneous, however (and his term misleading).

[5] A typical native Persian grammar is : 'A. Qarib and others, *Dastur-e zabān-e Fārsi barā-ye sāl-e sevvom va chahārom-e dabirestānhā* (Tehran, n.d.), where the four types of infinitive described above are discussed on pp. 37-38.

[6] At least one grammarian (among the earliest) adds two more categories: "abbreviated" or "appocopated" (*takhfifi*), and "secondary" (*thānavi*). By the former he means what is otherwise called *morakhkham*, and is the same as the past stem. He defines the "secondary" infinitive as one formed by adding /-(i)dǽn/ to the present stems of some verbs. His examples are: /baxtǽn/: /bazidǽn/, /pærhixtǽn/: /pærhizidǽn/, /gošudǽn/: /gošadǽn/, /næhoftǽn/: /næhandǽn/. (Gholām-Ḥoseyn Kāshef, *Dastur-e zabān-e Fārsi* [Istanbul, 1328 A.H./1909], pp. 127-129.) These examples, however, illustrate more than a single phenomenon, including that described in footnote 3 above. At any rate, the lack of parallelism referred to above is also present here. Such "secondary" infinitives are variants of "simple" infinitives, and so belong on the morphophonemic level.

substantives then served to create—certainly to strengthen—a preference in the language for forming and using compound verbs. So great has this preference become that compound verbs have been formed even where simple verbs existed, as we shall see later.

3.1. The term "compound" verb in Persian grammar is loosely defined as a verb consisting of a non-verbal element (which may itself be complex) and a simple verb, usually considered an "auxiliary". The examples provided actually represent several different phenomena. Their common feature is that they all translate simple, i.e., one-word, verbs in other languages, notably French, English, and other Western languages.[7] The imprecise definition, however, will not basically affect our discussion.

3.2. The non-verbal element in compound verbs may be Arabic (occasionally Turkic) or Persian. In the following examples, the non-verbal element is in each case Arabic: /ˀestedˀá/ "request": /ˀestedˀà kærdǽn/ "to request"; /jǽmˀ/ "addition": /jæ̀mˀ kærdǽn/ "to collect"; /jævàb/ "answer": /jævàb dadǽn/ "to answer"; /túl/ "length": /tùl kæšidǽn/ "to last"; /tæsmím/ "decision": /tæsmìm gereftǽn/ "to decide"; /ˀedamé/ "continuation": /ˀedamè dadǽn/ "to continue"; /vojúd/ "existence": /bevojùd ˀaværdǽn/ "to bring into being".

3.3. Compound verbs with native Persian non-verbal elements are illustrated by the following: /gúš/ "ear": /gùš dadǽn/ "to listen"; /yǽx/ "ice": /yæ̀x bæstǽn/ "to freeze"; /kár/ "work": /bekàr bordǽn/ "to use"; /dǽst/ "hand": /ˀæz dæst dadǽn/ "to

[7] It is, therefore, not surprising that the discussion of "compound verbs" is more prominent, and the list of such verbs longer, in grammars of Persian written by Westerners (who, in some cases admittedly, in others assumedly, have the foreign learners of Persian in mind). See, for example, the Lazard work cited in footnote 3 above, where the verbs we have in mind are discussed (pp. 284-294), under the headings "verbes à préverbe", "verbes 'composé' " (the largest group), and "autres locutions verbales". See also Ann K. S. Lambton, *Persian Grammar* (Cambridge, 1960), pp. 85-93, where all the verbs under discussion are considered "compound verbs". Among Iranian authors, at least one, having said that a compound verb is one "composed of two words having a single meaning", states that it is for this reason that such concepts are often expressed in simple verbs in some languages, and he cites the Arabic and French equivalents of several Persian compound verbs to prove his point. However, he applies this argument only to the type of compound verb in which the non-verbal element is a noun or an adjective, leaving out the type in which he considers the non-verbal element a prefix. See 'A. Khayyāmpur, *Dastūr-e zabān-e Fārsi*, 4th ed. (Tabriz, Iran, 1341/1962), pp. 59-60.

lose"; /porséš/ "question": /porsèš kærdǽn/ "to ask"; /kušéš/ "effort": /kušèš kærdǽn/ "to try".

In some cases, the Persian non-verbal element is itself derived from a simple verb which is still in use; e.g., /kušidǽn/ "to try": /kušés/ "effort": /kušèš kærdǽn/ "to try"; /pærværdǽn/ "to train": /pærværéš/ "training": /pærværèš dadǽn/ "to train"; /ʔazmudǽn/ "to test": /ʔazmayéš/ "test": /ʔazmayèš kærdǽn/ "to test"; /pærdaxtǽn/ "to pay": /pærdàxt/ "paying": /pærdàxt kærdǽn/ "to pay"; /porsidǽn/ "to ask": /porséš/ "question": /porsèš kærdǽn/ "to ask"; /xændidǽn/ "to laugh": /xændé/ "laughter": /xændè kærdǽn/ "to laugh"; /sotudǽn/ "to praise": /setayéš/ "praise": /setayèš kærdǽn/ "to praise"; /geristǽn/ "to cry": /geryé/ "crying": /geryè kærdǽn/ "to cry"; /ʔavixtǽn/ "to suspend": /ʔavizán/ "hanging, suspended": /ʔavizàn kærdǽn/ "to suspend"; /nalidǽn/ "to mourn": /nalé/ "mourning": /nalè kærdǽn/ "to mourn"; /pæžmordǽn/ "to wither": /pæžmordé/ "withered": /pæžmordè šodǽn/ "to wither".

One group of the all-Persian compound verbs needs special mention here. These are verbs of which the non-verbal elements are /bǽr/, /báz/, /forú/, etc., usually considered prefixes or adverbs: /bæ̀r nešæstǽn/ "to sit up (as on a horse)", /bàz yaftǽn/ "to find again, regain"; /forù nešæstǽn/ "to sit down"; etc. These verbs are reminiscent of such English verbs as look out, write up, write down, sit up, etc. This is the only group of Persian compound verbs which has decreased in size.

4.1. There is scarcely a simple infinitive for which there is no synonym in a compound infinitive; often there are several. There are, however, not a few compound verbs which are without simple-verb synonyms. Such is the case in /tærjomè kærdǽn/ "to translate"; /rahnemaʔì kærdǽn/ "to guide"; /bekàr bordǽn/ "to use"; /sæ̀br kærdǽn/ "to wait" etc. In many cases, a compound verb has at least one synonym which is a simple verb, e.g., /soʔàl kærdǽn/ ~ /porsidǽn/ "to ask"; /sŏrùʔ kærdǽn/ ~ /ʔaqazidǽn/ "to begin"; /hæræ̀kæ̀t kærdǽn/ ~ /jombidǽn/ "to move (intransitive)"; /zæmìn xordǽn/ ~ /ʔoftadǽn/ "to fall down"; /ʔèsm gozaštǽn/ ~ /namidǽn/ "to name"; /sæ̀ʔy kærdǽn/ ~ /kušidǽn/ "to try"; /ʔersàl daštǽn/ ~ /ferestadǽn/ "to send"; /fòwt kærdǽn/ ~ /mordǽn/ "to die"; /fèkr kærdǽn/ ~ /ʔændišidǽn/ "to think"; /peydà kærdǽn/ ~ /yaftǽn/ "to find".

The existence of a large number of compound verbs, along

with the simple verbs, has in some cases resulted in several synonyms, or near-synonyms; e.g., /sǽʔy kærdǽn/ ~ /kušidǽn/ ~ /kušèš kærdǽn/ "to try"; /mæjbùr kærdǽn/ ~ /vadaštǽn/ ~ /vadàr kærdǽn/ "to persuade"; /ʔeftetàh kærdǽn/ ~ /bàz kærdǽn/ ~ /gošudǽn/ "to open"; /pà šodǽn/ ~ /bæ̀r xastǽn/ ~ /bolæ̀nd šodǽn/ "to get up"; /mohævvæ̀l kærdǽn/ ~ /vagozàr kærdǽn/ ~ /vagozaštǽn/ "to make over (to)"; /bæ̀r gæštǽn/ ~ /moraje?æ̀t kærdǽn/ ~ /bàz gæštǽn/ ~ /bazgæ̀št kærdǽn/ "to return (intr.)"; /dærræftǽn/ ~ /gorixtǽn/ ~ /færàr kærdǽn/ "to flee"; /ʔamuxtǽn/ ~ /yàd gereftǽn/ ~ /færà gereftǽn/ "to learn".

4.2. The use of the term "synonym" as employed in the preceding paragraphs is justified only subject to certain restrictions. It is doubtful that there are any perfect synonyms—that is, two or more words, or word combinations, that are completely interchangeable—in Persian. There is usually some restriction on the use of each member of a group of supposed synonyms which distinguishes it from the other members; sometimes there is a network of overlapping restrictions. Even if the basic semantic content is to all intents and purposes the same in the whole group, there may be syntactic, stylistic, or other distributional features peculiar to each member. This is true of Persian verbs. Thus, /ræftǽn/ and /tæšrìf bordǽn/ both mean "to go", but the former is neutral while the latter is a polite form. The difference may be in the degree of formality: /sæ̀rf kærdǽn/ is a more formal synonym of /xordǽn/ "to eat", which is neutral. Another synonym, /sæ̀rf færmudǽn/, is both more formal and more polite. Euphemisms account for some synonyms. (1) /mordǽn/, (2) /fòwt šodǽn/, (3) /dæ̀r gozæštǽn/, (4) /mærhùm šodǽn/, (5) /sæqæ̀t šodǽn/, and several other words, all mean "to die". The first one is neutral, the rest are all euphemisms. In addition, (2) is formal, (3) is literary and/or formal, (4) is both formal and polite, (5) is quite impolite. As these examples indicate, often—though by no means always—the simple verb is neutral. A notable exception is /færmudǽn/, which can be used as a polite substitute for a number of verbs, sometimes for semantically opposite verbs, such as "to come in" and "to go out", "to sit down" and "to get up", etc.

4.3. Another type of restriction applies to the distribution of certain simple verbs and their compound-verb synonyms. It is grammatical in nature, and has to do with the relation of the verb to the rest of the sentence. The basic elements in a verbal sentence are subject, object, verb: /hæsǽn ketábra xánd/ "Hasan read the book". The core of such sentences, however, is the verb; a sentence may consist exclusively of a verb, which, as we have seen, embodies in its form an indication of the person and number of the subject, e.g., /rǽftæm/ "(I) went"; /míˀayænd/ "(they) are coming"; /nǽfæhmidid/ "(you) did not understand." An express subject is optional. The preceding examples do not contain such subjects; if they did, and if the subjects were pronouns, they would read: /mǽn rǽftæm/, /ˀišán míˀayænd/, /šomá nǽfæhmidid/, respectively. As for the object, some verbs do not need any: /ræftǽn/ "to go" and /xabidǽn/ "to sleep" are two such verbs. With some, the object is optional, e.g., /(ˀánra) šenídæm/ "(I) heard (it)", where /ˀánra/ "it (obj.)" is an optional object. The object precedes the verb, as in this example, unless it is a pronominal suffix, in which case it follows the subject-marking suffix, e.g., /šenídæmeš/. Still other verbs ordinarily require an object. /xordǽn/ "to eat" is an example. In Persian, one indicates the object of eating, e.g., "lunch", "supper", "fruit", "apples", etc. If he does not want to be specific, he uses a more general word, such as /qæzá/ "food", or even /cíz/ "thing": /cíz míxoræd/ "he is eating (some)thing". Or, provided that the context is clear, he can use a pronominal suffix to indicate the object: /xórdæmeš/ "I ate it". One way or another, a formal indication of the object is necessary.

Now, an object-requiring simple verb may have a synonym which is a compound verb consisting of a non-verbal element derived from that simple verb, (§ 3.3 above), plus an auxiliary verb; e.g., /randǽn/: /ranændegì kærdǽn/ "to drive", where /ranændegí/ "driving" is formed by adding the suffixes /-ændé/ + /-gí/ to the present stem /-ran/. In such pairs (or groups) an object will have to be furnished when the simple verb is used, e.g., /ˀotomobílra rándæm/ "(I) drove the car", or /rándæmeš/ "(I) drove it"; one does not just say /rándæm/. The synonymous compound verb, however, does not require an object; we can say /ranændegí kǽrdæm/. Strictly speaking, though, to say that we have, in this example, a (compound) verb without an object is not quite correct. Rather, we have a simple verb, /kǽrdæm/, with an object, /ranændegí/ "driving". The identicalness of the semantic content in /randǽn/ and /ranændegì kærdǽn/ is not relevant. That the two are not synonymous grammatically—and that /ranændegì kærdǽn/ is not actually a compound—can be seen in the fact that when the object of driving is indicated, we have to use the simple verb; we cannot say */ˀotomobílra ranændegí kǽrdæm/, as we can say, for example, /ˀotomobílra tæˀmír kǽrdæm/ "I repaired the car", where /tæˀmìr kærdǽn/ "to repair" is a compound verb (at least according to the criterion of substitutability), replaceable by a simple verb.

There may be other distributional restrictions involved in such cases of synonymy. Thus, /ranædegí míkonæd/ means "he drives as a profession"; or "he knows how to drive"; compare the English "I have a car, but I don't drive". We may take another verb: /neveštǽn/ "to write" and the corresponding /nevisændegì kærdǽn/. The simple verb requires an object; the corresponding combination cannot have one. In answer to a question about what someone is doing at the moment, in English we can say "he is writing", without specifying what he is writing. In Persian, we cannot just say /mínevisæd/. Nor, however, can we say /nevisændegí míkonæd/. The latter means "he writes", i.e., "he is a writer", writing as a profession, or at least as a hobby, etc. The closest Persian equivalent to the English answer to the hypothetical question is /cíz mínevisæd/ "he is writing (some)thing".

5.1. The number of compound verbs in Persian is large, and their number has been increasing. This fact, however, has caused investigators to overlook the relatively large body of verbs derived from other parts of speech. Grammarians generally cite less than a dozen such verbs. The verbs listed are: (1) /bælˀidǽn/ "to swallow", (2) /ræqsidǽn/ "to dance", (3) /fæhmidǽn/ "to understand", (4) /jængidǽn/ "to fight", (5) /tærsidǽn/ "to fear", (6) /ˀaqazidǽn/ "to begin", (7) /tælæbidǽn/ "to demand", (8) /tondidǽn/ "to speak in a rage", (9) /dærængidǽn/ "to delay", (10) /qarætidǽn/ "to plunder".[8] These forms originally replaced the earlier Modern Persian compound verbs consisting of the substantives /bǽlˀ rǽqs fǽhm jǽng tǽrs ˀaqáz tælǽb tónd dærǽng qarǽt/ and a simple verb, usually /kærdǽn/; e.g., /fæ̀hm kærdǽn/, /bæ̀lˀ kærdǽn/, etc. Today, only nos. 1-5 are in common use. Number 6, when used at all, is literary. Number 7 occurs almost exclusively in the negative past participle form, /nætælæbidé/

[8] See, for example, the Persian grammar cited in footnote 5, and M. J. Mashkur, *Dasturnāme*, 4th ed. (Tehran, 1345/1966), pp. 72-73. M. T. Bahār, *Sabkshenāsi ya tārikh-e taṭavvor-e nathr-e Fārsi*, I-III, 2nd ed. (Tehran, 1337/1958), I, pp. 315-317, also lists /xabidǽn/ "to sleep" and /cærxidǽn/ "to turn".

"un-asked for". Numbers 8-10 are not used in Contemporary Persian.[9]

The mere handful of examples given in grammars can be misleading, for the number of Persian verbs based on other parts of speech is in fact much larger. No reliable, exhaustive statistics are available yet, either of such verbs or of Persian verbs in general. Even from the statistics that do exist, however, we can see that the situation is quite different from what is represented, or implied, by the few examples given by grammarians.

The most complete list of Persian verbs published is that compiled by Moḥammad Bashir Ḥoseyn. Chiefly on the basis of this list, the number of verbs used in Modern Persian, including those no longer in use, is estimated at about 630.[10] Of these, about 170 are derived from members of other parts of speech which are still in use. About 100 of these verbs are no longer used in Persian, while the nouns, adjectives, etc., on which they are based are still part of the active vocabulary. Examples are: /ʔarezú/ "wish", /ʔarúq/ "belch", /ʔaqúš/ "embrace", /ʔahár/ "starch", /ʔaváz/ "voice", /ʔændúh/ "sorrow", /bavǽr/ "belief", /pǽnd/ "advice", /dám/ "snare", /sepás/ "thank", /šekár/ "hunt", /šækíb/ "patience", /gúš/ "ear", /negáh/ "look", /pór/ "full", /tæbáh/ "corrupt",

[9] R. Homāyun-Farrokh, in his *Dastur-e jāmeʿ-e zabān-e Fārsi*, 2nd. ed. (Tehran, 1338/1959), pp. 534-535, 872-875, seems to be more conscious of this process than other authors. Even in this grammar, however, whose chief merit is in the copious examples culled from over five-hundred primary sources (according to a note on p. 1130), we find no more than twenty examples, including those listed above.

[10] The list compiled by Moḥammad Bashir Ḥoseyn appears as an appendix to M. Moghaddam, *Rāhnemā-ye rishe-ye feʿlhā-ye Irāni dar zabān-e Avestā va Fārsi-ye Bāstān va Fārsi-ye konuni* (Tehran, 1342/1963). The list is an uncritical one. It consists of 1974 entries. Almost all the verbs listed, however, appear in three or more forms. For example, for each verb, both stems as well as the causative are given. Often the latter appears in both of the two possible variants, i.e., with the infix /-an-/ and /-ani-/; sometimes there are additional causative forms. In quite a few cases, the same verb appears in several pronunciation (or orthographical) variants, sometimes in misread forms due to the orthography. A score or so verbs are marked as being in the "Zand" language, i.e., are huzwarish forms for Persian verbs, without any indication as to the Persian words for which they stood. There may also be dialectal forms. Subtracting all the variants from the total, we are left with approximately 630 verbs. The list is based almost exclusively on secondary sources, which in most cases copy earlier secondary sources (chiefly on seven monolingual dictionaries and a Persian-English one), a fact which may account for some of the duplications (and errors). On the other hand, because of the limitation of the corpus, one may reasonably assume that the list, though the longest available, does not include all the Persian verbs.

/cǽp/ "left", /zír/ "below", /gǽrm/ "hot", /dír/ "late", /józ/ "except". Ḥoseyn's list includes even a few cases where the non-verbal elements (still in use) are themselves compound or complex forms, e.g., /pærváz/ "flight", /goftár/ "speech", /ˀasán/ "easy", /ˀærzán/ "cheap", /geramí/ "dear", /yeksán/ "alike". In all of these cases the underlying elements are still in use in Modern Persian, but the verbs formed on them are not.[11]

5.2. Despite the fact that many verbs of the type under consideration have gone out of use, there is still a fairly large number of cases where a verb is derived, or is derivable, from a word in another part of speech, and where both the verb and the underlying word are used in today's Persian. We say "derivable" because the relationship suggested between the verbs and the words from which they are said to be derived does not necessarily reflect the actual historical development in all cases. That is to say, whether, in actual fact, the underlying word, in any given case, is of older origin, with the verb having come later in history, is not our chief concern. Our chief concern is to provide the most convenient synchronic analysis, and this, as is sometimes the case, may in certain cases be no more than a convenient fiction. In these terms, then, we find at least about 70 verbs derivable from other parts of speech. The underlying words are listed here in alphabetical order.[12] It must be understood that these words, when functioning as verbs, serve as the present stems of the derived verbs. The past stem is in each case formed by the addition of /-íd/ to the present stem, and the infinitive by the addition of /-ǽn/ to the past stem:

---

[11] The above statements and approximate numbers do not take into account the facetious forming of verbs from a large number of other words, and apply only to the normal situation. The poet Ṭarzi Afshār, for example, of the latter part of the Ṣafavi period, made verbs from all kinds of words, including proper nouns; e.g., /ˀasudé/ "comfortable", /jonún/ "madness", /cún/ "how", /púl/ "money"; the names of the months, such as /ræjǽb/ "Rajab"; proper nouns and adjectives such as /dǽšte moqán/ "Dasht-e Moghān", /širván/ "Shirvan", /torkí/ "Turkish"; and many more. This poet's unorthodox treatment of the patterns of the language was not limited to the process discussed here, but included other parts of Persian as well. See Farrokh, *op. cit.*, pp. 535-536, A. Kasravi, "Enteqād-e maqāle-ye rāje' be Ṭarzi Afshār", in Y. Zokā', ed., *Chehel maqāle-ye Kasravi* (Tehran, 1335/1956), pp. 96-97, and Z. Mo'tamen, *She'r va adab-e Fārsi* (Tehran, 1332/1953), pp. 206-207. Ṭarzi's peculiarities of style represent individual idiosyncracies, and do not reflect the normal development of the language.

[12] Almost all the verbs listed appear in the Ḥoseyn list. He does not, however, indicate whether each verb is derived from another word.

1. /bǽlʔ/	"swallow" (a)[13]
2. /bǽs/	"enough" (b, c, d)
3. /bú/	"smell" (intr.)
4. /bús/	"kiss"
5. /cǽrb/	"rich in fat" ("to exceed in weight") (b, e)
6. /cǽrx/	"wheel" ("to turn", intr.)
7. /cǽsb/	"glue" ("to stick", intr.) (e)
8. /corúk/	"wrinkle" (c)
9. /dǽm/	"breath; bellows" ("to breathe into") (e)
10. /dów/	"running"
11. /dózd/	"thief" (b)
12. /fǽhm/	"understanding" (a, e)
13. /gǽnd/	"stink" ("to putrefy, become fetid") (b, e)
14. /gónj/	"volume" ("to be containable in") (d, e)
15. /gúz/	"fart"
16. /hærás/	"fear" (d, e)
17. /jǽng/	"fight"
18. /jómb/	"moving" (intr.)
19. /júš/	"boil" (intr.) (b)
20. /kéš/	"elasticity" ("to draw, extend, stretch") (e)
21. /kúc/	"migration"
22. /lás/	"flirtation" (d)
23. /lǽm/	"lolling" (d)
24. /lǽng/	"lame" ("to limp") (b, e)
25. /lǽrz/	"trembling" (e)
26. /líz/	"slippery, slipperiness" ("to slide", intr.) (b)
27. /lúl/	"wiggle" (d)
28. /nám/	"name" ("to name", i.e., "to give a name to") (d)
29. /náz/	"coquetry, pretended lack of interest" ("to feign disdain; to boast")
30. /núš/	"enjoying of beverages" ("to drink") (b, d, e)

[13] The infinitive in each case is to be understood to have a meaning more or less directly implied by the gloss given for the underlying word ("to swallow", "to be enough", etc.). When the relationship is not clear, or direct, the meaning of the infinitive is given in parentheses after the gloss. Similarly, in cases of ambiguity, a notation "intr(ansitive)" or "trans(itive)" has been added. The small letters in parentheses refer to the notes at the end of §5.2.

31. /pǽr/ "feather" ("to fly")
32. /pæsǽnd/ "choice, acceptability" ("to find acceptable and choose") (b)
33. /píc/ "turn, screw" (trans. and intr.)

34. /qæbúl/ "acceptance" (a, c)
35. /qǽlt/ "rolling" (intr.) (b)
36. /qáp/ "snatching" (b, d)
37. /qorómb/ "roaring sound" (e)

38. /rǽm/ "shying away" (as of a horse)
39. /rǽnj/ "suffering" ("to feel hurt") (e)
40. /rǽqs/ "dance" (a)

41. /sór/ "gliding" ("to glide, to slip", intr.) (b)
42. /šáš/ "urine"
43. /šǽl/ "crippled" ("to walk as a cripple") (b, e)
44. /šomár/ "number, counting" ("to count")
45. /šúr/ "spiritedness, commotion" ("to revolt")

46. /táb/ "lustre" ("to shine") (e)
47. /tælǽb/ "demand" (a)
48. /tæráš/ "scraping" (to shave) (e)
49. /tærǽk/ "crack" (intr.)
50. /tærǽq/ "cracking noise" ("to make a cracking noise") (d)
51. /tǽrs/ "fear"
52. /telefón/ "telephone" (d)
53. /telgeráf/ "telegraph" (d)
54. /tórš/ "sour, acid" ("to turn acid") (b)

55. /xáb/ "sleep"
56. /xǽm/ "bent, crooked" (intr.) (b)
57. /xæráš/ "scrape, scratch" (intr.)
58. /xerám/ "graceful walk" (e)
59. /xís/ "soaked" (intr.) (b)

60. /xorúš/ "roaring" (e)
61. /xóšk/ "dry" (intr.) (b)

62. /zíb/ "ornament" ("to become", i.e., "to be becoming") (b, e)

63. /ˀagáh/ "informed" ("to be informed") (b, d)
64. /ˀaqáz/ "beginning" (trans. and intr.) (d)
65. /ˀarám/ "calm and quiet" (noun and adjective) ("to repose") (b)
66. /ˀænjám/ "concluding, accomplishing" ("to end up in") (d)

Several observations may be made on the above verbs:

(a) Of all the verbs listed, only five (Nos. 1, 12, 34, 40, 47) are derived from Arabic words. Of these, /tælæbidǽn/, as we have seen, occurs in very limited usage. /ræqsidǽn/ alternates with /rǽqs kærdǽn/. /fæhmidǽn/ is the only Arabic-based verb which has no compound-verb synonym in Modern Persian. /qapidǽn/ is based on a Turkish word.[14] /telgerafidǽn/ and /telefonidǽn/ are the only verbs derived from recent Western loanwords.

(b) Of the underlying words, five (5, 54, 59, 61, 63) are clearly adjectives. Six (11, 13, 24, 26, 43, 65) are used both as adjectives and as nouns. Four (2, 30, 36, 41) are "preverbs". Five (19, 32, 35, 56, 62) do not seem to have a clear "part of speech" status. All others are clearly nouns.[15]

(c) In a few cases, all the forms of the verbs are not used. Thus, from /bæsidǽn/, only /bæsændé/ "sufficient" is used. /tælæbidǽn/, as already indicated (§ 5.1.), is limited in occurrence. /corukidǽn/ appears almost exclusively in the form /corukidé/ "wrinkled (often used of a face)". /qæbulidǽn/ is one of the few verbs in the language that occur only in the causative form, i.e., /qæbulandǽn/ "to make someone accept". It is interesting that this is one of the verbs based on Arabic words.

(d) Not all the listed verbs occur in all styles. Numbers 22, 23, 27, 36, 50 are used in informal style, as are their underlying words. In nos. 2, 16, 28, 30, 63, 64, 66 the verbs are used in the more formal and/or literary styles. Of the underlying words, 16, 44, 64 are somewhat more literary; 2 and 30 are used in the informal style also. /telgerafidǽn/ and /telefonidǽn/ are used in telegrams

---

[14] On the etymology of /qáp/, see ʿA. A. Dehkhodā, *Loghat-Nāma*, ed. M. Moʿin, Fasc. 57 (Tehran, 1339/1960), under *qāp zadan.*

[15] The terms "noun", "adjective", and "preverb" as here used are formally defined. A "preverb", briefly, is a word whose chief characteristics are that: (a) it is used in close-knit combination with a single simple verb, or one of a small group of such verbs, the combination forming a single unit in that it functions as—and is replaceable by—a simple verb, except that the verbal afixes are added to the stem of the simple verb, not to the preverb; (b) it cannot serve as subject or object (which substantives can). See my review of V. S. Rastorgueva, *A Short Sketch of the Grammar of Persian*, trans. Steven P. Hill, ed. Herbert H. Paper (*International Journal of American Linguistics*, vol. 30, no. 1, part 2; Indiana University Research Center in Anthropology, Folklore, and Linguistics, Publication 29) in *Language* XLI, pp. 338-345 (1965).

only. In no. 14, the noun is used only as a technical term in physics, while the verb is used in common speech.

(e) Of the simple verbs listed, some twenty (5, 7, 9, 10, 12, 13, 14, 16, 20, 24, 25, 30, 37, 39, 43, 46, 48, 58, 60, 62) seem to have no compound-verb synonyms, or at least not very-commonly-used ones.

5.3. We have seen that the words on which the verbs under discussion are formed serve as the present stems of the respective verbs. The reverse of this also happens sometimes; that is, the present stems of certain verbs ("real" infinitives) are used as substantives; e.g., /ʔæmbaštǽn/ "to store": /ʔæmbár/ "store"; /pendaštǽn/ "to imagine": /pendár/ "imagination"; /peyvæstǽn/ "to join": /peyvǽnd/ "link"; /foruxtǽn/ "to sell": /forúš/ "sale". There is one feature which can often distinguish the cases where verbs are derived from other words from those in which other words are derived from verbs. In the latter group of words, the verbal prefix /bé-/ (imperative and subjunctive marker) can, and often is, left out when the simple verb (usually one of a small group of so-called "auxiliaries"), is part of a compound verb. In the former group, this prefix is almost never left out.

It was also stated that the verbs in question form their past stems in /-íd/. Not all past stems in /-íd/, however, are based on other words. If they were, we could interpret the function of /-i-/ in the past stem to be the formation of verbs from other parts of speech. As it is, this /-i-/ seems to be an "empty" morph, without any semantic or grammatical (including morphophonemic) meaning.

6.1. Although, in the language as a whole compound verbs far outnumber simple verbs, the proportion of the two types can be expected to differ in the writings of different writers, and even in different styles. Among the recent authors, the scholar Aḥmad Kasravi (1890–1946) had a distinct preference for simple verbs.[16] He manifested this preference in his writings in several ways: (1) Where Modern Persian has a simple verb with one or more

[16] The examples of words used by Kasravi given in this paper are taken from secondary sources cited in footnote 20 below, as well as some primary sources, i.e., those writings of his which are not concerned with language. It must be said that, while in most cases he actually used the quoted verbs, in some instances he recommended using such derived verbs but had little or no occasion to employ them himself.

synonyms in compound verbs (§ 4.1.), he used the simple verb almost to the complete exclusion of the synonymous compounds. (2) He used, and/or recommended the use of, some of the archaic or obsolete simple verbs derived from substantives still in use (§ 5.1.), e.g., /pændidǽn/ "to give advice", /gæmanidǽn/ "to guess". (3) He formed new verbs from some Modern Persian substantives, e.g., /pærvá/ "attention": /pærvayidǽn/ "to pay attention", /cáp/ "printing": /capidǽn/ "to print".[17] (4) Certain lexical morphemes occur only in combination with other morphemes. He isolated some of these morphemes, used them by themselves, and also formed verbs from them. Thus, from /bihudé/ "useless", he isolated /hudé/ "result", and then formed /hudidǽn/ "to result".[18] Similarly, from /davtælǽb/ "volunteer", he isolated /dáv/ "claim", and formed /davidǽn/ "to claim". (5) He revived certain archaic substantives, such as /ʔák/ "defect", /zǽnd/ "explanation", /šovǽnd/ "reason"; and also formed verbs from them: /ʔakidǽn/ "to become defective", /zændidǽn/ "to explain", /šovændidǽn/ "to cause".[19] (6) When no other alternatives were available to him he coined—out of the blue, as it were—a number of verbs: /fæhlidǽn/ "to become engaged in", /fokidǽn/ "to be or become solid", /hekidǽn/ "to designate", /yufidǽn/ "to be changed (intr. counterpart of "to exchange")". (7) In the same way, he coined a number of substantives, such as /pǽrg/ "permission", and /pehǽl/ "doubt", and then derived verbs from them: /pærgidǽn/, and /pehælidǽn/. (8) He even coined verbs from complex forms. For example, from /bahǽm/ "together", which is a combination of /ba/ "with" and /hæm/ "also, and", he formed /bahæmidǽn/ "to unite" (intr.). In the literary style, there is a phrase consisting of /ʔæz/ "of, from" + /ʔán/ "that" + the connective /-e/ (the ezafe marker used in the major structure of modification) followed by a nominal phrase. The resulting construction expresses possession, and is somewhat similar to the so-called "long (or

[17] There is an older infinitive /capidǽn/ "to plunder" in use in Modern Persian. However, Kasravi suggested that this older infinitive, derived from Turkish, should be discarded, for "we have no need for it". See A. Kasravi, *Zabān-e pāk* (cited in footnote 20), p. 37.

[18] In dropping the /-e/ of /hudé/ in the infinitive, he imitated such pairs as /nalé/: /nalidǽn/, where the noun is derived from the verb.

[19] Kasravi uses the pronunciation /šovǽnd/ in place of the original /šævǽnd/, in order to make it different from an inflected form of /šodǽn/ "to become". See *Farhang-e Kasravi*, ed. Y. Zokā' (cited in footnote 20), under *shovand*.

second, or absolute) possessive pronouns" of English; e.g., /ʔæzáne mǽn/ "mine", /ʔæzáne hæsǽn/ "Ḥasan's", /ʔæzáne bæradǽreš/ "his (or her) brother's". Kasravi isolated the first part of the phrase, /ʔæzán-/, and formed the verb /ʔæzanidǽn/ "to possess". These verbs are reminiscent of certain English formations. Kasravi recommended deriving other words from the verbs he thus revived or invented, and in some cases he formed such derivations himself.

6.2. Kasravi's revival of certain simple verbs and invention of others was part of his conscious, insistent, and systematic efforts to "reform" and enrich the language. A major feature of his methods for achieving these goals was extensive use of derivation by affixation. Another feature was removing anomalies and irregularities, extending each grammatical rule to *all* the forms in its domain. Thus, of the two stems of each verb, he would use only one—that which would make it possible to form the past stems of all verbs (not some, as is actually the case) by adding /-(i)d/ to the present stems, thus making all verbs regular.[20]

6.3. Another contemporary scholar, Dr. Moḥammad Moghaddam, has recently suggested bringing into use the suffix (actually suffix complex) /-(æ)stǽn/ to form new verbs which in most cases would correspond to English verbs in *-ize*. Thus, he suggests as possible new verbs formed in this way: /bolúr/ "crystal": /boluræ stǽn/ "to crystallize", and /vižé/ "special": /vižæstǽn/ "to specialize". As in the case of Kasravi, Moghaddam's proposal is part of more extensive plans to "improve" the language, and to rid it of its foreign element, or at least of some of that element. He, too, preaches regularity— the extension of analogy to all forms without exception.[21] To my knowledge, however, he has not expressed—in print, at least—an opinion on the use of simple *versus* compound verbs. Nor does any preference on his part emerge from a partial examination of his writings.

[20] Kasravi discussed his views on language reform in numerous articles and in the book *Zabān-e pāk* (Tehran, 1322/1943). Some of his articles have been collected in *Zabān-e Fārsi va rāh-e rasā va tavānā gardānidan-e ān*, ed. Y. Zokā' (Tehran, 1334/1955). See also *Farhang-e Kasravi*, ed. Y. Zokā' (Tehran, 1336/1957), a glossary of some of the words Kasravi used.

[21] See his *Āyande-ye zabān-e Fārsi* (Tehran, 1341/1962); /-(æ)stǽn/ is discussed on pp. 19-20.

THE APPLICATION OF THE KAṬAPAYĀDI SANKHYA IN SOUTH INDIAN MUSIC

by Walter Kaufmann
Indiana University

THE MODERN system of South Indian music, formulated by Govinda (eighteenth century) in his *Saṃgraha Cūdāmaṇi* (one of the last treatises on music written in Sanskrit; reprinted, Madras, 1938), is the result of an evolution much less disturbed by foreign influences than that of the music of northern India. The Carnatic system bases its wealth of *janaka* and *janya* ragas upon 72 parent scales (*melas*, *melakartas*, "group-makers"). These 72 seven-tone scales, straight in ascent and descent, are organized according to their tone-materials. Before considering the relationship between the names of the scales and their numerical places in the system of the 72, it becomes necessary to list the *mela* names and show the remarkable and orderly changes of their scale degrees. The names of the *melas* are:

1. Kanakāngi
2. Ratnāngi
3. Gānamurti
4. Vanaspati
5. Mānavati
6. Tānarūpi
7. Senapati (Senavati)
8. Hanumattodi
9. Dhenuka
10. Nāṭakapriya
11. Kokilapriya
12. Rūpavati
13. Gāyakapriya
14. Vakulābharanam
15. Māyāmālavagaula
16. Chakravāka
17. Sūryakānta
18. Haṭakāmbari
19. Jhankāradhvani
20. Naṭabhairavi
21. Kiravāni
22. Kharaharapriya
23. Gaurīmanohari
24. Varunapriya
25. Māraranjani
26. Chārukesi
27. Sarasāngi
28. Harikāmbhoji
29. Dhīraśankarābharana
30. Nāgānandini
31. Yāgapriya
32. Rāgavardhani
33. Gangeyabhūśani
34. Vāgadhīśvari
35. Śūlini
36. Chalanāṭa
37. Sālaga
38. Jalārnava
39. Jhālavarāli
40. Navanītam
41. Pāvani
42. Raghupriya

43. Gavāmbhodi	58. Hemavatī
44. Bhavapriya	59. Dharmavati
45. Śubhapantuvarāli	60. Nītimati
46. Shadvidhamārgini	61. Kantāmani
47. Suvarnāngi	62. Rishabhapriya
48. Divyamani	63. Latāngi
49. Dhavalāmbari	64. Vāchaspati
50. Nāmanārāyani	65. Mechakalyāni
51. Kāmavardhani	66. Chitrāmbari
52. Rāmapriya	67. Sucharitra
53. Gamanaśrama	68. Jyotisvarūpini
54. Viśvambari	69. Dhātuvardhani
55. Śyāmalāngi	70. Nāsikabhūśani
56. Shanmukhapriya	71. Kosala
57. Simhendramadhyama	72. Rasikapriya

These 72 *melas* are grouped into twelve *chakras* (lit., "wheels"), each containing six *melas*. The scales of the first six *chakras* (thirty-six *melas*) employ the note F (*MA shuddha*), while those of the other six *chakras* (*melas* 37-72) use F# (*Prati MA*).

THE TWELVE CHAKRAS

CHAKRAS	MELAS
I. *Indu chakra*	1-6
II. *Netra chakra*	7-12
III. *Agni chakra*	13-18
IV. *Veda chakra*	19-24
V. *Bana chakra*	25-30
VI. *Rutu chakra*	31-36
VII. *Rishi chakra*	37-42
VIII. *Vasu chakra*	43-48
IX. *Brahma chakra*	49-54
X. *Disi chakra*	55-60
XI. *Rudra chakra*	61-66
XII. *Āditya chakra*	67-72

The names of the twelve *chakras* are chosen in such a manner that they serve the musician as a mnemonic device to establish the number of the *chakra*. As we have only one moon (*indu*), the word signifies the first *chakra*. The two eyes (*netra*) refer to the second *chakra*. *Agni* refers to the three sacred fires (*agni trayam*); *veda* implies the four vedas, *bana* points to the five *banas* of Manmatha;

rutu to the six seasons. There are seven *rishis*, eight *vasus*, nine *prajapatis* (*Brahmas*), ten *disis* (directions), eleven *rudras* and twelve *ādityas* (suns) mentioned in the puranas (legends).

All twelve *chakras*, that is, all 72 *melas*, have in their lower tetrachords the following notes (the unchanged notes of the first six *chakras* are C, F and G, while the unchanged notes of the second six *chakras* are C, F# and G):

TABLE I

Chakra	I:	C	D^b	E^{bb}	F	*Chakra*	VII:	C	D^b	E^{bb}	F#
,,	II:	C	D^b	E^b	F	,,	VIII:	C	D^b	E^b	F#
,,	III:	C	D^b	E	F	,,	IX:	C	D^b	E	F#
,,	IV:	C	D	E^b	F	,,	X:	C	D	E^b	F#
,,	V:	C	D	E	F	,,	XI:	C	D	E	F#
,,	VI:	C	D#	E	F	,,	XII:	C	D#	E	F#

From the first to the sixth *mela* within each *chakra* changes in the upper tetrachord occur in the following manner:

TABLE II

Chakra:	I	II	III	IV	V	VI	VII	VIII	IX	X	XI	XII				
Mela:	1	7	13	19	25	31	37	43	49	55	61	67:	G	A^b	B^{bb}	c
	2	8	14	20	26	32	38	44	50	56	62	68:	G	A^b	B^b	c
	3	9	15	21	27	33	39	45	51	57	63	69:	G	A^b	B	c
	4	10	16	22	28	34	40	46	52	58	64	70:	G	A	B^b	c
	5	11	17	23	29	35	41	47	53	59	65	71:	G	A	B	c
	6	12	18	24	30	36	42	48	54	60	66	72:	G	A#	B	c

The foregoing two tables, representing a summarization of involved theoretical terminologies, suffice to provide information concerning the changing degrees of the 72 *melas*. For instance, if the scale of *mela* 21 is to be ascertained, the second table is consulted, which shows that *mela Kiravāni* (21) appears in *chakra* IV. The first table provides the notes of the lower tetrachord standing to the right of the line in which the number IV appears: C D E^b F. The notes of the upper tetrachord of the twenty-first *mela* are shown in the second table at the right end of the third line containing the number 21: G A^b B c. Thus the whole scale of *mela Kiravāni* (21) is: C D E^b F G A^b B c. When the notes of the *melas* 37-72 are to be determined, F# has to be used instead of F, as mentioned before.

As South Indian musicians and theorists do not refer to our summarizations in the two tables stated above, they use the syllables *pā*, *śri*, *go*, *bhū*, *ma*, and *shā* for the six *melas* of each *chakra* and combine these syllables with the *chakra* names. Thus, *agni-bhū*, for instance, indicates the fourth *mela* of the third *chakra*, which is *Chakravāka* (16). The changes of the notes (excepting F and F#), as already indicated, occur only in the second, third, sixth and seventh degrees of the 72 scales in the same order as demonstrated in our two tables. Chakras I, II, III, and VII, VIII, IX use as second degree D^b; as third degree E^{bb}, E^b, and E, respectively. *Chakras* IV, V, VI and X, XI, XII use as second degree D, D, D# and as third degree E^b, E, E, respectively.

The first of the six *melas* (*pā*) in all twelve *chakras*, that is, *melas* 1, 7, 13, etc.; the second *melas* (*śri*) 2, 8, 14, etc.; and the third *melas* (*go*) 3, 9, 15, etc., use as sixth degree A^b, as seventh degree B^{bb}, B^b and B, respectively. The fourth *melas* (*bhū*) in all twelve *chakras*, that is, *melas* 4, 10, 16, etc.; the fifth *melas* (*ma*) 5, 11, 17, etc.; and the sixth *melas* (*shā*) 6, 12, 18, etc., use as sixth degree A, A, A# and as seventh degree B^b, B, B, respectively. The South Indian method of determining and describing the various scale degrees is somewhat cumbersome, because instead of simple tone letters, terms such as *shuddha RI* (D^b), *catusśruti RI* (four-*śruti Rishabha*, D), *shatśruti RI* (six-*śruti RI*, D#), *shuddha GA* (E^{bb}), *sādhārana GA* (E^b), *antara GA* (E), etc., are still in use.

The *Kaṭapayādi Sankhya* is the enumeration of *mela* names by referring to the letter groups headed by *ka*, *ṭa*, *pa*, and *ya*. Between every number of the 72 *melas* and their names exists a distinct relationship well known to the majority of South Indian musicians. If an outsider asks a southern musician for the number of a certain *mela* by merely mentioning the *mela* name, the musician, not always a well-educated person, will with very little hesitation provide the exact number. This feat, which first was admired as a great mnemonic achievement, is based upon an ingenious system which, until recently, was handed down from master to pupil in great secrecy. At the present time, however, several enlightened musicians and theorists of the South have lifted the veil. The system is based upon the order of the consonants of the Sanskrit alphabet, which serves as a basis for almost all other Indian alphabets. In contrast to western alphabets, this order of consonants consists of four groups:

(a) *Kādinava* group:

K	KH	G	GH	NG	CH	CHH	J	JH	(JN)
1	2	3	4	5	6	7	8	9	0

(b) *Ṭādinava* group:

Ṭ	ṬH	Ḍ	ḌH	Ṇ	T	TH	D	DH	(N)
1	2	3	4	5	6	7	8	9	0

(c) *Pādipancha* group:

P	PH	B	BH	M
1	2	3	4	5

(d) *Yādiashṭa* group:

Y	R	L	V	Ś	SH	S	H	(LH	KSH	DNY)
1	2	3	4	5	6	7	8	0	0	0

The letters in each of the four groups are numbered: in the first two groups from 1 to 9, in the third from 1 to 5 and in the fourth from 1 to 8. Some of the letters at the end of the first, second and fourth groups are not counted and are provided with zeros.

The relationship between *mela* name and *mela* number is determined in the following manner: the first two consonants of the *mela* name are taken and their numbers in the alphabet established. It is of no consequence whether the consonants belong to the first, second, third or fourth groups. These two numbers are then read in reverse order (right to left), and the two digits will represent the correct number of the *mela* in the system of the 72. A few examples may illustrate this system. Let us assume that the number of *mela Harikāmbhoji* is to be found. The first consonant of the *mela* name is H, which is 8 in the *yādiashṭa* group; the second consonant of the *mela* name is R, which is 2 (by chance) in the same group of letters. If we revert the numbers 82 into 28, we obtain the correct number of *Harikāmbhoji*. Another example is the *mela Kiravāni*. K is 1 in the *kādinava* group, and R is (as already known) 2 in the *yādiashṭa* group. We get the numbers 1 2. In reverse order, 21, they represent the correct number of *Kiravāni*.

A careful investigation of this *kaṭapayādi sankhya* shows that not all *mela* names can be ranged into this system. There are exceptions which appear in *mela* names where double consonants occur in the second place, that is, after the first vowel. In the following *mela* names, the second letter of the double consonants (following the first vowel) has to be counted:

Dharmavati: DH and M, 9 5, correct number 59
Gangeyabhūśani: G and G, 3 3, correct number 33
Jhankāradhvani: JH and K, 9 1, correct number 19
Ratnāngi: R and N, 2 0 (of the *ṭādinava* group), correct number 02
Shadvidhamārgini: SH and V, 6 4, correct number 46
Shanmukhapriya: SH and M, 6 5, correct number 56
Sūryakānta: S and Y, 7 1, correct number 17.

In all other *mela* names with double consonants after the first vowel (*Chakravāka*, *Divyamani*, *Viśvambari*, *Simhendramadhyama* and *Chitrāmbari*), the first letter of the double consonant is to be counted, thus the same rule is applied as in *melas* with single consonants.

The *kaṭapayādi sankhya* has also been used in the determining of the numbers of rhythmic units in Carnatic *tālas* and, furthermore, in a work entitled *Saṅgīta-Sāra-Saṅgraha* by one Akalaṅka, which may be of some interest. The author's name "is due to a misunderstanding of the opening verse of the work .... The word 'Akalaṅka' ... qualifies Śiva's holy name, Abhikyā .... One Tiruveṅkaṭa Kavi seems to be the author of this Telugu *kavya* [work, poem] on music dedicated to Śiva" (V. Raghavan, "The So-called Akalaṅka," *Journal of the Music Academy* XII, 1-4 [Madras, 1941], p. 39). The language in which this work is written is an inferior form of Telugu. The time of its origin cannot be ascertained, and the place of its origin is, most probably, Tanjore. The author employs new words for his twenty-four *śrutis* (not the usual twenty-two) which show *kaṭapayādi* prefixes. The *śruti* names in this work are:

1. Yina	13. Loka
2. Raga	14. Vaya
3. Lina	15. Suka
4. Ghana	16. Toya
5. Mana	17. Chhaya
6. Tana	18. Jaya
7. Sena	19. Dheya
8. Dana	20. Nara
9. Dhana	21. Kara
10. Naya	22. Khara
11. Paya	23. Giri
12. Thaya	24. Vira

The alphabetical numbers derived from the two consonants of these new *śruti* names when read in reverse order provide the appropriate *śruti* numbers. Although the adjusting of new *śruti* names to the *kaṭapayādi sankhya* could have been of value to musicians, the new method never became popular.

The author of the *Saṅgīta-Sāra-Saṅgraha* maintains that his *śruti* names also correspond to the twenty-four syllables of the *Gāyat-tri* [sic]. The famous *gāyatrī*, the most sacred mantram in honor of the sun, has each syllable, each word, filled with numerous mystic and transcendental allusions. Its text is:

> Tat savitur varenyam bhargo devasya
> Dhimahi dhiyo yo nah prachodayat.

The author alleges that, in addition to his *śruti* names, the tone syllables of the seven principal notes (*SA*, *RI*, *GA*, *MA*, *PA*, *DHA*, *NI*) are also derived from the sacred text of the *gāyatrī* and may be found in syllables 2, 6, 10, 15, 21, 23 and 7. T. R. Ṡrinivāsa Ayyangār in his preface to the previously mentioned *Saṃgraha-Cūḍāmaṇi* (p. xx) mentions "that it would be more appropriate, if the 17th and 20th syllables had been chosen . . . instead of the 23rd and the 7th."

This study could be extended to extra-musical fields where the ordering principle of the *kaṭapayādi sankhya* has been and still is employed. This system is an excellent tool for memorization and shows the general attitude of South Indians toward orderliness, neatness and a desire in their studies for classifying things.

OIRAT LITERARY RESOURCES AND PROBLEMS OF OIRAT LEXICOGRAPHY

by John R. Krueger
Indiana University

1. WESTERN AND EASTERN MONGOLIAN

THE historical events, religious texts and literary documents surrounding the Eastern Mongols, who ruled mighty China and even reached the West, and the resultant linguistic and scholarly attention lavished on them, seem literally and figuratively to outweigh the presumably equally meritorious materials of the Western Mongols, embracing the once mighty Oirat confederacy (which summoned the combined might of the Manchu lords of China and the Khalkha princes for its destruction) and the westernmost Kalmyks of the Don and Volga rivers, and Astrakhan.

Materials in Eastern Mongolian range from lapidary texts of the early 1200's down to present-day Khalkha writings in Cyrillic Mongolian of such practical bent as propaganda or agriculture. In contrast to this nearly 750-year range lies the strictly delimited period in which Oirat-Mongol and Kalmyk literary activity flourished. Because the Oirats did not develop their distinct orthography until the mid-17th century, and because later political developments resulted in its practical extinction in the mid-20th century, Oirat-Kalmyk literature is clearly preserved in time by definite *termini*. These borders may be set at exactly A. D. 1648 (in some sources, 1649), when Zaya Pandita devised the Oirat script, to 1917, when the Russian Revolution brought official abolition of the old script; and later 1943, when the Volga Kalmyk Republic was dissolved by the Soviet government—a period of around 300 years, a bit less if we consider that little original Script-Oirat material of interest to scholars or literary historians was composed after 1900 (the contents of such émigré periodicals as *Xoŋxo* of the 1920's appear to be based largely on the pre-1900 period). Various unofficial sources report the continuing private use of Oirat script in areas of Sinkiang and Western Mongolia; whether that limited usage will extend beyond the present generation of users cannot be known.

Since the materials in Eastern Mongolian have been so greatly favored over the Western Mongolian, by virtue of accessibility, content and importance, it follows that further investigation of Western Mongolian documentary sources should prove a rich field for scholarly study.

It is well recognized that a good general survey of the history of Mongolian literature is a badly needed item. Although popular works like Professor Walther Heissig's *A Lost Civilization: The Mongols Rediscovered*[1] do much to set the stage for the study of Mongolian history and culture, they cannot discuss any one topic in sufficient detail to enable the would-be specialist to acquire an evaluative survey of the present status of the discipline. For the Oirat-Kalmyk picture, however, several such surveys are at hand. A valuable and accessible general overview is N. Poppe's article, *Stand der Kalmückenforschung*,[2] which gives a clear and evaluative listing of anthropological, historical, literary and linguistic works touching on the Oirats and Kalmyks. For the linguistic side alone, a concise summary of phonology and morphological features is now at hand in Pentti Aalto's article *Schrift-Oiratisch*.[3] The *Kalmyk Manual* of A. Bormanshinow is a handy one-volume account with historical survey, bibliography, and readers with glossaries in both Cyrillic and Oirat scripts.[4] An evaluative bibliographical survey is that of D. Sinor, which lists thirty-nine works on Oirat-Kalmyk studies.[5]

Except for some Western Mongolian word-lists in Arabo-Persian historical writings (as Rashīd ad-Dīn), we may date the first substantive recording of Literary Oirat in exactly 1648, when Zāya

---

[1] Walther Heissig, *A Lost Civilization: The Mongols Rediscovered* (London: Thames and Hudson; New York: Basic Books; 1966), 271 pages. It is the English translation of his *Ein Volk sucht seine Geschichte: die Mongolen und die verlorenen Dokumente ihrer grossen Zeit* (Düsseldorf/Vienna: Econ-Verlag, 1965), 324 p.

[2] N. Poppe, "Stand der Kalmückenforschung", *Wiener Zeitschrift für die Kunde des Morgenlandes*, 52.346-379 (1955).

[3] Pentti Aalto, "Schrift-Oiratisch", *Handbuch der Orientalistik* 5(2).185-199 (1964).

[4] Arash Bormanshinow, *Kalmyk Manual* (New York: American Council of Learned Societies, Uralic and Altaic Project, No. 26; 1963), 306 p. The volume has not been formally published yet, but is available by the xerographic Duopage process (Bell and Howell, Cleveland 12, Ohio).

[5] D. Sinor, *Introduction à l'étude de l'Eurasie centrale* (Wiesbaden: Harrasowitz 1963), §§1889-1928, pp. 128-131.

Paṇḍita, a scholar and monk of a Khoshud noble family (1599–1662),[6] devised the Oirat script by making the ambiguous Uighur form of Mongolian writing more precise. With the aid of many assistants, he embarked on a whirlwind round of translating and editing, culminating in a total of from 177 to 200 works ascribed to him and his entourage. They have recently been listed, in Mongolian and Tibetan, in the Damdinsüren chrestomathy volume[7] (a similar but skimpier bare list is in A. Pozdneyev's chrestomathy, in the article rather misleadingly titled *Pervyi period razvitiya kalmytskoi literatury* [The Initial Developmental Period of Kalmyk Literature][8]). Unfortunately, of this sizeable output only a fraction survives—or at least is known to us—from the catalogued holdings of Western Mongolian collections. The fierce and prolonged internecine wars of the Oirats have taken their toll in the reduced numbers of literary manuscripts which survive.

When Western attention began again to be drawn to the Mongols in the early 1700's and 1800's by the works of such travellers as von Strahlenberg (1730) or Benjamin Bergmann (1804–1805), it was the Kalmyk Mongols of whom they spoke. The father of Mongolian studies, Isaac Jacob Schmidt, first made contact with Kalmyk Mongols near Sarepta and, it will be recalled, even worked as a Bible translator to them, though his later writings dealt more with Literary Mongolian and eventually with Tibetan. Contemporary with such mid-19th century Written Mongolian grammars and chrestomathies as those of Kowalewski and Popov is the first major Western study of a Kalmyk text, Bernhard Jülg's edition of the *Siddhitü kegür* tales.[9] Considering the fact that Mongolian studies were only beginning then in the West, it is a surprisingly careful edition, prepared with much forethought, though of course

[6] His biography in Mongolian by Ratnabhadra is now available, ed. B. Rinchen, *Rabjamba Caya bandida tuɣuji saran-u gerel kemekü ene metü bolai* (Corpus scriptorum mongolorum, V, no. 2, Ulaan Baator, 1959). Note that his biography is not in Oirat—moreover, it deals with his life, and not his literary works. There is an extract from it in the Ts. Damdinsüren chrestomathy, *Mongɣol uran ǰokiyal-un degeǰi ǰaɣun bilig* (One Hundred Choice Selections from Mongolian Literature) (Corpus scriptorum mongolorum, XIV, Ulaan Baator, 1959), selection 53, pp. 320-326.

[7] Ts. Damdinsüren, *op. cit.*, pp. 327-334.

[8] A. M. Pozdneyev, *Kalmytskaya khrestomatiya* ... (three eds., St. Petersburg, 1892, 1907, 1915), pp. 169-172 in the 2nd ed.

[9] B. Jülg, *Die Märchen des Siddhi-Kür* (Leipzig, 1866), 223 pp.

errors can be detected today.[10] This was followed by more studies of Oirat texts in the West (in which we include those printed in Russia), as Golstunskii's work on the Mongol-Oirat legal code of 1640,[11] Pozdneyev's folklore collection, the *Kalmytskie narodnye skazki*, his songs, then his large chrestomathy, an edition of Baza Bakshi's account of his pilgrimage to Tibet, and last, Pozdneyev's 1911 Kalmyk dictionary, which represents, however, only about a quarter of the material collected. Concluding the brief list of studies, one may mention the Kalmyk text of the Janggar epic, some publications in Kalmyk by Kalmyks (e.g., *Xoŋxo*) and a few 20th century European studies, such as Haenisch's edition of the Oirat *Altan Gerel* (Sanskrit *Suvarṇaprabhāsa*), one chapter of which he later separately edited. This short list virtually sums up the scholarly work on literary material. As Aalto aptly noted, and one

[10] A new ed. of the *Siddhitü Kegür* cycle (The Tales of the Bewitched Corpse, the *Vetālapañcaviṁsatikā*), considering the Kalmyk text and the several Mongolian versions now available (e.g., the 1925 Peking ed. by the *Mongγol bičig-ün qoriya*, 57 pp. with thirteen stories; now reproduced as *Special Paper No. Three* by The Mongolia Society, 1965, 60 pp.; and the 1928 Ulaan Baator ed. by the Urga UchKom (Learned Committee), which was reprinted at Mukden in 1957, 151 pp., containing the full 25 stories), would be a definite possibility today, and would also form a useful work for Mongolian studies.

In considering the Kalmyk version, it is possible to make improvements on Jülg's text, of which a few are sketched out here. His phrase *töüni xazāru kütölöd* (SK 3,10, cf. 3,19) cannot be "led by the bridle", for this would require *xazār-yēr*; it looks more like a directive suffix on the stem *γazā-* "outside", i.e., "led him towards the outside", or mayhap a distortion from *γazar* "earth, spot, place". It could be a combination of two readings with a copying error and loss of one, i.e., "he led him outside by the bridle". Further study is needed.

Jülg's treatment of the phrase *ava-dhüdi üzel* (SK 3,2), though correctly defined as *Mādhyamika* doctrine, is inadequate (cf. his p. 143-b, "das Wort war nicht zu enträtseln"). It is probably to be related to Sanskrit *avadhūta* "removed, repudiated, as of a philosopher", which is also doctrinally suitable. At SK 43,10 the word *čiloula-* "to petrify, turn to stone" is neither a good formation (one would expect **čiloura-* or **čilouǰi-*) nor particularly suitable to the context, whereas *čulγuyil-* "to tan" is well-suited to the story. At SK 6,2 something has happened in the phrase *ečige eke teǰīgēn künesü abād*. It is probably not to be connected with *teǰī-* "to nourish, feed" (hence, "taking provisions and nutriment of his parents") but may represent a distortion of the combined dative-ablative possessive *-dēčegēn*, hence "taking provisions from at his own parent's house". Finally, the source of the magical formula intoned to expel the ghosts (SK 5,4), *ha la ha la so hā*, may well be Skt. *halāhala* "deadly poison of the seas" (of Buddhist stories), plus *svāhā* (the other member of the pair, *hu lu hu lu* is merely an echo-phrase of the former).

[11] The bibliographic data for this and the following items is given in full in the checklist accompanying part 4 of this article.

must sadly echo, "Die oiratische Literaturgeschichte ist so gut wie unerforscht geblieben."[12]

2. LEVELS OF USAGE IN OIRAT

The unbroken continuity of the Uighuro-Mongolian vertical script conceals the fact that a considerable progression in morphological and lexical usage can be seen between the *termini:* there are archaic texts (e.g., the Stone of Genghis Khan and other inscriptions); there are pre-Classical texts, such as Buddhist sūtras in early translations; there is the *Blütezeit* of strictly Classical Mongolian writings, the Buddhistic xylographic output of the 17th and 18th centuries; and lastly, a degenerative usage seen in the last 200 years, culminating in a form of Uighuric script texts little better than Written Colloquial.

The student of Oirat must likewise contend with texts reflecting several disparate levels of morphological and lexical adaption, ranging from a "high" style slavishly patterned on Literary Mongolian, to a "low" style, a vulgarized transcription of colloquial and dialectal usage. At least three levels can be distinguished, though sometimes a given text reflects two levels, with forms sporadically cropping up from a higher or lower stage. It might be crudely compared to a badly-made American or Canadian edition of Shakespeare's plays which haphazardly or irregularly mixes British and American spellings and lets Elizabethan expressions like *How now?* occur side by side with "O. K."—only in the Oirat text the divergences are carried through in phonology, morphology and lexicon.

Because literary activity in Script Mongolian was well developed (though it had not yet reached its zenith), a long-established tradition of treating endings and grammatical forms had arisen, so that even at this time the written Mongolian language was remote from normal speech. It is not hard to see what happened. Sometimes works in Written Mongolian were Oiraticized simply by rewriting them in Script Oirat, with a not-always-consistent replacement of Oirat phonemics and graphemics for Mongolian ones. This level, as that which is most like Script Mongolian in vocabulary, phonology and morphology, I propose to call "Oirat Hybrid Mongolian" (abbreviated OHM), taking Edgerton's term

[12] Aalto, *op. cit.*, p. 188.

Buddhist Hybrid Sanskrit as model. It is in effect an Oiratified Mongolian written in Oirat script and with considerable betrayal of the source as Written Mongolian, e.g., frequent use of the converbum in *-run* (SK 3,15 *bürün;* SK 7,13 *ögüülerün*), the possessive-dative in *-dayan* instead of the contracted *-dān* (SK 3,3 *oyoun-dayan*), pronominal bases as *tegü-* for *töü-*, incomplete rounding as *edügē* for *ödügē* (MH 9-a, 13).[13] I would call the *Siddhitü Kegür* an example of this level.

The next level we may call the genuine Literary Oirat, the real standard Oirat literary language. In this style, the influence of Written Mongolian, while evident, is held to a definite minimum, possibly aided by the fact that the work in question may have been translated directly from Tibetan,[14] rather than being Oiraticized from a Written Mongolian model or by consultation with one. A certain degree of subjective judgment remains in deciding the amount of influence needed to make a given text cross the border from Level I to Level II or vice versa. Here we find the frequent use of grammatical forms which are uniquely Oirat and have no parallel in Classical Mongolian, e.g., AS 1-b, 11 *ülü serekēr* "so that they would not awake"; AS 3-b, 23 *odxuna* "if you go"; AS 2-b, 6 *töünēn* "with him"; M 1-b, 7 *γasalang-ēče nöqčikülē* "if one pass from suffering"; M 2-a, 21 *tere nada üzüülkü bolxulā* "if there be one who can demonstrate it to me". The *Medētei* (the Oirat version of the Mongolian *Üliger-ün dalai*) may be considered an example of this level.

Finally, we may describe a third level of Oirat writing, the Written Colloquial, or Written Kalmyk (we could also call it Written Oirat if the document were definitely known to originate in Oiratia rather than Kalmykia). These would be relatively recent compositions completely under the influence of the spoken

[13] The expansion of these abbreviations for texts, as SK and MH, will be found in a table at the end.

[14] This is the case with Zaya Pandita's Oirat version of the well-known Mongolian story cycle, the *Üliger-ün dalai*, as has been correctly noted by W. Heissig (*Mongolische Handschriften, Blockdrucke, Landkarten*, Wiesbaden, 1961, p. 166; "ist völlig unabhängig von der mongolischen Übersetzung" cf. p. *xviii*) and by Ts. Damdinsüren, *op. cit.*, p. 327. Some of his translations, such as this one, display an inordinate adherence to the Tibetan, e.g., with postposed demonstratives (cf. E. Haenisch's remarks on the Oirat *Altan Gerel*, *Weller Festschrift*, *Asiatica*, [1954] p. 199; "vor allem mit der Nachstellung des Attributs"). Although the detailed study of this version is not complete, there also appear to be some additional episodes not found in the Mongolian version, e.g., M 1-b, 19 to 3-b, 3.

language, written by persons probably knowing no Written Mongolian at all, who in effect transcribed as they spoke, with an occasional bow towards the conventions of representing sounds as at the middle level. An example of this level is the text first mentioned by B. Laufer, the *Dörbön oyirid mongxoli daruqsan touǰi kemēkü* (The Story of the Four Oirats Defeating the Mongols).[15] Such works write the *-luγā* past as *-lā/-lē*, use *-na/-ne* for the present-durative instead of the artificial *-mui/-müi*, write the colloquial ablative in a long vowel, *-ās/-ēs*, not *-āča/-ēče* (though by convention texts of higher level usually write only one of such pairs, viz., *-ēče*), and employ such spellings as *odō* for script *ödügē* (UXT 199,7). Sometimes these usages depart so far in appearance from the upper level forms that they are not readily recognized, e.g., (BB 2,1) *eberēn* for Mo. *öber-iyen* "one's own", cf. the spoken form *ewrēn*.[16] A knowledge here of any spoken dialect will be of more aid than dictionary searching. But even speaking modern Kalmyk will avail little in understanding the archaic epic phraseology of the Janggar, but that is a story unto itself.

Any given text may, moreover, occasionally cross levels, so that a purely colloquial form (which we may define for now as being one recorded solely in Ramstedt's dictionary) and with no script form hitherto recorded, will appear from time to time even in an OHM text—though the reverse, a Written Mongolian form, say *tegün-dür* "to him", would be unthinkable in a colloquial epic. More typical is a simple free variation, as in SK 6,8 *idegen eriküyin tula ende kürbei* ("arrived here in order to search for food", whereas only three lines previously, SK 6,3, we read *idē erikē odji* "went for seeking food". The latter uses the regular contracted Oirat form *idē* "food", and the Oirat purposive ending in *-kV̄*; yet the

[15] The text under this title is none other than the Ubashi Xung Taiji story ed. by Galsang Gomboyev in 1858 (*Istoriya Ubaši-khuntaidžiya i yego voiny s oiratami*), appearing as a *Priloženie* (Supplement) to his ed. of the *Altan tobči* (St. Petersburg, 1858), 234 pp., pp. 198-224. It was further ed. by K. Th. Golstunskii, *Ubaši khuntaidžiin tūdži...* (St. Petersburg, 1864). Berthold Laufer ("Skizze der mongolischen Literatur", *Keleti Szemle*, vol. VIII [1907], p. 215; and in the Russian revision, *Očerk mongol'skoi literatury* [Leningrad, 1927], p. 50) thought them to be distinct works, as did (perhaps following him) Poppe (*op. cit.*, WZKM 52.376-7) and Aalto (*op. cit.*, p. 198). Heissig, who was able to see the text itself, has correctly identified it (*op. cit.*, p. 6, §8). There is now also a Written Mongolian translation in Damdinsüren's chrestomathy (*op. cit.*, selection 38, pp. 184-188).

[16] G. J. Ramstedt, *Kalmückisches Wörterbuch* (Helsinki, 1935), p. 129-b.

environments are much alike. Lastly, one may observe blends, in which an Oirat base has a literary ending (less often vice versa), e.g., SK 3,11 *döü-yuγān* "his own younger brother (obj.)" and SK 3,5 *töün-luγā* "with him".

3. OIRAT TEXTUAL AND LEXICAL PROBLEMS

Just as it would be possible to learn to play the pipe organ without ever studying the piano, or the viola without studying the violin, it would be feasible to learn Oirat without knowing or studying Written Mongolian. In practice, however, every student of organ comes to his instrument with the rudiments of piano technique, different though this may be, and violists are notoriously recruited from the ranks of violinists. Likewise, every Western investigator of Oirat-Kalmyk has been well grounded in Script Mongolian, and has of course profited from a considerable transference of learning between the two branches. Nonetheless, the careful learner of Oirat will observe that more could be said about the exact circumstances for employment of letters in the Oirat script, and that variations and conventions, apparent to a reader knowing Mongolian already, demand a more careful description.

For instance, present transcription practice varies between a strict letter-for-letter replacement and an interpretative transcription changing it to what it ought to be. Thus, the common word *köböün* "boy, child" is actually written *küböün*, with the distinguishing tick that separates *kö* from *kü* omitted by convention (on the grounds, I presume, that since a syllable in *ö* occurs later in the word, it is not necessary to indicate *ö* more than once unequivocally). Consequently, Pozdneyev's dictionary gives the word as *küböün*[17] (and anyone who has ever studied Mongolian will probably recognize the word and not look it up anyway). Faced with such added examples as *külgülö-* "to ride, travel" (SK 3,12) or *kündölöng* "athwart, crosswise" (SK 7,11), as against *tögünčilen* "thus, in this way" (SK 4,9), *öbögün* "old man, oldster" (SK 6,6) or *bölügē* "was, been" (SK, 6,8), one might conclude that *ü* may occur before *ö*, and vice versa, *ö* before *ü*. This, however, would be contrary to the known phonological propensity of other Mongolian languages. A closer inspection reveals the "rule" that *kü* or *gü* are (generally) written for *kö* and *gö* before or after another *ö*

[17] A. M. Pozdneyev, *Kalmytsko-russkii slovar'* (St. Petersburg, 1911), p. 294-a.

of the same word. The literal transcriptions thus stand for the normative transcriptions of *kölgölö-*, *köndölöng*, *öbögön*, and so forth.

Variation also exists at present in the practice of writing *c* or *č* and *ǰ* or *ž*. The solution of the present writer is to transcribe *č* and *ǰ* only before *i* and elsewhere to write *c* and *z* (which accords more closely with the pronunciation and standard Mongolistic transcription). Similarly, it is probably better to reflect the graphemics by writing *ou*, *öü* (etc.) instead of *ô* or *ö* with a circumflex, so as to create a closer one-for-one relationship (and, by the way, to make the later computer-processing easier). Other minor points could also be raised, as words of the type of Mo. *anggida* "separately", most often seen written as *angkida* etc. in Oirat (M 141-a, 13). The transcription employed by the late E. Haenisch falls particularly short of a desired standard, e.g., *ds* for *z*, *î* for *iyi* and use of only *k* for both *k* and *q*.

The stems of verbs present more problems to a strictly structural and objective analysis of Oirat unhampered by Written Mongolian antecedents. First, there are cases of variation in stem forms, as *sed-* (SK 7,11) and *sede-* (BB 2,7) "to think, contrive" (Mo. *sedü-*), or *zal-* (SK 3,13) and *zala-* (M 138-b, 25) "to guide, direct; invite" (Mo. *ǰala-*). Second, because of later contraction and the widespread apocopation characteristic of Kalmyk, the status of stems after formative suffixes remains unclear, unless one collects many examples on which to base a decision. Whereas *böküyildü-* clearly is the stem of *böküyildüǰi* "they bowed to one another" (SK 43,17), should one say that *dayilda-* is the stem of *dayildaxu* "fighting together" (UXT 3-b, 8) in the light of Written Mongolian *dailaldu-* id.? Even a clear-cut formative morpheme like *-la/-le* (forms verbs from nouns) is treated in a number of ways, e.g., *kündüle-* "to honor, entertain" (PC 17,7) < *kündü* + *le*, as opposed to *könggölö-* "to lighten, disrobe" (SK 41,3) < *könggö/n* + *le*.

Following texts alone, one is hard put to discover whether a given *n*-stem noun has a stable or fleeting *n*, without yielding to the temptation to reconstruct them on the basis of known Mongolian forms. Should one, on first meeting *künesü* "provisions (acc.)", with the characteristic Oirat loss of stem-final *n* in the accusative, reconstruct a nominative *künesün* until actually seen?

Although correspondences are great between Oirat and Mongolian, it is true that the lexicon does differ. Though by applying simple and well-known laws of vowel contraction and substitution of consonant equivalents, one can readily see that Oirat *izour* < Mo. *iǰaγur* "root, origin", *öbdüq* < Mo. *ebüdüg* "knee", or *öšölö-* < Mo. *ösiyele-* "to take revenge", there are also sometimes familiar words with meanings differing from those of Mongolian, e.g., Mo. *qaγalγan* "door, portal, gate" means "path, road, way" (Oirat *xālγa, xāluγa*), SK 44,12 (though in OHM it may occur with the Mo. meanings, e.g., AS 1-b, 7 and nearly everywhere in SK); Oirat *balγasun* "house, building, establishment" (and thence, perhaps, "quarter, district, city"), as at M 134-a, 29, whereas only the meaning "city" is known to Mongolian (cf. Oirat *abxui balγad* "trade quarter, commercial district", AG 94,18; M 3-b, 8).

Oirat texts have a number of lexical peculiarities unknown to other Mongolian languages. Late 19th century texts, as for instance those of historical content, abound in references to Russian places, persons and items of material culture. Examples are the Russian names of the months, which Buriat also uses (*april, maya, iyuli*, etc.), names of Russian provinces and cities (*oringburg* / *oron buurg* "Orenburg"; *kīve* "Khiva"; *šara tuu* "Saratov"; *seber* "Siberia"; *simbiyir* "Simbirsk", and others). Words of social, political or technical content, and weights and measures, are also encountered, as *polkobniq* < Russ. *polkovnik* "colonel" (PC 16,12), *kinigine* < Russ. *knyaginya* "princess" (PC 12,17), *pistul* "pistol" (BB 3,1), *beredengki* "Berdan gun, single-shot gun" (BB 3,1), or *pud* "pood, a weight" (PC 4,16).

New lexical formations and borrowings are also found, as *asxan* "evening"[18] (UXT 200,9), cf. Turkish *akşam* < Arabic, or the very interesting word *tetürü(ü)* "on the contrary, on the other hand" (MH 11-a, 2; MH 15-b, 29). This last seems to be a loan from Uighur *tätrü*,[19] though it is recorded in the *Hua-i i-yü* of

---

[18] The fact that Ts. Damdinsüren uses it in his Mongolian translation of this story (*op. cit.*, pp. 185-a, 17) is first vitiated by his gloss (*oroi ni* "in the evening"), and, second, cannot be considered conclusive proof that it exists in Literary Mongolian, in the light of the frequent use in such modern translations of archaic forms as *ügüülerün* (an introductory *verbum dicendi*) or *bülüge* "was", when even 17th century texts occasionally use the colloquial *bilē*. The citation by Ramstedt (*Kalmückisches Wörterbuch* [Helsinki, 1935], p. 16-a) *asqan, asqun* is his own back-formation.

[19] W. W. Radloff, *Versuch eines Wörterbuches der Türk-Dialecte*, vol. III (reprinted The Hague, 1960), col. 1093.

1389[20] and also cited by Poppe.[21] There are also new formations made on familiar stems, but not recorded in that precise form, although the meaning is always clear, e.g., *ügeče-* "to discuss, agree, contract" < *üge* "word" (UXT 3-b, 20); *dailya-* "to wage war" < *dain* "war" (M 141-b, 2); or *duqčira-* "to grow drowsy" (SK 43,12), cf. Mo. *duγ ki-* id.

Quite a number of totally new words, not listed in standard Mongolian dictionaries and rarely if ever seen in Classical texts, are also found in Oirat texts. Samples are *külčin* "demon" (SK 10, 18), *iböü* "beggar, indigent" (M 142-a, 9), *ibaqla-* "to deride, torment" (SK 44, 16), *tekelceq* "square, quadrangle" (UXT 203,1), *ilimel* "smooth, polished" (SK 46,07) and *ulbu*, *ulba* "quilted jacket" (UXT 3-b, 1). Present research may, of course, reveal in the near future other citations in texts or dictionaries for these. For some words, no sources or parallels have yet been unearthed—some of these may rest on distortions or textual errors. Examples are *merdün* "kind of tree" (AS 3-b, 6), which may be graphically corrupted from *amiri* (< Skt. *āmra* "mango"), and *šimin* "kind of animal" (MH 5-a, 20).

Buddhistic texts have some characteristics of their own, and an earlier query as to the phonetic equivalent of some Buddha names[22] can be answered by the discovery that, although usages like *angšobiye* "Akṣobhya" (PC 2,4) do occur, the absence of Oirat equivalents for many names, e.g., *Kāśyapa*, is because they are translated, viz., *gerel sakiqči* (M 142-b, 19).

As an aid to the parallel study of Oirat and Mongolian, it has been found useful always to enter the Classical form of the Mongolian equivalent to an Oirat word, when it can be readily located. Some words, such as those mentioned, occur only in Oirat, but many others would seem to have Mongolian forms, though they may not actually be recorded in any dictionary under just that derivation. These would include **kögelǰirgene* for Oirat

---

[20] M. Lewicki, *La langue mongole des transcriptions chinoises du XIV*e *siècle...*, II, *Vocabulaire, Index* (Wroclaw, 1959), p. 79 "renversé". See also S.E. Malov, *Pamyatniki drevnetyurkskoi pis'mennosti* (Moscow, 1951), p. 429-b.

[21] *Grammar of Written Mongolian* (Wiesbaden: Harrassowitz, 1954), p. 59.

[22] John R. Krueger, "Sanskrit Loanwords in Kalmyk" (*Kalmyk Monograph Series*, II; pp. 181-189), p. 185.

kögölǰirgönö "dove, pigeon" (SK 4,2,[23] **qaγurγal* for Oirat *xourγal* (SK 33,12) "ditch, pit", **gedelǰe-* for Oirat *gedelze-* "to nod, bob head" (SK 5,18), or **ormuγla-* for Oirat *oromoqla-* "to put into tufts" (AS 4-a, 21).

When reading texts with a view towards eventual lexicographical compilation, one of the most difficult problems is treating errors, variants and anomalous forms. It is hard to decide on the basis of citations alone whether any given form represents a standard of usage (without imposing the standard of Classical Mongolian); thus, *ēd tabar* occurs once (MH 5-a, 7) as against repeated uses of *ed tavar* "goods" with short vowel as expected (MH 7-a, 27)—hence, the former is anomalous.[24] The stem *bariu-* (MH 9-a, 21) which puts one in mind at once of *bari-*, *bariul-*, is seen in its context to be an error for *barui-* (*baruyi-*) "to be gloomy". It would seem that one has no choice in a lexicon but to prepare cross-references throughout and thereby presume to solve problems for later readers of edited or unedited texts. When variant forms are equally represented in a corpus of texts, only more citations will establish the standard usage, e.g., *mangǰi* (PC 7,1) and *mangzu* (PC 22,17) "Manchu"; *torγon* (SK 11,12) vs. *toroγon* (MH 15-b, 1) "silk"; or *paradiga bud* (AG 1, 11) and *paridkya bud* (M 203-b, 18) "Pratyekabuddha". In the light of such a well-known metathesis as Mo. *gulir* ∼ *guril* "flour" or *kürel* ∼ *küler* "bronze", is one justified to presume that *tölör* for *töröl* "birth, rebirth" (MH 18-a, 3) is no more than a *lapsus?* A curiosity is the form (four citations to date) *dabtaγār* "fifth", where Mo. has only *tabduγar* with t-.

Were one to embark on Oirat lexicographical work, it would be necessary to resolve these and other problems by establishing firm procedures and guidelines.

---

[23] It does occur in Ts. Zhamtsarano's ethnography of the Darkhats, his *Darqad, köbsügül naγur-un uriyangqai...* (Ulaan Baator, 1934), p. 44, line 1, but he too has a penchant for using Buriat and Oirat words. Cf., too, my remarks on the word, reviewing G. Doerfer's "Ältere west-europäische Quellen zur kalmückischen Sprachgeschichte...", *Asiatische Forschungen*, XVIII (Wiesbaden, 1965), in a forthcoming issue of *Oriens*.

[24] An interesting variant on this very common phrase is at M 192-b, 29, *ed dbyiq* < Mo. *ed* + Tib. *dbyigs* id. (Jäschke, *Tibetan-English Dictionary*, p. 390-a).

4. TEXT RESOURCES IN OIRAT-MONGOLIAN

Although Zwick wrote a dictionary in 1853,[25] and Jülg's *Glossarium* to the *Siddhitü Kegür* tales of 1861[26] contains around 2500 words or entries, neither one can be considered very complete or useful for more extensive reading at the present time. Pozdneyev, whose knowledge of Oirat was unexcelled, spent much time compiling a large Oirat-to-Russian dictionary,[27] and accumulated 23,000 entries; but he was unable to find publication support for the entire work, a fate which might equally befall a similar work in our day. The compromise was to make a selection of 6,000-odd entries, chosen by a committee of Kalmyk educators interested in a practical school dictionary for students.[28] As a result, the dictionary, in addition to the hardship of being in Russian, a language more distant for us than German or French, is of limited value, if indeed copies are available for use or purchase. The early short native glossaries compiled by Kalmyks are virtually inaccessible, and may be disregarded for the purposes of a literary dictionary.

A brighter side to the picture is the fact that Oirat is a Mongolian language and shares with Written Mongolian a large similar vocabulary, so that with some judicious speculation and experience, the equivalents to Oirat forms can also be discovered from a Mongolian dictionary. But this is a cumbersome and unsure task; hence, it is evident that the production of an extensive Oirat-to-English dictionary is a *desideratum* of high priority in Mongolian studies. Owing to the many internal struggles of the Oirats and Khalkhas, there is an unusual paucity of manuscripts, and since relatively little text-editing has been done in Oirat studies, the amount of texts available in the West, first in transcription and second in published (script) form, is sufficiently limited as to make the compilation of a dictionary a feasible project. After exploiting

[25] H. A. Zwick, *Das Handwörterbuch der westmongolischen Sprache* (Donaueschingen), 1853.

[26] Bernhard Jülg, *Die Märchen des Siddhi-Kür, Kalmückischer Text mit deutscher Übersetzung und einem kalmückisch-deutschen Wörterbuch* (Leipzig, 1866), 223 pp., of which pp. 137-223 are the Glossary.

[27] A. M. Pozdneyev, *Kalmytsko-russkii slovar'* (St. Petersburg, 1911), 306 pp.

[28] The fate of the remaining slips was never definitely established, but Poppe assures me from his personal knowledge that all trace of them was lost, and that even thirty years ago there was no hope of discovering them (cf. *op. cit.*, WZKM 52.365).

the known printed and transcribed resources, attention could be directed to extant unedited texts. Those accessible in the West are only some more than one hundred in number. Such a lexicographical project, consequently, shrinks to manageable size. If at a later date easy access to Soviet, Mongolian and Tuvinian holdings of *Oiratica* becomes possible, the entire Oirat literature could be encompassed.

Next, we should wish to survey, in brief form, extant materials in Oirat script (not considering the various phonetic or dialect studies recorded only in Western transcriptions), both printed and transcribed from printed (or xylographic) works, to which such manuscript and blockprint resources can be added as are known at present. Unfortunately, printed texts and transcribed texts, if the originals are no longer accessible, can suffer from an enormous flaw, which one may be inclined to forget, namely, that we are at the mercy of the earlier editor. Today, in some cases, we have no way of knowing how accurately the editor read or misread.[29] One would expect high standards of Pozdneyev, but it is definitely known that the spellings he employs in his dictionary differ from the original texts, cf. the trenchant remark that he "has in hundreds of cases artificially changed half-contracted groups . . . , although the Oirat manuscripts show no complete contraction."[30]

With a view to encouraging the production of an Oirat-Mongolian dictionary (which should, it goes without saying, be only a citation dictionary quoting words that actually occur in texts, in the form that they occur, rather than taking over from other sources words not verified in documents), we give next our present notes on Oirat text resources. To spare lengthy, and here unnecessary, bibliographical citation, only the essential features of identification

[29] A good example is afforded by Pozdneyev's ed. of the Bāza bakshi pilgrimage account *Skazanie o khoždenii v Tibetskuyu stranu*... [St. Petersburg, 1897], 260 pp.), where the following phrase occurs (BB 1,7): *ödügē bi... dēreki tüüjiyin γarulγan bolun, lungdun üzeqsen*.... This is translated into Russian (p. 122) as *nıně ya... pročitav vıšeoznačennıya skazanIya i nastavlenIya* ("Now I, ..., having read the above-noted statements and precepts..."). The word *γarulγan* "outcome, lineage" has been grossly misunderstood and the entire sense of the passage distorted as a consequence. It should be "Now I, ..., being the historical (?) outcome of this above lineage, read the prophetic instruction...", i.e., because he, Bāza Bakshi, is the spiritual descendant (rebirth) of the aforementioned party, it is particularly appropriate for him to make a pilgrimage to Tibet.

[30] *Central Asiatic Journal*, vol. 3, p. 210.

are given now, as the works are fully listed in the earlier cited items by Poppe and Bormanshinow, and can thus be readily identified.

A CHECKLIST OF OIRAT TEXT RESOURCES (IN OIRAT SCRIPT OR MADE FROM SCRIPT)

A. Available as published in the West (including Russia)

1. Script texts

a. Bible versions and portions. A number of translations are known,[31] beginning with I. J. Schmidt's *Evangelium St. Mathæi* (1815), followed by the Synoptic Gospels and Acts (1822). A. M. Pozdneyev also translated the New Testament in 1896 (2 vols., a copy at the Univ. of Washington). In my possession is the Schmidt *Gospel of John* (1820), 145 p., as reprinted (reduced?) in 1878.[32]

b. H. A. Zwick, *Grammatik der westmongolischen ... Sprache* (1851), contains as a *Sprachprobe* in script the second chapter of the *Üliger-ün dalai* (Oirat *Medētei*, text M), pp. 118-124, the same text in Oirat as was given in Mongolian in Schmidt's 1831 *Grammatik der mongolischen Sprache*. Various copies are available.

c. The Ubashi Xung Taiji story (same as "How the Four Oirats Defeated the Mongols"), as edited by Galsang Gomboyev (pp. 198-224 of his *Altan tobči* ed. of 1858), and further edited by Golstunskii in 1864. A differing copy in the Laufer Notebooks (see B. *infra*). No location for Golstunskii ed. known; Gomboyev at Univ. of Wash.

d. B. Jülg, *Die Märchen des Siddhi-Kür* (Leipzig, 1866). Text on p. 3-48, with translation and glossary to the thirteen stories. Various copies available.

e. A. M. Pozdneyev, *Obraztsy narodnoi literatury mongol'skikh plemën*, I (St. Petersburg, 1880), contains some songs in Oirat script.[33] A copy at Univ. of Washington.

---

[31] A special study of all Mongolian Bible translations is in preparation by this writer, and will appear separately at a later date. I may refer here to Laufer, *op. cit.*, pp. 255-259; to the standard catalogue, T. Darlow and H. Moule, *Historical Catalogue of the Printed Editions of Holy Scripture*, vol. 2 (London, 1903–11, reprinted, New York, 1963), pp. 1111-1116; and to my private list of the holdings in the American Bible Society library (New York).

[32] *British Museum General Catalogue of Printed Books*, vol. 215 (London, 1965), p. 358-b, item six.

[33] Cf. Poppe, *op. cit.*, WZKM 52.371, n. 6.

f. K. Th. Golstunskii, *Mongolo-oiratskie zakony 1640 goda . . .* (St. Petersburg, 1880), with the Kalmyk text of the important 1640 legal code. (I know of no U.S. location.)

g. A. M. Pozdneyev, *Kalmytskiya skazki* (Kalmyk Tales), appearing originally in the *Zapiski VOIRAO* (Mémoires of the Oriental Division of the Imperial Russian Archaeological Society), vol. III–X (1888-1896), in ten parts.[34] Of these (Kalmyk text with Russian translation), the first six parts appeared separately as *Kalmytskiya narodnyya skazki* (Kalmyk Folk Tales) (St. Petersburg, 1892, 150 p.), Kalmyk text only. No U.S. location for the 1892 version is known, but a number of libraries have the *Mémoires* (e.g., New York Public, and Princeton Univ.), and there is a complete photocopy set in the Library of the Society for the Preservation of Kalmyk Culture (Philadelphia).

h. Pozdneyev, *Pamyatniki istoričeskoi literatury Astrakhanskikh kalmykov* (Astrakhan Kalmyk Historical Literature Monuments), St. Petersburg, 1885 (size not given). Lithographed texts of some Kalmyk historical works; no known location.[35]

i. Pozdneyev, *Skazanie o khoždenii v Tibetskuyu stranu . . .* (St. Petersburg, 1897), 260 p. Kalmyk text (pp. 1-119) of the account of Bāza Bakshi's pilgrimage to Tibet, with Russian translation. A copy at Univ. of Washington.

j. W. L. Kotwicz, *Kalmyckie zagadki i poslovitsy* (St. Petersburg, 1905, 110 p.). Oirat script text, with parallel Russian translation of Kalmyk proverbs and riddles, some transcribed. A copy at Univ. of Washington.

k. *Taki Zulān Xāni . . . . Jangyarīn arban bölöq* (St. Petersburg, 1910), 336 p., lithographed. Kalmyk text of the famous Janggar epic; copies at Univ. of Washington, the Kalmyk Society library in Philadelphia, and some others.

l. B. Vladimirtsov, *Obraztsy mongol'skoi narodnoi slovesnosti* (Leningrad, 1926). A work similar to Entry *e supra*; mostly in Cyrillic transcription, but has a few Oirat songs and poems in script. A copy at Univ. of Washington.

m. Pozdneyev, *Kalmytskiya khrestomatiya* (1st ed., St. Petersburg, 1892; 2nd ed., 1907; 3rd ed., 1915). A Kalmyk reader entirely in Oirat script, intended for use in the upper classes of Kalmyk national schools, containing some twenty selections from history, literature, Buddhism and epics; 191 p.

---

[34] See *ibid.*, p. 372, n. 3, for the full citations.

[35] Cf. the remarks by Poppe, *op. cit.*, p .351.

n. *Хоŋхо* (Khongkho): A Kalmyk periodical published 1925–1927 in Czechoslovakia by Kalmyk refugees and émigrés there. Although briefly mentioned before[36] no full bibliographical citations for pagination and contents have been published yet. For this reason, the contents are briefly sketched out here. All volumes are lithographed editions.

Issue I, 1925. pp. i-x, preface in Russian by B. N. Ulanov; xi-xxix, preface in Oirat script; contents 1-233, songs, fables, tales in Oirat script only; no Russian text.

Issue II, 1926. pp. i-ix, Oirat preface by Ulanov; xiv-xxv, Russian preface; contents 1-312, tales, songs, fables, legends, etc., in Oirat script; concludes with Oirat alphabet tables.

Issue III, 1927. *Kalmytskaya khrestomatiya* . . . compiled by Shurguchi Boldyrev in 1906, pp. i-vi, Russian preface by Ulanov; xvi-xvii, compiler's preface; contents, 1-255, proverbs, tales, biographies, etc., in Oirat script.

Issue IV, 1927. contains an Oirat translation of N. N. Pal'mov's sketch of Kalmyk history (*Očerk istorii Kalmytskogo naroda za vremya yego prebyvaniya v predelakh Rossii*); pp. i-vi, preface in Oirat; vii-xi, preface in Russian; text, 1-240 in Oirat script. The translation was made by Shamba N. Balinov.

[For the above and other data, I thank Dr. Arash Bormanshinow, a Kalmyk intellectual (Slavic Department, New York Univ.), who says that the Philadelphia Kalmyk Society preserves the apparently only existing copies.]

o. Other émigré periodicals, as the Prague journal *ulan zalāt*, and the Paris journal *Kovyl'nye volny*, also contain material in Oirat script. There are reportedly sets, almost complete, in the Hoover library at Stanford, California.

p. Princess Nirgidma de Torhut, *Dix-huit chants et poèmes mongols* . . . (Paris, 1937). Gives Oirat text, transcription and music of eighteen songs.

q. B. Rinchen, "Version oïrate des chansons de Guesser; *Tod üsgiin Geser*", *Corpus scriptorum mongolorum* IX (1) (Ulaan Baator, 1960), 176 p. A lithographed edition of an Oirat version of the Gesar epic.

r. A. Bormanshinow, *Kalmyk Manual* (New York, 1963: ACLS Uralic-Altaic Project No. 26), 306 p. A historical and bibliographical manual, with reading selections in Cyrillic and

[36] *Ibid.*, p. 377, n. 5.

Oirat script; the Oirat on pp. 249-255, 262-264, 268-270 and 274. They are brief tales drawn from entries j, m and p.

s. MINOR ITEMS. There are isolated Oirat illustrations in various books, of which we mention the following. In N. P. Shastina's *Russko-mongol'skie posol'skie otnošeniya* XVII *veka* (Russo-Mongolian diplomatic relations of the 17th century) (Moscow, 1958), there are three diplomatic documents of 1691 in Oirat script, letters to the Russian Czar. In W. Heissig's *Mongolische Handschriften, Blockdrucke, Landkarten* (Wiesbaden, 1961) are a number of illustrations (see preface) of Oirat materials, such as a sample page of the Manuhari, materials on divination, and others. An Oirat document is also illustrated in L. S. Pučkovskii's catalogue of the Mongolian collections in Leningrad, *Mongol'skie, buryat-mongol'skie i oiratskie rukopisi i ksilografy Instituta Vostokovedeniya*, I (Moscow/ Leningrad, 1957).

2. Transcribed texts

a. Erich Haenisch, *Altan Gerel, die westmongolische Fassung des Goldglanzsutra* ... (Leipzig, 1929) 122 p., in transcription only.

b. E. Haenisch, "Kapitel XVII von Jalavāhana aus dem ... Altan Gerel," in the *Weller Festschrift, Asiatica* (1954), pp. 198-213. Transcribes the 17th chapter, with translation and parallel texts in other languages.

c. G. J. Ramstedt, Sh. Balinov, P. Aalto, "Kalmückische Lieder," in *JSFOu* 63 (1962), pp. 1-127; gives transcription of fifty songs and poems recorded by Ramstedt (one sample illustration in script).

d. N. Poppe, "An Oyrat Vajracchedikā Fragment from Turfan," in CAJ 7, pp. 170-178 (with the fragment illustrated, in script). Transcription and translation of brief extract from the *Vajracchedikā.*

e. N. Poppe, "The Mongolian Versions of the Vessantarajataka," in *Studia Orientalia* 30 (2), pp. 1-92. Gives Oirat and Mongolian texts in transcription, with translations.

f. N. Poppe, The *Üsün debisker-tü xān* (1968). (Cf. Heissig, *op. cit.*, §§ 49-50, pp. 36-37; § 502-IV, p. 271).

g. MINOR ITEMS. There are also isolated brief transcriptions from Oirat texts in other works, e.g., E. Haenisch, "Kalmückische Fragmente", UAJb 25.283-294 (1954), giving some Kalmyk correspondence of I. J. Schmidt; G. Kara, "Le colophon de l'Altan Gerel oïrat", in *Acta Orientalia*

(Hungary) 10 (1960), pp. 255-261; E. Haenisch, "Zwei viersprachige Inschriften zum Dsungarenkrieg ...", in *Miscellanea Academica Berolinensia* (Berlin, 1950), pp. 224-247, with Oirat parallel text of two quadrilingual inscriptions.

B. Available as unpublished in the West

1. LAUFER NOTEBOOKS (see the account at JAOS 86, 3, pp. 173-174)
   a) Book I, the *Manuhari Okin tenggeri* story (cf. Heissig, *op. cit.*, § 148, page 94). A translation by this writer has been completed, to appear in an Indiana Univ. International Affairs Center Publications series. (I must here thank Dr. G. Doerfer of Göttingen for aiding me in securing a photocopy of the original in Göttingen.)
   b) Book II contains the *Ubashi Xung Taiji* story (cf. *supra* A.l.c); the *Külil gtorma*, a brief lamaistic text of divination (Heissig, *op. cit.*, § 506-a); the *Arthasiddha*, a brief *jātaka* of 160 lines (Heissig, *op. cit.*, § 156 and § 504-b). A translation of the latter has been completed, and appeared in *The Mongolia Society Bulletin*, vol. 6, pp. 29–33 (1967).
2. The Vienna *Vajracchedikā* (see the article in CAJ 2, pp. 155-157), and J. R. Krueger, "Remarks on the Oirat *Vajracchedikā* in Vienna" (*Kalmyk Monograph Series*, 2 [1966], pp. 223-227; of which a microfilm and photocopy in my possession (the Vienna copy is, however, incomplete).
3. The Oirat version of the *Üliger-ün dalai*, the *Medētei mede ügeyigi ilaγuqči kemēkü sudur*, (Heissig, *op. cit.*, § 285, pp. 165-167.) A photocopy in the possession of the author is now under study. B. Rinchen (Ulan Bator) will soon publish another copy.
4. Other U.S. collections. I have at present no information about any holdings of Oirat manuscripts or xylographs in U.S. libraries. There are only some copies of the printed or lithographed Kalmyk works of Section A-1 above, and the hand-copied materials of the Laufer Notebooks (section B-1 preceding). Aalto's statement that in Chicago they "besitzen mehrere oiratische Werke" is simply a misunderstanding.[37] The Library of the Philadelphia Society for the Preservation of Kalmyk Culture, previously referred to, has the printed materials mentioned, and there are some standard Buddhistic sūtras and other works in the possession of individual Kalmyks and at the Buddhist temples in New Jersey.

---

[37] Aalto, *op. cit.*, p. 198.

5. Western European holdings
Copenhagen (The Royal Library) possesses the *Altan Gerel* (which Haenisch made the basis of his 1929 ed.; see section A.2.a above), in two versions, and a work titled *nöqčisödiyin tala tōloxoi oriši̇bo.*
Helsinki has six items in the University Library, and nine items in the library of the Finno-Ugric Society, one learns from the catalogue of the late G. J. Ramstedt's collection.[38]
In Germany, thanks to the *Verzeichnis der orientalischen Handschriften*, I (Wiesbaden, 1961),[39] it is an easy matter to tot up the Oirat-Kalmyk items in the various German libraries. These are found at only four locations: Dresden, Göttingen, Marburg and Tübingen (one item in Berlin is duplicated elsewhere). About 122 different works are represented (the figure depending a bit on exactly how they are counted).

Dresden	59 items	less 18	duplicates, etc.	=	41
Göttingen	17 items	less 4	duplicates, etc.	=	13
Marburg	56 items	less 32	duplicates, etc.	=	24
Tübingen	71 items	less 27	duplicates, etc.	=	44
	203 items in Oirat-Kalmyk				122

As to holdings in other European cities, such as London, Stockholm and Paris, there seem to be no Oirat items listed in earlier catalogues of collections in those cities.

6. Materials in the U.S.S.R. and in the Orient
From the Pučkovskii catalogue of the Leningrad collection, thus far dealing only with law and history,[40] one can find his items 101-111 as listing four histories in nine copies, and his items 260-262, two law-sets in three copies. From N. Poppe, Sr., I have this kind information about other cities: in Leningrad there is a lot of Oirat material; in Moscow, none at all; in Vladivostok, much; in Kiev, some; in the Astrakhan archives, very much; and in Kazań, none now (it was transferred to Leningrad and elsewhere).
The recent Poppe-Hurvitz-Okada catalogue of the Toyo Bunko *Mongolica*[41] did not mention any Oirat holdings. There may be

---

[38] Aalto, "G. J. Ramstedt's mongolische Bibliothek" JSFOu 57, 4 (1953-4), pp. 1-26.

[39] W. Heissig, *op. cit.*

[40] L. S. Pučkovskii, *Mongol'skie, buryat-mongol'skie i oiratskie rukopisi Instituta Vostokovedenia*, I, items 101-111 (pp. 137-146), items 260-262 (pp. 263-265).

[41] N. Poppe, L. Hurvitz, H. Okada, *Catalogue of the Manchu-Mongol Section of the Toyo Bunko* (Seattle/Tokyo, 1964).

other library or private holdings in Japan which include Oirat items.

A recent private report from Mongolia states that a sizeable trove of Oiratica has been found in Kyzyl, the capital of Tangnu Tuva, amounting to over one thousand items. If even ninety percent of those were duplicates of known works, there would still be over one hundred new or unknown works there.

5. APPLICATION OF COMPUTER-PROCESSING TO OIRAT LEXICOGRAPHY

Since it is evident that there is a great need for a new and adequate dictionary of Oirat, based on actual usage in texts, this writer has endeavored to apply some of the rapid processing techniques of computers to this field. In order to benefit from high speed electronic manipulation of data, the researcher must carefully and systematically organize his transcription and material. The first task was to devise a workable transcription scheme to replace Oirat graphemes with the letters and symbols available on the IBM keypunching equipment. Without recounting the reasons behind every choice, suffice it to list here (in a Mongolian order[42]) the set of symbols chosen:

A E I O * V N X Q) B P F S $
T D L M C Z J Y K K' G R W H

Most of these will be self-evident, except asterisk * as ö, rounded ü as letter v (vee), "close-parenthesis") for γ, dollar sign $ for š, and omission of diacritic on č and ǰ, since no confusion can arise. The symbol for length (the *udaan*) was "period", e.g., XA.N for "xān". A little practice enables one quickly to read texts in this transcription.[43]

---

[42] The order developed here adheres closely to the standard order as used, for instance, in Kowalewski's dictionary. It is very similar to an earlier Mongolian order for computing purposes developed for the writer's Mongolian reverse dictionary (Uralic and Altaic Series, vol. 88). Other known orders for Oirat are the following. In Jülg's glossary, a e i o u ö ü n b x k γ g m l r t d y z c s š h. In Pozdneyev's Kalmyk dictionary, a e i o ö u ü n x q γ b s š t d l m c/č j/z y k' k g w r z' p. In Bormanshinow's *Kalmyk Manual* (cf. p. 133, "the order of letters in this Glossary is traditional"), a e i o u ö ü n m l γ g x k b s š d t z č z c y.

[43] A definite drawback is the difficulty of treating the Galik letters, which requires developing a complex subsidiary system. For the present, I have not marked them specially, on the grounds that there are so few and that the foreign words

The next task was to organize the eighty columns available on the basic punchcard so as most fruitfully to utilize all space. The following fields were designated: col. 1 = blank (for internal machine operations); cols. 2-9 for coded location of text by letter symbol, folio or page, column or side, and line (e.g., UXT 9-a, 21 = "Ubashi Xung Taiji, folio 9 recto, line 21"); col. 10 blank for visual set-off; cols. 11-23, thirteen spaces for entry of the Oirat form; cols. 24-39 for entry of the Classical Mongolian dictionary form; cols. 40-53 for first or primary English definition; cols. 54-69 for second or extended English definition; cols. 70 to end 80 for third or other definition.

During the summer of 1966 this writer had the privilege of reading and studying various Oirat texts with Professor N. Poppe, under whom many ideas were developed and problems resolved. Our reading for the term embraced several hundred pages of historical, Buddhistic, literary, narrative and other texts, drawn from printed works and from manuscripts. Cards were prepared daily and verified for accuracy of definition, transcription, Mongolian equivalent, prior occurrence, etc. (This work, by the way, is definitely slower and more demanding than traditional hand and file-slip methods, but once it is correctly done, the data are permanently recorded and can be sorted and transferred by the program in a negligible amount of machine time.)

This regimen produced a file of 3,906 data cards (of which perhaps 25% are repetitions or second cards for the same entry). First, a print program produced a raw data file, i.e., cards sorted according to their occurrence in the stories in the order read (which later proved to be useful as glossaries to given texts for students). The cards themselves, I might digress to say, were also color coded so that all words from the same work or class of works were on red, brown or green, as the case was.

The first effective test of the sort-program with new modified internal sequence (i.e., Mongolian instead of Latin order) was run on the second field, the Oirat text form. About 6½ minutes of machine time produced an Oirat-ordered sort of the entire summer's vocabulary building work, and immediately brought together all duplications overlooked in the hand preparation, as

---

in which they chiefly occur are well known anyway. An advantage found in Oirat is that, because the script is not ambiguous like Classical Mongolian, there need be no stage of "interfiling" to merge the letter pairs t/d, o/u, k/g, and so forth.

well as casting out errors and other slips passed over in checking. (This print-out was double-spaced for later write-in use as a rough-draft, or "pre-edit" dictionary copy.)

A more elaborate sort-and-merge program was written to blend the first, second and third English definitions into a single English dictionary order (and, incidentally, to shuffle the fields so that the code-location was, for instance, last). The same 3,906 cards yielded an English-to-Oirat dictionary of 8,917 entries sorted in $13\frac{1}{4}$ minutes machine time. (Not every card always bore the full three permissible entries.) When considering the repetition of synonyms, I would estimate that at least 6,000 English words are given Oirat definitions.

Later, it was found useful to prepare smaller sorts, for example, an Oirat sort of only the green cards, namely, glosses to the *Siddhitü Kegür* stories, which were then checked against Jülg's glossary for completeness; and a sort made on the Classical Mongolian forms.

The approximate time required to prepare the nearly 4,000 entry cards was between eighty and one hundred working hours and punching time. It is clear that the use of machine technique has virtually revolutionized this kind of lexicography. Although the sorts in their present form are still only sorted raw data, they provide a nucleus from which an edited copy of an Oirat dictionary could slowly be compiled, after additional verification, re-reading texts in the light of the context and other occurrences.

6. CONCLUSIONS

Western Mongolian or Oirat-Kalmyk literary and historical documents being far less studied than Eastern (Classical) Mongolian writings, there is a considerable need for basic reference works, among which an extensive citation dictionary of Oirat ranks very high. Since the range of Oirat literature is both circumscribed in time, and the materials available (in printed or transcribed form) in the West are also limited in amount, the preparation of a dictionary would be a feasible project to undertake, requiring some years of work. A good nucleus to such a dictionary would be formed by carding the vocabulary of available known printed and transcribed texts; then, as previously unstudied manuscript texts in East or West were brought in over the years, nearly the whole of Oirat literature could be encompassed. Lastly, the modern development of high speed electronic computer-processing of literary data makes it possible cheaply to have accurately sorted preliminary listings of various kinds at hand from which to make the final edited dictionary copy.

Abbreviations of Texts

AG	Altan Gerel
AS	Arthasiddha
BB	Bāza Bakshi
M	Medētei (the *üliger-ün dalai* in Oirat)
MH	Manuhari
PC	Pozdneyev Chrestomathy
SK	Siddhitü Kegür
UXT	Ubashi Xung Taiji

ADDENDA. Since the completion of this article the following information has come to light: W. Heissig has published *Mongolische volksreligiöse und folkloristische Texte* (Wiesbaden, 1966), 256 pp., containing ten Western Mongolian texts, some illustrated.

To n. 10 may be added that Ts. Damdinsüren has published *Tibetan and Mongolian Tales of Vetala* (Ulan Bator, 1963). During a European study tour in 1968, the author photocopied over 75 Oirat works from Germany and Denmark (over 2,200 exposures), to be the basis for ongoing research. A number of Oirat items not listed in the Heissig-Sagaster *Verzeichnis* (1961) were discovered in Dresden, and will be described in a supplemental catalogue. The materials for the proposed dictionary have been partly revised, and expanded to about 5,000 cards. A study of three Oirat diplomatic documents of 1691 will appear in *Central Asiatic Journal*, vol. 12. The collection of rare Oirat books has lately made good progress in the MPR; see the report by Zh. Tsoloo, translated in the *Mongolia Society Bulletin*, vol. 6, pp. 73–75 (1967).

THE OLDEST PRESERVED CODEX OF THE BABYLONIAN TRADITION*

by I. O. Lehman, F.R.A.S.
Visiting Professor, College of Jewish Studies, Chicago

1. RECENTLY Dr. Orlinsky has made available again C. D. Ginsburg's "Introduction to the Masoretico-Critical Edition of the Hebrew Bible",[1] adding an introduction of his own. In the introduction he reviews the Bible editions made since Ginsburg and the problems as they now stand. Since Ginsburg's day a number of important sources have become known which have never been examined critically. It will, therefore, be an important addition to Ginsburg's work to analyze the tradition of the oldest preserved Bible codex of the Elkan Adler collection.

The study of the Bible texts goes back to antiquity. Their discussion was based on ancient and often divergent manuscripts. The ancient versions bear manifold witness to that fact. All modern editions of the Hebrew text are based on medieval manuscripts. When, largely in the nineteenth century, the study of the versions was based on a scientific footing, the impression arose that in many places the Hebrew text was "corrupt". There is hardly a page in the *Biblia Hebraica* which does not make that claim and which supplies remedies sometimes ingenious and sometimes to a degree wilful. The text is that of Ben Asher, or, in our editions at least, what was turned into, and claims to be, Ben Asher. It is on the whole a uniform text. The discovery of texts with superlinear vocalization of non-Tiberian Hebrew traditions (occurring in Rabbinic texts, too) has shown that that uniformity is artificial. Our Hebrew Bible

* Paper read before the American Oriental Society in Philadelphia on 21 April 1966 (Hebrew manuscript studies no. 5). The writer is indebted to the authorities of the Jewish Theological Seminary of America for permission to study this manuscript, claimed by the late Elkan Adler as the oldest preserved Bible codex of the collection. The disastrous fire in the Seminary library raging overhead when the writer was sitting in the reading room merely caused an interruption. As our sages have said: "the messengers fulfilling a religious commandment suffer no harm" (Pes. 8b) and "he who is keeping a *miṣwah* experiences no evil"(Midrash Koheleth Rabba, VIII, 9).

[1] New York, 1966 (first published in 1897).

text is usually that compiled by Jacob b. Ḥayyim in the 16th century, with some modifications. All our grammars and dictionaries are based on that text. In reality it is an eclectic text. Since many grammatical features presented in it are more or less artifical or, perhaps better, follow the rules of one school, attempts have been made in recent decades to show what pre-Tiberian Hebrew grammar was like. A comparison of medieval manuscripts with ancient consonantal texts shows that in antiquity the principles underlying the consonantal traditions of the sacred text were different, and many passages described as "corrupt" are in fact in order. One such principle was made the subject of our study at the recent Bible congress in Detroit.[2] If we could obtain a pure Ben Asher text, it is claimed by Kahle, on the basis of manuscripts which can be traced directly back to Ben Asher, we should then have the best text available at the time, and many of the involved problems would become easier. That claim was made for the Leningrad Codex B 19a, which Ginsburg had already described as "the oldest dated manuscript of the entire Hebrew Bible (A.D. 1009), with the official list of the variations between the Babylonians and the Palestinians".[3] That manuscript, however, contains quite a number of Ben Naphtali readings;[4] moreover, the masorah does not agree with the actual text of the manuscript.[5] Further, various alterations were made in the manuscript; their occurrence has not normally been recorded in the apparatus of the *Biblia Hebraica*. Besides, in many places where the apparatus of this standard edition should have mentioned that a certain passage is the subject of a masoretic discussion, the apparatus remains silent.

2. There is no reason why the Ben Asher tradition should be so much better than that of Ben Naphtali. The Babylonian Gaon

[2] See the the writer's article "A Forgotten Principle of Biblical Textual Tradition Rediscovered" (Hebrew manuscript studies no. 3) in JNES, April, 1967. There the writer tried to show how the neglect of a study of ancient manuscript traditions has led to serious misunderstandings of the sacred text.

[3] C. D. Ginsburg in "Recueil des travaux rédigés en mémoire du...M." Daniel Chwolson, 1899, p. 151.

[4] See F. Perez-Castro in *Sefarad*, XV, p.I ff. The writer originally made the suggestion to Dr. Castro to investigate the *Biblia Hebraica,* which seemed to be no pure Ben Asher text, as had been claimed until then.

[5] See A. Rubinstein in *Sefarad*, XV (1965), pp. 16-26 and F. Diaz Esteban, *op. cit.*, XVI (1966), pp. 3-11.

Saadia (d. 942) had already polemized against Ben Asher. In fact, one of Kahle's four Ben Asher manuscripts,[6] the Cairo Codex, drops out because of its many Ben Naphtali readings. On the occasion of the Bonn Bible congress in 1962 we wrote a paper on the Damascus Pentateuch,[7] which still has notes vocalized with old Babylonian superlinear vocalization and dates from about the 9th or 10th centuries. In the Jewish Theological Seminary of America there is another manuscript, which has been claimed as the oldest Bible of the Elkan Adler collection, hailing from Persia and supposedly dating back to the 9th century. As far as we are aware, it has never in any publication been studied in detail. Before its true date can be discussed, a detailed analysis will be necessary.

This manuscript is written on rough parchment.[8] It is a folio size written in three columns in Babylonian square characters[9] with 21 lines to a column on 111 more or less damaged sheets.[10] The correspondences of certain prophetic sections to the Haftaroth lessons were entered by a later hand, which shows that the manuscript was actually used in the liturgy. The Haftaroth correspond to those of an oriental ritual;[11] the script is not Sephardi. The

[6] The British Museum codex 4445; Leningrad codex B 19a; the Aleppo and Cairo codices. Kahle's suggestion that Ben Naphtali followed Aaron b. Moses b. Asher's father now appears very unlikely (see also A. Diez-Macho in the G. R. Driver Jubilee Volume, *Hebrew and Semitic Studies*, 1963, p. 16f).

[7] Cp. *The Damascus Pentateuch and Its Manuscript Tradition According to Ben Naphtali*, Oxford, 1962.

[8] Not "vellum", which term is wrongly used in most of our catalogues.

[9] For the appearance of Babylonian square characters see, for example, P. Kahle, *Masoreten des Ostens* (1913), pl. 16a and S.A. Birnbaum, *The Hebrew Scripts* (1954-57), p. 189 (Codex Petropolitanus of 916) and p. 190 (tombstone of 1232), although the method of mixing up tombstone and other inscriptions with manuscripts is not free from objection.

[10] In a number of cases the margins were cut; in other cases the binding paper covers up a number of masoretic notes.

[11] The Haftaroth added much later differ repeatedly both from the Ashkenazi and the Sephardi ritual and no doubt follow an oriental *minhag*: a) Haft.Berē'shīth begins Isa. *42*, I (against Ashk. and Seph. *42*,5); b) Haft. Wa-yiḳrā' here ends Isa. *44*,28 (against Ashk./Seph. *44*,23); c) Haft. hillūlā' starts at Isa. *61*,10 (Ashk. & Seph. Haft. Niṣṣābhīm); d) Haft. 'Eḳebh here begins Jer. *2*,1 (against the current Isa. *49*,14f.); e) Haft. Debhārīm here begins Jer. *6*, 16 (against the current Isa. *1*, If.); f) Haft. Be-har here covers Jer. *16*,19-*17*,14 (against the current Jer. *32*, 6-27); g) Haft. 'Aṣartā' (i.e.I. day of Shābhū'ōth) varies: it begins also at Ezek. *1*,1 but at the end jumps to Ezek. *3*,12 (against the current *3*,1–12); h) Haft.Ḥōlā' de-Phisḥā' (i.e. Shabbath ḥol ha-mō'ēdh Pesaḥ) comprises Ezek.

manuscript was rebound by its discoverer, the late Elkan Adler (d. 1938). The *dallal*[12] who sold Adler this manuscript in October 1896 in Teheran claimed that it came from a genizah in Yezd. The province of Yezd is situated between Isfahan in the west, Khurasan in the east, and Kerman in the south. Yezd is famous for its silk textiles. The surviving remnants of parchment show that their first owner must have been a man of considerable means.[13] There were no doubt Jewish silk merchants in that area. The discoloring of the pages and the damage to the material, particularly noticeable in the book of Isaiah, with which the manuscript begins, is in fact of a kind found in manuscripts, which were already meant for burial in a genizah. Texts exposed to burial conditions, which show very similar features, may be seen, for example, in the Biblioteca Palatina in Parma (Italy), where the writer examined them some years ago. The pages have been reset, but extensive illegible passages are beyond repair, even though the material is still quite firm. The manuscript comprises the Latter Prophets, of which only the following pieces have been preserved: Isaiah, chap. *17*, 3 to the end; Jeremiah; Ezekiel *1*, 1-*6*, 13 and chap. 40 to the end; further, parts of the Minor Prophets.[14] An attempt was made in the Middle Ages, it seems, to re-use the manuscript and many letters have been retraced; on some such occasion some Ben Naphtali readings were turned into Ben Asher, sometimes—though more rarely—the opposite was true. An 11th century author emphasizes the equal reputation of Ben Asher and Ben Naphtali.[15] The letters are suspended from the lines or at times stand between the lines. The manuscript is supplied with masora magna and parva. There are no traces any more of Babylonian superlinear vocalization. The Tiberian vocalization is well established (it is hardly older than the 9th century). Already the masorah has sometimes a slightly ornamental form like circles (folio 37a), half-circles (f. 40a), roof-

---

45,9–25 (against the current Ez.*37*,1-14 and finally i) Haft. Wa-yēṣē' varies: Hos.*11*,7–12,14 (against Ashk.*12*.13–*14*,10 and Seph.*11*,7–*12*,12). Although the other haftaroth, as far as they are preserved, agree with the current tradition, the differences are significant.

[12] I.e., auctioneer, broker.

[13] One piece of prepared parchment of that size would cost in England about 30 shillings, i.e. five dollars.

[14] Hosea; Joel *1*,1–*4*,7; Mich. *5*,6 to the end; Naḥ.; Ḥab; Zeph. *3*,20; Hag.; and Zech. *1*,1–15.

[15] See L. Lipschütz, *Textus*, IV, p. 3 (1964).

like arrangements (f. 41a), etc. However, this manuscript has a textual tradition which is of immense interest.

3. The character of the manuscript from Yezd (hereafter called Y) may be characterized in a three-fold way: by a description of Ben Asher and Ben Naphtali readings (hereafter called BA and BN, respectively); by the difference between eastern or Babylonian and western or Palestinian readings (called E and W respectively); and by an examination of the kethibh and ḳerē and certain other notes in the masora magna and parva. Since Lazar Lipschütz in 1960, on the basis of a Leningrad manuscript originally discovered by Kahle, for the first time published Mishael b. Uzziel's *Kitāb al-khilaf*,[16] it has after three-quarters of a millennium of confusion in the preserved manuscript lists become possible to see what really were the differences between BA and BN. For determining the reliability of manuscripts and printed editions in this respect, Mishael b. Uzziel's treatise is of the greatest value. As far as printed editions are concerned, we shall for purposes of comparison limit ourselves to three recent standard editions: (1) The *Biblia Hebraica*, edited by Kittel-Kahle on behalf of the Württembergische Bibelanstalt. Stuttgart, 1937 ff. This edition is based on one manuscript, the Leningrad Codex B19a of ca. 1009. (2) The Hebrew Bible, edited by N. H. Snaith on behalf of the British and Foreign Bible Society. London, 1958. This edition is based on three manuscripts, a Lisbon one of 1483, a Yemenite one of ca. 1460-80 for the Hagiographa, and a third British Museum manuscript. (3) The *Qoren Bible*, edited by D. Goldschmidt, A. M. Haberman and M. Medan on behalf of the Qoren Publishers, printed in Jerusalem, 1962. This edition is based not on one manuscript, but on what is found in "most manuscripts[17] and accepted printed texts. . .." The *Kitāb al-khilaf* quotes as authorities Abū

[16] In *Textus*, II, p. aleph ff. (1962).

[17] While there can be no doubt about the careful scrutiny of the editors, concerning their claim it should be borne in mind that there are hundreds of Bible codes in European countries, quite apart from the vast Russian collections (the second Firkovitch collection alone comprised over 2300 Bible manuscripts; whether they have all survived the invasion of Russia in the last war is not known); but they have not even been classified, since the great Hebrew manuscript cataloguers of the 19th century, like Steinschneider, Neubauer, etc., dealt with Bibles in a rather summary fashion. There are further ca. 700 Bible codes in the JTSA and in HUC in Cincinnati.

Saʿīd and Abū ʿImrān, or, with their Hebrew names, Aaron b. Moses b. Asher (BA) and Moses b. David b. Naphtali (BN). Ben Asher lived in Tiberias in the earlier half of the 10th century. Although a descent going back as far as Ezra is claimed for him, our manuscript study no. 3 implicitly shows that at least as far as the knowledge of ancient manuscript traditions is concerned, the claim is not borne out by the facts. Maimonides (d. 1204), like most scholars, according to the Hilkhoth Sefer Torah,[18] had already relied on a carefully corrected Ben Asher codex, which came from Jerusalem and was at that time kept in Fostat.[19] Moses b. David b. Naphtali was Ben Asher's contemporary and presumably also lived in Tiberias. Elijah Levita[20] is responsible for the claim that the westerners follow Ben Asher and the easterners Ben Naphtali. Things are not so simple, though: all preserved Bible codes more or less show the influence of Ben Asher. The Adler manuscript (Y), however, is likely to throw light on whether in Babylonian codes Ben Naphtali readings were at one time favored.

Since the Book of Jeremiah is the best preserved in Y, it may be convenient to begin our analysis with this book in order to obtain a clear picture of the character of Y.[21] There are altogether 51 passages where BA and BN differ. The *Biblia Hebraica* has no clear cases now where the Leningrad Codex B 19a (hereafter abbreviated as L) follows BN in Jeremiah.[22] But Y shows 25 to 26 such cases (namely *2*, 6; *3*, 9; *7*, 33; *10*, 20; *14*, 18; *21*, 9; *22*, 24; *22*, 28; *25*, 29; *26*, 12; *27*, 15; *29*, 18; *29*, 23; *32*, 35; *34*, 1; *35*, 15; *36*, 23; *37*, 13; *37*, 19; *38*, 11; *42*, 1; [*43*, 2]; *44*, 26; *44*, 28; *50*, 9; *51*, 3). There are some deviants, which do not exactly follow one school or the other, as must be expected in manuscripts of that age.

While in Jeremiah, L has no clear cases of BN readings (if any corrections have rightly been interpreted in the printed text of the

---

[18] VIII,4.

[19] Whether that codex personally corrected by Ben Asher is really identical with the Aleppo codex now in Jerusalem is rather doubtful (see M. Cassuto in Ha'ares of 2.I.1948; but now M. Gottstein in *Textus*, I (1960), p. 17 ff.; on BA's karaism see S. Szyszman in Rev. Bibl. 73,4 (1966), p. 531 ff. If the hand in *Textus*, V (1966), pl. II-III is that of the Aleppo codex, that of *op. cit.*, I, pl. I ff. is not or vice-versa!

[20] *Massoreth ha-massoreth*, ed. C. D. Ginsburg, p. 144.

[21] At the time of the Seminary fire our study was based on this book alone.

[22] However, in 6 to 7 cases the text was later turned into BA without the editors remarking that these are not original readings of the manuscript. The same applies mutatis mutandis to the other Biblical books.

Biblia Hebraica), there are a number of deviations. In *14*, 18 (against BA כִּי and BN כִּֽי), L reads כִּֽי with ga'ya, which tends towards BN. On the other hand, in *18*, 11 (against BA אִישׁ and BN אִֽישׁ), L reads plain אִישׁ. In another case L has a mixed reading: in *51*, 3 (against BA אֱֽל־ידרך ... וְאֱֽל and BN אֱֽל־ידרך ... וְאֱל), L reads אֱֽל־ידרך ... וְאֱל, i.e. the first אל with ga'ya but not the second.[23]

In Y, a number of alterations have been made in the differences between BA and BN, showing that at that time the text was still under discussion. There are first a number of small differences, showing that in Y we are dealing with a careful tradition; for example, in the following BN readings, compared with the lists of Mishael b. Uzziel, Y also has a maḳḳeph: *22*, 24 (Y's BN אִֽם־יהיה with maḳḳeph and ga'ya against BA without ga'ya); *22*, 28 (Y's BN אִֽם־כלי with maḳḳeph and ga'ya against BA without ga'ya). In a number of cases, the original BN text was later altered to adapt it to BA, which also occurs repeatedly, for example, in the Damascus Pentateuch. In Y, that applies in three cases: *25*, 29; *29*, 18; *44*, 26. In *43*, 2 (against BA בן־הוֹשַֽׁעיה and BN בן הֽוֹשעיה), the text of Y exhibits both readings: בן־הֽוֹשַֽׁעיה.[24] That is clearly not original, but the BN reading seems to have been added later. There is evidence in this manuscript that BA readings have been turned into BN elsewhere too. That can only have been done at a time when the dispute between the two schools was still felt to be a live issue. There is one case, too, where the text of Y follows BA (*52*, 12), but the BN reading is recorded in the masora parva. In various cases, unfortunately, where the masorah might have been informative, the text has now become illegible.

The result is that in the Jeremiah text of L, genuine BN readings are practically non-existent, whereas they constitute 50 % of Y In his introduction to Ginsburg, Dr. Orlinsky raises the question whether it is really facetious to speak of BN manuscripts with BA readings. Y now shows for the first time among the ancient codes preserved to us that such manuscripts did exist. Owing to its relatively good preservation, the Jeremiah text of Y is the best example illustrating the character of Y, since the other books have either suffered too much or are too short.

---

[23] Lipschütz, *op. cit.*, II, *ad loc.*, prints אֱל right through.

[24] The sources differ in putting ga'ya to the right or the left of the vowel.

The Book of Isaiah coming in the manuscript before Jeremiah, is in Y preserved only in parts (Isa. *17*, 3–*66*, 24), and even there the passages in question have repeatedly become illegible or have been lost. Only 13 out of 34 passages exhibiting the BA/BN differences can still be compared. Here L has 11 BA readings and two BN ones (namely *34*, 11 and *63*, 7). Imperfect as the picture is now, it seems likely that in the Isaiah text of Y, the number of BA readings was higher than in that of Jeremiah. Y follows BA in nine cases and BN in four (namely *24*, 18; *28*, 4; *38*, 4; *63*, 7), although the proportion of BA/BN readings might have been different had the whole text been preserved. It is remarkable that there are cases where L follows BN and Y follows BA, as in *34*, 11. Otherwise they differ in *38*, 4, where L has BA and Y, BN; in *63*, 7, both have BN (i.e. plain אֲשֶׁר instead of אֲשֶׁר with ga'ya, which is BA). There is one case (Isa. *24*, 18), where the text originally seems to have followed BN (BA: וֱהיה ; BN: וְהיה), i.e. the text first had a waw, which, however, faded; then waw was added on top; the text was apparently altered into וֱהיה with ga'ya later on.

From the Book of Ezekiel no more than the sections Ezek. *1*, 1–*6*, 13 and *40*, 7–*48*, 35 are preserved. There are merely 13 passages out of 45 in the whole of Ezekiel where the BA/BN differences can now be traced. In these passages, L has 11 BA and two BN readings (namely *1*, 3 and *4*, 6). Y, on the other hand, has six BA and seven BN readings (*1*, 3; *4*, 6; *40*, 18; *42*, 1; *44*, 6; *46* 3 and *46*, 23). There are some special cases: in *1*, 3, both L and Y prefer the simpler reading without ga'ya (עַל־נהר), which is BN. In one case (*45*, 17), the alteration disagrees with both BA and BN: against BA (בְּכָל־מועדי בית ישראל, with ga'ya) and BN (without ga'ya), the present text in Y now has בכל, which was formerly בְּכָל. i.e. BA originally. There are two cases in Y (*4*, 6 and *40*, 18) where the text was originally BN but was later altered to adapt it to BA. The Book of Isaiah is too badly damaged to obtain a clear picture, but things are different in the Book of Ezekiel. The proportion of BA/BN readings, though incompletely preserved, shows that there are some 50 % BN readings, which agrees with the results obtained from an analysis of the Book of Jeremiah.

In the Dodekapropheton of Y, entire books are now missing, namely Amos, Obadiah, Jonah, Malachi and most of Zephaniah. In Hosea, L in all 8 cases follows BA, but Y follows BA in 4 and BN in four cases (*2*, 24; *9*, 12; *11*, 9; *12*, 10). Two of the readings in Y deserve special mention: in *7*, 14 (against BA יְיֵלִילוּ without ga'ya and BN יְיֵלִילוּ with ga'ya[25]), Y now reads יְיֵלִילוּ, but originally it had יְיֵלִילוּ, i.e. BA). In 11, 9, the ga'ya of the BN school (וְלֹא־אִישׁ) was later erased to adapt the text to BA. Here a comparison of L and Y confirms the preceding results: while L here regularly follows BA, Y has 50 % BN readings.

Regarding the two passages in the BOOK OF JOEL where BA and BN differ, both L and Y agree to the same tradition: in *2*, 17, they follow BA (וְיֹאמְרוּ חוסה ה׳ with ga'ya) and in *4*, 3, BN (וַיִּתְּנוּ without ga'ya). The previous results regarding Y are thus confirmed by the Book of Joel.

Of all the remaining differences between BA and BN in the Dodekapropheton, no more than one passage has been preserved, which, however, is interesting: Hag. *1*, 12. Compared with BA (בֶּן־שאלתיאל with ga'ya) and BN (בֶּן־ without ga'ya), L clearly follows BA, but Y originally had BA,[26] which later on was turned into BN.

Although comparatively little has been preserved of the Latter Prophets in Y, it is sufficient to show beyond doubt that in this manuscript we have the sole surviving witness still existing in codex form of a vanished type of manuscript, where there are 50 % BN readings and where alterations were still made to adapt the text also to Ben Naphtali

4. Another approach to determine the character of this manuscript is to analyze its relationship to the differences between eastern and western readings (hereafter called E and W, respectively). The manuscript begins with Isa. *17*, 3, but before *37*, 36, all recorded E/W differences have become illegible.[27] In Isa. *37*, 36, Y (like L) has the grammatically correct form ויצא מלאַך ה׳ (Ms. Orientalis 2201 [in the British Museum], hereafter Ms. Or. 2201, records as Babli: מלאָך); in *38*, 14, Y (like L) has the W spelling כסוס (the E kethibh is כסיס); in *44*, 27, where according

---

[25] C. D. Ginsburg in the apparatus of his Bible edition of 1894, which has to be used with great caution, (II, p. 1050) prints יְלִילוּ without ga'ya for BN (a typical case showing how the lists were confused in later medieval manuscripts!), but Lipschütz correctly has יְלִילוּ *ad loc.*

[26] Lipschütz here points according to Add.; *q.v.* in *Textus,* II, *ad loc.*

[27] When differences are not recorded here, it means that the passages in question are either illegible or have been lost altogether.

to the Chwolson list[28] plene ונהרוֹתיך is the W reading and defective ונהרתיך the E one, Y (against L) reads ונהרותיך, i.e. the W reading[29]; in *46*, 8, Y (like L) has הָשִׁיבוּ פושעים without waw, the W reading (against E והשיבו, as is recorded in the masora parva of Y *ad loc.*); in *48*, 13, Y (like L) has וימיני טפחה שמים (whereas Ms. Or. 2201 records as Babli: טִפְּחָה); in *53*, 4, Y (like L) reads plene yodh ומכאבינו, the E reading following the Chwolson list (against W defective in the yodh מכאבֵנו, which would then have a singular form).[30] Of three cases here concerning the E/W differences in אל/על, Isa. *56*, 3 and *56*, 7 are now illegible; but in *56*, 6, Y (like L) has הנלוים על, which in the Chwolson list is given as E (against W: אל).[31] In *57*, 6, Y (like L) reads העלִית מנחה with ḥireḳ, grammatically the more frequent form (but Ms. Or. 2201 records as Babli: העלֵית). In *57*, 10, Y (like L) reads לא אמרתְּ נואש, which, following the Chwolson list,[32] is W (against E אמרתי)[33]. In *59*, 6, Y (like L) has מעשיהם מעשֵׂי־און, which according to Chwolson is W (against E מעשה). In *66*, 2, Y (like L) has וחרד עַל־דברי, the W reading (against E אל).

There are some 24 recorded differences in E/W readings occurring from Isa. *17*, 3–*66*, 24 (different lists vary slightly). Only 11 of these are still legible. The picture is therefore rather incomplete. We have to single out that group where the E reading is supported by one manuscript only, namely Isa. *37*, 36; *48*, 13; *57*, 6. In these three cases, all the readings as they stand in L and Y are grammatically simpler; the readings in Y and L would all be western, if Ms. Or. 2201 does not record here an *isolated* opinion of E/W differences in the passage in question. Following Ch. there then remain two E readings (*53*, 4; *56*, 6) and six W readings (*38*, 14; *44*, 27; *46*, 8; *57*, 10; *59*, 6; *66*, 2). Relying on the E/W differences recorded in Ch., the Book of Isaiah, incomplete as the evidence is, in any case shows a majority of W readings.

---

[28] Cp. Ginsburg on the basis of the Leningrad Codex of ca.1009 as cited by M. Daniel in Chwolson, *op. cit.*, p. 151f.

[29] But in the Bible, Ginsburg edition, II, 1894, p. 793 that is recorded as the E one (no note in *Bib. Heb.*[3]!).

[30] But the Ginsburg edition, II, p. 804 records a reading like Y's without *waw* (i.e. מכאֹבינו) as W and with waw (ומכאוֹבינו) as E (no note in *Bib. Heb.*[3]!).

[31] Not recorded in Ginsburg edition and Kittel-Kahle at all !

[32] Hereafter abbreviated as Ch.

[33] See note 31.

Because it is well preserved, the Book of Jeremiah is our principal witness here too.

In the BOOK OF JEREMIAH there are over 50 differences between E and W readings, all of which have been preserved in Y (again, different lists differ slightly in the number of such differences recorded). In Jer. *2*, 20, the W reading is על־כל־גבעה; that is read also by Y and L (E omits כל[34]); in *4*, 30, Y (against L) follows the E kethibh בפיך (W: בפוך, into which the text of Y was corrected later on); in *5*, 17, Y (against L) follows the E text (אתה בֹּטח defective;[35] but W: בוטח plene); in *6*, 6a Y (like L) has W: כרתו עצה (against E: עֵצָהּ with mappiḳ hē'); in *6*, 6b, Y (like L) has W: כֻּלָּהּ עשק (against E: כלו); in *8*, 7, Y reads ותר וסיס וְעָגוּר with *waw* in עָגוּר, which according to Ch. is the W keth. (E keth. is וסיס ועגיר with *yodh* in ועגיר); L has the keth. וסוס ועגור;[36] in *9*, 23, Y originally follows the E reading חסד וּמשפט וצדקה with waw before משפט (against W: without waw; *sic* L). But later the original waw was blotted out to adapt the text to W.[37] A particularly interesting case occurs in *10*, 13, showing how easily people thought divergent readings to be "wrong": here the text first had מקצה הָארץ with the הָ *standing out into the margin*; this is a western tradition. This reading actually appears in the LXX (ἐξ ἐσχάτου τῆς γῆς), the first edition of the whole Bible, Soncino, 1488 and the Complutensian Polyglot, i.e., הארץ as the kethibh *and* ḳerē. But then in Y the letter hē' was erased leaving only the ḳamaṣ (*sic* L) in agreement with a note in the masora parva: בק̇ הארץ. To have a kethibh ארץ and a ḳerē הארץ is the current W tradition (against E kethibh *and* ḳerē ארץ, which seems to have been the original text of the copyist's Vorlage[38]). In *10*, 18, Y reads with E והצרֹתי להם without waw following Ch. (against W plene והצרותי; *sic* L).[39] In

[34] According to Ms. Add. 15251; cp. also *Bib.Heb. ad loc.*

[35] Also, for example, the Codex Petropolitanus, ed. H. L. Strack, *ad loc.* reads בֹּטח.

[36] Ginsburg, Bible, II, p. 838 *ad loc.* records an opinion according to which the readings are: W kethibh וסיס (*sic* Y); E kethibh: וסוס. Ch. does not bring an E/W difference in וסיס/וסוס, but in Codex Petropolitanus *ad loc.* וסוס was corrected into וסיס. The apparatus in *Bib. Heb.*[3] does not record here an E/W difference at all!

[37] The versions seem to support the E reading (LXX, Vetus Latina and Pesh, *ad loc.*).

[38] Since no room was left for either the ה or the ḳamaṣ.

[39] Ginsburg edition II, p. 483 records the contrary! And *Bib.Heb.*[3] has nothing.

11, 11, Y (against L) has a marked E reading:[40] וְאַל אשמע (W: ולא). The masora parva records another opinion taking ואל merely as a kethibh: ולא ק̇.[41] In *12*, 14 the text of Y originally read הנגעים בַּנַּחלה without a dagesh in the nūn;[42] according to Ms. Addition (hereafter, Ms. Add.) 15, 251, that is the E reading (against L בַּנַּחלה, the W reading).[43] In *13*, 18, Y (like L) reads with W plene השפילו (against E defective: השפלו); in *13*, 20, Y (like L) has with W: שאי (in the masora parva: שאו ק̇), whereas E has kethibh and ḳerē שאו;[44] in *15*, 14, Y (like L) has the W reading תוקד (against E kethibh תיקד). In *23*, 35 we have another correction: the text of Y (against L) originally read איש אֶל־רעהו, which is the E reading, but later it was corrected into the W one: על. In *26*, 24 the opposite occurs: the original W reading (*sic* L) אחיקם בֶּן־שפן was later corrected into the eastern one (בני שפן) and an apparently later masoretic note adds in the margin: בן ק̇. In *26*, 8, the W reading is אֶל־כל־העם (thus L) and the E one: על־כל־העם (thus Y). In *27*, 19, the text in Y (against L) originally read כה אמר ... עַל העמדים ועל־העם, according to Ch. the E reading[45] (against W: אֶל, into which the text was corrected later); similarly, in *29*, 7, we have in Y (against L) the E reading: הגילתי אתכם (i.e. as kethibh; ḳerē [הגל[יתי), whereas W reads: הגליתי; similarly in *29*, 22, Y (against L) reads with E כצדקיהו וּכְאֶחָאב (against W: וכאחב.[46] Again in *32*, 11, there is in Y (against L) an E reading את החתום וְאֶת המצוה with a second ואת (the masora parva *ad loc.* remarks: בבלאי כת̇ ואת), which was later blotted out (against W: את החתום והמצוה); likewise in *32*, 19, Y (against L) has with E the kethibh דרכי בני אָדָם and the ḳerē הָאָדָם, whereas W has plain בני אדם. Also in *32*, 34, Y (against L) with the kethibh orientalis reads ושימו (with the ḳerē noted in the masora parva

---

[40] Thus Ch.; Ginsburg edition II, p. 485; *Bib.Heb.*[3].

[41] That is in fact recorded by Ginsburg too as a divergent opinion.

[42] Ginsburg edition, II, 847 has a misprint here for the E reading.

[43] A dot like a dagesh does now appear in the *nūn*, but a careful comparison shows that the vocalizer makes a clear round dot, whereas here a little line representing the dagesh was added later to adapt the text of Y to the W reading.

[44] While the LXX seems to support W, E seems to be supported by Pesh., Targum and Vulgate.

[45] Also occurring in the Babylonian ms.Eb 22 (*see Bib.Heb.*[3] *ad loc.*).

[46] Here is also a reading *ad loc.* ascribed to BN as a ḳerē וּכְאֶחָיו (*sic* Codex Tzufutkale no. 84); see Ginsburg's Introduction, p. 248, but not recorded in Mishael b. Uzziel's lists.

ק [ויש]ימו), whereas W has plain: וישימו. But in *33*, 3, Y (like L) reads וּבְצֻרוֹת with W (against E kethibh ונצרות). In *34*, 2a Ms. Add. 15251 records צדקיה as an E reading, which is found in Y (against W: צדקיהו; thus L); but following Ms. Or. 1474 in *34*, 2b, the third word (אמר ה׳) כֹּה in the E tradition (against W) starts a new verse, which is found neither in Y nor L. According to Ms. Add. 15251 the E reading in *35*, 3 omits the dagesh forte in חבצניה (i.e. E: חֲבַצִּנְיָה against W: חֲבַצִּנְיָה; but Y (like L) here follows the W tradition. In *35*, 11, in the reading אל־הארץ following Ch., Y (like L) has the E reading[47] (against W: על); similarly, in *35*, 17, the E reading has plene waw יוֹשְׁבֵי ירושלם followed by Y (and L)[48] against W defective ישבי.[49] Likewise there is clearly an E reading in Y (against L) in *36*, 23 (E ויהי בקרא against W ויהי כקרא), with the masora parva adding in the margin of Y: כק ק. Y (like L) goes with the W reading הנפש הַזֹּאת in *38*, 16 against the E kethibh הנפש הזה.[50] In *39*, 11, Y (like L) reads ויצו ... עַל ירמיהו, which is the W reading (against E: אל). The example in *42*, 6 is somewhat inconclusive: the scribe first wrote אנחנו, then, erasing it, wrote אנו (in the masora parva: אנחנו ק), which is the W reading (thus also L) and apparently meant originally, whereas the E kethibh *and* ḳerē is אנו. In *44*, 18, the text in Y has been corrected; it originally read וּלְהַסֵּךְ־לה, which is the E reading, but was later turned into the W one: והסך (thus L) with a *later* masoretic note in the margin of Y: ולהסך ק. The note presupposes a later masorete referring to a deviating Babylonian reading! In *44*, 25, Y (like L) with W reads ובידיכם מְלֵאתם, whereas Ms. Or. 2201 maintains that the E reading is מְלאתם with shewa. But in *45*, 1 again Y (against L) clearly has the E kethibh בשנַת הרביעית (ḳerē in the masora parva: [בש]נה ק), whereas the W reading is: בשנה. According to Ms. Add. 15251, in *45*, 4, Y (like L) reading כל־הארץ הִיא follows W (against E: לי היא). In *46*, 2, Y (like L) originally read עַל־נהר־פרת, the W reading; but later it was corrected into אֶל, the E one, with a masoretic note apparently added later: על למער[באי]. It is significant that in the same way as sometimes readings are corrected into Ben Naphtali, sometimes the western readings are also corrected into eastern ones, whereas in the surviving codes usually

---

[47] *Sic* Ch., Ginsburg edition, II, p. 897 against *Bib. Heb.*[3] II, p. 772, which calls על "Or." = E.

[48] No note in *Bib. Heb.*[3]!

[49] For the special case of Jer. *36*, 12 see section 5.

[50] Cp. Ms. Add. 15251.

the opposite is the case. In *46*, 16,[51] on the current text found in L קוּמָה וְנָשֻׁבָה (Y has נשובה), a W reading, the masora parva in Y remarks לבבלא קומו ק וכת קומה. Y (against L), therefore has the E reading here. In *48*, 1, according to Ms. Add. 15251, Y (like L) follows the W reading וְחַתָּה with a dagesh (against E וחתָה with a rapheh stroke). In *48*, 17, on the other hand, in Y (against L) we have the E kethibh אֵיךְ נשבר against W: איכה (the masora parva in Y remarks: למערבא איכה כת); in *48*, 31,[52] Y (like L) has the W reading יֶהְגֶּה (against E ḳerē אֶהְגֶּה). In *48*, 36, we have in Y (like L[53]) the defective E reading כַּחֲלִלִים יהמה (against W plene כחלילים). In *48*, 41, the text in Y (against L) originally had והמצדות נתפשו (the right downstroke is heavier than the rest of the letter!), the E kethibh later corrected into נתפשה, the W reading. In *48*, 44, Y (like L) reads הַנָּיס מפני הפחד (in the masora parva: ׳י); according to Ch., הניס is the E kethibh and ḳerē; Y and L, therefore, follow the W reading (W kethibh הֵנִיס and ḳerē הַנָּס).[54] In *49*, 19,,, Y (unlike L) reads ומי יְעִידֶנּוּ with a defective waw of the Hifʿil פיו and the suffix 3. p. sg. m.; according to *Bib. Heb.*,[3] the form ending in -nū is the E kethibh spelling, all defective יְעִדֶנּוּ; Ginsburg (II, 925) spells יְעִידֶנּוּ as the E kethibh.[55] Ch., however, takes the form with plene waw and defective yodh, of the Hifʿil as E.[56] Y does not record a ḳerē in the masora parva. If the *Bib. Heb.* and Ginsburg are right here, Y's יְעִידֶנּוּ and L's יְעִידֵנִי are the E and W readings, respectively. Likewise in *49*, 20, according to Ch., Y (like L) follows the E reading with plene waw: ומחשבותיו (as against W with defective waw: ומחשבֹתיו[57]). In *50*, 6, with its reading הרים שובבים (i.e. kethibh שׁוֹבָבִים, ḳerē שׁוֹבְבוּם), Y (like L) follows the W reading (against E kethibh *and* ḳerē שׁוֹבְבוּם). In *50*, 9,[58] Y (unlike L) originally read מעיר ומעלה

---

[51] Not recorded in Ch., but in *Bib. Heb.*[3] and Ginsburg.

[52] See no. 51.

[53] Not recognised in *Bib. Heb.*[3]

[54] *Bib. Heb.*[3] is not sure mentioning "K[ethibh] Occ. הֵנִיס (?)" (*sic*). Ginsburg, *op. cit.* II, p. 924 has like Ch.: W kethibh הניס; ḳerē הַנָּס; according to G. the E kethibh is הַנָּס.

[55] Taking the -nī form as ḳerē (יְעִידֵנִי).

[56] I.e. E: יועדני; W: יעידני (defective waw and plene yōdh).

[57] *Bib. Heb.*[3] has no note and Ginsburg edition II, p. 925 reverses the E/W readings: The defective reading does appear, for example, in the editions of Soncino 1488, Lisbon 1492, etc.

[58] Not in Ch.

אֶל־בבל, the E reading,[59] later corrected into על, the W reading (thus L). In *50*, 11, according to Ch., Y in ותצהלי כאבִּירים (with plene yodh) curiously has the W reading and L on the contrary with defective yodh (כאבִּרים), the E reading.[60] In *50*, 20, Y (unlike L) originally read בימים הָהֵמָּה,[61] the E reading; but later the medial mem was corrected into a final one turning it into the W reading (thus L). But in *50*, 29, Y (like L) has the W reading אֶל־בבל (against E: על). In *51*, 46, in Y (unlike L) there is again a clear E reading: מֹשֵׁל על־משל (with the note in the masora parva למערבא ומשל) without waw copul (against W: ומשל as in L). Finally there is the last E/W difference in Jeremiah: in *52*, 2, Y (unlike L) reading יהויָקים plene follows E (and L follows W), if *Bib. Heb. 3*[62] and Ginsburg[63] are right (against W defective: יהויָקם).[64]

In summary, the Book of Jeremiah contains some 57 to 58 E/W differences. L has here seven to eight E readings against some 50 W ones, i.e. roughly over 5 % E readings, which, by the way, shows again that the Leningrad Codex B 19a is a superior but not a pure Palestinian BA text. The latter has already been proven by Dr. Castro for the BA/BN differences.

Y in Jeremiah contains as many as 13 corrections in the E/W differences. Eleven times the eastern readings were turned into western ones (*4*, 30; *9*, 23; *10*, 13; *12*, 14; *23*, 35; *27*, 19; *32*, 11; *44*, 18; *48*, 41; *50*, 9; *50*, 20); and twice (*26*, 24; *46*, 2) the western readings into eastern ones. Here we are confronted with a result we have already seen in the BA/BN differences: such alterations in both directions are possible only at a time when the issue was still felt to be a live one, and that can be the case only at an early period. It is only natural to find a majority of Ben Asher and western corrections, since the Ben Asher school soon displaced Ben Naphtali, and all deviant codes either had to be corrected or buried. It was in fact a stroke of rare luck which enabled as skilful a collector as Elkan Adler to rescue from oblivion this codex, which was doomed to destruction.

---

[59] Cp. *Bib. Heb.*[3] *ad loc.*

[60] Ginsburg edition II, p. 928 agrees with this explanation of the E/W difference here; not recognised in *Bib. Heb.*[3].

[61] Cp. a Babylonian fragment (Eb 22) the E reading הָהֶמָּה.

[62] *Ad loc.*

[63] *Op. cit.*, II, p. 936.

[64] But according to Ch. it is W: יהויָקים and E: יהויָקם. In *52*, 32 the ḳerē המלכים, according to Y, is an E reading.

There is one curious case (*50*, 11) where Y follows W and L follows E. Otherwise, while L has 6 E readings, all of them in the second half of the book (*35*, 11; *35*, 17; *48*, 36; *49*, 20; *50*, 11; *52*, 2) on the whole L shows a consistent western text. That is not the case with Y. Here in Jeremiah alone we have 37 E readings (*4*, 30; *5*, 17; *9*, 23; *10*, 13; *10*, 18; *11*, 11; *12*, 14; *23*, 35; *26*, 8; *27*, 19; *29*, 7; *29*, 22; *32*, 11; *32*, 19; *32*, 34; *34*, 2a; *35*, 11; *35*, 17; *36*, 23; *44*, 18; *45*, 1; *46*, 16; *48*, 17; *48*, 36; *48*, 41; *49*, 19; *49*, 20; *50*, 9; *50*, 20; *51*, 46; *52*, 2; [*52*, 32][65]), i.e. over 55 % eastern readings. That shows clearly that Adler's codex (Y) is in fact a Babylonian codex. As far as the writer is aware, this is the first time that it has become possible to show in one of the surviving Bible codes of such antiquity that there were Bibles which followed the eastern readings as consistently, as all the Bibles we now have follow the western ones.

The different E/W readings preserved from the remaining books of the Latter Prophets are again too few to form a clear picture of the exact percentages. The data are added here merely for completeness' sake. In Ezek. *1*, 1–*6*, 13 and *40*, 7–*48*, 35, all that is preserved in Y, there are only six E/W differences. In *1*, 13, Y (unlike L) follows the E kethibh כמראה הלפידים הוא[65a] (against W: היא; thus L). In *5*, 11, Y (like L) follows the W reading וגם אני אֶגְרַע (against the E kethibh אגדע).[66] In *42*, 8, Y (unlike L) has אֶל־פני היכל, the E reading (against W: על). In *43*, 20 we have another adaptation of an E to a W reading. Y (unlike L) originally reads with E: אֶל־ארבע קרנתיו. The masora parva still notes how the Palestinians differ: למע[רבאי] על, but the Y text was later adapted to W's על too. Further, in *43*, 26, Y (unlike L) has the E kethibh וכפרו את המזבח[67] with the masora parva יכפרו ק (against W: יכפרו). Likewise in *44*, 3, when Y

---

[65] On this reading see section 5.

[65a] Also in the Babylonian fragment Eb 10.

[66] The more forceful E kethibh is actually supported by Symmachus, Targum and Vulgate, and therefore is no doubt the older reading. Actually the beautiful Bible of Naples ca. 1492 and that of Brescia 1494 print אגדע as kethibh *and* ḳerē.

[67] ḳerē יכפרו. The E kethibh is supported by LXX and Pesh., beginning as it does a new verse with וכפרו. E kethibh וכפרו is treated as kethibh *and* ḳerē in the Prophets of Soncino 1485-86 and the Rabbinic Bible of Felix Pratensis, Venice, 1517.

(like L) reads לֶאֱכוֹל־לחם with plene waw, that is really an E reading (against W defective לאכל).[68]

The result of the analysis on the whole confirms what we found in Jeremiah. Among six cases there is one where an E reading was turned into a W one (*43*, 20); but while L has only one E reading (*44*, 3), Y has five out of six (*1*, 13; *42*, 8; *43*, 20; *43*, 26; *44*, 3); the passages are too few to estimate a percentage, but in any case Y's Ezekiel no doubt had over 50 % eastern readings too.

In the preserved remnants of the MINOR PROPHETS there now occur in Y no more than nine E/W differences. In the BOOK OF HOSEA there are three differences, all of which have been preserved. In *4*, 12, we read in Y (as in L) וּמַקְלוֹ יגיד לו, the W reading (against E: וּמִקּוֹלוֹ). In *14*, 1, Ms. Harley 5710–11 (British Museum) records the defective reading יפלו עלליהם (without waw) as western. That is read by Y and L (against E plene עוללירהם, if that is a genuine E/W difference[69]). In *14*, 5, Y (unlike L) has a clear E reading: שב אפי מִמֶּנִי with the masora parva remarking נו ק; the W reading is: מִמֶּנּוּ. In JOEL there are two E/W differences, only one of which is preserved. In *1*, 12, Y (unlike L) reads as kethibh מן־בני אדם and as ḳerē in the margin מבני, which is the E reading (against W: plain מן־בני אדם). The text of the other E/W difference (*4*, 7) breaks off in the middle.

In the remaining text of MICHAH (*5*, 6–*7*, 20), two E/W differences have survived. In *6*, 5, Y (unlike L) reads מי־יעץ בלק with the masora parva remarking מה ק, i.e. the E reading (against W: מה־יעץ). In *7*, 5, in the reading אל־תבטחו בְּאַלוּף with plene waw Y (like L) follows the W reading (against E defective באלף).[70] The two E/W differences in NAḤUM have been preserved. In *2*, 12, Y (like L) reads ומרעה הוא, the W reading (against E kethibh היא and ḳerē הוא); but in *3*, 8, Y (unlike L) reading plene התיטיבי מנא אמון follows the E kethibh with the ḳerē הֲתֵיטְבִי (against W kethibh and ḳerē הֲתֵיטְבִי). In ḤABBAKUK one out of two E/W differences has been preserved. In *2*, 16, Y (unlike L) follows

[68] Not recognised in *Bib. Heb.*[3]. In Ginsburg, *op. cit.* II, p. 1032 the reverse is recorded! The western reading occurs in the *ed. princeps* of the whole Bible, Soncino, 1488, and the Brescia Bible of 1494.

[69] This E/W difference, however, is recorded neither in Ch., *Bib. Heb.*[3] or Ginsburg edition II, p. 1056. To take this as an E/W difference may perhaps be an isolated opinion, because in this passage elsewhere (cp. Ginsburg *ad loc.*) simply a variant is recorded.

[70] Thus according to Ch.

the E reading וקיקלון אֶל־כבודך (against W על). No other E/W differences have been preserved in the Minor Prophets.

If we leave out Hos. *14*, 1 as an apparently isolated opinion, in the remaining eight passages there are in L western readings only, whereas Y has five eastern readings (namely Hos. *14*, 5; Joel *1*, 12; Mic. *6*, 5; Nah. *3*, 8 and Ḥab. *2*, 16), i.e. again over 50 % eastern readings. It follows therefore from an analysis of Jeremiah, Ezekiel and the Minor Prophets that, quite apart from the script, Y is clearly a predominantly Babylonian manuscript.

5. There remain for us to examine groups of terms which occur from time to time in the masora parva and likewise show Y to be Babylonian in origin. For lack of space only a few of the masoretic readings can be quoted here.

(a) The group making references to the readings of the בבלאי and מערבאי, respectively, i.e. what we have called E/W readings. As is to be expected in manuscripts of that age, we find here E/W differences which are not mentioned, for example, in Ch. In the famous passage where Rabh-shakeh addresses the Judeans (Isa. *36*, 12), Y brings an E/W difference:[71] Y and L following the current text read .... שלחני ... לדבר ... הלא עַל־האנשים הישבים על־החומה But the masora parva of Y has a clearly superior and so far unrecorded E reading אֶל־האנשים. The *Bib. Heb.*[3] could adduce for that reading so far the LXX only. In the re-assertion of the Lord's sole godhead in Isa. *46*, 6, Y and L with the current text read: ויעשהו אל יסגדו אף ישתחוו.[72] But the masora parva of Y here records an E reading ויסגדו. That this is an old tradition may be seen from the LXX: καὶ κύψαντες προσκυνοῦσιν αὐτοῖς.

Such references occur in the Book of Jeremiah too. In Jer. *28*, 4, Y (against L) has in the text ואת יְכָנְיָהוּ[73] taking as an E reading יכניה (thus L), which seems to be an isolated opinion.[74] In Jer. *41*, 12 where the current texts read וימצאו אתו אֶל־מים רבים (*sic* L),

[71] No record in Kennicott, Ch., *Bib. Heb.*[3] and Ginsburg edition II, 778, *ad loc.*

[72] Again in the Ch., Ginsburg edition and *Bib. Heb.*[3] apparatuses no difference is recorded.

[73] Not recorded in Ch., *Bib. Heb.*[3] and Ginsburg edition; further, in Jer. *28*, 1 Y reads צדקיהו later corrected into צדקיה.

[74] What occurs in one manuscript as an E/W difference may occur in another as a kethibh/ḳerē or the latter as a sebhir. The whole discussion whether "the masoretes" were correctors (cp. S.R. Driver, Samuel, 2nd ed., p. XXIX) or selectors suffers from the fact that: a) The Hebrew Bible manuscripts have not even been classified. b) Instead of working with printed and mostly eclectic texts one would

Y has the reading עַל מים רבים,[75] recording in the masora parva לבבלא ג׳ אל. The current text is, therefore, here considered as an E reading. A remarkable case occurs in *48*, 31;[76] here the masora parva of Y remarks on the text as it is in Y and L : ... איליל ... אזעק ... קיר־חרש יֶהְגֶּה : בבל̇ והגה כת̇, i.e. the text of Y, יהגה, is taken as western against E והגה (usually against W יהגה we find E kethibh יהגה and ḳerē אהגה), because the E kethibh is assumed to be והגה and the ḳerē, יהגה. Another interesting case occurs in *52*, 32: here usually a kethibh/ḳerē is recorded,[77] but Y (against L) claims this as an E/W difference: regarding the W reading ממעל לכסא מלכים, the E reading has the kethibh מלכים with the ḳerē הַמְּלָכִים. Accordingly, Y would have here an E reading.[78] Other readings of the בבלאי and מערבאי have already been discussed in the text. There thus exist three new cases of E/W differences according to Y (*36*, 12; *41*, 12; *52*, 32), of which the first is the most interesting.[79]

(b) Another group of differences distinguishes between the קדמאי and בתראי, the anteriori and posteriori. In Jer. *2*, 15, the current text runs עריו נִצְּתָה מבלי ישב[80] (*sic* L). It will be observed that all the verbs are Ḳal ישאגו ... נתנו קולם ... וישיתו ... לשמה, denoting aspects of active destruction. The kethibh נִצְּתָה or the

---

have to work with individual manuscripts where the masorah still agrees with the text. The readings seem to have differed in local schools not always for philological or exegetical reasons. Dr. Orlinsky (in Supplement to *Vetus Testamentum*. Congress vol., 1960, p. 184ff.) ingeniously suggests that "the masoretes" selected the three best manuscripts. However, a comparison of masoretic notes in different *old* manuscripts makes one wonder whether the general notion of "the masoretes" can be maintained. There were besides agreements marked differences. The matter requires further study; for example, in a number of cases, old and good eastern traditions seem to have been overruled in the ascendency of the Palestinian Bible text. The *scriptio plena* or *defectiva* is a frequent point of disagreement between eastern and western readings. They show by the way that there was no final decision concerning one canonic text taken in the second century.

[75] The letter ל looks as if an attempt was made at one time to correct it.

[76] Not in Ch.

[77] Thus in *Bib. Heb.*[3] and Ginsburg edition II, p. 938 *ad loc.*; not in Ch.

[78] המלכים actually occurs in the parallel in II. Ki. *25*, 28; cp. also LXX in Jer. *52*,32 ἐπάνω τῶν βασιλέων τῶν μετ' σὐτοῦ.

[79] The small number of new differences is also an indication of an early text. The later British Museum Ms. Harley 1528 has 215 BA/BN differences already against 117 in Mishael b. Uzziel. See L. Lipschütz in *Textus*, IV, 1964, p. 4.

[80] The kethibh as an old fem. sg. Nif. may be derived from יצת = to burn or נצה = to devastate.

ḳerē נִצְּתוּ have always been taken as a Nifʿal, which is somewhat weak. Now the ḳadhmā'ē mentioned in Y handed down a tradition [ר]ה חסֹ, i.e. נצת מבלי ישב. This is a much more forceful reading when the "principle of ambivalence" is applied:[81] נצת מ͡בלי ישב, i.e. נִצְּתָם מבלי. Understanding נצת in the sense of תץ is supported by the LXX, Pesh. and some manuscripts[82] meaning with reference to the eighth century destruction by the Assyrians, in exact parallelism: "*they* have made his land a *desolation*; his cities—*they have destroyed them being uninhabited*". On *6*, 23, the masora parva of Y records that in the verse קשת וכידון יחזיקו/אכזרי הוא ולא ירחמו the ḳadhmā'ē read like MT and the bathrā'ē, הֵמָּה.[83] On MT *8*, 10 לכן אֶתֵּן את נְשֵׁיהֶם לאחרים according to the masora parva, while the ḳadhmā'ē read אתן את נשיהם, the bathrā'ē read אתן את בניהם [84] The parallel between בניהם־יורשים (10aα) and קטן־גדול (10aβ) is rather good but is supported neither by the versions nor elsewhere in Rabbinic literature. However, the reading of the bathrā'ē here seems to be influenced by the parallels in Jer., chap. 6.[85] On *9*, 9, מעוף שמים ... נדדו הלכו the ḳadhmā'ē read like MT but the bathrā'ē נדו; the latter form of a *verbum mediae geminatae* is possible but nowhere used in MT. In MT *14*, 12, יעלו עֹלָה ומנחה the bathrā'ē simply have a plene reading עוֹלָה. On the other hand, while Y has עָרִיצִים plene in *15*, 21a and L, defective עָרִצִים, the ḳadhmā'ē record: יוד חסֹ. In *15*, 14, there is again a marked divergence. While the ḳadhmā'ē follow MT in reading אש קדחה באפי עֲלֵיכֶם תוקד, the bathrā'ē, no doubt under the influence of Jer. *17*, 4, read עַד עוֹלָם תוקד, for which there is evidence also in other manuscripts.

(c) Further, there are references to "corrected books" (ספרי מוגהי), some of them of considerable interest: in Isa. *36*, 15,

---

[81] Cp. O. Lehman in JNES, April, 1967.

[82] Further, although עיר is fem., a suffix -ūn before m in fast speech would be assimilated to m.

[83] P. Volz, Jeremiah, 2nd ed., 1928, p. 82, proposed אכזרים; Targum *ad loc.* read the plural אַכְזְרָאִין אִינּוּן. Perhaps this conceals some reading like אכזריהמא (ה)?

[84] Where תן seems to stand for [א]תן. — For MT נשיהם MS. Kennicott 237 has שניהם; בניהם is unrecorded.

[85] Similar examples are already found in the readings of the masoretes (cp. A. Sperber in *HUCA*, XVII, 1943, p. 304f. and elsewhere in medieval Hebrew manuscripts (cp. O. Lehman in *The Register of the Chicago Theological Seminary*, April, 1967).

regarding MT הצל יצילנו ה׳ לא תנתן העיר וג׳ (*sic* L)[86] Y records that in corrected scrolls the reading is ולא, which is smoother. This is actually found in the LXX, Pesh., and the prints of Soncino, 1485-86 and the ed. princeps of the entire Bible, Soncino, 1488. A very interesting reading according to Y occurs in the "corrected books" in Isa. *37*, 10, which changes the meaning considerably. Sennacherib is appealing to King Hezekiah and the Judeans. According to MT he says: "Let not your god in whom you trust deceive you *saying* 'not (לאמר לא) shall Jerusalem be given into the hand of the kind of Assyria' ". But according to the corrected scroll referred to in Y, the text reads "thus you shall say to Hezekiah . . . let not your god in whom you trust deceive you *informing him* [i.e. the king] (לאמר לו): Jerusalem will be given into the hand of the king of Assyria." This forceful reading has remained unrecorded in our standard Hebrew Bible editions.[87] But it can now be shown from the Dead Sea Scroll of Isa. 1 that this reading may indeed be old; the text there reads: אלוהיכה אשר אתה בוטח בוא לאמר לוא תנתן ..., i.e. [in whom] you trust; [go] to inform him[88] etc.

(d) There is a fourth group of readings ascribed to the dārōmā'ē, the meridiani. In Jer. *31*, 29 they read, instead of אבות אכלו, בֹּסֶר: בְּשֶׂר: with sīn. But unlike the bathrā'ē who seem to have used various deviating readings, hardly enough material has been preserved in Y to obtain a clear idea about the character of these dārōmā'ē. The variant spelling recorded in Y may be old too, for a similar variant was found already in the famous Codex Severus, which at the second destruction of Jerusalem was taken to Rome. Vespasian had it preserved in the imperial palace. In the passage in Gen. *27*, 27 ריח בני כריח שָׂדֶה (the fragrance of my son is like the fragrance of the field), instead of MT שדה (with sīn) the Codex Severus read סדה (with samekh). A. Epstein adds the

[86] Without any note in the apparatus of the *Bib. Heb.*[3]

[87] Not listed in the differences of passages changing לא/לו, respectively, cp. S. Frensdorff, Ochlah w'Ochlah, 1864, p. 105-106.

[88] With ambivalence of בוא. For the form לוא in לאמר לוא being the dative, see Isa. *36*, 22 ויגידו לוא את דברי וג׳. The traditional translation is thereby of course not excluded. But it is ancient practice already to read one text in more than one sense. One wonders whether in Isa. *37*, 10 (and the parallel in II Kings *19*, 10) LXX λέγων οὐ μὴ παραδοθῇ Ἰερουσαλὴμ does not perhaps hide Hebrew לאמר לו לא תנתן וג׳.

remark: "I do not know what סדה in CPD may mean".[89] This, however, is not a meaningful but an orthographic variant of the kind which was frequent in the first centuries in mishnaic and paitanic texts.[90]

(e) Finally, there is a group difference in kethibh/ḳerē readings, where Y sheds fresh light on problems which have been discussed for centuries and remained obscure up to the present day.

When C. D. Ginsburg in 1899 copied the list of E/W differences from the Leningrad Codex of ca. 1009,[91] under Jer. *32*, 11 he came across a passage which puzzled him. The verse runs ואקח את־ספר המקנה את החתום הַמִּצְוָה והחקים ואת הגלוי (in the American Jewish Version cheerfully translated by: I took the deed of the purchase both that which was sealed, *containing* the terms and conditions, and that which was open). MT is rather odd. It is clearly an ancient *crux interpretum.*[92] As an E reading, Ginsburg found ... אֶת החתום וְאֶת המצוה; but as a differing W reading again אֶת החתום וְאֶת? המֹ[צוה]. If the readings had agreed, they would not have been recorded as differences. Comparing the passage with the Codex Petropolitanus of 916 Ginsburg found the E text וְאֶת המצוה, but a marginal ḳerē there remarks on את לא קֹ והמצוה קֹ: ואת המצוה; instead of ואת המצוה we should read והמצוה. According to the view of this masora parva, the kethibh is ואת המצוה and the ḳerē והמצוה. But the reading found in the *ed. princeps* of the prophets, Soncino 1485-86, and the first complete Bible, Soncino, 1488, is והמצוה, i.e. as kethibh *and* ḳerē (cf. Vulgate *ad loc.*). If Ginsburg had found the right Talmudic passage, he could easily have corrected the reading in the list of E/W readings of Codex 19a of ca. 1009, which originally was no E/W difference at all.

Before Ginsburg, Norzi in *Minḥath Shay* had already discussed

---

[89] Ginsburg in Chwolson *op. cit.*, p. 52.CPD are the lists giving the Codex Severus readings.

[90] Cp., for example, Dan מִשְׂתַּכַּל ... בקרניא (Dan. *7*, 8) with Mishn. מסתכל; שִׂיד (Am. *2*, 1) with Mishn. סִיד etc.; cp. also M. Segal, *Diḳdūḳ leshōn ha-Mishnāh*, 46.

[91] Ginsburg in Chwolson, *op. cit.*, p. 156, 173.

[92] Vulgate: et stipulationes et rata presupposes וְהַמצוה וְהַחקים; Targum כהלכתא וכידחזה takes it like כמצוה וכחקים. Correspondingly, Rashi paraphrases כשהוא חתום כדת וחוק (when it was sealed according to law and statute). Ḳimḥi takes it like a construct ספר המצוה והחקים.

the various opinions concerning this passage. When he somewhat loosely refers to "Nedharim, section 'ēn bēn ha-muddār (hanā'āh mē-ḥabhērō)", i.e. "regarding him that is forbidden by vow to have any benefit from his fellow there is no difference . . .", he means section IV. Among the Bible passages "written but not read" Norzi lists את of המצוה. He then forwards two opinions on where את המצוה is to be found: according to Rabbenu Nissim in Deut., Sidra Wā-'ethḥannān. But, it is added, "that does not occur in the books we have". The second opinion, that of Rashi, is that the passage in question occurs in Jeremiah. "In my opinion" adds Norzi, "this refers to the fact that the word את seems superfluous". He further remarks that according to another opinion this is an E/W difference; the W reading being אֶת החתום הַמצוה (as we have it today) and the E reading, את החתום ואת המצוה. This would seem to solve Ginsburg's puzzle, but it would mean correcting the list of the Codex B19a of ca. 1009 (W omits ואת). In reality Norzi had the wrong reading to start with, and apparently even in the early half of the tenth century things were no longer clear in the masorah.

The next scholar to refer to the talmudic list of passages which are "written but not read" is S. Frensdorff.[93] He used the masoretic material available at the time. He lists eight cases, three from the Former, four from the Latter Prophets and one from Ruth: 1) אם in בני המלך מתו כי אִם אמנון לבדו מת (II Sam. *13*, 33);[94] 2) אם in ויען אתי ... חי ה׳ ... כי אִם במקום אשר יהיה שם אדני ... כי שם יהיה עבדך (II Sam. *15*, 21). The analogy of the oath כי כאשר נשבע ... כי כן אעשה־לו (II Sam. *3*, 9) shows that אם has wrongly been introduced here, apparently from the following אם־למות אם־לחיים (v. 21bβ);[95] 3) נא in יסלח [נא] ה׳ לעבדך (II Kings *5*, 18). This case is different

---

[93] Ochlach W'Ochlah, p. 98.

[94] Although the parallel in v. 32 has כי אמנון, כי אם is defensible (cp. S. R. Driver, Sam., *ad loc.*). Already the Codex Petropolitanus lists אם as a kethibh we-lō' ḳerē, but Leningrad Codex B 19a has אם only. On the other hand, the Complutensian Polyglot, and Felix Pratensis' Bible of 1517 have כי only (as kethibh and ḳerē); cp. Vulgate, Pesh., etc. Originally this seems to have been a duplicate reading: a) כִי אמנון לבדו מת; b) אִם אמנון לבדו מת > כי אם. Either reading makes good sense.

[95] Codex Petropolitanus again lists this as a kethibh we-lō' ḳerē. Vulgate has quoniam throughout, apparently = כי. L, however, has אם only, which in the formula of an oath is less good.

from the two preceding ones, for already talmudic texts had here a word נא,[96] which is missing in our modern Bible texts.[97] Frensdorff lists two cases of dittography: 4) Jer. *51*, 3 (ידרך ידרך) and 5) Ezek. *48*, 16 (חמש חמש); and 6) Ruth *3*, 12: אם in ועתה אמנם כי אִם גאל אנכי. As for אם, the latter case is mentioned in Ned. 37b as, a kethibh we-lō' ḳerē.[98] There are two additional cases in Frensdorff § 98:7: Jer. *38*, 16 (חי ה׳ אֶת אשר עשה לנו הנפש הזאת) and 8) *39*, 12 (ואל תעשה לו מאומה רע כי אִם כאשר ידבר וג׳). It is, however, remarkable that the passage referred to by Norzi no longer occurs in this masoretic list of kethibh we-lō' ḳerē, a clear indication that in the later Middle Ages the talmudic passage had already been obscured and displaced by others.

A. Sperber[99] in discussing the list of such cases in Ned. 37b rightly observed that the talmudic list of five cases was later expanded into eight. The talmudic list compared with § 98 contains: 1) II Kings *5*, 18 (נא; no. 3 above); 2) a reading זאת המצוה; 3) Jer. *51*, 3 (ידרך; no. 4 above); 4) Ezek. *48*, 16 (חמש; no 5 above); 5) Ruth *3*, 12 (אם; no. 6 above). It will be seen that the masoretic list left out one talmudic case and added four new ones (nos. 1, 2, 7 and 8); three of them being other cases of אם. Sperber already saw that 6) את אשר later replaced the talmudic case :זאת המצוה. The question is, where does the passage זאת המצוה implying a kethibh we-lō' ḳerē occur in the Bible? Sperber, no doubt relying on Norzi, considered the passage untraceable. In reality

---

[96] Cp. Ned. 37b.

[97] Frensdorff clearly refers to the first יסלח in v. 18, but the note in *Bib. Heb.*[3] refers to the second יסלח נא ! נא is missing also in the LXX (*ἱλάσεται κύριος* : cp. the second יסלח נא with *ὑλάσεται δὴ κ.*), Vulgate, etc. According to Ned. 37b and this masorah, the talmudic reading was twice ... לדבר הזה יסלח נא (v. 18a) בהשתחותי ... יסלח נא (v. 18b), but the targumic text like Lagarde's LXX omitted נא both times. This is the case also in the Prophets, Soncino, 1485; the Soncino Bible of 1488; the Naples edition of Soncino ca. 1492, etc.

[98] There is, however, a deviating opinion, which no doubt in analogy to v. 9 end (כִּי גֹאֵל אתה) reads here too כִּי גֹאֵל אנכי with כֹ as kethibh *and* ḳerē. That is actually found in the Complutensian Polyglot. Some Hebrew and Greek manuscripts also read כי only. The versions differ: the Alexandrinus and Vaticanus do not seem to have read עתה. One might think of a conflated reading: ( ) וכי אמנם גאל אנכי (this, though, leaves the second kī unexplained). ועתה ( ) אם גאל אנכי

[99] *Op. cit.*, p. 299f.

Rashi when referring to Jeremiah meant Jer. *32*, 11 and Rabbenu Nissim when referring to Wā-'ethḥannān meant Deut. *6*, 1. Only instead of Norzi's ואת המצוה, one has to read זאת המצוה. The talmudic passage has never been found in any manuscript as is shown also by Kennicott's material.[100] Even the Codex Petropolitanus of 916 no longer knew the right tradition. It can now also be stated that Rashi had the better tradition, for in the Adler manuscript from the Yezd genizah (Y) in Jer. *32*, 11, the text actually reads החתום זאת המצוה, the reading quoted by Ned. 37b. Y is unique in this reading, another indication of the great age of its consonantal tradition. Later on, however, an attempt was made to erase the word זאת to adapt the text to that of our current Bibles. A note in the masora parva, being somewhat later than the original masorah, then added the remark: בבלאי כתׄ זאת. As Chwolson's and Norzi's discussions show, what originally was a case of kethibh/ḳerē later became a difference of the בבלאי (or מדנחאי) and מערבאי.[101]

As for cases of ḳerē we-lō' kethibh, the talmudic passage lists seven cases,[102] of which only two occurring in Jeremiah can be

---

[100] On *32*, II, Kennicott observes on ואקח את ספר המקנה את החתום המצוה: את 2⁰: ואת in eleven manuscripts; החתום: ה *sup. ras.* 93; והמצוה: in 9 + 1 mss. (i.e. 1 "*primo*"); את המצוה in 2 mss.; ואת המצוה in 5 mss.

[101] The two other cases of kethibh we-lō' ḳerē in Ned. 37b taken from the Prophets are less interesting as dittographies. But even here Y has a tradition of its own. In Jer. *51*, 3 Y originally read no dittography: אל יִדְרֹךְ ( ) הדרך with the masora parva remarking ידרך כתׄ [ולא קרי], although actually Y's text does *not* exhibit the dittography. A later hand, noticing this discrepancy, added a second ידרך. The first of Frensdorff's additional Jeremiah passages (*38*, 16) listing את אשר as a kethibh we-lō' ḳerē is not in agreement with talmudic tradition and is therefore missing in the original text of Y (but it does occur in the text of L and Q). The reading is secondary both from a masoretic and a syntactical point of view. But a later hand added את in the text of Y, accompanied by a later note in the masora parva (את כתׄ ולא קׄ). In the other Frensdorff passage (Jer. *39*, 12) Y like L has כי אִם כאשר ידבר (an erased masoretic note seems to have been [כתׄ] ו[לא] קׄ). This reading also seems to be based on a duplicate reading

ואל תעש לו מאומה רֽע { כי אם ()אשר / כאשר } ידבר אליך כן עשה עמו

both of which are syntactically defensible.

[102] In Ned. 37b: 1) II Sam. *8*, 3 (להשיב ידו בִּנְהַר־ [פְּרָת]) with the ḳerē supplied from I Chron. *18*, 3; 2) II Sam. *16*, 23 (כאשר יִשְׁאַל־ [אִישׁ] בדבר);

checked. Here Y shows the following evidence: in Jer. *31*, 38, Y reads הנה ימים [ ] נאם ה׳, where according to Ned. 37b the ḳerē is בָּאִים[103] and Y has in the masora parva באים ק. In Jer. *50*, 29, Y has אל יהי [ ] פלטה remarking in what is left of the masorah: לה ק.[104] Y, therefore, simply follows talmudic and masoretic tradition without any deviations.

f) Last, there remains the question of any majuscules (in Isa. *56*, 10)[105] or minuscules (Jer. *14*, 2).[106] As is normal, it seems, in such early codes none are found in Y. With regard to Jer. *39*, 13[107] (וּנְבוּשַׁזְבָּץ), with small final nūn, the masora parva remarks: בן ג ק נונין זעיר; i.e. as to *-bān* there are three cases (Jer. *39*, 13; Isa. *44*, 14; Prov. *16*, 28) where minuscule nūns are written. Actually, however, the scribe wrote a zayin at the end. This is, therefore, really a case of kethibh (ז־) and ḳerē (ן). The other example (Isa. *44*, 14) has faded. There is then no traceable case in Y of majuscules and minuscules.

6. None of the scholars who have expressed an opinion concerning the date of Y have made a detailed study of its textual tradition. It is not enough to look over the shapes of the letters and the Tiberian vocalization as it now appears. None of the Bible codices in our possession has altogether escaped the influence of Ben,

---

האלהים 3)Jer. *31*, 38; 4)Jer. *50*, 29; 5) Ruth *2*, 11 (הגד הגד לי[אֶת] כל אשר עשית) which according to one tradition is given as a reading of the מדנחאי! 6) Ruth *3*, 5 (אשר תֹּאמְרִי [אֵלַי] אעשה); 7) Ruth *3*, 17 (אָמַר [אֵלַי] אל־תבואי). Again, in the later masorah (cp. Frensdorff, *op. cit.*, § 97) the list of such cases was expanded to ten, adding: 8) Jud. *20*, 13 (ולא אבו [בְּנֵי] בִּנְיָמִן לשמע), which is actually a case of "ambivalence", not "haplography" as in Ginsburg, p. 313; 9) II Sam. *18*, 20 (כי עַל־[כֵּן]־בֶּן המלך); 10) II Kings *19*, 37 (ואדרמלך ושראצר [בָּנָיו] הִכֻּהוּ) but see *Bib. Heb.*[3] *ad loc.*; 11) Isa. *37*, 32 (ה׳ [צבאות]), where, however, our texts have this word already. No doubt instead of Isa. *37*, 32 the parallel (II Kings *19*, 3) should be read in Frensdorff's list, where צבאות is actually missing. In fact, in the masora parva of Y, Isa. *37*, 32 is—rightly—not given as a ḳerē we-lō' kethibh.

[103] But באים appears as kethibh *and* ḳerē in the prints of Soncino, 1485-86; the Brescia Bible of 1494; the Complutensian Polyglot and before that in the LXX, Vulgate (veniunt), Targum, Pesh., etc.

[104] לה appears as a kethibh *and* ḳerē in the prints of Soncino, 1485-86; Sonc. 1488; Brescia 1494 and the Complutensian Polyglot; cp. also לה in v. 26 end.

[105] Cp. Frensdorff, *op. cit.*, § 83.

[106] *Op. cit.*, § 84.

[107] *Op. cit.*, § 178.

Asher. Elkan Adler, who owned the manuscript, suggested the ninth century.[108] Dr. Murtonen, who saw the manuscript in New York, seemed to tend towards the 11th century as a conservative estimate. Mr. Luzki in his typed catalog suggests the "tenth to eleventh century".

Usually the copyist and the vocalizer are two different persons. That seems to have been the case here too. The vocalizer, it is true, on the whole followed the developed Tiberian system of vocalization. That rules out a date as early as the ninth century.[109] But the Vorlage used by the copyist was clearly a Babylonian manuscript. It contained over 50 % eastern readings, which, as far as the writer is aware, has been proved for no other surviving Bible codex. Ben Asher and Ben Naphtali flourished about the middle of the tenth century. This constitutes the *terminus a quo*, since the constant disagreements about one reading or another cannot be older than the dispute between these two schools. Mishael b. Uzziel compiled his *Kitāb al-khilaf* listing the differences between BA and BN about the middle of the eleventh century.[110] That is usually done at a time when the knowledge of such minute differences is about to be forgotten. In fact, by the twelfth century the school of BA had carried the day, and Maimonides (d. 1204) took BA as a model codex. The middle of the eleventh century, therefore, is likely to constitute the *terminus ad quem*. The manuscript shows that various readings were turned into BA and some into BN. The latter case is so rare in the surviving codices that it seems reasonable to assume that this was done at a time when the issue was still felt to be a live one. Moreover, the manuscript, contains some 50 % BN readings. The Vorlage of the manuscript, therefore, clearly favored this school, which becomes less likely after the second half of the eleventh century. Moreover, the masora parva contains various readings which are recorded nowhere else, as far as is known at present, and therefore must go back to a very early time. We should also bear in mind another aspect. This is the time of the marked rivalry between the Palestinian and Babylonian schools, which came to a head in the famous controversy about the calendar between the Babylonian

---

[108] *United Synagogue Recorder*, IV, I, January, 1924.

[109] Cp. P. Kahle, *Vetus Testamentum*, I, 1951, p. 165.

[110] On differences between the masoretes see P. Kahle, Cairo Geniza, 2nd ed., 1959, p. 75f.

Gaon Saadia (d. 942) and the Palestinian Ben Meir. The Palestinian school adopted the text of Ben Asher. Saadia polemized against Ben Asher.[111] It seems, therefore, likely that there was a time in Babylonia when they favored Ben Naphtali.[112] The consonantal traditions emerging in the Vorlage of the manuscript from the genizah in Yezd are clearly older than the 10th to 11th century system of vocalization used. Considering the various aspects, we may sum up by saying manuscript Y is unique among the preserved codices. It really comes from a genizah; it contains a Babylonian consonantal text of a controversial kind and, for the reasons stated, should be dated between the last decades of the tenth and the early half of the eleventh century. This manuscript is, therefore, one of the most valuable of the Seminary collection.

APPENDIX I: *Correspondence Table of E/W Readings in the Book of Jeremiah*

Jer.	*Y*	*L*	*Comp*	*S*	*Q*
2,20	W	W	W	W	W
4,30	E	W	W	W	W
5,17	E	W	W	W	E
6,6[a]	W	W	W	W	W
6,6[b]	W	W	W	W	W
8,7	W	W	W	W	W
9,23	E	W	W	W	W
10,13	E	W	W	W	W (kethibh and ḳerē הארץ)
10,18	E	W	E	E	E
11,11	E	W	W	W	W
12,14	E	W	W	W	W
13,18	W	W	W	W	W
13,20	W	W	W	W	E

111 In the poem ʾessāʾ meshālī, published by M. Lewin. Jerusalem, 1943.

112 It has been generally assumed that Elijah Levita (in *Massoreth ha-massoreth*, ed. C. D. Ginsburg, p. 113f.) was wrong in associating Jewry in the eastern orient with favoring BN readings (thus Kahle and Lipschütz, *op. cit.*, p. 13.) Levita lived in Italy in the former half of the 16th century. Many Hebrew manuscripts now found in various European libraries were at one time or another in Italy, the well known Mediterranean bridge for Jewish travellers to and from the Orient. It is not at all unlikely that Levita still saw manuscripts of a type similar to Y, which have since disappeared.

	Jer.	*Y*	*L*	*Comp*	*S*	*Q*
	15,14	W	W	W	W	W
	23,35	E	W	W	W	W
	26,8	E	W	W	W	W
	26,24	W	W	W	W	W
	27,19	E	W	W	W	W
	29,7	E	W	W	W	W
	29,22	E	W	W	W	W
	32,11	E	W	W	W	W
	32,19	E	W	W	W	W
	32,34	E	W	W	W	W
	33,3	W	W	W	W	W
	34,2[a]	E	W	W	W	W
	34,2[b]	W	W	W	W	W
	35,3	W	W	W	W	W
	35,11	E	E	E	E	W
	35,17	E	E	E	E	W
	36,23	E	W	W	W	W
	38,16	W	W	W	W	W
	39,11	W	W	W	W	W
(accord. to Y:)	41,12	E	E	E	E	E
	42,6	W	W	W	W	W
	44,18	E	W	W	W	W
	44,25	W	W	W	W	W
	45,1	E	W	W	W	W
	45,4	W	W	W	W	W
	46,2	W	W	W	W	W
	46,16	E	W	W	W	W
	48,1	W	W	W	W	W
	48,17	E	W	W	W	W
	48,31	W	W	W	W	W
	48,36	E	E	E	E	W
	48,41	E	W	W	W	W
	48,44	W	W	W	W	W
	49,19	E	W	W	W	W
	49,20	E	E	E	E	W
	50,6	W	W	W	W	E
	50,9	E	W	W	W	W
	50,11	W	E	E	W	E
	50,20	E	W	W	W	W
	50,29	W	W	W	W	W
	51,46	E	W	E	W	W
	52,2	E	E	E	E	E
(accord. to Y:)	52,32	E	E	E	E	E

Comparing L (based on Leningrad Codex B 19a), the Complutensian Polyglot (Comp), the Snaith edition of the Hebrew Bible (S), and the Qoren (Q) edition, it is seen that they all have some eight to nine eastern readings, whereas the Manuscript from Yezd (Y) has some 52 E/W differences and some 31 eastern readings. If we bear in mind that in some E/W differences where Y is credited with a western reading, it is supported only by one manuscript, the percentage of eastern readings in Y might even be greater. In any case, while none of the current Bible editions has a purely western text, Y's text is overwhelmingly eastern or Babylonian.

APPENDIX II: *Conspectus of BA/BN readings in Jeremiah*

Jer.	*Y*	*C*	*L*	*S*	*Q*	
1,7	BA	BA	BA	BA	BA/BNm	(m = mixed)
2,6	BN	BN	BA	BA	BA	
2,22	BA	BN	nBA	BA	BN	(n = now)
3,9	BN	BN	BA	BA	BN	
4,16	BA	-1)	BA	BA	BA	(1) = illegible)
5,22	BA	BN	BA	BA	BA	
7,13	BA	2)	BA	BA	BA/BNm.	(2) = diff. reading)
7,25	BA	BA	BA	BA	BN	
7,33	BN	BN	BA	BA	BA	
9,3	BN	BN	BA	BA	BA	
9,16	BA	BN	nBA	BA	BN	
10,20	BN	BN	BA	BA	BA	
10,24	BA	BA	BA	BA	BN	
11,7	BA	BA	nBA	BA	BN	
14,14	BA	BA	BA	BA	BA	
14,18	BN	BN	sBN	BN	BN	(s = similar to)
15,17	BA	BN	BA	BN	BN	
18,11	BA	BN	nr	BN	nr.	(nr = neither BA/BN)
21,9	BN	BN	BA	BA	BA	
22,24	BN	BN	BA	BA	BA	
22,28	BN	BN	BA	BA	BA	
23,25	BA	BN	BA	BA	BA	
25,14	BA	BA	BA	BA	BA	
25,29	BN	-1)	nBA	BN	BN	
26,12	BN	BN	nBA?	BN	BA	
27,15	BN	BA	BA	BA	BA	
29,18	BN	BN	BA	BA	BA	
29,23	BN	BN	BA	BA	BN	

Jer.	*Y*	*C*	*L*	*S*	*Q*	
32,35	BN	BN	BA	BA	BA	
34,1	BA	BN	BA	BA	BA	
34,1	BN	BN	BA	BA	BN	
35,15	BN	BN	nBA	nr.	nr.	
36,12	BA	BN	BA	BA	BA	
36,23	BN	BA	BA	BA	BN	
37,10	BA	BA	BA	BA	BA	
37,13	BN	BN	BA	BN	BN	
37,19	BN	BA	BA	BA	BA	
38,6	BA	BA	BA	BN	BA	
38,11	BN	BN	BA	BN	BA	
38,17	BA	BN	BA	BA	BA	
39,5	BA	BN	BA	BA	BA	
42,1	BN	BA	nBA	BA	BN	
43,2	(BN)	BN	BA	BA	BN	
44,14	BA	BA	BA	BA	BA	
44,26	BN	BN	BA	BA	BA	
44,28	BN	BN	BA	BA/BNm	BA/BNm	
48,13	BA	BN	BA	BA	BA	
48,19	BA	BA	BA	BA	BA	
50,9	BN	BN	BA	BA	BN	(acord. to H[113])
51,3	BN	BA/BN	BA/BN	BN	BA	
51,10	BA	BA	BA	BA	BA	
52,12	BA	BA	BA	BA	BA	

A comparison of the five texts shows that the Codex Cairensis (C), dated "895", with two cases illegible and one different reading, has the largest number of BN readings (some 34 cases) and cannot possibly be even an older form of BA, as Kahle suggested. Y has some 50% (25 to 26 cases) BN readings; Y and C go together in only 20 cases of BN and 11 cases of BA, i.e. they constitute different traditions. Neither S nor Q are anything like pure BA texts: in S, there are 11 cases which are not BA (one is neither BA nor BN; one is mixed and nine are BN); in Q we find even 20 such cases (i.e. two neither BA nor BN, three mixed and 15 cases of BN). As a Bible text, L is still superior as a BA text to S and Q and can now be confronted with Y, which is largely a BN text.

113 Source H given by Lipschütz in his article in *Textus*, vol. II, p. 64.

A 15TH CENTURY ṢAFAVID PROPAGANDIST AT HARĀT*

by R. M. Savory
University of Toronto

Preface

Some years ago I collected all the material then available relating to the activities of Muʿīn al-Dīn ʿAlī Ḥusaynī Sarābī Tabrīzī, known as Qāsim al-Anvār, the eminent 15th century Ṣafavid *dāʿī*.[1] Since that time the publication of new material, in particular by Jean Aubin and Saʿid Nafīsī,[2] has made it possible to draw in the picture with firmer strokes, though some areas still remain obscure.

Historical Introduction

On Friday 23 Rabīʿ II 830/21 February 1427, as the Tīmūrid ruler Shāhrukh was leaving the Masjid-i Jāmiʿ at Harāt, he was stabbed in the stomach by a man named Aḥmad the Lur, who had approached him on the pretext of wishing to present a petition. The wound was not lethal, and Shāhrukh recovered.[3] The would-be assassin was cut down by the royal guards.

A court of inquiry was set up, presided over by Shāhrukh's son Mīrzā Bāysunqur. Aḥmad the Lur, who alone could have provided a clue to the motive for the attack, had been killed, but a key was found among his belongings which, it was discovered, fitted the lock of a merchant's chamber or office (*ḥujra*) in one of the bazaars. Aḥmad the Lur apparently plied the trade of

* In its original, shorter, form, this paper was read at the 176th meeting of the American Oriental Society, held at Philadelphia, April 1966.

[1] See R. M. Savory, *The Development of the Early Ṣafawid State under Ismaʿīl and Ṭahmāsp*, unpublished thesis, London 1958, pp. 107-123.

[2] J. Aubin (ed.), *Matériaux pour la Biographie de Shāh Niʿmatullāh Walī Kermānī*, Tehran/Paris 1956; Saʿīd Nafīsī (ed.), *Kulliyyāt-i Qāsim-i Anvār*, Tehran 1337s./1958-59.

[3] The article by V. F. Büchner in *Encyclopaedia of Islam* 1st ed., vol. 2, 1927, pp. 798-99 (Ḳāsim-i Anwār), contains the erroneous statement that "the king, S̲h̲āh-Ruk̲h̲, was murdered by a Ḥurūfī in 830" (1426/7). Actually, Shāhrukh continued to reign for another twenty years, until 850/1447.

ṭāqiya-dūz, or maker of the *ṭāqiya*,[4] a tall, round hat which was used either on its own or as a base around which to wind a turban.

The residents of the bazaar named various persons who had frequented Aḥmad the Lur. One of these was Mawlānā Maʿrūf, a celebrated calligraphist, scholar and poet, formerly at the court of the Jalā'irid ruler at Baghdad. Mawlānā Maʿrūf was arrested and interrogated. He declared that the man behind the attack was ʿAḍud b. Mawlānā Majd al-Dīn Astarābādī, the leader of a group of Ḥurūfīs, who night and day held secret meetings and engaged in discussions of an impious and heretical nature (*mubāḥatha-yi kufr wa zandaqa*). The Ḥurūfīs were then arrested. They confessed to a conspiracy against the life of Shāhrukh, but asserted that Aḥmad the Lur had anticipated them in this design. Despite this disclaimer, which, incidentally, failed to save their lives, there is little doubt that Aḥmad the Lur was, in fact, a member of this Ḥurūfī group. The reference to hat-makers (*ṭāqiya-dūz*), and a reference elsewhere to drapers (*bazzāzān*), indicate the social class from which the Ḥurūfīs drew their adherents at Harāt. At this juncture the Ṣafavid *dāʿī* Qāsim al-Anvār fell under suspicion, because Aḥmad the Lur had been seen in his company. Qāsim al-Anvār was expelled from Harāt, lived for a while at the court of the Tīmūrid ruler Ulugh Beg at Samarqand, and finally returned to Kharjird in Khurāsān, where he died in 837/1433.

This, in the barest outline, is an account of events at Harāt in the year 830/1427.

Problems Connected with Qāsim al-Anvār's Activities as a dāʿī

Qāsim al-Anvār was born in 757/1356 in the Sarāb district of Tabrīz in Ādharbāyjān. At an early age he became a disciple (*murīd*) of the second Ṣafavid *shaykh* Ṣadr al-Dīn Mūsā at Ardabīl. After completing his training there *summa cum laude*, he went to Gīlān, where "he sated the thirst of postulants with the limpid water of gnosis." From Gīlān he went to Khurāsān. His stay at Nīshāpūr was cut short by the opposition of the *ʿulamā*, and he moved to Harāt, from which base he disseminated the Ṣafavid *daʿva* in Khurāsān for more than half a century. At Harāt, he achieved instant success as a *murshid* (spiritual director). He possessed a magnetic personality; every sceptic who approached him

[4] See R. P. A. Dozy, *Dictionnaire détaillé des Noms des Vêtements chez les Arabes*, Amsterdam 1843, pp. 280 ff.

became his convert, until most of the notables and sons of *amīrs* at the Tīmūrid capital became his disciples. When he was expelled from the city in 1427, "people lined the street on both sides from the ʿIrāq gate to the end of the avenue."

1. The first question to be asked is, was Qāsim al-Anvār a Ḥurūfī? E. G. Browne, the only scholar until recent times who has paid any attention to Qāsim al-Anvār, thought he might be. Influenced, perhaps, by his predilection for the heterodox and the heretical, he says: "there is good reason to suspect that Qásimū'l-Anwár was at any rate something of an antinomian, even if he had not some quasi-political relation with the Shiʿite partisans of the still uncrowned Ṣafawīs, or with the still more irreconcilable Ḥurúfí heretics."[5] After quoting one of Qāsim al-Anvār's poems, Browne comments: "although the traces of the Ḥurúfí influence in this poem are unmistakeable, it cannot on such evidence alone be proved that Qásimu'l-Anwár was actually a member of that sect, though his association with an admitted disciple of Fadlu'llāh of Astarábád and the suspicion which he thereby incurred afford strong corroboration of this conjecture."[6]

In my view, Qāsim al-Anvār was definitely not a member of the Ḥurūfī sect. Had he been, it is unlikely that he would have escaped execution. Many Ḥurūfī doctrines, in particular that of *ḥulūl* ("incarnationism"), were definitely heretical, and the Ḥurūfī sect had operated as an underground organization ever since the execution of its founder in 796/1393-4.

The label "Ḥurūfī" was a convenient one to use in the 15th century Muslim world as a means of getting rid of one's enemies. Browne thought he saw traces of Ḥurūfī ideas in one poem, but the overwhelming impression given by Qāsim al-Anvār's poetry is that he was a convinced and sincere Ṣūfī, using language which had been the stock-in-trade of Ṣūfīs everywhere for several centuries. His heroes are all Ṣūfīs of the "regular" rather than the "irregular" type, and it is inconceivable that he would have been held in such high regard by such eminent contemporary Ṣūfīs as Shāh Niʿmat Allāh Valī had he been tainted by Ḥurūfī ideas.[7] If one is looking

[5] E. G. Browne, *A Literary History of Persia,* vol. III, Cambridge 1951, p. 475.

[6] *Ibid.*, p. 479.

[7] According to the source quoted by Aubin, p. 38, the infant Qāsim al-Anvār is said to have been brought before Shāh Ni ʿmat Allāh Valī, who extolled his great qualities.

for "unmistakeable" influences in Qāsim al-Anvār's poetry, I suggest the *ghazals* of Jalāl al-Dīn Rūmī.

2. If we allow that Qāsim al-Anvār was not a Ḥurūfī, are we to absolve him of complicity in the attempt on Shārhukh's life? Even Browne does not go as far as to suggest that he was a party to this plot. There is nothing unusual, however, in the fact that Ḥurūfīs were involved. The Ḥurūfīs imitated the Isma'īlīs in many respects, for instance in the use of mystic numbers, and they also used assassination as a means of revenging themselves on their enemies. Qāsim al-Anvār, however, had nothing to gain by such an action; on the contrary, the reaction might have undone the work of half a century of patient propaganda activity in Khurāsān. The Ṣafavid *da'va* had not yet entered its militant phase, and the organization of the Ṣafaviyya had not yet reached the point at which its leaders could hope to effect a successful revolution.

3. If, then, Qāsim al-Anvār was *not* a Ḥurūfī, and was *not* involved in the assassination attempt, why was he expelled from Harāt? He was, of course, *suspected* of complicity, because the would-be assassin happened to lodge in property owned by him, and one is, to some extent at least, known by the company one keeps. But in my view the political and religious authorities merely used this as a convenient excuse to get rid of a man whose influence among the people had become a source of embarrassment to them. The suggestion made by some sources, notably the *Maṭla'-i Sa'dayn*,[8] that Mīrzā Bāysunqur expelled Qāsim al-Anvār from the city because of a personal grudge, is clearly absurd. In fact it was Bāysunqur who interceded for Qāsim al-Anvār before the court of inquiry, according to the *Sharafnāma*.[9] Nor is the suggestion that he was expelled because he displayed independence of spirit and a lack of proper respect towards Shāhrukh and his sons, an adequate explanation. Dawlatshāh is, I am sure, nearer the mark when he says that "intriguers represented to Sulṭān Shāhrukh that it was not expedient for that Sayyid to remain in that city, because the majority of the young men had become his disciples, and it might be that mischief would derive from that situation."[10] This

---

[8] Kamāl al-Dīn 'Abd al-Razzāq Samarqandī, *Maṭla'-i Sa'dayn* (ed. Muḥammad Shafī'), vol. II, 2nd ed. Lahore 1941, Part 1, p. 593.

[9] Sharaf al-Dīn Bitlīsī, *Sharafnāma* (ed. V. Véliaminof-Zernof), St. Petersburg 1860-62, pp. 88-9.

[10] *Tadhkirat al-Awliyā'*, quoted in Nafīsī, p. 12.

view is confirmed by the eminent Tīmūrid *amīr* and *littérateur* ʿAlī Shīr Navā'ī, in the *Majālis al-Nafā'is*, who states that Shāhrukh became alarmed at the "public turmoil" (*hujūm-i ʿāmm*), and "granted Qāsim al-Anvār permission to go to Samarqand." Navā'ī adds significantly that this treatment by officialdom merely increased Qāsim al-Anvār's popularity.[11] Another version of Navā'ī's work says that Shāhrukh, because of the size of the crowds of people who came together on account of their love of Qāsim al-Anvār, feared a revolt.[12] The word used for "revolt", *khurūj*, is the one used to describe Ismaʿīl's "coming" in 905/1499, when he emerged from hiding in Gīlān to carry through the final stages of the Ṣafavid revolution. It seems probable, therefore, that this picked Ṣafavid *dāʿī* was expelled because he had been too successful in his mission, and constituted, in the eyes of the political authorities, a threat to the state.

4. Just how unorthodox were the ideas and views of Qāsim al-Anvār? On the one hand, we have the weighty testimony of Jāmī, in the *Nafaḥāt al-Uns*. People, he says, "were divided on the question of accepting or rejecting" Qāsim al-Anvār. Most of the disciples of Qāsim al-Anvār, he says, "were beyond the pale of the Islamic faith (*az rabqa-yi dīn-i islām khārij būdand*), and had entered the sphere of *ibāḥat* (i.e., abrogation of the requirements of Islam) and contempt for the canon law and the *sunna*." Jāmī admits, however, that Qāsim al-Anvār himself was "undefiled by all this." In Jāmī's opinion, Qāsim al-Anvār's excessive absorption with the nature of the Divine Unity, and his readiness to range over the whole field of speculation and inquiry, enabled unscrupulous people to pervert his esoteric teachings for their own purposes. Qāsim al-Anvār, he says, although innocent himself, was aware of the corrupting influence exercised by his disciples on more "orthodox" Ṣūfīs.[13]

We have to remember that Jāmī was, "in spite of his mysticism, a thoroughly orthodox Sunnī"[14] and he may well have been scandalized by beliefs and practices which were commonplace among Ṣūfīs of the more ecstatic type. It is difficult to believe that, had Qāsim al-Anvār been guilty of *ibāḥat* and contempt for the

[11] *Ibid.*, p. 18.
[12] *Ibid.*, p. 20.
[13] Savory, pp. 116-17.
[14] Browne, vol. III, pp. 521, 541.

canon law and the *sunna*, he would have been held in such high esteem by two such champions of orthodoxy as the Tīmūrid rulers Shāhrukh and Ulugh Beg. On the contrary, he and his disciples would have been liable to impeachment on a charge of heresy. Doctrines which could be classified as *ibāḥat*, "making licit what is illicit," constituted a threat to the existing political institution, and would have been suppressed ruthlessly.

We should also remember that Jāmī, depending as he did on Tīmūrid patronage, may in some degree be considered the "official spokesman" of Tīmūrid Sunnism. It is not unreasonable to suppose, therefore, that he would wish to show the Ṣafavid propagandist in the most unfavorable light. The *Nafaḥāt al-Uns* was written in 883/1478-9. By that date the Ṣafavids had entered the final phase of their preparations for revolution. Abandoning peaceful missionary methods, they had committed themselves to a policy of armed rebellion to achieve their ends, and the Tīmurīds were one of the obstacles which stood between them and supremacy in Iran.

There is a curious passage in the *Nafaḥāt al-Uns* which supports my contention that Jāmī was making a deliberate attempt to discredit the Ṣafavid shaykhs and, in particular, Shaykh Ṣadr al-Dīn Mūsā, head of the Ṣafavid Order from 735/1334 to 794/1391-2. Jāmī states that, *after* Shaykh Ṣadr al-Dīn Ardabīlī, Qāsim al-Anvār turned for guidance to Shaykh Ṣadr al-Dīn [ʿAlī] Yamanī, a companion of Shaykh Awḥad al-Dīn Kirmānī. Jāmī further states that Qāsim al-Anvār is reputed to have thought highly of Shaykh Ṣadr al-Dīn ʿAli Yamanī, and to have displayed great devotion toward him. Jāmī does not record Qāsim al-Anvār's attitude toward the Ṣafavid *shaykh*. Finally, Jāmī alleges that he saw the "genealogy of discipleship" (*nisbat-i irādat*) of Qāsim al-Anvār, written by the hand of some of the latter's followers, and in this document Shaykh Ṣadr al-Dīn ʿAlī Yamanī was mentioned, *but not* Shaykh Ṣadr al-Dīn Ardabīlī.[15]

Jāmī's allegations seem to have no foundation in fact. First, Shaykh Ṣadr al-Dīn ʿAlī Yamanī's name is mentioned only by Jāmī and by works based on Jāmī, the majority of them of late date. Second, this Shaykh Ṣadr al-Dīn ʿAlī Yamanī cannot be traced in any of the *tadkhiras* or elsewhere. Third, the Awḥad al-Dīn Kirmānī who is mentioned as being "one of the companions"

---

[15] See Savory, p. 115.

(*aṣḥāb*) of Shaykh Ṣadr al-Dīn ʿAlī Yamanī, died in 635/1237-8. Even if Shaykh Ṣadr al-Dīn ʿAlī Yamanī had lived for thirty years after the death of his "companion," he would still have died nearly a century before Qāsim al-Anvār was born. Further, even if Shaykh Ṣadr al-Dīn ʿAlī Yamanī were the disciple of Awḥad al-Dīn Kirmānī, as is alleged by the 17th century *Safīnat al-Awliyā'*,[16] he must still have died at least half a century before the birth of Qāsim al-Anvār.

A further piece of evidence may be submitted in support of the argument that Shaykh Ṣadr al-Dīn Mūsā Ardabīlī was the spiritual guide whom Qāsim al-Anvār revered above all others. In his poems, Qāsim al-Anvār uses the following forms of *takhallus*, or *nom de plume:* Qāsim, Qāsimī, Qāsim-i Anvār, Shāh Qāsim. All these forms are variants of the nickname Qāsim-i Anwār, which was bestowed on him by Shaykh Ṣadr al-Dīn Mūsā Ardabīlī as a result of a vision experienced by Qāsim al-Anvār during his initial period of spiritual training.[17] The fact that Qāsim al-Anvār uses exclusively the variant forms of this soubriquet in his poems, points not only to his having become a disciple of Shakyh Ṣadr al-Dīn Mūsā at an early age, but also to his continuing devotion to Shaykh Ṣadr al-Dīn Mūsā above all other spiritual directors.

Finally, the document showing the "genealogy of discipleship" which Jāmī alleges he saw, a document containing no mention of the name of Shaykh Ṣadr al-Dīn Ardabīlī, has too much appearance of a *deus ex machina*. The very words which Jāmī no doubt intended to clinch its authenticity, are to me an indication of its spuriousness. The document, says Jāmī, was "in the handwriting of some of his convinced followers" (*bi-khaṭṭ-i baʿḍ-i muʿtaqidān-i vay*). The very vagueness of the statement condemns it. Surely the authorship of such an important document would be known and attested, and its contents incorporated in *tadhkiras* and historical chronicles. Further, the oral tradition in matters of this kind is of paramount importance. Qāsim al-Anvār's "convinced followers" would not need to carry around a certificate to prove their *murshid's* devotional lineage. They would *know* whose disciple he was, because the information would have been passed on by word of mouth among the Ṣūfī Community, by Ṣūfīs who had worked with him in Gīlān, or who had accompanied him to Khurāsān from Ādharbāyjān. In

---

16 Nafīsī, p. 35.

17 Savory, p. 112.

another way, too, Jāmī has overplayed his hand. Had he confined himself to the assertion that Qāsim al-Anvār found Shaykh Ṣadr al-Dīn Mūsā inadequate as a *murshid* and later turned for guidance to Shaykh Ṣadr al-Dīn ʿAlī Yamanī, this would have had *prima facie* credibility—always supposing that the latter *shaykh* could be identified. By stating that Shaykh Ṣadr al-Dīn Ardabīlī was not even mentioned as one of Qāsim al-Anvār's spiritual directors, he presumes too much on our credulousness.

It is impossible to avoid the conclusion that Jāmī's account in the *Nafaḥāt al-Uns* is pure fabrication. The most likely motive for his attempt to discredit Shaykh Ṣadr al-Dīn Mūsā was the desire to minimize the effects of the Ṣafavid *daʿva* in Khurāsān.

5. In attempting to arrive at a balanced picture of Qāsim al-Anvār, it is important to emphasize his close connection, not only with the Ṣafaviyya, but also with other Ṣūfī Orders active in the Middle East in the 15th century, such as the Naqshbandīs, the Niʿmat Allāhīs, and the Khalvatīs. The spiritual affinity between the Ṣafaviyya and the Khalvatiyya, the heterodox Ṣūfī Order which gave the Ottomans so much trouble in Anatolia, was first pointed out by H. J. Kissling.[18] The statement by Jāmī, that the *khalvat* (cell) of Qāsim al-Anvār at Harāt was close to that of Mawlānā Zahīr al-Dīn Khalvatī,[19] now assumes a new significance. It is corroborated by Qāsim al-Anvār himself in his *Risāla dar bayān-i ʿilm*. In this treatise, Qāsim al-Anvār states that, in 779/1377-8, he was living at Harāt in the "new convent" (*khānaqāh-i jadīd*), as a neighbor of Mawlānā Ẓahīr al-Dīn Khalvatī (died 800/1397-8).[20] This new convent was probably founded by Qāsim al-Anvār for the purpose of effecting the spiritual direction of the people of Harāt and their induction into the Ṣafavid Order. A reference to the "Cemetery of the Khalvatīs" (*Gūristān-i Khalvatīyān*) at Harāt in 783/1381[21] indicates that the Khalvatīs had been present at Harāt for some time, probably from the middle of the 14th century.

Even more important were Qāsim al-Anvār's relations with Shāh Niʿmat Allāh Valī Kirmānī (731-834/1331-1431), the founder

---

[18] H. J. Kissling, *Zur Geschichte des Derwischordens der Bajrâmijja*, in *Südost-forschungen*, XV, 1956, p. 249.

[19] Savory, p. 142.

[20] Nafīsī, pp. 83, 402.

[21] Muftī Ghulām Sarvar Lāhūrī, *Khazīnat al-Aṣfiyā*, vol. II, pp. 302-303, quoted in Nafīsī, p. 84.

of the Niʿmat Allāhī Order. The friendship, based on mutual respect, which developed between these two men led to a close and continuing relationship between the Ṣafavids and Niʿmat Allahīs after the establishment of the Ṣafavid state.[22] Shāh Niʿmat Allāh Valī and Qāsim al-Anvār were considered by 15th century gnostics to be of equal rank as *murshids*.[23]

6. New evidence, much of it of an internal nature, makes it clear not only that Qāsim al-Anvār directed a flourishing convent (*khānaqāh; langar*) at Harāt as a centre of the Ṣafavid *daʿva*, but also that he commenced operations in Khurāsān at a very much earlier date than has hitherto been supposed. We now know that he was actively engaged in spreading the Ṣafavid *daʿva* at Harāt as early as 779/1377-8, that is, fourteen years before the death of his *murshid*, the Ṣafavid *shaykh* Ṣadr al-Dīn Mūsā[24] and three years before Tīmūr began his onslaught on the Iranic world.

---

[22] See Savory, pp. 142-148, and Aubin, *passim*.

[23] Nafīsī, p. 95.

[24] The *marthīya*, or elegaic ode, which Qāsim al-Anvār composed on the occasion of his *murshid*'s death, was written at Harāt. There is no mention in Qāsim al-Anvār's writings of Ṣadr al-Dīn Mūsā's successor, Khvāja ʿAlī, and this again suggests that the *dāʿī* was not in Ādharbāyjān at the time of Ṣadr al-Dīn Mūsā's death (see Nafīsī, p. 83).

THE *YÜEH CHÜEH SHU*, AN EARLY TEXT ABOUT SOUTH CHINA

by Axel Schuessler
Wayne State University

THE larger *ts'ung-shu's* which contain historical works include a smaller text, *Yüeh chüeh shu*,[a] that usually is listed under the category *tsa-shih*,[b] right after another work with a somewhat similar topic, the *Wu Yüeh ch'un-ch'iu*,[c] "Spring and Autumn of the States of Wu and Yüeh."[1]

The *Yüeh chüeh shu* (*YCS*) was supposedly written during the later Han Dynasty, and its contents cover the early history of the southern states of Wu and Yüeh (that is, the later half of the Chou period). Since sources for early Chinese history, especially those of regions at the periphery of Chou civilization, are not abundant, it is justifiable to take a closer look at this little book, although it will not surprise us with the discovery of new basic facts about that part of early China.

The *YCS* is not uniform in either content or style. The following table of contents, arranged by chapters, will show this; there are fifteen chapters (*ch'üan*) or nineteen *pien*:[2]

Chapter 1 A is obviously some kind of an early preface to the book, discussing in a question and answer form problems about the book itself (author, title, etc.). In the *Szu-pu ts'ung-k'an* edition it is even labeled "preface" and is not an integral part of the text.

Chapter 1 B "King P'ing of Ching" (state of Ch'u) tells about Wu Tzu-hsü, whose father and brother have been executed by

[1] This article is a résumé of my doctoral thesis "*Das Yüe chüe shu als hanzeitliche Quelle zur Chan-kuo Zeit*", Munich 1965. Here in this summary I cannot go much into detail as far as philological arguments are concerned, but can merely pick out the more important and interesting points.

[2] As a basis for discussion, the extensively commentated edition of Chan Tsung-hsiang, reprinted in the series of the Shih-chie shu-chü, T'ai-pei 1962, is used; but here, the *YCS* and the *Wu Yüeh ch'un-ch'iu* are quoted from the Szu-pu pei-yao edition. There is only an occasional disagreement among the various *YCS* editions (Szu-pu ts'ung-k'an, Szu-pu pei-yao, Han Wei ts'ung-shu, etc.), the most important being only that in the Szu-pu ts'ung-k'an text in chapters two and eight a few sections are divided differently.

King P'ing; Wu Tzu-hsü escapes to the state of Wu where he becomes minister and later finds a chance to revenge his father's death at the grave of this king of Ch'u.

Chapter 2 describes the topography of the state of Wu.

Chapter 3 consists of thirteen sections:

The first and second section repeat Wu Tzu-hsü's revenge on King P'ing which was told in chapter 1 B; here the corresponding passage of the *Kung-yang chuan*[3] is to a large extent copied. In the third section, Fan Li, the cunning minister of King Kou-chien of Yüeh, explains to his sovereign his thoughts for preparing his state to finally conquer the rival state of Wu. The fourth section takes the occasion of the death of King Ho-lü of Wu to elaborate on a passage of the *Kung-yang chuan*,[4] explaining that for referring to the death of, for example, a small official, a different term is used than for the death of a duke, and again a different one for the passing away of a king. It also relates briefly how Chung-erh became duke of the state of Chin, and Hsiao-po the lord of the state of Ch'i.

Chapter 4 is about the thoughts and theories of Chi Ni, who seems to have been an adviser at the court of Kou-chien of Yüeh.

Chapter 5 describes how the conquest of Wu by the rival Yüeh came about: the weak and gullible King Fu-ch'ai of Wu got rid of his able minister Wu Tzu-hsü and gave away his country's grain-resources to Kou-chien.

Chapter 6 is a collection of biographies of the ministers Wu Tzu-hsü and Po P'i from Wu, and Fan Li from Yüeh.

Chapter 7 A is again a short biography of Fan Li.

Chapter 7 B is the account of the alleged trip of Confucius' disciple Tzu-kung to various states, including Wu and Yüeh. It is identical in text with the corresponding part of chapter 67 of the *Shih-chi*.

Chapter 8 contains the same type of topographical accounts as chapter two, but dealing with Yüeh.

Chapter 9 presents more theories of Chi Ni.

Chapter 10 deals again with the ruin of the state of Wu, this time demonstrating the deplorable character of King Fu-ch'ai by

[3] Ting kung, 4th year.

[4] Chao kung, 4th year, 11th month.

showing his desperate reactions to the interpretation of evil omens.

Chapter 11 tells about the fabrication of famous bronze swords by Wu and Yüeh masters.

Chapter 12 A relates the final ruin of Wu to the nine schemes of Wen Chung, another counselor of King Kou-chien of Yüeh.

Chapter 12 B explains in detail how to interpret the colors of the sky as omens when one is setting out on a military expedition. At the end of the chapter is added a list of capitals of the feudal states.

Chapter 13 gives Fan Li a chance to explain at length his political theories.

Chapter 14 A turns suddenly from the milieu of the middle Chou period to that of the end of the Warring States period, telling how the Lord of Ch'un-shen, who served under the Kings K'ao-lieh and Yu of Ch'u (they ruled together from 261 to 227 B.C.) was enfeoffed with the former state of Wu.

Chapter 14 B describes the characters and lives of Fan Li and Wen Chung from Yüeh, King Fu-ch'ai and Wu Tzu-hsü from Wu.

Chapter 15 is drafted in the same style as chapter 1 A, this time, however, discussing personalities and subjects as they are presented in the *YCS*. It has to be regarded as a counterpart to chapter 1 A.

It is evident that chapters 1 A and 15 are of later date than the rest of the *YCS*, originally not belonging to it, so that we can eliminate these two from further investigations.

As is the case with many ancient texts, the *YCS* seems at some time to have had more chapters than it has today. It now consists of fifteen chapters (*ch'üan*) or nineteen *pien*.[5] From the bibliography *Ch'i-lu* by Yüan Hsiao-chi (479-536) as quoted in the *cheng-i* commentary to chapter 65 of the *Shih-chi*, down to the *T'ang-shu* (completed in 945 A.D.), it is stated that the *YCS* consisted of sixteen *ch'üan*, whereas the *Ch'ung-wen tsung-mu* of 1042 A.D. knows only of fifteen *ch'üan*, reporting at the same time that the text formerly was subdivided into twenty-five *pien*, while at the time

[5] A complete collection of all the information available on the *YCS* is done by Hsü I-fan, "Yüeh chüeh k'ao", *Wen-lan hsüeh-pao*, VI, 1937, 1-36. Very informative also is the *Erh-shih-wu shih pu-pien*, vol. IV, Shang-hai 1956.

of the bibliography of 1042 there were only twenty *pien* left. Chao Hsi-pien,[6] a Sung scholar, suggests calling the first *pien* (1 A) *ch'üan* 1 in order to reach the original number of sixteen *ch'üan*, a procedure which doesn't prove whether a chapter has been lost or not.

There is other evidence, however, that the *YCS* is smaller now than it used to be. Li Shan, the commentator of the *Wen-hsüan* who lived about 660 A.D., and the encyclopedia *T'ai-p'ing yü-lan*[7] give us the title of a chapter not to be found in today's text: *Wu Tzu-hsü shui-chan ping-fa*[d] ("The Laws of Riverboat Warfare by Wu Tzu-hsü"). In addition there are quite a number of quotations supposedly from the *YCS* which now can no longer be found in it.[8] Some of these would easily fit into the topographical chapters, whereas many others deal with the political and military theories of Wu Tzu-hsü, so that one gets the impression that there really used to be a chapter on the theories of this able minister of Wu, on which there is little information in the present text.

A glance at *YCS* excerpts in encyclopedias, the *I-wen lei-chü* of the 7th century, and the *T'ai-p'ing yü-lan* of the 10th, shows that the wording is practically identical with today's text. The *YCS* was first discovered in 1192 A.D. and then edited in 1208 by Hsü Ting-fu at K'uei-chou. Hsü says, however, that he compared three copies and picked out the passages common to all three of them, taking these to be the original text,[9] that is, the present one.

The diversity of subjects dealt with gives rise to the following questions: is it possible to distinguish different strata of the text? And is it at all possible to single out an original version or nucleus of the *YCS*? To find an answer, there are, on one hand, revealing parallels to the various topics in other early works, and, on the other hand, helpful quotations from the *YCS* found in commentaries or encyclopedias.

For the following discussion, the chapters are arranged according to their subject, though it is sometimes hard to draw a definite line

[6] *Erh-shih-wu shih pu-pien* IV, 5274.

[7] *Wen-hsüan* ch. 22 and 35; *TPYL* 315, 2a.

[8] The quotations, as collected by the Ch'ing scholar Ch'ien P'ei-ming, are on pp. 252-257 of Chang Tsung-hsiang's edition. Also the *Ku-wei shu* ch. 32 quotes a lengthy paragraph supposedly from the *YCS*; s. M. Kaltenmark, "Ling-pao: Note sur un terme du Taoisme religieux", *Mélanges* II, 1960, 559-588. The *Szu-k'u ch'üan-shu ts'ung-mu t'i-yao* gives the titles of 12 lost *pien* of an "Enlarged *YCS*".

[9] *YCS*, postscript in the SPPY edition.

between one subject and another. The number of pages covered by a subject group is added here in parentheses to give an idea of their distribution.

1. Topography: chapters 2 and 8 (48 pp.).
2. Monographies or historical tales: chapters 1 B; 3, sections one and two; 5; 7 B; 10; 11; 14 A (48 pp.).
3. Treatises on political philosophy by famous statesmen: chapters 3, section 3; 4; 6, section 1; 9; 12 A and B; 13 (34 pp.).
4. Biographies of these statesmen: chapters 6; 7 A; 14 B, sections 1-4 (14 pp.).
5. Earliest Chinese history (from Emperor Yao to the Duke of Chou): chapter 3, sections 5-7 and 9-13 (7 pp.).

The first group, concerning topography, consists of chapters 2 and 8, not considering the list of the capitals of feudal states added to chapter 12 B; the latter is completely out of place, so that we can assume that it was not part of the original text. Here follows the translation of a few typical sections from these two chapters:

From chapter 2:

Section 1 (p. la). Formerly Wu's first lord was T'ai-po. At the time of the [beginning of the] Chou, King Wu enfeoffed T'ai-po with the territory of Wu. [From T'ai-po] to Fu-ch'ai, one counts twenty-six generations or a thousand years. At the time of Ho-lü, the great hegemon, the city of Wu was walled in; within this wall are two smaller ones, leading down from the Hsü mountain. Two generations later, in the twenty-third year of the reign of Fu-ch'ai, King Kou-chien of Yüeh destroyed it.

Section 2 (p.la). Ho-lü's palace was at the village[10] Kao-p'ing.

Section 3 (p.la). There are two archery-towers: one at the village Hua-ch'ih-ch'ang, and one at the village An-yang.

Section 23 (p.2b). The mound outside the Wu gate ("Sorcerer's gate") was Ho-lü's ice-house.

Section 57 (p.4a). The Hai-yen district was originally called Wu-yüan hsiang.

Section 94 (p.6a). The large gates at all villages in Wu were built by the Lord of Ch'un-shen.

Section 111 (p. 7b). King K'ao-lieh of Ch'u annexed Yüeh as

[10] The term "li"[e] here seems to signify "village".

far as Lang-ya. More than forty years later, the state of Ch'in annexed Ch'u, and forty years after that, Han annexed Ch'in. From the beginning of the Han until now there are 242 years. And from the time when Kou-chien moved to Lang-ya until the twenty-eighth year of the Chien-wu era [that is, 52 A.D.], there are altogether 567 years.

From chapter 8

Section 15 (p. 3b). The wall of the village Yang-ch'eng was built by Fan Li; to the West it reaches to the canal. It has one canal gate and two highway gates.

Section 36 (p. 4b). The boat house was Kou-chien's boat house; it is fifty miles[11] from the district capital.

Section 47 (p. 5b). The T'u mountain is the one where emperor Yü took his wife. It is fifty miles from the district capital.

In these two chapters a chronological arrangement is attempted, starting with T'ai-po or the legendary emperor Yü and going through the times approximately up to the end of the former Han Dynasty, and chapter 2 gives the date 52 A.D. (in section 111, see above). This leads to the conclusion that these chapters were written at the beginning of the later Han period, around 52 A.D. It is also interesting to note that the two earliest commentaries which make use of the *YCS*, the *chi-chie* on the *Shih-chi* in the early sixth century and the commentary on the *Waterclassic*, *Shui-ching chu*, in the sixth century, quote only from these two chapters, while Ou-yang Hsün (557-641) in his encyclopedia *I-wen lei-chü*, and Li Shan (ca. 660 A.D.), commentator of the *Wen-hsüan*, make extensive use of these chapters. That indicates that the chapters are the most characteristic ones of the whole work.

These chapters have textual parallels only in the *Wu Yüeh ch'un-ch'iu* (*WYCC*), as mentioned at the beginning, which was supposedly written about the same time as the *YCS*. As the title of it shows, it deals with the history of the states Wu and Yüeh in chronological order. Sections 2 and 3 of chapter 2 of the *YCS* (see above) definitely have a close textual relationship with *WYCC* chapter 4,[12] where, however, the elements of the village names are differently arranged; the *WYCC* writes An-li-hua-ch'ih and P'ing-

---

[11] "li".[e]

[12] P. 12b.

ch'ang. Three more sections have parallels in the *WYCC*.[13] The first section of chapter 8 about Emperor Yü has connection to *WYCC* chapter 6,[14] only the *YCS* is shorter than its counterpart, and also other sections have a connection with the *WYCC*.[15] The tale of Confucius' visit to King Kou-chien of Yüeh is identical in wording in both texts.[16] It is difficult to say which of the two texts transmits the more original version. Since, however, the *YCS* specializes in topography, and at the same time is not the type of text which is likely to have invited later scholars to manipulate it in order to prove certain points they fancied, we may assume that the *YCS* variants are the more reliable.

In the second group of historical tales, it is more complicated to come to a conclusion as to when the chapters received the shape in which they are written down in our text. That the chapters from this group are mentioned only from the seventh century on does not necessarily prove that they did not exist earlier. Since almost all of the subjects dealt with in this category have parallels in better known works like the *Tso-chuan*, *Kuo-yü*, *Chan-kuo ts'ê*, *Shih-chi*, *Wu Yüeh ch'un-ch'iu* and others, it is only natural that one looks in vain for quotations from these chapters of the YCS. As a matter of fact, chapters of this group are quoted exclusively in encyclopedias, the commentator Li Shan using only chapter 11, an account of the famous swords fabricated in these two southern states, this account being paralleled only to some extent by the *WYCC*.[17]

The chapter with the most parallels in other texts is 1 B. Although its title says "King P'ing of Ching", it is evident that the key figure is Wu Tzu-hsü. Here follows a summary of this chapter:

Wu Tzu-she, minister of King P'ing of Ch'u, falls into disgrace and is about to be executed by order of the king. Because both, of Wu Tzu-she's sons immediately leave the country, the king tries to call them back to liquidate them as well in order to prevent later revenge. The first son, Wu Tzu-shang, full of filial piety, comes back and is promptly executed with his father, whereas the second

[13] Sec. 4 and 5 on p. la have connection to *WYCC* ch. 4, p. 12b and 1b; and sec. 20 on p. 2a-b has connection to *WYCC* ch. 4, p. 7a.

[14] Pp. la-b, and 3b-4a.

[15] Sec. 2 on pp. 1b-2a has connection to *WYCC* ch. 10, p. 11a; and sec. 5 to 12 on pp. 2a-b have connection to ch. 8, p. 2a.

[16] Sec. 1 on p. 1b is identical with the corresponding part of *WYCC* ch. 10, p. 10a.

[17] *WYCC* ch. 4, p. 7a-b.

son, Wu Tzu-hsü, starts a journey, the description of which is a challenging objective for this chapter's writer.

Arriving first in the state of Cheng to the North of Ch'u, Wu Tzu-hsü decides to go on, climbing a "high mountain" of "heng-ling",[f] which can be interpreted as the proper name of an unidentifiable mountain range, or has to be translated by "mountain range running from East to West". There he overlooks the states of Chin and Ch'i, but decides, however, to turn to the South. At the Yang-tzu river a fisherman takes pity on him, ferries him to the other shore, feeds him, and urges him to flee in order to escape his pursuers. Tzu-hsü asks the friendly man to keep his flight secret, and the latter assures him by killing himself. Later, he reaches the river Lai (also called Ling) near the town of Li-yang to the West of the city of Wu. There he encounters a girl washing silk in the river and asks her for something to eat. After feeding him, she kills herself for the same reason as the fisherman did.

Finally, he reaches the city of Wu, where he begs in the market-place. After three days, he catches the eye of the market-supervisor who promptly runs to King Ho-lü to tell him of this odd-looking man. The bright king remembers hearing about the tragedy of Wu Tzu-she and his sons and knows immediately that the beggar is Wu Tzu-hsü, whom he keeps as a close advisor.

Several years later, the army of Wu, under the command of Wu Tzu-hsü, supports the little state of Ts'ai in a war against Ch'u. Ch'u, of course, is quickly and completely defeated, Wu Tzu-hsü taking that occasion to beat and flog the grave of the late King P'ing.

The successor of P'ing, King Chao, realizes that he cannot live in peace as long as Tzu-hsü is Ch'u's enemy, and asks him politely to take over the affairs of the state of Ch'u. But as an upright and honest man, Tzu-hsü refuses.

In comparing this account with its parallels, one notices first of all that the *YCS* abbreviates or interpolates at some points in order to avoid the introduction of people who are irrelevant for the chapter in question. That Wu Tzu-she fell into disgrace with King P'ing is actually the result of a court intrigue. Chien, the son and heir-apparent of P'ing, was at odds with the minister Fei Wu-chi; the latter, having fears for the time when Chien would become king, falsely accused him of planning to overthrow his father. Chien's instructor Wu Tzu-she inevitably got involved in the plot and was put to death by the king, while Prince Chien managed to escape to the state of Sung and finally to Cheng, where he eventually was murdered. A second instance of simplification we find near the end of the same chapter, where it says that Wu Tzu-hsü comes to "King Ho-lü". All other texts agree, however, that at that time the king in Wu was Liao, Ho-lü being merely a prince who cared very little about the refugee from Ch'u. A third example is in chapter 10. The first half is *en bloc* identical with the *WYCC* version;[18] this identity, however, abruptly stops where Wu Tzu-hsü comes into the picture: the *YCS* continues on its own, and the name Wu Tzu-hsü is not mentioned through this chapter.

This phenomenon of cutting sources is, of course, not unfamiliar to early Chinese historiography, the most famous example of this being Szu-ma Ch'ien's *Shih-chi*. But in our case it clearly indicates that the writer did not intend to write history, as did the writer or compiler of the *WYCC*, but rather wanted to give the reader a lively character portrait. In fact, in chapter 5 we are surprised that from the occasionally tiresome dialogues evolves an "objective" account of King Fu-ch'ai of Wu, who is usually depicted as a villain by whose despotic whims and evil character the state of Wu was ruined. Here we meet a weak, undecided, but not necessarily wicked, king who does evil deeds and brings about final disaster because his intelligence and character are not fit for the job of ruling a country. At the end, of course, it is made clear that Wu came to an end because Fu-ch'ai committed evil deeds, not because he himself was evil.

The episode of chapter 1 B which has the most parallels is the flight of Wu Tzu-hsü from Ch'u to Wu. The *Tso-chuan*[19] says only that he went to Wu, but states that prince Chien escaped to Sung and Cheng. In the *Chan-kuo ts'ê*[20] one learns that Tzu-hsü passed the Chao pass, Ling-shui (Lai-shui), and then reaches the market-place of Wu. The *Lü-shih ch'un-ch'iu*[21] tells of him climbing the "T'ai-hang" mountain and then turning to the Yang-tzu and Wu. The *WYCC*[22] and the *Shih-chi* chapter 66 agree that he fled to

[18] *WYCC* ch. 5, pp. 4b-5b.

[19] *Chao kung* 20th year; James Legge, *The Chinese Classics*, V, Hong Kong 1960, p. 676.

[20] *Ch'in* III, 9.

[21] Ch. 10, sec. 4.

[22] Ch. 3.

Sung and Cheng (with or following Prince Chien), came to the Chao pass and the Yang-tzu, the *WYCC* adding Lai-shui and the marketplace of Wu.

The *YCS* version corresponds very well to the *Shih-chi* and *WYCC*, so that one may draw the conclusion that this chapter of the *YCS* represents the Han period state of the Wu Tzu-hsü legend. Comparisons with other episodes, also from other chapters of this second group, do not contradict this assumption, and the similarity in style and purpose of all the chapters in question strongly suggests that our assumption holds true for this entire group. It also proves that the writer was not only familiar with the traditions as handed down by the *Shih-chi* and *WYCC*,[23] but also with the tradition of the *Lü-shih ch'un-ch'iu*, for the latter's "T'ai-hang" certainly corresponds to the *YCS*. In both versions we find the elements *ta* or *t'ai*,[g] *hang*[h] (<*g'âng or *g'ang) or *heng*[i] (<*g'wang). The pattern of this episode is in both texts identical, too.

The *YCS* author apparently also had acquaintance with other old traditions. At the beginning of chapter 1 B we are told that Wu Tzu-hsü's brother Wu Tzu-shang fled to the state of Wu while Tzu-hsü went to Cheng. No other text mentions the flight of Wu Tzu-shang; only the *Tso-chuan*[19] mentions something that could explain this *YCS* statement: it states that Tzu-shang was prefect of T'ang, which was a small town in the border area between Ch'u and Wu and may very well have belonged to Wu at that time; hence the *YCS* statement which connects him with Wu. Also in chapter 3 of the *YCS*[24] one encounters very un-Confucian opinions that say that Emperor Yao had no compassion for his son and Emperor Shun had no filial piety. These remarks obviously escaped the Confucian idealization of the golden age, and the *YCS* therefore could well reflect an old tradition.

Before passing to the next group, it may be worth noting that

[23] That the *YCS* used the tradition of the *WYCC* and not *vice versa* is shown by the following detail: according to the *YCS* version, the fisherman first warns Tzu-hsü by a song containing instructions for him to wait hidden in the reeds till nightfall in order to be taken across the river unseen. Only the *WYCC* explains the need for this caution: the fisherman has passengers aboard who could recognize the fugitive.—This song of the fisher is partly corrupted in the *YCS* and only fully understandable with the *WYCC* version.

[24] P. 2b.

parallels are also to be found in the *Kuo-yü*,[25] as well as the works already mentioned.

The chapters with stress on political thought have parallels in the *WYCC*. Chapter 4 is also known as a separate text which is summarized by Alfred Forke.[26] Some of these chapters have already been quoted by Li Shan. Since the philosophical dialogues are framed in an historical event with which the reader of the *YCS* is already familiar, and since these chapters are very similar in style to the historical tales, one is tempted to suggest that the chapters of this group and the preceding one are composed by the same person, with the exception of chapter 12 B; it does not start, as all the other chapters of the *YCS* do, with the word "formerly", and does not mention any person, nor is it styled in dialogue fashion as is the rest of the *YCS*.

From a different brush (or brushes) originate the short biographies of the fifth category. Their style is extremely short and pregnant, and they are less well done than the pictures of personalities given by the historical tales; but here the persons Fan Li, Wu Tzu-hsü and Po P'i (a statesman in Wu, colleague of Tzu-hsü) are reduced to mere Platonic schemata filled with conventional virtues and vices and biographical data. The reader gets the impression that a smart scholar, after reading the other parts of the *YCS*, felt a lack of biographical information for some persons and then added his historiography.

Finally, the sections of chapter three about early history obviously do not fit into the general context of this work about Wu and Yüeh, not having any connection with these southern states. One can trace a few scattered sentences back to the *Lü-shih ch'un-ch'iu*[27] and *WYCC*.[28]

Nothing has yet been said about the author of the *YCS*, because there is no dependable information about him. The bibliography in the *Sui-shu* states on this point that Tzu-kung, the disciple of Confucius, was the author. This is impossible, simply because many events mentioned in the *YCS* took place long after his lifetime. But it is an indirect hint that the chapter, 7 B, about Tzu-kung's trip to Wu and Yüeh was a firmly established part of the

[25] In describing the defeat of Wu, the *YCS* ch. 5 partly paraphrases *Yüeh-yü*, II, 6-7.

[26] *Geschichte der alten chinesischen Philosophie,* Hamburg 1927, 500-503.

[27] Sec. 5 corresponds to *Lü-shih ch'un-ch'iu,* ch. 11, sec. 4.

[28] Sec. 9 corresponds to *WYCC*, ch. 6, p. la-b.

text by that time, this fact prompting the association of him with the book. The *Sung-shih* goes so far as to propose, albeit reluctantly, Wu Tzu-hsü as an alternative author.

Not much clearer is the question of how to interpret the title *Yüeh chüeh shu*. The crucial character is *chüeh* "to cut off, make an end to", etc., and on this western scholars disagree as much as their earlier Chinese colleagues did, the most common but not very convincing interpretation being, "The book about Yüeh making an end [to the state of Wu]". It is curious that the words "Yüeh chüeh" had the same archaic rime: *gi̯wat dz'i̯wat, so that one is reminded of the common adverbs of the type *·iog-d'iog "pretty". Nor is there any answer to the question: why is just "Yüeh" in the title while half the work deals with Wu?

After comparing the *YCS* with parallel versions in other texts and taking information gathered from bibliographies and quotations of this book elsewhere into consideration, one can now sum up and draw the following conclusions, and answer the questions of strata and original version raised earlier.

The chapters on topography are the ones dated to the later Han Dynasty, and at the same time they are the most distinguishing ones of the whole work. They apparently are the nucleus of the book, chapters on historical tales and political thought being grouped along with them (and, maybe, from the same author or compiler), or added to them between the later Han period and the sixth or seventh century A.D. Of younger origin are a few short biographies, on the one hand, and two chapters forming a preface and a postscript, on the other. Most likely a separate treatise on thought was incorporated into the text (chapter 12 B), whereas other parts of the *YCS* seem to be lost, or at least eliminated by the revision done by the *YCS*'s first publisher Hsü Ting-fu around 1200 A.D. It is probable that the wording was not subjected to major interpolations at some later date, since: 1) chapters two and eight are of no interest for such purposes; 2) the quotations from the *YCS* found elsewhere do not disagree with today's version; and 3) the historical tales make a consistent impression. The *YCS*, then, appears to be an early form of what was later to develop into the gazetteers which are so common in more recent Chinese history.[29] As in the gazetteers,

[29] This idea was already expressed by Joseph Needham, *Science and Civilisation in China*, vol. III, Cambridge, Mass., 1954-1962, p. 512.

the subjects of the *YCS* (topography, history, description of personalities and their thought, even a paragraph on the language) have only one thing in common: they are relevant to a specific geographical area.

CHARACTERS

a 越絶書

b 雜史

c 吳越春秋

d 伍子胥水戰兵法

e 里

f 横嶺

g 大太

h 行

i 横

ON THE ORIGINAL MEANING OF TAITTIRĪYA UPANIṢAD 1.11.1-4

by R. Morton Smith
University of Toronto

IT IS generally agreed that the early Upaniṣads no longer mean what they did. Part of the reason is the emergence and triumph of the classical ideology of India, represented conspicuously by Śankara. Long before his time, however, any historical sense of Indian society of the 7th-6th centuries B.C. was lost. English translations also tend to lack this historical sense, and even have overtones of Victorian earnestness. Here we shall seek to recover the original meaning of Taittirīya Upaniṣad 1.11.

This section is normally taken as a unit. However, there is a curious mixture of 2nd person singular imperatives and neuter singular gerundives. We suggest that the imperatives represent the original text, and the gerundives a subsequent commentary, which is still early, perhaps from the 5th century B.C. We have here the graduating formula, as it were, for brahmins, along with an exposition of its meaning.

TEXT:

1.11. *vedam anūcyācāryo'ntevāsinam anuśāsti / satyaṃ vada dharmaṃ cara / svādhyāyān mā pramadaḥ / ācāryāya priyaṃ dhanam āhṛtya prajātantuṃ mā vyavacchetsīḥ —*

"Having taught the Veda, the teacher instructs the pupil further: Speak the truth; do your (caste) duty; do not neglect Vedic study. Having paid a satisfactory fee to your teacher, do not cut the thread of progeny."

There is a very great deal of difference to an English reader between "Practise virtue" and "Do your (caste) duty". Both meanings would have been the same to an Indian, especially before Buddha; but it is the latter meaning that translates the sense for us. The pupil here is a brahmin, and this kind of generalized ethic is a late development in society. Truth, while the central virtue in India, is especially the virtue of brahmins; it also belongs to kings by virtue of their original religious connection with *ṛta*.

The brahmin youth cannot marry before he has ended his studentship, and this is not technically completed until it has been paid for. Begetting offspring is a religious duty, and therefore should not be undertaken in an improper religious state, such as an incomplete studentship. Does the emphasis on the satisfactory fee here indicate the developing economy of the 7th-6th centuries? The above brief instruction is followed by this commentary:

> *satyān na pramaditavyaṃ dharmān na pramaditavyaṃ kuśalān na pramaditavyaṃ bhūtyai na pramaditavyaṃ svādhyāyapravacanābhyāṃ na pramaditavyaṁ devapitṛkāryābhyāṃ na pramaditavyam* —
>
> "One should not be neglectful of truth; one should not be neglectful of caste duty; one should not be neglectful of health; one should not be neglectful of wealth; one should not be neglectful of study and teaching; one should not be neglectful of rites to the gods or ancestors."

The word *kuśala* is classically used for general well-being, and "nice" as opposed to "nasty"; here it may complement *dharma*; *dharma* would be the caste duty, and the use of *kuśala* would connote "Behave properly in things/dealings outside the caste."

TEXT

> 1.11.2 *mātṛdevo bhava / pitṛdevo bhava / ācaryadevo bhava / atithidevo bhava* —
>
> "Be one having mother as a god, father as a god, teacher as a god, a guest as a god."

COMMENTARY:

> *yāny anavadyāni karmāṇi tāni sevitavyāni no itarāṇi / yāny asmākaṁ sucaritāṇi tāni tvayopāsyāni no itarāṇi* / (1.11.3) *ye ke cāsmac chreyāṁso brāhmaṇās teṣāṃ tvayāsanena praśvasitavyam / śraddhayā deyam aśraddhayādeyam śriyā deyaṃ hriyā deyam bhiyā deyaṃ saṁvidā deyam* —
>
> "What actions are irreproachable, these are to be practised, not (the) others; what are our good deeds, these are to be thought on, not (the) others. (3) Which brahmins are better than us, they are to be consoled with a seat by you (sic!). Giving should be with faith; no faith—no giving; giving should be with riches (i.e. liberal). Giving should be with modesty; giving should be with fear; giving should be with complete knowledge."

The commentary in 1.11.2 is somewhat surprising, and bespeaks an age of individualism. This is the only Vedic occurrence of *anavadya*, except for Maitr. Up. 7.1.1, which only dates from the 2nd century B.C.; the word is attested by the epic, and it would look as if this word were a later interpolation into the commentary. This can be supported by the use of *karman*, which in .2 here is a general word for "deed", while in .4 *karmavicikitsā* is a "doubt on ritual action". We suggest that such an interpolation would have been made when the commentary in .3 was made inoffensive.

The moral criticism of a teacher or a parent is not a part of Indian tradition. The normal brahmin is not a miserable sinner, with a lot of *duścarita*, "evil deeds", implied. What then is the meaning of our *sucaritāni*, "good works"? The interpretation of the whole phrase should be, "What things of us have been well performed, these things are to be practised by you, not others," i.e. "our good (old) habits are to be practised, and no innovations (not others)": by the time the early commentary was made, there were innovating heretics; the commentary is post-Buddha, perhaps from the 5th century B.C. This interpretation may be open to doubt; but the defenders of the vulgate ask us to believe an Indian teacher, guru, dismissing his pupil after having had him in the house for several years with the message "Don't beget till you've paid up; and for God's sake, avoid my vices."

"Hold your father as a god, hold your mother as a god" was in no need of comment or explanation, but "Revere your teacher" was; no innovations were allowed as these were irreverent, conceited or wrong-headed, or all together. We should now expect a simple comment on *atithidevo*; but this needs retranslation. Again the vulgate shows a most unwonted humility, a unique modesty that does not, on reflection, carry conviction. The teacher is speaking to his pupil, and no brahmin would expect a pupil to meet as a commonplace, or expect his pupil to expect to meet as a commonplace, a better brahmin than his teacher. And consoling him with a seat is not very meaningful. Monier-Williams explicitly explains the passage in his dictionary, which suggests that he found it strange. The first thing to do is to join *asmad* and *śreyas* in a compound, meaning the people who have more *srī* than us, our betters; the brahmins now belong to them, and the punctuation should be before, not after *brāhmaṇās*. That is to say that when the commentary was first composed (soon after 500?), the great still had their *purohitas*, and we should respect brahmins employed in the service of our own (royal) patrons or their friends. This explains the "employed", *āyukta* (1.11.4).

We now come to the seat, *āsana*: this could be authentic, but "chairs" are not all that common in early times, and in view of the duty to a guest, it is very little to suggest the true reading was *aśanena*, "with food"; as early as Pali, the sibilants collapsed to a single one, so that with a Prakritic pronunciation, no emendation is needed. However, we must emend *-śvasitavyam* to the nominative plural *-śvasitavyās*: the corruption is not scribal, but due to the removal of an objectionable sentiment, viz. that brahmins could have betters, which was impossible to credit after the fall of the Mauryas in 185 B.C., but still quite possible before the liquidation of the old families by Mahāpadma Nanda, circa 500 B.C.. The point of hospitality is not offering a man a seat, and turning him out before dinner, but offering him food; and there are careful rules about whose food, not whose seat, should be accepted, and whose not. The usual compounds for "refresh" are *ā-*, *pratyā-*, *samā-*, *śvāsayati*, but an original *prāśu-āśayitavyāḥ*, "should quickly be caused to eat", would be purely conjectural. It might be held that the eating is sufficiently mentioned in the giving, *deyam*.

"It should be given with faith; it should not be given with non-faith". Faith in what? If we keep the translation "with faith", we suggest that the faith is that the recipient is an orthodox brahmin, not a heretic; brahmins were early attracted to the heresies, and this qualification would again give point to the use of "employed", *āyukta*, in .4. Or we could regard the faith to be at the receiving end, which would give the same effective sense. If we translate *śraddhayā* as "willingly", this seems to be epic, and so the word would belong to the final corrector, but then it also takes the point out of *aśraddhayā adeyam*.

I suspect *srī*, *hrī*, *bhī* represent a mystic sound mantra, such as is later found in tantra. And at this point we should re-think the passage; Who is to do the giving? If it is the brahmin, as it should be from the context, it amplified *atithideva* well; we may remember the Homeric society, where a guest may prove to be a god, and should therefore be treated with a meticulous reverence. This would equally apply here. In this case, it might be better to take *śraddhayā deyam. . . adeyam* as a later interpolation, "willingly. . . not to be given unwillingly". It would also be possible to read the passage as *śraddhayā ādeyam aśraddhayā adeyam*, "That which is going to be received willingly is not to be given unwillingly", the point being that the brahmin guest confers a favor by receiving.

The vulgate translation "It should be given with sympathy"

is just wrong; *sam-vid* means "to know thoroughly", or as a noun, "consciousness, agreement, news". Who is the brahmin to have sympathy for when he gives? For his guest? "I'm sorry for you having to eat my wife's cooking"? The brahmin is conventionally the fit recipient, not the source of giving. The duty of hospitality in Vedic times is a religious act; by the 7th-6th centuries B.C. the religious act is not effective unless performed with (full) knowledge. Giving is a rite, therefore giving without understanding is no virtue and brings no merit any more than performing a rite without knowing it does. There is no attestation of *saṁvid* in the meaning "sympathy" other than for the purposes of this passage, though after the Buddhist ideal of compassion had been formulated it might suit Śankara very well. When the passage is taken out of context and applied to generalized giving, then, in the brahminical reaction of the 2nd and subsequent centuries B.C., one (i.e. a non-brahmin) should give, i.e. to brahmins with *srī*, *hrī*, and *bhī*, liberally, with due sense of inferiority, and with proper fear.

TEXT (FUSED WITH COMMENTARY ?)

> 1.11.3 *atha yadi te karmavicikitsā vā vṛttavicikitsā vā syād* .4 *ye tatra brāhmaṇāḥ saṃmarśino yuktā āyuktā alūkṣā dharmakāmāḥ syur yathā te tatra varteran tathā tatra vartethāḥ*,
>
> "then what doubt on rite or conduct may be yours, what thinking brahmins there are there, experienced, employed, not dried up, loving the dharma, as they would behave, so you should behave".

alūkṣā is not very clear; *lūkṣ/rūkṣ* "make dry/emaciated" in ŚpB, "be irritated" in Jātakamālā; we suspect the word refers to a *vanaprastha* or *saṇnyāsin*, the rights of such to be irritable on any intrusion being well known.

This passage is repeated with *athābhyākhyāteṣu ye tatrabrāhmaṇāh*. . . This may be the original, and explained by *karmavicikitsā* etc.; "rite" and "conduct" make a good pair; the vulgate "deeds" and "conduct" are virtually synonyms, and do not make good sense of *vā*. . . *vā* "either. . . or". *abhy-ā-khyā* in Buddhist and Jain writers and the Kauśikasūtra gets the (restricted) meaning "accuse falsely, calumniate". When the early commentator lived, it may well not yet have acquired this restriction, hence the subsequent explanation, "i.e. a doubt on rite or conduct".

We have already noted *āyukta*, "employed brahmin"; in the

economic expansion of the 6th-3rd centuries brahmins are more and more leaving their caste duties, to the disgust of the writers of the early *Dharmasūtras*. Loss of patrons and greater opportunities for new trades such as money-lending contribute to the same result; while quite a few brahmins enter the heresies, e.g. Prakudha Kātyāyana, Pūrana Kāśyapa, Gautama Indrabhūti, Maudgalīputra and many others.

Lastly, the contents of Tait. U 1 are summarized,

eṣa ādeśa, eṣa upadeśa eṣā vedopaniṣat etad anuśāsanam.

"This is the doctrine and this is the explanation (thereof); this is the mystery teaching of the Vedā, and this is the instruction (thereof)."

THE FIRST CHINESE DICTIONARY PUBLISHED IN EUROPE

by B. B. Szczesniak
University of Notre Dame

THE present short paper is concerned with the first Chinese dictionary published in Europe, by Michael Boym (1612–1659), a prominent Polish scholar, perhaps the first Sinologist of the true learning, who contributed most considerably to the foundation of Chinese studies in the Western World. Boym, in spite of his short life, was the author of several studies on Chinese language, medicine, geography, botany, and cartography. But his lexical contributions are practically unknown to the historian of Sinology.[1]

Before publication of Michael Boym's Chinese-Latin dictionary in 1667 there were some manuscript vocabularies compiled by the Dutch and Portuguese,[2] and by the Jesuit missionaries in China for their use while working among the Chinese. Several short vocabularies, lists of Chinese words and their Latin equivalents, are preserved in the Vatican Library in the Fondo Borgia Cinese.[3] However, the first published dictionary was that by Boym.

Boym's vocabulary is quite modern, not only for his time but by present standards. It combines the use of characters and their Romanized transliteration with marks of tonations and with Latin equivalents of the Chinese words. For this purpose Boym used the inscription of the famous Nestorian stele discovered in 1625 in Hsi-an Fu. From the rubbing of this important monument, which he brought to Rome in 1652, a facsimile engraving was made in reduced size, with numbered Chinese ideograms of each column

[1] For Boym's lexicographical contribution to Chinese studies, see Boleslaw Szczesniak, "The Beginnings of Chinese Lexicography in Europe with Particular Reference to the Work of Michael Boym (1612-1659)," *Journal of the American Oriental Society*, vol. 67, 1947, pp. 160-165; *idem*, "The Writings of Michael Boym," *Monumenta Serica*, vol. XIV, 1949-1955, pp. 481-538; *idem*, "Athanasius Kircher's *China Illustrata*," *Osiris*, vol. X, 1952, pp. 385-411.

[2] Henri Cordier, *Bibliotheca Sinica*, 5 vols. (Paris, 1902–1925), vol. III, cols. 1626-1638, vol. IV, cols. 1588-1592; J.J.L. Duyvendak, "Early Chinese Studies in Holland," *T'oung Pao*, vol. XXXII, 1936, pp. 293-344.

[3] Paul Pelliot, "Michael Boym," *T'oung Pao*, 1934, p. 137.

of the text. The text was transliterated according to the system used among the various missionaries, giving genuine pronunciation and with numbers indicating the proper characters on the facsimile engraving. For the proper tonations of the pronunciation Boym put special marks above the transcribed words. He compared his tone markers to the notes of the musical scale, Ut Re Mi Fa Sol. The student of the Chinese language had a pretty exact system of pronunciation and knowledge of Chinese ideograms and their Latin meanings. The literal translation of the inscription, including its characters, constituted therefore, a small basic vocabulary. This vocabulary was published in an elaborate volume, the *China illustrata*[4] by Athanasius Kircher, which appeared in Latin in 1667, in Dutch in 1668, and in French in 1670. Because of the difficulty of printing Chinese characters at that time in Europe, this was a somewhat unusual dictionary. The reproduction of the Inscription of Hsi-an Fu also showed a well-worked text of the Chinese script.

In the French edition of *China illustrata*, Kircher included Boym's vocabulary in a conventional form, but without characters and with only the French equivalents of the transcribed Chinese words.[5]

The appearance of a Chinese-Latin dictionary with ideograms undoubtedly stirred the interest of the readers of the very popular *China illustrata*, especially of the "curious savants" so typical of seventeenth century European culture and of the humanists in particular. This was the century of unscrupulous plagiarism of all kinds, practiced also by the Jesuits among themselves.

---

[4] See pp. 325-336 of Athanasius Kircher's important book of the Baroque period but written following the models of the Renaissance: *Athanasii Kircheri e Soc Jesu China monumentis qua sacris qua profanis, nec non variis naturae et artis spectaculis, aliarumque rerum memoriabilium argumentis illustrata, auspiciis Leopoldi Primi, Roman Imper. Semper Augusti, munificentissimi mecaenatis*, Amsterdami, apud Jacobum a Meurs, in fossa vulgo de Keysergracht, anno M.DC.LXVII.

[5] See pp. 324-367 of *La Chine d'Athanase Kirchere de la Compagnie de Jesus, illustrée de plusieurs monuments tant sacrés que profanes, et de quantité de recherchés de la nature et de l'art. A quoy on à adjusté de nouveau les questions curieuses que le Serenissime Grand Duc de Toscane a fait dépuis peu au P. Jean Grubere touchant ce grand empire. Avec un Dictionnaire Chinois et Francais, lequel est tres-rare, et quie n'a pas encores paru au jour.* Traduit par F. S. Dalguié. A Amsterdam, Ches Jean Jansson a Waesberge, et les Heritiers d'Elizée Weyerstraet, l'an MDCLXX. Avec privilege.

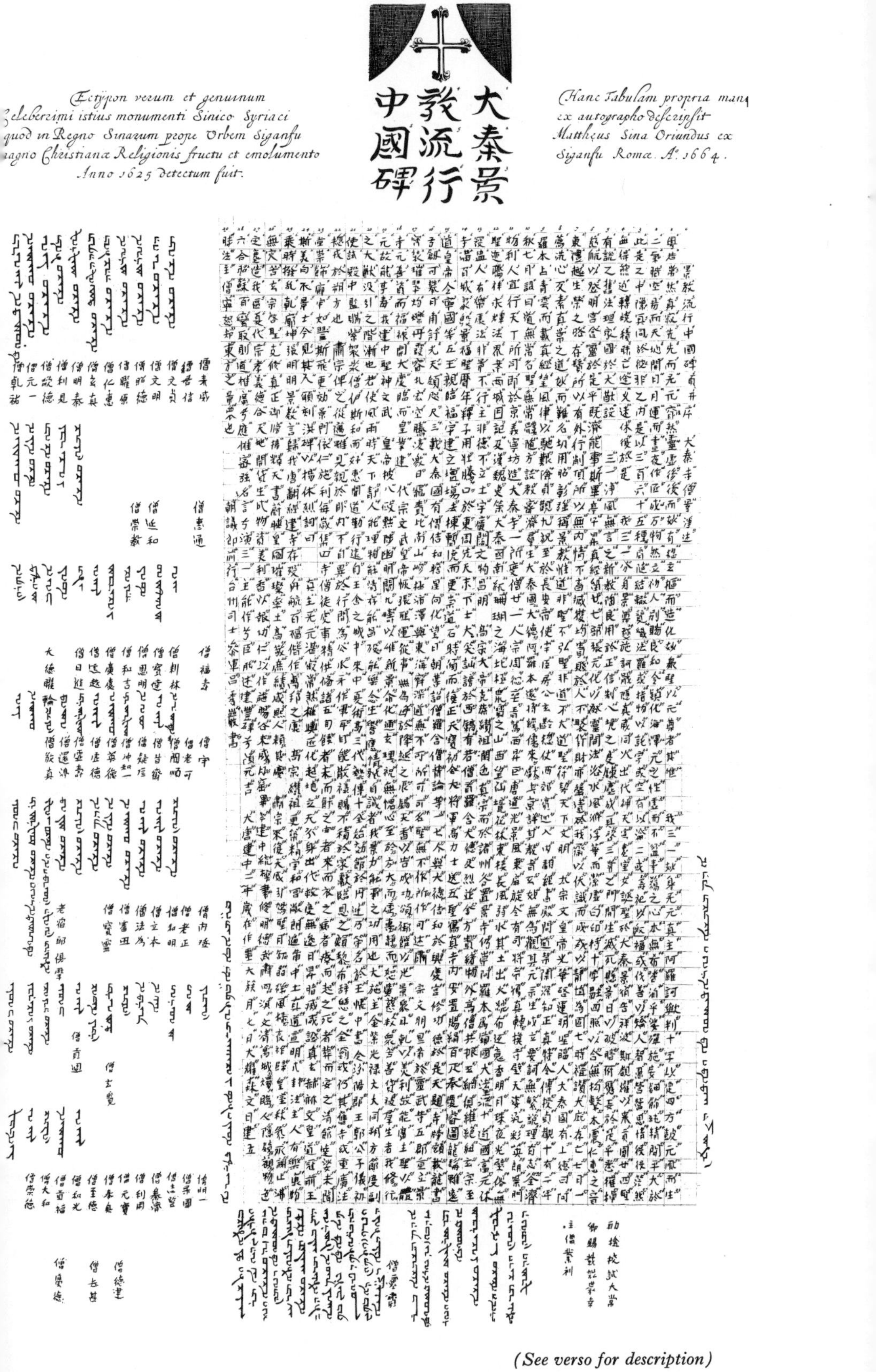
大秦景教流行中國碑
Ectypon verum et genuinum
Celeberrimi istius monumenti Sinico Syriaci
quod in Regno Sinarum prope Urbem Siganfu
magno Christianæ Religionis fructu et emolumento
Anno 1625 detectum fuit.
Hanc Tabulam propria manu
ex autographo descripsit
Mattheus Sina Oriundus ex
Siganfu Romæ. Aº. 1664.

(See verso for description)

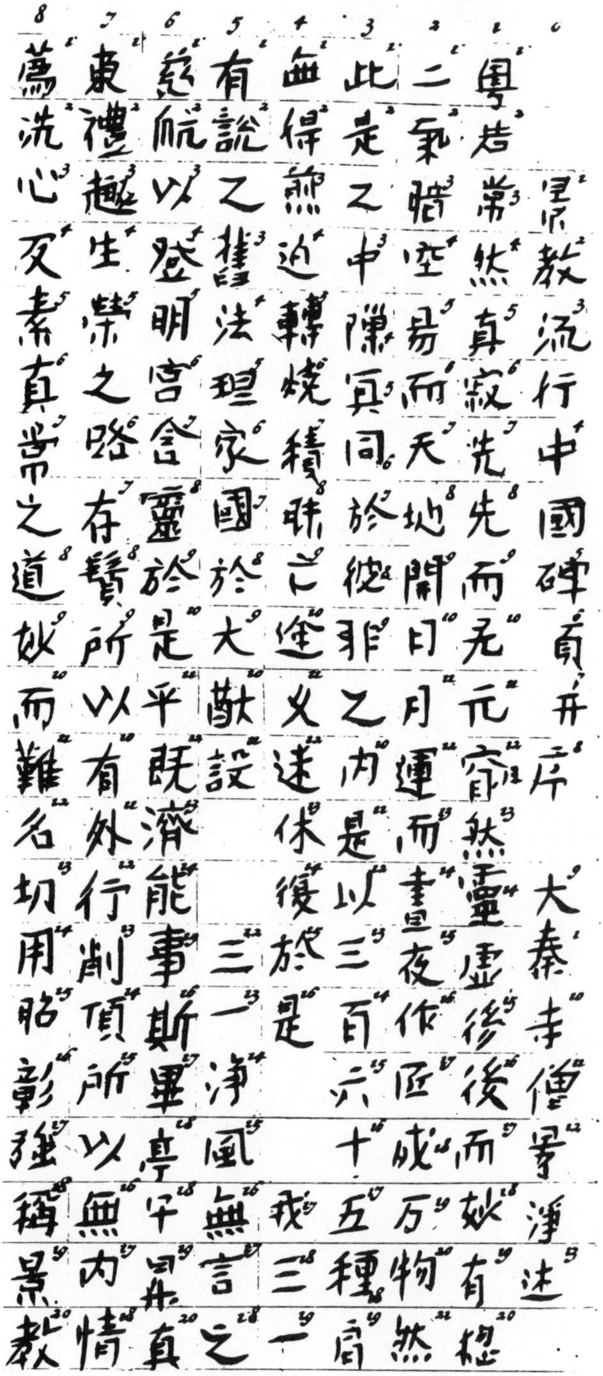

Slightly enlarged section of the Hsi-an Fu Inscription.

page 219 (recto) The Hsi-an Fu Inscription with numbered Chinese characters as equivalents to the Romanized transliteration in order of the columns of the Inscription. (Michael Bohm's Chinese Dictionary in *China illustrata*, 1667)

INTERPRETATIO I.

Quâ

Characterum Sinicorum, qui in Monumento Sinico continentur, pronunciatio genuina per Latinos Characteres exprimitur.

7. *Chum* 8. *Kuĕ* 9. *Poeŷ.*

4. *Kiaó* 5. *Lieû* 6. *Hiñ*

1. *Ta* 2. *Cyń* 3. *Kim̀*

4. Col.
1. *uû*
2. *tĕ*
3. *cyeñ*
4. *pĕ*
5. *chueǹ*
6. *xaŏ*
7. *cyĕ*
8. *mŏ*
9. *vaǹ*
10. *tû*
11. *kieù*
12. *mî*
13. *hieū*
14. *fŏ*
15. *yú*
16. *xí*
17. *rigò*
18. *ſañ*
19. *yĕ*
20. *fueñ*
21. *xim̃*
22. *kiḿ*
23. *suǹ*
24. {*mî*, *xí*, *ŏ*}
25. *cyĕ*
26. *yǹ*
27. *chiñ*
28. *gueý*
29. *tûm*
30. *giǹ*
31. *chŏ*
32. *taý*
33. *xim̀*

3. Col.
1. *sú*
2. {*xí*, *chî*}
3. *chum̃*
4. *kiĕ*
5. *miñ*
6. *tum̂*
7. *yú*
8. *poý*
9. {*ſî*, *chî*}
10. *nuý*
11. *xí*
12. *ỳ*
13. *ſañ*
14. *pĕ*
15. *lŏ*
16. *xĕ*
17. *ú*
18. *chum̃*
19. *kieñ*
20. *ſuŷ*
21. *kiĕ*
22. *chĕ*
23. *kiḿ*
24. *chĕ*
25. *fá*
26. *lŏ*
27. *hoĕ*
28. *chî*
29. *uĕ*
30. *ỳ*
31. *tŏ*
32. *sum̂*
33. *hoĕ*

2. Col.
1. *lĭ*
2. *kî*
3. *ngañ*
4. *chim̂*
5. *ý*
6. *lĭ*
7. *tieñ*
8. *tý*
9. *kaỳ*
10. *gĕ*
11. *yuĕ*
12. *yuñ*
13. *lĭ*
14. *cheú*
15. *yĕ*
16. *só*
17. *cyaḿ*
18. *chim̂*
19. *tam̂*
20. *uĕ*
21. *gên*
22. *liĕ*
23. *sŏ*
24. *giñ*
25. *piĕ*
26. *sú*
27. {*leam̂*, *hŏ*}
28. *liḿ*
29. *chiñ*
30. *hoá*
31. *haỳ*
32. *hoén*
33. *yueñ*

1. Columna.
1. *yĕ*
2. *giû*
3. *cham̂*
4. *geñ*
5. *chiñ*
6. *cyĕ*
7. *syeñ*
8. *syeñ*
9. *lĭ*
10. *uû*
11. *yueñ*
12. *siaŏ*
13. *geñ*
14. {*lim̂*, *hiñ*}
15. *heú*
16. *heú*
17. *lĭ*
18. *miaó*
19. *yeù*
20. *sum̃*
21. *hiueñ*
22. *kiû*
23. *lĭ*
24. {*saó*, *hoá*}
25. *miaó*
26. {*chum̂*, *xiḿ*}
27. *ỳ*
28. *yueñ*
29. *suñ*
30. *chè*
31. *kî*
32. *gueý*

o.
1. *Kim̀*
2. *kiaó*
3. {*lieû*, *hiñ*}
4. {*chum̂*, *kuĕ*}
5. *poeŷ*
6. *sum̂*
7. *piñ*
8. *siú*
9. {*Tá*, *cyń*}
10. *xí*
11. *ceñ*
12. {*kim̀*, *cyḿ*}
13. *xŏ*

34. *tieñ*

First page of the Hsi-an Fu Inscription in the Romanized text with marks of tones and numbers of the words corresponding to the numbers of the Chinese characters, in Michael Boym's Chinese Dictionary in *China illustrata*, 1667.

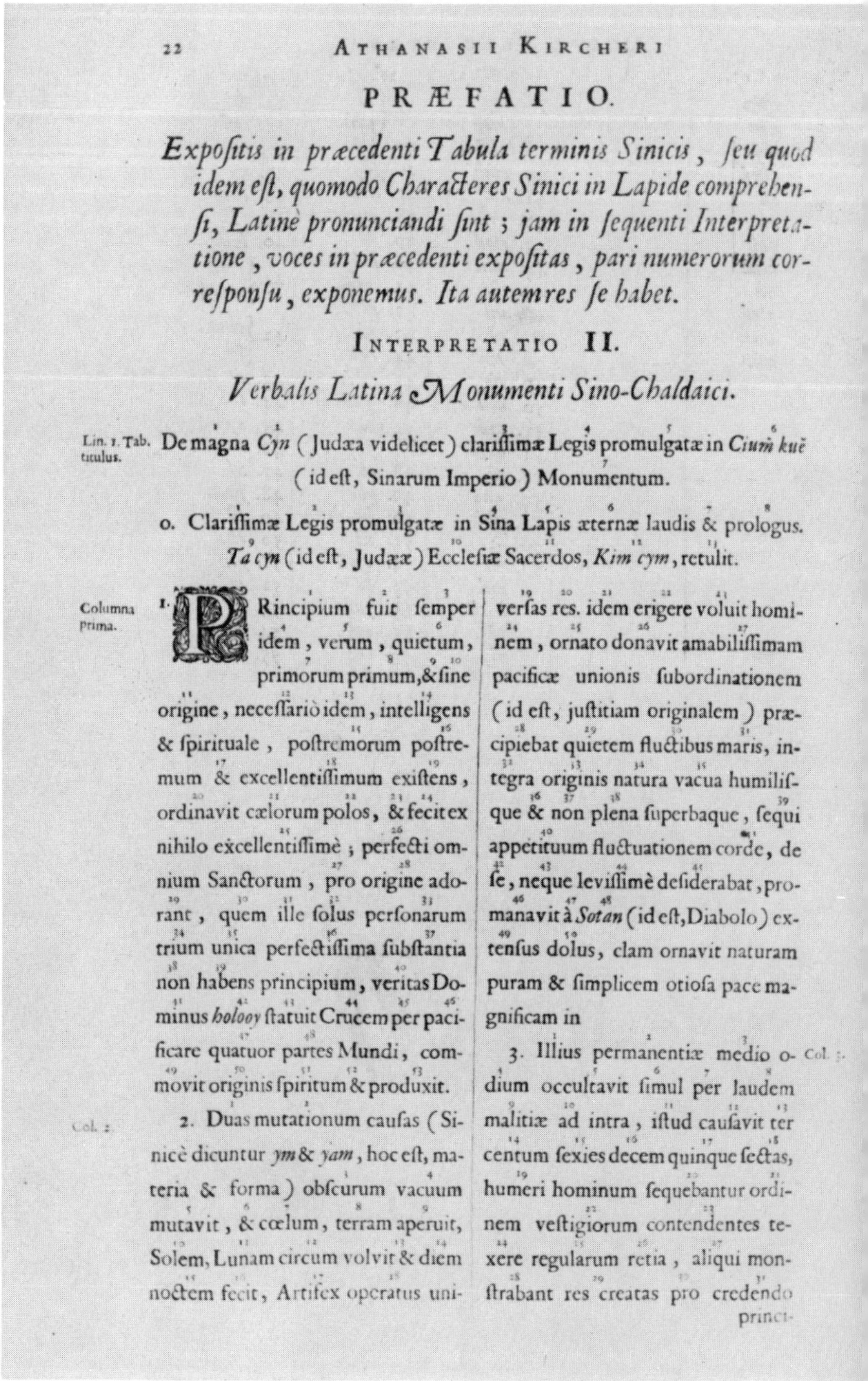

22 ATHANASII KIRCHERI

PRÆFATIO.

Expositis in præcedenti Tabula terminis Sinicis, seu quod idem est, quomodo Characteres Sinici in Lapide comprehensi, Latinè pronunciandi sint; jam in sequenti Interpretatione, voces in præcedenti expositas, pari numerorum correspon su, exponemus. Ita autem res se habet.

INTERPRETATIO II.

Verbalis Latina Monumenti Sino-Chaldaici.

Lin. 1. Tab. titulus. De magna *Cyn* (Judæa videlicet) clarissimæ Legis promulgatæ in *Cium kuë* (id est, Sinarum Imperio) Monumentum.

o. Clarissimæ Legis promulgatæ in Sina Lapis æternæ laudis & prologus. *Ta cyn* (id est, Judææ) Ecclesiæ Sacerdos, *Kim cym*, retulit.

Columna Prima. 1. PRincipium fuit semper idem, verum, quietum, primorum primum, & sine origine, necessariò idem, intelligens & spirituale, postremorum postremum & excellentissimum existens, ordinavit cælorum polos, & fecit ex nihilo excellentissimè; perfecti omnium Sanctorum, pro origine adorant, quem ille solus personarum trium unica perfectissima substantia non habens principium, veritas Dominus *holooy* statuit Crucem per pacificare quatuor partes Mundi, commovit originis spiritum & produxit.

Col. 2. 2. Duas mutationum causas (Sinicè dicuntur *ym* & *yam*, hoc est, materia & forma) obscurum vacuum mutavit, & cœlum, terram aperuit, Solem, Lunam circum volvit & diem noctem fecit, Artifex operatus universas res. idem erigere voluit hominem, ornato donavit amabilissimam pacificæ unionis subordinationem (id est, justitiam originalem) præcipiebat quietem fluctibus maris, integra originis natura vacua humilisque & non plena superbaque, sequi appetituum fluctuationem corde, de se, neque levissimè desiderabat, promanavit à *Sotan* (id est, Diabolo) extensus dolus, clam ornavit naturam puram & simplicem otiosa pace magnificam in

3. Illius permanentiæ medio odium occultavit simul per laudem malitiæ ad intra, istud causavit ter centum sexies decem quinque sectas, humeri hominum sequebantur ordinem vestigiorum contendentes texere regularum retia, aliqui monstrabant res creatas pro credendo Col. 3.

princi-

First page of the literal Latin translation of the Hsi-an Fu Inscription with the numbered words corresponding to the numbers over the Chinese characters and to their transliteration in Michael Boym's Chinese Dictionary in *China illustrata*, 1667.

Boym's vocabulary, a great curiosity in itself, became a source of deep interest to two "home-made" scholars, Andreas Müller (1630–1694) and Christian Mentzel (1622–1701). These two amateurish German orientalists had close connections with Poland, the country of Boym. Mentzel studied in Frankfurt on the Odra, and in Königsberg or Królewiec, in East Prussia, at that time a Polish dependency. From 1658 he was the librarian of Kurfurst Friedrich Wilhelm of Brandenburg in Berlin. Müller was born at Grefenhagen, also on the Odra, and worked as a Protestant pastor in Starogard in Poland, and died in Szczecin in Polish-speaking Pomerania.[6]

The extensive descriptions of China and the Far East in *China illustrata* attracted the imagination and curiosity of these two savant-librarians, who showed vivid excitement about the Chinese dictionary in particular, which together with some other of Boym's papers was edited by Kircher, the prominent Jesuit polyhistor (1602–1680).[7] Their disposition to inquire into exotic things coincided with the character of Boym's work, which was in the library at Berlin. Mentzel and Müller were in close relationship with Andreas Cleyer, a senior medical officer of the Dutch East India Company in Java, who, like them, proved to be a plagiarist. These three unscrupulous orientalists were members of a strange academy, Academia Naturae Curiosorum in Frankfurt on the Main. They unfortunately became friends of Philip Couplet (1624–1692), a missionary and Jesuit Procurer of China and Japan. Couplet mishandled some of Boym's papers, leaving them temporarily with Andreas Cleyer, and later sold them to the Berlin Library. Some of Boym's translations of Chinese medical essays were published by Cleyer under his own name in 1682, with no mention of the original translator.[8]

In 1672, five years after Kircher's publication of *China illustrata*, Müller issued his essay on the Hsi-an Fu inscription, with a long complicated Baroque title: *Monumenti Sinici quod anno Domini MDC XXV terris in ipsa China erutum*, etc. The title can be rendered in English as follows: The Chinese monument which

---

[6] See Szczesniak, "The Beginnings of Chinese Lexicography," p. 164.

[7] See n. 1, *ut supra*.

[8] Szczesniak, "The Works of Michael Boym," pp. 517-521, and nn. 96-110; Julius Klaproth, *Verzeichniss der Chinesischen und mandshuischen Bücher und Handschriften de Königlichen Bibliothek zu Berlin* (Paris, 1822), pp. VII-VIII, 153-180.

in A.D. 1625 was excavated in China and which in the eighth century was erected,. . . presently its inscription is translated, edited and paraphrased with amendments of errors, and with added musical tones, with removed defects of the text as published by Athanasius Kircher, now issued by Christian Müller.[9] As we see, he did not credit Boym with the authorship, and furthermore, as the title indicates, he falsely ascribed to Kircher the marks of tonations, which constituted an important contribution to the system of Romanization of the Chinese language. Kircher was ignorant of the Chinese language. Müller did not improve Boym's work. He preserved misprints and added many errors, an evident proof of his ignorance. Müller's knowledge of Chinese, as Thomas Hyde, an orientalist from Oxford, concluded, was "dubious or rather null."[10] Eusèbe Renaudot (1646–1720), a prominent author and student of Oriental relations with the Western World, was astounded by Müller's claim of correcting Boym's translation of the Chinese text of the Nestorian monument. Renaudot did not believe that Müller was able to introduce any emendation into the translation. He also criticized Müller's fantastic interpretations of the contents of the Nestorian inscription.[11] Savant Müller pretended he had invented a key to the Chinese language, *Clavis Sinica*, but he did not do it. Gottlieb Siegfried Bayer (1694–1738), in his *Museum Sinicum*[12] justly observed about Müller's proposed method of the study of the Chinese language, that "it would

[9] *Monumenti Sinici quod Annó Domini MDXXV terris in ipsa China erutum; seculo vero octávo Sinice ac partim Syriace, in saxo perscriptum esse adeoque dogmatum et rituum Romanae Ecclesiae (ante annos quippe mille in extremo Oriente receptorum) antiquitatem magnopere confirmare perhibetur, lectio seu phrazis, versio seu metaphrasis, translatio seu paraphrasis, plane uti celeberrimus polyhistor, P. Athanasius Kircherus, Soc. Jesu presbyter Romanus, in China sua illustrata anno MDCLXVII. singula singulariter edidit. Ceterum tonos vocibus addidit, inq; nonnullis novae hujus editionis exemplis Kircherianae defectus supplevit, errata sustulit, omnia vero minio indicavit Andreas Müllerus, Greiffenhagius.* Berolini, ex officina Rungiana, anno MDCLXXII.

[10] Thomas Hyde, *Historia religionis veterum Persarum...* (Oxford, 1700), p. 41, and table V.

[11] Abbé Eusèbe Renaudot, *Anciennes relations des Indes et de la Chine de deux voyageurs mahométans...* (Paris, 1718), p. 241; see also English translation of the work, *Ancient Accounts of India and China by Two Mohammedan Travellers...* London, 1733.

[12] *Museum Simcum in quo Sinicae linguae et litteraturae ratio explicatur,* vol. I (Petropoli, 1730), p. 38.

be easier to teach fish to sing, than man to speak by his method."[13]

In his second essay on the Christian Inscription from Hsi-an Fu, entitled *Hebdomas observationum de rebus Sinicis*, Müller reprinted Boym's observations on the original text with a few incongruent remarks, which were supposed to show his Sinological learning, and with a chaotic evaluation of the inscription.[14]

His friend Christian Mentzel, went a step further in tackling the rare, exotic dictionary. He collected Chinese words with their Latin meanings, from Boym's vocabulary text in *China illustrata*, copied the Chinese characters, and in 1685 published in conventional form the Boym vocabulary. In the title, however, he presented himself as the author who had made the vocabulary on the basis of material from Chinese authors. The long Latin text of this *opusculum*, beginning with the words *Sylloge minutiarum lexici Latino-Sinico-Characteristici. . .*,[15] implied that this dictionary was Mentzel's own, compiled from original Chinese sources. However, the only material he used was Boym's Latin translation of the famed inscription. He selected 288 words, which he put into alphabetical order with their corresponding characters, transliteration and meaning. Mentzel had a good idea how a Chinese dictionary should be compiled, but he did not know the Chinese language. He repeated Boym's inaccuracies and misprints and in addition obscured the whole work by ignorant copying of characters. The vocabulary was of no value for any practical purpose.

Although Boym's lexical effort was an object for exploitation by two ignorant self-styled orientalists, it advanced interest in the Chinese language, in its nature and its origin. In 1686–87 Shen Fu-tsung, a Chinese scholar brought to Europe by Philip Couplet, appeared at Oxford. The scholar helped Thomas Hyde to learn

[13] Professor Donald Lach made a glaring mistake in his article, "The Chinese Studies of Andreas Müller," *Journal of the American Oriental Society*, vol. 60, No. 4, p. 568, expressing an opinion that "Müller was one of the outstanding German authorities on Chinese subjects. He had read practically everything on China written in western languages." [sic!]

[14] *Hebdomas observationum de rebus Sinicis... quibus adiunguntur tria capita examinis illi monumenti Sinici autor. Andreas Müllerus, Greiffenhagius.* Coloniae Brandenburgicae, ex officina Georgii Schultzi, Elect. Typogr. 1674.

[15] *Sylloge minutiarum lexici Latino-Sinico Characteristici, observatione sedula ex auctoribus et lexicis Chinensium characteristicis eruta, inque specimen primi laboris ulterius exantlandi erudito et curioso orbi exposita a Christiano Mentzelio D. Seren. Elect. Brandenb. Consil. et Archiatro.* Norimbergae, anno MDCLXXXV.

some words, especially numbers and the units of time-reckoning, in Chinese. Hyde, an English Orientalist and lecturer in Persian, showed for a short time a strong interest in lexical studies of the Chinese language, but he eventually realized the hopelessness of his intention.[16]

As late as ca. 1710, Etienne Fourmont (1683–1747), a self-made French Sinologist, worked on a Mandarin dictionary with another Chinese scholar imported by the Jesuits, a missionary convert named Arcadius Hoang (died in Paris, 1716). The scholar appeared, however, to have been of no real help to Fourmont, who was not able to finish his project; and what Fourmont left of his work included the material which Couplet had acquired. The French student of Chinese was acquainted with Boym's vocabulary and knew his plagiarists, whom he condemned. He displayed a true sense of respect for Boym's Sinological contributions, but he was also an amateur Sinologist, a dabbler. Fourmont published in 1742 *Lexicon Sinicum*, a Chinese-Latin dictionary inserted in his *Meditationes Sinicae.*[17] It was taken from Boym's papers which were left by Couplet in the Sainte Geneviève Jesuit house in Paris. It had been published in the French edition of *China illustrata*, *La Chine illustrée* (Amsterdam, 1670), from where Fourmont took it and acknowledged Boym's authorship.[18] Therefore, the second Chinese dictionary by Boym, compiled in conventional form, suffered an appropriation similar to the previous one. In his *Chinese Meditations* Fourmont speculated that the Greek language

---

[16] J. L. L. Duyvendak, "Bodleiana," *T'oung Pao*, vol. XXXIV, 1938, pp. 228-230; see also Hyde, n. 10.

[17] *Meditationes Sinicae, in quibus; I° consideratur linguae philosophicae atque universalis natura qualis esse aut debeat aut possit; II° lingua Sinarum Mandarinica, tum in hieroglyphis, tum in monosyllabis suis, ea mente inventa ac talis esse* ostenditur; III° datur eorumque *hieroglyphorum ac monosyllaborum atque inde characterum linguae Sinicae omnium... lectio et intellectio;* IV° *idque omne, progressu a libris mere Europaeis (de Sina tamen) ad libros mere Sinicos facto...* Author Stephanus Fourmont... Lutetiac Parisiorum, Musier le Père, 1737.—With this work is connected another book, a grammar of the Mandarin language with Chinese characters. *Linguae Sinarum Mandarinicae hieroglyphicae grammatica duplex, latine et cum characteribus Sinensium. Item Sinicorum regiae bibliothecae catalogus denuo... editus...* Author Stephanus Fourmont. Lutetiae Parisiorum, H. L. Guerin, 1742.

[18] Etienne Fourmont, *Catalogue des ouvrages de monsieur Fourmont L'Aine, professeur en langue arabe en College Royale de France, associé de L'Académie Royale des Inscriptions et Belles Lettres, interprête, et sou-bibliothequaire du Roy, etc.* (Amsterdam, 1731), pp. 47-48.

was borrowed from Chinese.[19] Fourmont's Sinological works are undoubtedly not his own.

The appearance of the Boym Chinese dictionaries happened at a time when European pride in its cultural preeminence was harmed by the realization that there were other countries of perhaps greater eminence and of much older culture than the European, countries with considerably perfected administration as well. Interest in Sinical studies has constantly been impeded by the lack of Chinese vocabulary. Boym helped to advance the beginnings of Sinological studies in the age of the Enlightenment, and was also conspicuous for his admiration of the Chinese Empire.[20]

[19] See the very rare pamphlet by Daniel Webb, *Some Reasons for Thinking that the Greek Language was Borrowed from the Chinese*; *In Notes on the Grammatica Sinica of Mons. Fourmont* (London, 1787).

[20] A portion of this paper was read to the Far Eastern Section at the annual meeting of the American Oriental Society, March 23, 1967, at New Haven, Connecticut.

THE SEVEN CASTES OF MEGASTHENES

by J. A. B. van Buitenen
University of Chicago

ONE OF the most curious problems presented by Megasthenes' *Indika* as preserved principally by Strabo, Arrian and Diodorus Siculus[1] is that of the seven population groups in which, according to him, Indian society was divided. It has been pointed out frequently that these seven groups make no sense. They obviously cannot be identified with the *varṇas*, which are four. It is also out of the question that the seven groups exhaust the number of *jātis* that existed in Candragupta's time.[2] In the best study, to my knowledge, on the subject of Megasthenes' account of Indian society Barbara Timmer comes to the following conclusion:[3] "The mutual sequence of the seven classes is therefore determined by different motivations: first, by Indian conceptions; second, by their social functions; third, by incidental qualities such as number; and for the rest by the author's whim." These "Indian religious conceptions" amount to the fact that the Brahmins are placed first and are declared to be the most highly honored group. The division into seven groups she attributes to a partially mistaken application by Megasthenes of the common Brahministic notion that class and profession coincide, so that he identified every professional and vocational group as a class or caste.[4] While this is a fetching notion, it is hard to understand why Megasthenes identified

[1] For the reader of Dutch the most convenient compilation of the materials here discussed is found in Barbara C. J. Timmer's *Megasthenes en de Indische maatschappij* (Thesis, Amsterdam 1930); others will have to rely on J. W. McCrindle, *The* Indika *of Megasthenes and Arrian*, now reprinted as *Ancient India as Described by Megasthenes and Arrian* (Calcutta 1960) and *Ancient India, As described in Classical Literature* (Westminster 1901); the Greek and Latin sources are collected in E. A. Schwanbeck, *Megasthenis Indica* (reprinted Amsterdam 1966).

[2] Arrian reports, somewhat incredulously, that according to Megasthenes there were 118 "tribes" in India (McCrindle, *The* Indika, pp. 198-99), which may well correspond to castes; the number itself may be based on the usual 108 in the sense of a hundred, or fairly large indefinite number.

[3] Op. cit., p. 68.

[4] P. 67.

only *seven* vocations; physicians and lawyers, for instance, are not recognized among them.

While many of Miss Timmer's results should be retained, it may be worthwhile to return to this old problem and suggest a new interpretation which may bring some clarity to it. It has become customary to translate Megasthenes' *groups* by "class, caste,"[5] and we may well wonder whether this is not a misnomer, since the groups correspond to neither.[6] The only *varṇa* discernible is that of the Brahmins, but in his description Megasthenes clearly refers to only a small group among the Brahmins, namely, the professional priests. To identify the soldiers with the kṣatriyas is stretching the point beyond reason; and if we identify the artisans and tradesmen with the vaiśyas, are we to consider all the peasants śūdras? And that these seven groups were the only castes of the time militates against historical evidence. It therefore prejudices the question by calling these groups "castes."

On the other hand, it is true that Megasthenes himself identifies them in caste terms when he says that the groups do not intermarry, that members of the groups are not permitted to adopt the vocation of another group, and that vocations thus are hereditary.[7] Also, from his description of the manners of India, it is clear that he observed the lack of commensality which we would attribute to their differences in caste.[8] We are thus faced with the fact that Megasthenes knew about caste and erroneously assumed that the seven groups corresponded to castes. I am inclined to go a step further than Miss Timmer and submit that the application of caste to the groups was *completely* mistaken and that, if one of the groups happened to be a caste also, it was by accident.

This leads us to assume that the application of notions of class

---

[5] Particularly since McCrindle; more recently, A. L. Basham, *The Wonder That was India* (London 1954), p. 101; spoke more cautiously of Megasthenes' "seven occupational classes."

[6] Among others and most recently, R. C. Majumdar, "The Indika of Megasthenes," (JAOS, 1958), pp. 273ff., finds in these "castes" an occasion to impugn Megasthenes' veracity: "His description of the seven castes, which are unknown to Indian literature or tradition, may be cited as an example (sc. of Megasthenes' unreliability), where, on a few basic facts, he has reared up a structure which is mostly inaccurate and misleading." But translating them as "castes" in the first place produces the inaccuracy; cf. also his note p. 231, in reprint of McCrindle, *Ancient India*.

[7] Timmer, op. cit., pp. 53-55 for the sources.

[8] Cf. Timmer, p. 263, corresponding to Strabo, 15.1.53.

and caste to the seven groups can only be confusing and that we should look for another principle of classification in order to understand why Megasthenes mentioned just these groups. For even if they were not castes, they might still be a correct division of society, however rough.

He enumerates them in this order: philosophers, peasants, herdsmen (including hunters), artisans-tradesmen, soldiers, inspectors, and officials; and, though incomplete, this looks like a rough and ready inventory of population during Candragupta's time. It is possible to argue that Megasthenes himself has drawn up these groups from personal observation, but there is an important argument against it. He mentions carefully the relation of each group to the treasury; and though such information could no doubt have been acquired by interviewing the groups once he had listed them, it is far more likely that he simply went to a treasury official and asked for the information.

Megasthenes, after all, was an ambassador, and envoys are rarely courtesy visits. He was sent by Seleukos Nikator, who spent most of his life warring for Alexander's bequest of the Middle East. In 307 or 306 Seleukos had invaded Northwest India, no doubt to claim Alexander's old conquests. Troubles elsewhere forced him in 304 to stop his campaign, and in fact he completely abandoned all claims to the territory in a treaty with Candragupta in which he actually ceded the Paropanisadic country, Arachosia, and Gedrosia for five hundred elephants. It was after concluding this treaty that Megasthenes was sent to India, to keep a check, one cannot help thinking, on Candragupta's own intentions. An army of 400,000 men, as Megasthenes attributes to the Maurya,[9] is a considerable force on a warring neighbor's flank. A country's military power depends on its revenues, and one may safely assume that Megasthenes, himself a general, investigated the tax basis of the country.

Looked at from this point of view, Megasthenes list makes excellent sense. It is an official list: the seven groups are in fact seven *treasury or tax categories*.

1. Philosophers: tax-exempt and occasionally to be paid out of the treasury.

[9] Strabo I, 53, p. 709; H. L. Jones, *The Geography of Strabo* (New York 1932) translates "40,000," which Majumdar wants to accept; but Arrian 12, 2-4 says that the soldiers are the second most numerous group (after the peasants), which makes us prefer 400,000.

2. Agriculturalists: free from military service and in theory tenants of the king's land as Crown demesne, paying 25% in rents.
3. Herdsmen: pay cattle taxes, but may receive grain grants for clearing the jungle of game.
4. Artisans-tradesmen: pay taxes, with the exceptions of weaponsmiths and shipwrights, who are paid out of the treasury.
5. Soldiers: including horses, elephants and their handlers, entirely paid out of the treasury.
6. Inspectors:[10] entirely paid out of the treasury.
7. Officials: entirely paid out of the treasury.

We have therefore two basic groups: those who pay taxes *into* the treasury, and those who receive money *from* the treasury—respectively, (2), (3) and (4); and (5), (6) and (7). This leaves the category of the philosophers, who are in neither category, being tax-exempt and not paid out of the treasury, except in incidental cases at New Year.

This classification of the population by people who neither pay nor receive, those who only pay (with specific exceptions), and those who only recieve,[11] seems to me a very sensible one from the point of view of the fiscus, and at the same time resonant of

[10] To translate *epískopoi/éphoroi* as "spies" is to narrow unduly the significance of this group; they constitute a government service which, since it is listed separately, was clearly budgeted separately from Army and Ministries, as secret services usually are. Their use of prostitutes as "stool pigeons"(for which Kanṭilya also allows) is not at all surprising. The information thus elicited would be of at least three kinds: on criminal underworld activity generally, even though prostitution itself was legal; on the amount of discretionary income of possibly undertaxed citizens (these kinds of information would no doubt emerge from the city courtesans who, according to Strabo, are distinguished from camp-following prostitutes); and on unrest in the army (from camp followers). The service as a whole is approximately that of a police force—criminal, political as well as military —a service not accounted for among Megasthenes' three principal government departments (Timmer, pp. 177-78); Strabo, 15.1.50-52.

[11] It is revealing to what extent Megasthenes' account is saturated with what one might call fiscal attitudes: the army is really overpaid and makes merry in peacetime on government money (Timmer, pp. 155-56); Strabo 15.1.47; of the three principal departments, the first, the ágoranómoi, collects revenues from lumberjacks, carpenters, smiths and miners; the second, the astunómoi, includes a *pañcāyat* to encourage the flow of foreign money, one for vital statistics "for the sake of taxes," one for commerce which makes sure that merchants dealing in more than one product are doubly taxed and one that supervises the 10% sales tax. This consistent interest in taxation should point to the preoccupation of both Megasthenes and his informant.

Indian classification. There is A, there is B, and there is neither A nor B; the last group could as easily have been placed last in the list, but it is obviously put first as a sign of respect either by Megasthenes' informant or by Megasthenes himself.

It is noteworthy that after the description of the seven groups Megasthenes resumes the topic of the philosophers in greater detail.[12]

Miss Timmer curiously rejects this interpretation because "members of the same class often relate differently to (the treasury)."[13] This is true, but every tax category usually has its minor exceptions. Again in the listing there seems to be sensible order: those who all pay taxes (2); those who all pay taxes, but may be recompensed for special services (3); those who all pay taxes with the exception of weaponsmiths and shipwrights. Of the last one it is at once noted with typical accountant's precision what happens to the products; the weapons go to the general for distribution, the ships go to the admiral for rental.

I see a similar order in the categories (5), (6) and (7). First, no doubt the largest recipient of expenditures is the Army,[14] followed directly by Intelligence, which surely was military as well as fiscal, and finally the Government.

The only mistake Megasthenes made was to think of these fiscal population groups as castes and to apply to them what he knew of caste. The mistake is understandable, especially since the groups obviously included castes. And it might have been a simple misunderstanding. *Jāti* may mean any group[15] that can be classed together, and Megasthenes, upon asking a revenue official, "How many *jātis* are there in the country?" could well have received the answer, "These seven."

---

[12] Which may indicate that the description of the philosophers was the last one; but the point is tenuous.

[13] P. 69.

[14] According to Arrian, the second largest group of the population.

[15] Megasthenes seems to have used only *meros* and *genea*, or "parts" and "kinds" in his original account; both words are sufficiently neutral and both are translatable by *jāti*, when speaking of population groups.

FROM THE CHINESE TO THE KOREAN, JAPANESE, AND VIETNAMESE SYSTEMS OF WRITING: THREE CASES OF LINGUISTIC NATIONALISM*

by Joseph K. Yamagiwa
University of Michigan

IN THE early years of their development the Korean and Japanese writing systems passed through a number of stages which show some striking similarities. The parallelism is by no means complete, but it seems possible to speak of a typology of evolution when we discuss the adaptation of the Chinese system of charactery to the writing of two languages, Korean and Japanese, which are not at all genetically related to the Chinese language. Chinese, we here assume, is a qualified member of the Sino-Tibetan group of languages, whereas Korean and Japanese, whose precise relationship is still being debated, seem relatable to the Altaic family.[1]

In both Korea and Japan no written script had been devised prior to the advent of the Chinese charactery. In both cases it was the Chinese characters that were first learned, and items in the Chinese language, mainly inscriptions, that were first written. The same process of adapting the Chinese writing system to the native languages included use of the characters for their logographic values, that is, in expressing Korean and Japanese words and roots, though often imperfectly, and the use of the Chinese characters as representations of Korean and Japanese syllables, that is, as phonetic symbols. In both Korea and Japan, shapes were invented that stood for the native syllables, and, finally, the Chinese and

* The author wishes to acknowledge the assistance he has received from Professors Frits Vos of Leiden University, William E. Henthorn of Princeton University, and Miles McElrath of the University of Michigan, in checking the details of this paper that have to do with the Korean language and system of writing.

[1] Hattori Shirô, throughout the collection of articles gathered in *Nihoñgo no keitō* (The Affinities of the Japanese Language) (Tōkyō, Iwanami Shoteñ, 1959), takes a very cautious view with respect to the relationship between Korean and Japanese. Samuel E. Martin, in "Lexical Evidence Relating Korean to Japanese," *Language*, Vol. 42, No. 2 (April-June, 1966), pp. 185-251, has recently provided a list of 350 correspondences between Korean and Japanese lexical items, divided into three groups in accordance with degree of "fit" in form and meaning.

syllabic characters were used together in the writing of the Korean and Japanese languages. Only in Japan was a system of markings also invented which would permit the reading of a Chinese text as a series of Japanese sentences. More in Korea than in Japan, the forms standing for the syllables were compounded of other shapes to which vowel and consonant values could be given.

The Chinese characters, taken to still another area of East Asia, Annam (part of what is today Vietnam), suggested the creation of a system of characters known as *chữ' nôm.* In Vietnam, however, the Chinese characters and *chữ' nôm* are today almost entirely replaced by the letters of the alphabet, introduced first by Western missionaries in the sixteenth century and then sponsored under the French protectorates of the nineteenth century.[2]

Studies of the Korean, Japanese, and Vietnamese writing systems usually have very little to say concerning the political and other conditions under which the vernaculars in the respective non-Chinese areas have asserted themselves. The present paper will discuss:

I. The relationship between language and nationalism and the conflicts which occur when rival languages are found in a single nation

II. The adaptation of the Chinese writing system in Korea and Japan: parallel developments

III. The adaptation of the Chinese writing system in Korea and Japan: divergent developments

IV. Linguistic concerns related to the development of the Korean and Japanese writing systems

V. Paralinguistic concerns relating to their development

VI. The sociopolitical reasons behind the divergent developments in Korea and Japan

VII. The Vietnamese case

VIII. Prospects for the vernaculars in other areas of Asia, Africa, and elsewhere in the world where newly emergent countries face the problem of preserving their native languages.

We need here to say that this excursion into typology is being undertaken with more daring than diffidence, and with greater

[2] For a description of *chữ' nôm,* see Nguyễn Đình Hoà, "Chữ' nôm, the Demotic System of Writing in Vietnam," *Journal of the American Oriental Society,* Vol. 79, No. 4 (October-December, 1959), pp. 270-274. Section 7 of the present paper owes a great deal to Professor Nguyễn's article.

reliance on materials in English and Japanese than in Korean or Vietnamese, but it is the very existence of these materials, many recently published, which has suggested this attempt at a subject that is basically paralinguistic and cross-cultural.[3]

I

The close relationship that exists between language and national aims is freshly illustrated on every continent today.[4] In nations like the United States, England, and Japan a common language makes for a feeling of oneness and community. In Asia and Africa the rising tide of nationalism brings in each country a desire to use one's own language, rather than the language of a colonial power, as the language of communication. Today, in India several native languages contend for dominance and the right to replace the

---

[3] For a treatment in English of the ways in which the Chinese writing system was adapted in Korea, see the articles by Frits Vos in *Papers of the CIC Far Eastern Language Institute: The University of Michigan, 1963*: "Korean Writing: *the hyang'ga*," "Korean Writing: *idu* and *han'gŭl*," and "History of the Korean Language." Specifically on the development of *han'gŭl*, see G. K. Ledyard, *The Korean Language Reform of 1446: the Origin, Background, and Early History of the Korean Alphabet*, University of California, Berkeley, 1966; abstract in *Dissertation Abstracts A: The Humanities and Social Sciences*, Vol. 27, No. 4 (October 1966), pp. 1031A-1032A. For a discussion of the *han'gŭl* by a Korean scholar see Lee Ki-moon (Yi Kimun), *Kug'ŏ p'yogi-bŏp ŭi yŏksa-jŏk yŏn'gu* (A History of the Written Characters and of Language Studies in Korea) (Seoul, 1963). This work has a 23 page résumé in English. Western, Korean, and Japanese works on the Korean language and writing system are listed in B. H. Hazard, Jr., etc., *Korean Studies Guide* (Berkeley and Los Angeles, University of California Press), chaps. 14 and 15, pp. 145-163. For a treatment in English of the adoption of the Chinese charactery in Japan, see G. B. Sansom, *A Historical Grammar of Japanese* (Oxford, 1928), chap. 1, pp. 1-68. For the Japanese bibliography on the Japanese writing system, see the article by Yamada Toshio in Joseph K. Yamagiwa, ed., *Japanese Language Studies in the Shōwa Period* (The University of Michigan Center for Japanese Studies Bibliographical Series, Number 9; Ann Arbor, 1961), pp. 134-141; also, Yamada's article on the development of the Japanese writing system and Tsukishima Hiroshi's on Japanese historical linguistics in the forthcoming second volume of *Current Trends in Linguistics*, ed. by Thomas A. Sebeok. For a comparison of the ways in which the Koreans and Japanese adopted the Chinese charactery see Kōno Rokurō, "*Kojiki* ni okeru kañji shiyō (The Use of the Chinese Characters in the *Kojiki*)," in *Kojiki taisei* (A Compilation of Studies of the *Kojiki*), Vol. 3 (Tōkyō, Heiboñsha, 1957), pp. 155-205.

[4] The propositions stated in this section derive greatly from suggestions found in Alfred Pietrzyk, Janet R. Duckett, and Kathleen P. Lewis, *Selected Titles in Sociolinguistics* (Washington, Center for Applied Linguistics, 1964).

language (English) used by the colonizing power, the language under which the country was formerly ruled. The attempt to designate one language (Hindi) among many possible rivals as the official language of the country may in itself be divisive, so much that the language riots of 1956 and 1965 led to the death of many Indians. Some degree of national unity is lacking or lost and the country is weakened when no single language prevails, as in Belgium, where French and Flemish are spoken. This is also true of Switzerland with its French, German, Italian, and Romansh, and the Philippine Republic with its rash of local tongues.

Although it may be argued that factors extraneous to language, such as geographic features, the workings of a strong central authority, the influence of a dominant social class, and acceptance of common traditions, can create a sense of unity, it is language through which the authority is applied, and it is language that plays an almost inexorable part in developing a nation's sense of its own unity. Possony has shown that language differences, along with racial and religious differences, and allegiance to different political, legal, and educational systems, have helped to shape and to give identity to the nations located between the Rhine River and the Urals.[5] When a new nation rises, or when a local tribe seeks independence, it may substantiate its drive for autonomy by pointing to its possession of a separate language.[6] One may thus speak of linguistic unity as one of the conditions under which real national unity will develop.

Where several languages are spoken in a nation, other factors, such as the need of a common stand against an outside enemy, may keep it unified. In the case of Switzerland, an army trained for mobility in the high mountains, both in summer and winter, and neighbors on four sides which have had very little to show in the way of military success in the twentieth century, have helped to preserve the nation from invasion. Possibly, the polylingual capacities of its people, plus generations of experience in the art of hospitality, have also induced acceptance of Switzerland's inviola-

---

[5] Stephan T. Possony, "Political and Military Geography of Central, Balkan, and Eastern Europe," *Annals of the American Academy of Political and Social Sciences*, 232 (1944), p. 3.

[6] This seems to be the case with some mountain tribes in northern Cambodia; according to a report in the *New York Times*, September 25, 1964, these tribes point to ownership of a single language as a reason for seeking independence from Cambodia.

bility. Language by itself will not prevent attack, but an invading power faces special problems if the language of the country it has invaded is different from its own.

When in any nation a minority exists which insists on the preservation of some native tongue, like Welsh in Wales and Basque in southwest France, some amount of resistance to the central government is the rule. Wales is not completely subservient to England nor the Basques to France.

Emerging from colonialism or semi-colonialism, a nation may try to preserve as best it can its native tongue. But this native tongue may be too far lost to achieve revival, and in India, even though Hindi-Urdu has been designated as the national language, communication between north and south best takes place, at least among the educated minority, in English, the language of India's former masters.

Effective communication requires that a standard or common language be adopted. The existence of different languages and dialects, mutually unintelligible to the speakers, sparks an attempt to establish one of the languages or dialects as the standard. Usually, it is the language of the capital of the country, in most cases the center for artistic, cultural, and religious life as well as for government, which is adopted as the model. Sometimes, as has happened in modern Japan, a national agency like a Ministry of Education, working with committees of scholars and literary men, will support a deliberate attempt to establish a single standard language. This is reminiscent of the French Academy. In actuality, the chosen standard is rarely if ever adopted in all its details, for languages, including those chosen as models, change, and speakers of dialects tend to adopt the forms of the standard language simply because it is more prestigious to talk the language spoken at the sources of power. Consequently, there is something illogical and even pathetic in planned attempts made to change the language of dialect speakers, because dialects will in any case change toward the usages of the capital. On the other hand, the establishing of a standard language does help to spread it, especially when its use is emphasized in the schools, on radio and television, and in public print. Since in provincial areas the influence of the local dialects cannot be obliterated, dissemination of the standard helps at least to create a series of "common languages," spoken when speakers of two different dialects talk to each other. In this case, one of the two speakers may well come from the capital and control more effectively the language taken as standard. Speakers of two different dialects talking to each other generally adjust their languages in the direction of standard speech, thus making for a higher level of communicability.

Minority languages may be suppressed when used as vehicles of ideas conceived to be inimical to national purposes. These minority languages need not be obliterated, though this has been done, or virtually done, in the case of Ainu in northern Japan. The teaching of minority languages may be permitted, but the content of education is scrutinized.[7] Speakers of minority languages are apt to avoid using them, especially in countries where speaking anything other than the dominant national language suggests inability to accommodate oneself to the mores of the host state. Bilingualism in this situation is something less than an asset. In times of tension, the language schools established by immigrant minorities are viewed with suspicion, especially when the tension felt is between the host country and the homeland of the minority group.

Efforts to suppress minority languages may bring about political problems, or may be a symptom of them. When, as in the Philippines, the minority languages are spoken by local groups who are exposed also to two foreign languages, Spanish and English, the situation becomes highly complicated. The attempt there to spread the use of the Piripino (basically Tagalog) language in addition to Spanish and English is obstructed by those speakers of Visayan, Ilocano, and other languages who seek precedence for their own tongues. Since by fiat each student in the universities of the Philippines must elect Spanish and English, some feel that too much time is being devoted to language learning at the expense of "subjects with content value," and others feel that less effort should be expended in learning Spanish and more in learning English.

Viewed against this background of languages in conflict throughout the world, what can we learn from the rival purposes to which the Chinese and Korean languages were put in Korea and the Chinese and Japanese languages in Japan in the earliest period of heavy Chinese influence on these two countries?

---

[7] This has happened in Thailand, where the textbooks used in the Chinese language schools, supported by the local Chinese communities, were being rewritten in 1964.

II

The Korean language has its ancestors in a group of languages of northeastern Asia. As early as the fourth century A.D., the languages of Koguryŏ, in the northern part of the Korean peninsula, and of Silla, found in the south, were presumably related but different. But it is the language of Silla on which scholars working on the relationship between Korean and Japanese concentrate, because it is this language in which the largest number of extant Korean writings remain.[8]

Even before, in 108 B.C., four Chinese commanderies had been established in northeast Korea, and early envoys from Korea and Japan possibly saw their names written in the Chinese characters. In time, Chinese became a second language for Korea's educated elite. In Japan, Chinese artifacts, including metal mirrors containing inscriptions, arrived possibly as early as the first century A.D., and the Chinese language and characters arrived by the end of the fourth century, when Wani, possibly a Chinese person who had lived in Korea, is said to have come with a copy of the *Lun yü*, or Confucian Analects.

Hardly phonemic, but well enough adapted to the Chinese language, the Chinese characters were by no means the perfect medium for writing the Korean and Japanese languages. The Korean and Japanese writing systems developed as they did because the Korean and Japanese languages differed from Chinese in a number of significant ways, all of which helped to dictate the development of new systems of charactery:

[8] Lee Ki-moon relates the language of Koguryŏ to Japanese on the basis of some cognates found for the numerals three, five, seven, and ten, and for some fourteen other words, mainly nouns. He also finds that three words in the language of Kaya, according to him related to that of Koguryŏ, possess cognates in Japanese. Regrettably, the number of cognates from Koguryŏ and Kaya which he is able to adduce is only a handful; as Lee himself states, the total number of words in Koguryŏ and Kaya recorded in Korean works numbers only 50 or so. Lee Ki-moon, "A Genetic View of Japanese," *Chôsen gakuhô* (Journal of the Academic Association of Koreanology in Japan), No. 27 (April, 1963), pp. 97-98, 103. Lee, pp. 97-98, accepts the statement found in the *Wei shih* that Koguryŏ is related to the languages of Puyŏ, Okčŏ, and Ye, found in Manchuria and northern Korea at the beginning of the Christian era. He therefore suggests that Japanese, through Koguryŏ and Kaya, is related to some of the languages once spoken in northeastern Asia. For a bibliography of Japanese work on the affinities of the Japanese language, including Korean, see the chapter by Kamei Takashi entitled "The Relationship of Japanese to the Other Languages of East Asia," in Yamagiwa, ed., *Japanese Language Studies in the Shōwa Period*, pp. 84-87.

a. In Chinese syntax the subject came first, the verb next, and the object, where required, third, whereas in Korean and Japanese the order was normally subject-object-verb.
b. The Chinese lexicon was essentially monosyllabic, the Korean and Japanese polysyllabic; Korean personal and place names were modeled on the Chinese, Japanese names were formed on native Japanese morphemes.
c. Chinese words were not inflected, the Korean and Japanese verbs, adjectives, and specifiers (copulas) were.
d. A complicated system of honorific and humble usages based on the verbs, not found in Chinese, was found in both Korean and Japanese.
e. The Chinese had only a few particles, the Koreans and Japanese many, with the great majority standing postpositionally to the words, phrases, and clauses that they governed.
f. The Chinese syllables were both open and closed, the Korean syllables too were open and closed, but the Japanese were only open.

In addition, it is possible to note that Chinese accent depended, as today, on pitch differences, with the syllables taking different levels of height and also showing rising and falling contours or both, that Korean accent may have depended on different levels and contours of pitch, and that Japanese accent too depended on tonic contours found among the successive syllables of a phonological word. Differences in accent, however, were not to play so important a role as factors a-f in shaping the changes which the Chinese charactery underwent in Korea and Japan; that is to say, neither the Korean nor the Japanese writing systems attempted to indicate accent in any consistent way. Japanese accent is shown in the twelfth century dictionary *Ruijū myōgishō;* it was only with the invention of the *han'gŭl* signs in the fifteenth century that attention was given to indication of accent in Korean.

The following sections describe the development of the Korean and Japanese systems of writing.

a. The earliest writings in both Korea and Japan no doubt consisted of inscriptions and documents written in Chinese. The Chinese texts first taught to the Koreans by their Chinese mentors and to the Japanese by their Chinese and Korean teachers were probably learned as texts in a second language; that is to say, the Chinese materials were probably read as anyone reading a foreign language might read them, in the order of the written symbols, in pronunciations approximating those given to these characters in the Chinese language.[9] But both the Koreans and Japanese found that their oral renderings of Chinese could not take the place of communication in Korean or in Japanese and that it was necessary to seek methods of writing that were more appropriate to their own languages. In effect they were bilinguals of a curious sort, speakers of one language but writers of another.

b. The first adaptations by the Koreans and Japanese of the Chinese writing system are found in a series of inscriptions, cut on stone or in metal and dating from the middle of the sixth century.[10] The earliest datable examples are found in Silla, in four "hunting monuments" or border markers. In these inscriptions the Korean and Japanese verb endings are only rarely shown; suffixes of honorific value may be, especially in the Japanese cases; the particles are only rarely written; and the syntax often shows marked Korean and Japanese characteristics, with characters normally indicating a verb and its object in Chinese inverted in the Korean and Japanese representations. This last characteristic is especially to be noted in a Korean inscription dated 732 (or possibly as late as 792); the ordering of the characters is exactly as in Korean, but the verb endings and particles, with one exception, must be supplied in the reading. Both the Korean and Japanese inscriptions show the first uses of the characters for their phonetic values; a marked difference between the Korean and Japanese cases consists in greater use of the Chinese characters by the Japanese to represent words of native provenance.

c. The characters used in Korea for their phonetic values, when employed by government clerks in writing village registers, contracts, etc., later came to be known as *idu*, "government servants' writing." These documents were so written that Chinese words and phrases, expressed in the Chinese characters, were used together with Korean suffixes, that is, with verb endings and particles found in Korean but not in Chinese and expressed in the Chinese characters or in abbreviations thereof. The characters used in the same texts for both logographic and phonetic purposes were known as *hyangch'al*.

---

[9] For Japanese, Misawa Mitsuhiro, *Kokugoshi gaisetsu* (Outline History of the Japanese Language) (Kyōto, Sañwa Shobō, 1958), p. 14.

[10] We here follow Kōno, "*Kojiki* ni okeru kañji shiyō," sections 2 and 3, pp. 161-175; and 5 and 6, pp. 182-205; also, in some of the details, Vos, "Korean Writing: the *hyang'ga*" and "Korean Writing: *idu* and *han'gŭl*" (see n. 3, above).

In Japan the Chinese characters used to represent the syllables of the Japanese language are called *mañyōgana*, from their use in the *Mañyōshū* (Collection of a Myriad Worlds), the great anthology of the eighth century which contains approximately 4,500 poems. In the Chinese language the pronunciations carried by the Chinese character generally took the shape (C)(y)(w)V (C,y,w).[11] In time, the importation of Chinese loan words into the Japanese language had the effect of making a very simple syllabic structure more complex; in the Heiañ age (794-1167), the Japanese syllables in V and CV were augmented by others in CyV, CwV, ñ (syllabic), and in k, s, t, and p when followed by a CV syllable in which the C was also k, s, t, and p, respectively. But since the tradition of syllables in CV was exceptionally strong, a Chinese syllable beginning and ending in a consonant was usually converted into two Japanese syllables. The resulting configuration was most frequently CVCu. A Chinese character could thus be read as a Japanese word in one or more syllables. In its one-syllable Japanese pronunciation it could also be used phonetically to express a single syllable belonging to another word. A character taking a Japanese pronunciation in two or more syllables could also be used to express only the first of these syllables, or, used with full pronunciation, to render a homonym. Rarely, two characters would be used to express more than two syllables.

d. Both the *idu* in Korea and *mañyōgana* in Japan were next written in smaller size when used to show the particles and inflectional elements. The writing thus began to distinguish these "functional" elements from the more "conceptual" words which were still written in larger size. In Japan this writing of characters in larger and smaller size is found in the *norito*, or Shiñtō prayers, and *señmyō*, or Imperial proclamations. These too were "governmental" forms since Shiñtō was the native religion and the *señmyō* came from the source of power, the Emperor, but the *norito* and *señmyō* clearly have a more solemn air about them than do the documents, contracts, and deeds in which the *idu* were used in Korea. Twenty-seven *norito* are found in the *Eñgishiki* (Detailed Supplementary Code of the Eñgi Period

[11] We here follow Samuel E. Martin's formulation for the Ancient Chinese syllable in *The Phonemes of Ancient Chinese* (Supplement to the *Journal of the American Oriental Society*), No. 16 (April-June, 1953), p. 23.

[901–923]). Twenty-seven *señmyō* are recorded in the *Shoku-Nihoñgi* (Continuation of the Chronicle of Japan), compiled in 887, and a twenty-eighth example in the historical work known as *Takahashi ujibumi* (Records of the Takahashi Clan), completed in 792. Some of the *norito* probably go back to pre-Nara times, that is, to the seventh century, whereas the earliest *señmyō* are dated in the Nara period (710–794). The use of larger and smaller size characters in the *señmyō* gave the name *señmyōgaki* to this form of writing. We need to note, again, that in the Korean materials the more meaningful elements expressed in the Chinese characters were read in pronunciations borrowed from the Chinese language, whereas in the *señmyō* these same conceptual elements were more often read as representations of Japanese words.

The *idu* were sometimes called *t'o*, and their use in writing to show particles and inflectional elements was known as *hyŏnt'o*, or *t'o* that have been 'hung' in writing." As some *idu* came to be used more regularly than others in the writing of particular syllables, they underwent a process of abbreviation, often by selection of one part of the characters. Sometimes, parts of two characters were combined in order to represent single two-syllable Korean particles. These new characters came to be known as *kugyŏl*, "orally transmitted secrets." The *kugyŏl* are traditionally, but no doubt erroneously, ascribed to Chŏng Mongju (1337–1392).

The same process of selection and abbreviation took place in Japan at the end of the Nara period (710–794) and the beginning of the Heiañ (794–1185), in particular in the eighth and ninth centuries, therefore much earlier than in Korea, and yielded the *katakana* or more angular form of the syllabary. It was the Buddhist priests who created the *katakana*, as they marked their Chinese texts with *mañyōgana* for reading as Japanese. According to Nakada, the *katakana* appear to be based on the cursive forms of the *mañyōgana*.[12] The priests and government clerks also invented the *hiragana* or cursive form of the syllabary from rapidly written renderings of the Chinese characters. When used, as the *kugyŏl* were, to represent the particles and inflectional elements, the *kana* in Japan are known as *okurigana*.

[12] Nakada Norio, *Koteñpoñ no kokugogaku-teki keñkyū: sōroñ-heñ* (A Study of the Ancient Texts Bearing Reading Marks: General Remarks) and ... *yakubuñ-heñ* (Deciphered Materials) (Tōkyō, Kōdañsha, 1958).

e. The literary use of *hyangch'al* is illustrated in a cycle of eleven verses found in the *Kyun'yŏ-jŏn*, a biography of the priest Kyun'yŏ (917–973), written in 1075, in "The Dirge," written by Koryŏ King Yejong in 1120, and in fourteen *hyang'ga*, "regional songs," which may in some cases go back to seventh century Silla and which are recorded in the chronicle *Samguk yusa* (Remains of the Three Kingdoms), written by the priest Iryŏn (1206–1289). The complexities of the Korean writing may be judged from Kōno's interpretation of the phrase which he transcribes *durə-sa jari bo-gon* "when I did enter and looked at the bed," found in a *hyang'ga*. This phrase is written with seven characters of which the first, read *dur*, means "enter"; the second, read *rə*, repeats the final consonant of the verb and indicates that the verb is in its conjunctive form; the third, read *sa*, is an expletive particle, rendered by the word "did" in the translation; the fourth and fifth, read *jari*, or possibly *ja-dai*, means "a place to sleep"; the sixth, read *bo*, means to "see"; and the seventh, read *gon*, combines the conjunctive particles *go* and *n*, the former merely showing that the verb is being used conjunctively, and the latter conveying the idea "when."[13]

It is often assumed that the use of the characters in Japan for their phonetic values, to represent the particles and the inflectional elements, is modeled after that in Korea. But, as Kōno argues,[14] this is exceedingly difficult to prove. Only a few inscriptions remain from early Korea. The dates of the four Korean inscriptions cited by *Kōno* are 591, 719, 758, and ?792, respectively, whereas those of four Japanese documents are 596, 605, 607, and 623, and the date of the *Kojiki* (Record of Ancient Matters), the first Japanese chronicle, also cited by Kōno, is 712. The Korean inscriptions, moreover, come from Silla alone and not from the kingdoms of Paekche and Kara or Karak (Mimana). The usage in Silla must have been influenced by that in Paekche.

It is mainly in the case of the *idu* and *mañyōgana* that the question

---

[13] Kōno, "*Kojiki* ni okeru kañji shiyō," p. 198. In this passage Kōno relies heavily on Ogura Shiñpei, *Kyōga oyobi ritō no keñkyū* (Studies in the *hyang'ga* and *idu*) (Keijō [Seoul], Keijō Teikoku Daigaku, 1929), and on Yang Chudong, *Koga yŏn'gu* (A History of Ancient Korean Poetry), rev. and enl. ed. (Seoul, Pangmun ch'ulp'ansa, 1954). For a second interpretation of this line, see Vos, "Korean Writing: the *hyang'ga*," p. 27.

[14] Kōno, *op. cit.*, pp. 204-205.

arises whether any influences extended from Korea to Japan or vice versa. Kōno states that "the use of the Chinese characters in the *idu* and *t'o*, one may think, probably forms the original pattern for the use of the Chinese characters in ancient Japan."[15] Eñdō Yoshimoto and Hayashi Ōki, too, are willing to concede the possibility that the *mañyōgana* were related to the *idu*, although they point to the fact that the phonetic use of the characters in the transcription of foreign place and personal names was already found in ancient China. Some of the *mañyōgana* appear to be used in pronunciations similar to those found in Korea.[16]

III

Both Japan and Korea begin with inscriptions that were written entirely in the Chinese language; initially, their writers do not give positive evidence of having identified the elements in their own languages. The Japanese and Koreans trod the same path of arranging the characters in accordance with Korean and Japanese syntax, respectively, without indication of particles and inflectional elements, and then of indicating these suffixed forms. In the case of the verb *-tamau*, attached to other verbs to indicate honorific meaning, and in the case of the particles meaning "with, by means of" and "as for, if," the Japanese used the same characters as the Koreans. But the earliest extant materials in which the characters are used phonetically in order to write proper names and poetry are found earlier in Japan than in Korea. The development of the *mañyōgana*, *katakana*, and *hiragana* in Japan took place more quickly than the invention of the *han'gŭl* (which we shall presently discuss) in Korea, and Korean writing, as evidenced by the heavy load carried by loan-words from China, shows much greater reliance on the Chinese lexicon. So far, however, the Koreans and Japanese appear to have adapted the Chinese writing system to their own uses in such a way as to suggest a typology of development.

We need, on the other hand, to refer to two further developments, one coming in the late eighth and early ninth century in Japan and

[15] Kōno, "Ritō [the Japanese reading of the characters for *idu*]," in Kokugo Gakkai (Japanese Language Association), *Kokugogaku jiteñ* (Dictionary of Japanese Language Studies) (Tōkyō, Tōkyōdō, 11th printing, 1964), p. 948.

[16] Eñdō Yoshimoto and Hayashi Ōki, "Mañyōgana," in Kokugo Gakkai, *op. cit.*, pp. 889, 890.

the other not coming till the fifteenth century in Korea, in which the Japanese and Koreans did not emulate each other:

a. In order to read Chinese texts in such a way that they would in effect be translated into Japanese, the Japanese began by using comma-like signs to mark phrases, clauses, and sentences; they also wrote numbers along the sides of the characters to indicate the order in which they should be read. Later, dots, commas, hooks, vertical lines, etc., written in a variety of inks, were added at the four corners, sides, between or superimposed on top of the Chinese characters, or placed at the margins above or below the writing and even at the backs of the pages, to show how particular characters should be read and which inflectional endings, suffixes, and particles should be inserted into the readings. In later times, check-marks were used to indicate inversions. The use of these check-marks and of the numbers permitted the Japanese to convert the Chinese sequence of verb-object into the Japanese sequence of object-verb. Ultimately, the check-marks and numbers were used with the characters for "low," "mid," and "high," and for "D," "C," "B," and "A" in such a way that the order of reading agreed quite well with Japanese syntax. The whole process of marking was called *kuñteñ*.

One series of markings, often used in *kuñteñ*, is known as *okototeñ*, which was perhaps suggested by the Chinese method of indicating tone. The name *okototeñ* comes from the fact that in one of the favorite marking systems the dot placed at the upper right hand corner of a character was pronounced *o*, indicating the accusative particle, whereas a dot just below it signified the word *koto*, meaning "fact." The *okototeñ* are today classified in eight groupings, of which four of the earliest are graphed as follows:

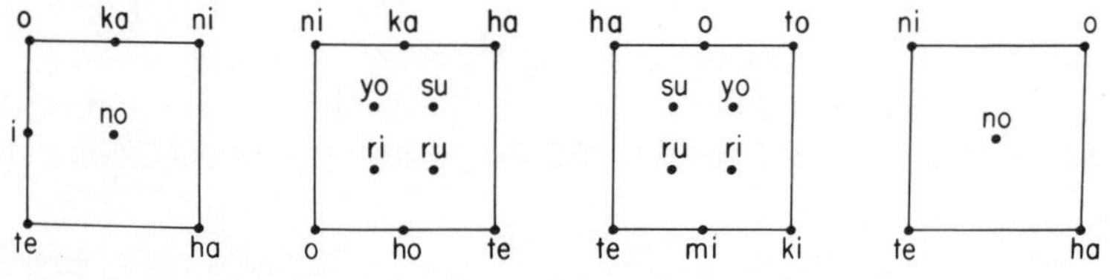

Since, in the system shown farthest to the right, the dots at the four corners, read in clockwise order beginning with *te*, yield *tenioha*, the markings were also known as *teniohateñ*, a name that developed in the Kamakura period (1185–1333). The term *tenioha* came to be applied to the particles as a word-class. Also found are the *teniharuteñ* and *nishihakateñ* systems of marking, peculiar to particular families of scholars.

The style mixing the Chinese characters and *katakana*, a species of *kanamajiribuñ*, or written format, using the Chinese characters and one of the two kinds of *kana*, originated in the *kuñteñ* markings.[17] The year 828 marks the date of the earliest extant Buddhist materials showing these signs.

b. In the fifteenth century the Korean writing system showed a remarkable development unmatched in Japan. It is signaled by the promulgation in 1446, under King Sejong, of the *han'gŭl*, a set of twenty-eight written shapes, each standing for a consonant or vowel and formed in such a way that the signs for consonants of the same type, velars, dentals, labials, spirants and palatals, and laryngals, take similar configurations, and the vowels too are symbolically distinguished in the shapes chosen. The use of the configurations in combination permitted representation of the Korean syllables. A system of diacritical markings even permitted the representation of accent. However, because of sound change and closer analysis of the language, the twenty-eight shapes are now reduced to twenty-four. The *han'gŭl* signs agree almost perfectly with the linguist's ideal of a single sign for each phoneme.[18] Strict adherence to the representation of morphemes, however, makes the configurations difficult to learn, since polysyllabic words suffering morphophonemic changes may still be rendered as combinations of morphemes. The very fact that the *han'gŭl* were created implies acceptance of the idea that the Chinese characters were inadequate for the writing of the Korean

[17] Kasuga Masaji, "Katakanamajiribuñ no kigeñ ni tsuite (On the Origin of the Style Written in a Mixture of *kañji* and *katakana*)," *Kokuñteñ no keñkyū* (Studies in the Old *kuñteñ* Materials) (Tōkyō, Kazama Shobō, 1956), pp. 293-306, especially p. 305. Like Nakada (see reference at n. 12), Kasuga contradicts the supposition, formerly held, that the *katakana* came from abbreviations of the characters, written in smaller size in *señmyōgaki*, to express the particles and inflectional elements of the Japanese language. As Kasuga explains, the development of the *katakana* in *kuñteñ* materials and the use of lesser size characters in *señmyōgaki* probably occurred at the same time, independently of each other.

[18] Edwin O. Reischauer and John K. Fairbank, *East Asia: the Great Tradition* (Boston, Houghton Mifflin, 1960), p. 435, state: "Han'gŭl is perhaps the most scientific system of writing in general use in any country."

language. The shapes taken by the *han'gŭl* and their close reference to the Korean phonemes are a clear departure from the pictorial shapes representing entire syllables found in Chinese charactery. The *kana*, in comparison, were mere extensions of the Chinese characters, since they represent syllables in their totality without reference, as far as their forms are concerned, to particular phonemes. The joint employment of the Chinese characters and *han'gŭl* today is known as *kukhanmun* and agrees with the Japanese *kanamajiribuñ*. However, the Chinese characters used in *kukhanmun* are still read in their pronunciations borrowed from the Chinese language, whereas in *kanamajiribuñ* the Chinese characters may be read either in their borrowed pronunciations or as the representations of Japanese words with the same or similar meaning. After World War II, North Korea went over to exclusive use of *han'gŭl*—despite its close political ties to Mainland China!

c. In the sixteenth century Westerners appeared in both Korea and Japan, and in time both the Koreans and Japanese became conscious of the possibility of writing their languages in romanization. Although today an effort is made to teach the romanization of Korean and Japanese words to school children, their actual use comes mainly in signs on stores and other establishments catering to the Western traveler, and the weight of tradition lies heavily on the side of the charactery.

IV

In their attempts to adapt a badly suited foreign writing system the Koreans and Japanese evidenced considerable concern in matters that are in large part linguistic:

a. Implicit in the phonetic use of the Chinese characters, as *idu* or as *mañyōgana*, was the concept of the syllable. Because of earlier and heavier infusion of monosyllabic Chinese elements into the Korean language, reinforced by the syllabic nature of the Chinese writing system, the Koreans probably found the concept of the syllable and use of a charactery, read as single syllables, quite easy to accept. The Japanese, too, must have soon discovered that the Chinese characters were pronounced as single syllables. It was probably under Chinese influence that the alternation of lines of five syllables and seven, characteristic of Japanese verse, became fixed by the end of the seventh century. In earlier Japanese poetry the lines had contained a varying number of syllables, generally from three to eleven. Study of Chinese poetry, which in some common forms was composed of lines either of five syllables alone or of seven syllables alone, probably reinforced in the Japanese the concept of syllabification which to some extent was already important in Japanese verse.

b. Study and use of the Chinese language and writing system stimulated study by the Koreans and Japanese of their own languages. The phonetic use of the Chinese characters as *idu* and as *mañyōgana*, the way in which characters of a larger size were used in representing the meaningful words and those of lesser size, the inflectional and other functional elements, the joint use of the Chinese characters with *han'gŭl* in Korea and the joint use of the Chinese characters with the two forms of the syllabary in Japan could not have taken place without some kind of analysis of the Korean and Japanese languages.

c. The creation of the *han'gŭl* may owe part of its inspiration to study of foreign systems of writing other than Chinese,[19] but it is still a major achievement, since its configurations are based on close study of articulation and therefore of the phonology of the Korean language. The *kana*, too, identify the consonants and vowels of the Japanese language, but fall short of phonemicity because they represent syllables in their entirety, with none of the parts representing particular consonants and vowels.

d. The *kuñteñ* markings which permitted the reading of Chinese texts as Japanese, so that nouns were read with the proper particles and verbs and adjectives with their proper suffixes, also show significant understanding of their language on the part of the Japanese.

e. The ordering both of the *han'gŭl* and the *kana*—the latter

[19] Ledyard believes that at least five and perhaps seven of the *han'gŭl* shapes were borrowed from the Mongol ḥPhags-pa script, which also suggested the squareness of the forms (*Abstracts*, p. 1031A). Kōno suggests that the use of single Chinese characters to express Korean morphemes consisting of single consonants anticipates the use of particular shapes to represent the phonemes in *han'gŭl*. Kōno, "*Kojiki* ni," p. 202. Vos states: "Many attempts have been made to reduce the origin of the Korean alphabet to other systems of writing, such as Chinese seal characters, Sanskrit, Tibetan, Jürčen, Uighur-Mongol, and ḥPhags-pa. All these comparisons, however, are restricted to incidental resemblances of a few letters and are far from convincing." "Chinese writing: *idu* and *han'gŭl*," p. 33.

in the *gojūoñzu* or "table of fifty sounds," which was devised in the Kamakura period (1192–1333)—may have come from study of the order in which the consonants and vowels are presented in the Sanskrit alphabet. The ordering of the *kana* may also derive in part from the manner in which initial consonants and rhyming remainders are shown in the Chinese rhyme tables.[20] It is interesting to note that the ordering of the consonants with which the *han'gŭl*, *kana* and the Sanskrit letters are pronounced goes basically from the back of the mouth to the front, and not vice versa, as in modern Western treatments of phonetics.

f. Indication of accent on Japanese words goes back to the eleventh century and is especially to be noted in the *Ruiju myōgishō*. Indication of tone in Korea came with the invention of *han'gŭl*. Here again, the Japanese and Koreans show that they had well learned their Chinese lessons. The Chinese method of indicating tone by means of dots placed at the four corners of the characters was known to the Japanese scribes as early as the tenth century. Dots were used by the Koreans, too, in marking tone on the *han'gŭl* signs.

V

The motivations that lay behind the development of the writing systems in Korea and Japan, the attitudes with which the new forms of writing were regarded, the ways in which the systems were employed in written materials both documentary and literary, and the development of calligraphy show additional points of similarity in Korea and Japan. On the other hand, the Japanese possibly showed more playfulness than the Koreans in the way they manipulated both the Chinese characters and *kana*.

a. The several systems of charactery which developed in Korea and Japan could not have arisen unless the deficiencies of a previously developed system of charactery had been acutely felt. In a sense, each new system was found wanting. Thus, the

[20] Vos, *op. cit.*, p. 33, states: "It is, of course, not impossible that the phonetic classification (the order of the alphabet) has been inspired by foreign examples. The fact that the Korean *e*... is regarded as a diphthong could have come from the fact that the *e* (as well as the *o*) is metrically a long vowel in Sanskrit." Cf. Morioka Keñji, "Gojūoñzu no hairetsu (The Arrangement of the Table of Fifty Sounds)," *Kokugo to kokubuñgaku* (March, 1951).

shortcomings of *idu* as a transcriptional system both of Korean and of Sino-Korean led to the invention of *han'gŭl*.[21] The need for a set of characters that could easily be written led to the formation of the *kana*. In both Korean and Japanese materials are found specific references to the problems caused by the use of the Chinese characters and to the need of a system of writing that would more adequately represent the native languages. Thus in the preface to his proclamation concerning the *han'gŭl*, King Sejong wrote:

> The sounds of the language of our country are different from those of China and have no correspondence with the Chinese characters. Therefore, it often happens that when simple folk want to say something they are in the end unable to express their feelings. Because of this regrettable situation we have made twenty-eight new letters with the wish that everybody will study them easily and that they will be practical for daily use.[22]

Similarly, in the preface to the *Kojiki*, dated 712, Ō no Yasumaro, writing in Chinese, tells of the problems he faced in transcribing the recitations of Hieda no Are:

> To relate everything in ideographic transcription would entail an inadequate expression of the meaning; to write altogether according to the phonetic method would make the story of events unduly lengthy. For this reason have I sometimes in the same sentence used the phonetic and ideographic systems conjointly, and have sometimes in one matter used the ideographic record exclusively. Moreover, where the drift of the words was obscure, I have by comments elucidated their signification; but need it be said that I have nowhere commented on what was easy?[23]

Despite Ō no Yasumaro's evident concern, not everything in the *Kojiki* is even today clear. Hieda no Are probably belonged to a guild of narrators known as the Kataribe. In a sense, before it was adopted, the Chinese charactery was forced to contend with these oral reciters of ancient matters.

In the *Kogo shūi* (Gleanings from Ancient Words), dated 807, Iñbe Hironari states the reasons why his family should deserve

[21] See Ledyard, *Abstracts*, p. 1031A.

[22] Vos, *op. cit.*, pp. 31-32.

[23] B. H. Chamberlain, *Translation of "Ko-ji-ki"... or "Records of ancient matters,"* 2nd ed., with annotations by W. G. Aston (Kōbe, J. L. Thompson and Co., 1932), pp. 13-14.

precedence over its rivals, the Nakatomi, in the management of Shiñtō ceremonies. These reasons he states in the form of a written memorial to the throne. Although he is convinced that the older method of oral transmission is to be preferred, he memorializes the Emperor in writing:

Tradition says that writing was unknown in old Japan, so that all people, whether high or low, youthful or aged, handed down from hoary antiquity their sacred traditions verbally among themselves, memorizing them from one generation to another. When, however, the art of writing was introduced, the Japanese began to discard the old simple way of transmitting orally their family traditions under the prevailing influence of the new tendency to ostentations and frivolity which caused the people to revolt against the ancient simplicity and despise those who remained faithful to the old mode of oral transmission. Hence change after change occurred in the traditional accounts they handed down during long centuries, and obviously no one nowadays is competent to decide the true origin and exact nature of these cherished and venerable traditions. Even though there certainly exist some official histories and private family records which describe ancient things as they actually were, yet Your Imperial Majesty's humble servant Hironari finds that there still survive some others not mentioned in those written documents, which would probably by degrees sink into oblivion unless Your Imperial Majesty's humble servant Hironari make so bold as to endeavour to bring them to light.[24]

In 720 the difficulties created when Buddhist documents written in Chinese were being rendered in Japanese caused the government to issue an order to read these Buddhist materials in the pronunciations borrowed from Chinese. Among the scholars who tried to determine the readings to be given to the characters used in writing the *Mañyōshū* are Minamoto no Shitagō, 911–983, the priests Señgaku, 1203– ? 1273, and Keichū, 1640–1701, Kamo no Mabuchi, 1697–1769, and Tachibana Chikage, 1734–1808.

The motivations that lie behind the several developments in Korea and Japan thus become clear: to work toward the formulation of writing systems that would assist in better communication. In addition, in Korea, it appears that by the fifteenth century, when the *han'gŭl* were promulgated, the need had

[24] Iñbe Hironari, *Kogoshūi. Gleanings from Ancient Stories*, trans. by Geñchi Katō and Hikoshirō Hoshino (Tōkyō, The Zaidañ-Hōjiñ-Meiji-Seitoku-Kineñ-Gakkai [Meiji Japan Society], 1925), Preface.

arisen specifically to reflect in better fashion the sound changes that had occurred in morphemes and words borrowed from the Chinese language.

b. Both the Koreans and Japanese were at first agreed that composition in the characters that they themselves had developed was less prestigious than writing in the Chinese language, using only the Chinese characters. This attitude is seen in particular in the men, who more than the women were versed in Chinese. In Korea the *han'gŭl* were generally scorned by educated men, who thought that it was more appropriately written by women and children. In both Korea and Japan, the Chinese characters were the vehicles for government and law. In Japan, the *katakana* were used mainly by novice priests and students marking their *kuñteñ* texts, and the *hiragana* became the charactery in which the women wrote their fiction, diaries, and miscellanies. It was in their poetic exchanges with women that the men used the *hiragana*. Generally, men wrote their diaries in Chinese. But in the *Tosa nikki* (Tosa Diary), Ki no Tsurayuki wrote in *hiragana*, concealing the fact that he was a man. In the opening sentences he writes: "Diaries are things written by men, I am told. Nevertheless I am writing one to see what a woman can do."

Typical of the attitude taken to women who were well versed in the Chinese characters is the following passage from the diary of Murasaki Shikibu, famed authoress of the *Geñji monogatari* (The Tale of Geñji):

> There is a lady, Saémon-no Naishi, who unreasonably cherished hatred of me. I was not at first aware of it, but later heard of much criticism of me in my absence. Once the King was listening to a reading of my Genjimonogatari, and said, "She is gifted, she must have read the Chronicle of Japan." This lady heard of it, and unreflectingly spread abroad among the courtiers the idea that I am very proud of my learning, giving me the name of "The Japanese Chronicle Lady"—it is laughable, indeed! I am reserved even before the maids of my own house; how then should I show my learning in Court? When my elder brother Shikibu-no-Jō was a boy he was taught to read "Chinese Historical Records." I listened, sitting beside him and learned wonderfully fast, though he was sometimes slow and forgot. Father, who was devoted to study, regretted that I had not been a son, but I heard people saying that it is not beautiful even for a man to be proud of his learning, and after that I did not write so much as the figure one in Chinese. I grew clumsy with my [writing] brush. For a long time I did not care for the books I had already read. Thus I was ashamed

to think how others would hate me on hearing what Lady Saémon said, and I assumed an air of not being able to read the characters written on the Royal screen. But the Queen made me read [to her] the poetical works of Li T'aipo, and as she wished to learn them I have been teaching her since the Summer of two years ago the second and third volumes of that collection very secretly when none were present. Her Majesty and I tried to conceal it, but His Majesty the King and the Lord Prime Minister finding it out, the latter presented to the Queen many poetical books which he had copied. I think that bitter Saémon does not know it yet. If she did, how she would criticize me![25]

c. A basic distinction is discernible in the types of written material for which the Koreans and the Japanese used, on the one hand, the Chinese language and the Chinese charactery, and, on the other, their native vernaculars and the charactery that they had themselves developed.[26] The *Shan-hai ching* (Book of Mountains and Rivers) and *San-kuo chih* (History of the Three Kingdoms) were perhaps the first two Chinese works imported into Korea; the first came to Paekche in the third century and the second to Koguryŏ later. In Japan it was perhaps the *Lun-yü* (The Confucian Analects) which first came, brought by Wani, at about the end of the fourth century. The study of these writings prepared the Koreans and Japanese or their teachers to produce the earliest writings found in Korea and Japan in their respective domains. Thus composed in Chinese were inscriptions, government documents, chronicles and histories, and commentaries on the Buddhist scriptures, materials that were all pragmatically oriented and therefore non-literary in nature. In Koguryŏ, in northern Korea, the Chinese inscription on a monument erected in honor of King Kwanggaet'o (391-412) consists of 1,759 characters, and in 600 came an official history of the kingdom. In Paekche, in southwest Korea, official documents were being written after the middle of the fourth century, an official history was being compiled in the third quarter of the same century, and diplomatic messages and requests for commentaries on the

---

[25] Annie Shepley Ōmori and Doi Kōchi, trans., *Diaries of Court Ladies of Old Japan* (Tōkyō, Keñkyūsha, 1935), pp. 138-139.

[26] The remarks on Korean writings which follow owe a great deal to Peter H. Lee, *Korean Literature: Topics and Themes* (Association for Asian Studies Monographs and Papers, no. 16; Tucson, University of Arizona Press, 1965). For a discussion of the division of function between writings in Chinese and in Japanese in Japan, see Sansom, *op. cit.*, pp. 51-68.

Nirvāna sūtra and *Book of Songs* were being sent to China in the fifth and sixth centuries—all in Chinese. In Silla, in southeast Korea, Chinese was the official language by the second half of the fourth century; inscriptions were soon incised on monuments and a national history compiled.

The early use of the Chinese characters in Japan has a similar history. Wani, quickly asked to serve as a teacher, was followed by other Chinese and Koreans. Soon the Japanese, too, were writing inscriptions in Chinese. Buddhism arrived in 538 (some say 552); by the end of the century, Prince Shōtoku was composing the first Japanese commentaries, written in Chinese, on the Buddhist sūtras. He was also the supposed author of a "constitution" in seventeen articles which was a compendium of Confucian, Buddhist, and native Japanese wisdom. The *Kujiki*, reportedly the first history, was also compiled, but it was lost in a fire in 645.

A national university was established in Silla in 651 and in Nara in the following century. The Chinese classics were the main items studied, and in Korea in particular there was frequent exchange of scholars with China, where many Koreans were able to pass the civil service examinations of the T'ang dynasty. Because of its use as a textbook, the Chinese *Wen-hsüan* (Anthology of Literature) was well known; it made the writing of parallel prose a favorite activity among the educated in Korea and became a model for the *Mañyōshū* in Japan, where the laws of the land, commentaries on these laws, the Imperial decrees known as *shōsho* and *chokusho*, which ranked next to the *señmyō* in importance, the full range of documents exchanged by government offices, and diaries written by men in high office were all written in Chinese.

The Koreans and Japanese, having mastered a foreign language and charactery, also wrote both poetry and prose in Chinese. The total volume of Chinese writings was apparently more substantial in Korea than in Japan. During the Koryŏ dynasty (918–1392) adoption of the civil service examinations modeled on those of China further enhanced the study of Chinese writings. Parallel prose continued to be written, but gradually yielded its position as a favored mode of writing to pre-Han and Han styles. A military coup in 1170 forced the scholar-statesmen to retreat into the countryside and mountains, where they were able to practice the writing of poems, often under Taoist, Zennist, and T'ien-t'ai influence. In the early fourteenth century Neo-Confucianism arrived in Korea, approximately 170 years before its advent in Japan. Many poets worked in the Koryŏ dynasty. This was also the age which produced chronicles like the *Samguk sagi* and *Samguk yusa*, along with biographies of monks and kings. But it was Neo-Confucian philosophy, T'ang poetry, and the Sung poet Huang T'ing-chien that attracted the scholars and literary men. In the sixteenth century a fission divided the Neo-Confucianists from those more inclined to literature. The latter were well versed in most of the varieties of Chinese poetry and prose, but their disagreements with the philosophers continued into the seventeenth century.

The first Japanese collection of Chinese poetry is the *Kaifūsō* (Remembrance of Things Past). Compiled in 751, it was followed by at least six more anthologies of Chinese poetry in the Heian̄ period. The earliest Japanese chronicle, *Kojiki* (Records of Ancient Matters), was written in Chinese characters in 712; the earliest extant history in Chinese, the *Nihon̄gi* (Chronicle of Japan), written in 720, was modeled on the (Chinese dynastic histories; it was followed by five more of the *Rikkokushi* (Six National Histories), all written in Chinese and compiled before the end of the Heian̄ era.

With the development of the phonetic use of characters the Koreans and Japanese were able for the first time to set down in writing whatever they could previously transmit only by word of mouth. The myths, legends, anecdotal narratives, stories, and traditions of the people could still be rendered in Chinese, but use of the characters as *idu* and as *man̄yōgana* now permitted the Koreans and Japanese to transcribe their native songs and poetry. Hence in Korea the *hyang'ga* were recorded in the *Samguk yusa* and *Kyun'yŏ-jŏn*, as were other varieties of poetry, including the *chang'ga*, the "long poems" of the Koryŏ dynasty, certain of the *akchang* or eulogies of the Yi dynasty, the *sijo*, or short lyric, which came to be identified as an independent form in the Koryŏ period, and the *kasa*, used as a song to accompany the form of performance with drum beats and hand clappings also known as *kasa*, and remaining in examples that go back to the middle of the fifteenth century. One of the *akchang*, it should be noted, was the *Yongbi ŏch'ŏn ka* (Hymn to Flying Dragons in Heaven), in 125 cantos, which was composed in *han'gŭl* and presented to King Sejong in 1445, one year before his proclamation decreeing that *han'gŭl* be used in the writing of the Korean language.

In Japan, the *mañyōgana* were used in writing down the *tañka* (the five-line, 31-syllable poem whose lines run 5-7-5-7-7 syllables), the *chōka* (long poem), and other forms of poetry in the *Mañyōshu*. The Japanese poems and proper names, along with much of the *Kojiki*, that went in the *Nihoñgi* are similarly in *mañyōgana*. At the Yakushiji near Nara is a stone, representing the Buddha's foot, on which is inscribed a group of twenty-one poems which add an extra seven-syllable line to the *tañka*. The *Kiñkafu*, dated 981, records twenty-one songs rendered to the accompaniment of the *koto*. Other materials quote the songs of the *kagura* and *saibara*, that is, the dances performed at the Shiñtō shrines, and the folk songs of the provinces. The *norito* or Shiñtō prayers and the *señmyō*, the most important variety of Imperial proclamation, were both composed in Japanese; clearly, the words intoned at religious exercises and the most serious pronouncements of the Emperor could not be rendered in Chinese.

Having a system of writing as easily written as the *hiragana* permitted the Japanese of the Heiañ period to pour out a steady stream of poems, diaries, and fiction. Both in volume and in artistic sensibility these writings mark a high point in the history of Japanese literature. By 905, when the second major collection of Japanese poetry, the *Kokiñshū* (Collection of Ancient and Modern Times), was compiled, it was the *hiragana* that were mainly used in writing poetry. Six other anthologies were compiled under Imperial command before the end of the Heiañ period, and to their number may be added numerous private collections. These anthologies collect examples of the *tañka*, which was now the main vehicle of communication between men and women in love and among all poets writing of nature.

In the meantime prose works written by women in *hiragana* were undergoing steady development, and reached high achievement in the fiction, diaries, and miscellanies produced by such accomplished authors as Murasaki Shikibu and Sei Shōnagoñ. From the former came the *Geñji monogatari* (Tale of Geñji) and from the latter the *Makura no sōshi* (Pillow-book). Only toward the end of the Heiañ period did the men venture, and then with only moderate success, into the field of narrative writing. It was then that the *rekishi monogatari*, or historical tale, began to be written. The *Eiga monogatari* (Tale of Glory), *Ōkagami* (Great Mirror), and *Imakagami* (Contemporary Mirror) were all composed, it is probable, before the end of the Heiañ period. Since they were historiographical in intent, their writing by men agrees with the composition of the *Six National Histories* in Chinese. In the *Ōkagami*, it should be noted, two aged men, said to be 150 and 140 years old in one version, recount the events of the past, and a young man presumably writes down what they say. The combination of recitants and scribe found in the *Ōkagami* recalls the joint composition of the *Kojiki* by Hieda no Are and Ō no Yasumaro and reminds us of the strength of the oral tradition, even at a time when the Japanese had achieved a relatively supple system of writing.

Lee makes the point that not having a system of charactery which could adequately express their language was one of the reasons why the people of Koryŏ did not develop a vernacular poetry, whereas possessing the *idu* and *han'gŭl* led respectively to the writing of poetry in Silla and of literature in general in the Yi dynasty.[27] It was, in fact, not till the invention of *han'gŭl* that Korean fiction really received its start; prior to its invention, the Koreans composed their novels and shorter stories in Chinese. More fiction in Chinese was written in Korea than in Japan, but Japan was richer in fiction in the vernacular, which also flourished at an earlier date in Japan, partly because the *hiragana* were invented earlier than the *han'gŭl*. It seems possible to argue, therefore, that possession of an easily written script not only promotes the creation of a voluminous literature, but, given the further advantages of a courtly life spent in sensitive enjoyment of aesthetic pleasures, a literature of quality. Collections of Buddhist stories, glossaries of words found in Chinese texts, and three dictionaries, the *Shiñseñ jikyō* (Mirror for Characters, Newly Compiled), *Wamyō ruijushō* (Selection of Japanese Words, Classified), and *Ruiju myōgishō* (Selection of Japanese Meanings, Classified), should also be included in the roster of works written in Japanese. By the end of the Heiañ period appear the first examples of governmental documents in Japanese, the *nyōbō hōsho*, which were memoranda dictated by the Emperor and written by women attendants at the palace.

More poetry, fiction, diaries, and miscellanies were written in

[27] Lee, *op. cit.*, p. 15.

Japanese, using either the *mañyōgana* or the *hiragana*, than in Korean. Japanese literature, written mainly in *hiragana*, came quite early; the *Geñji monogatari* was written by Murasaki Shikibu in the first two decades of the eleventh century, within 170 years after the formulation of the *hiragana*.

The best narrative writing was done by women. Like the other ladies of the Heiañ court, Murasaki Shikibu enjoyed the privileges of observation and participation in the round of activities, artistic, religious, and to some extent governmental, that went on in the palaces. Early invention of the *hiragana* permitted development of a wide range of Japanese literary genres, produced in a shorter period of time, than was possible in Korea.

d. Control of the writing system permitted both the Koreans and Japanese to become concerned with the aesthetics of handwriting. But in Korea brushmanship was limited to the Chinese characters until the *han'gŭl* were formed, whereas in Japan it was quickly extended to the *kana* as well. In the listing of nouns and phrases entitled *ametsuchi*, and in the poem beginning *tawi ni*, each of the *kana* is used once, and once only. The *irohauta* came later. All three listings were used in practicing the writing of characters. The handwriting of Ki no Tsurayuki remains to this day a model for writing with the brush.

Many passages in Heiañ literature attest to the fact that both men and women took pains to write elegantly the poems that they exchanged. After a night's dalliance, a man's poem, tied to a branch of flowers, would be carried to the home of his lady-love, who was obliged to answer in kind. The custom arose of reading a person's character in the way he wrote. Kaoru, the unfortunate anti-hero of the final chapters of the *Tale of Geñji*, wrote in a less interesting and less distinguished hand than the more graceful Niou.

e. The shapes that make up the Chinese characters are susceptible of playful manipulations. In both Korea and Japan, parts of two or more characters are used to form still other characters. The *kugyŏl* character pronounced *hana* is made up of parts of two other characters pronounced *ha* and *na*, and the character for "water" is written above the one for "rice-field," as the written representation of *tap*, "wet rice-field." So in Japan parts of the *katakana* read *ko* and *to* are combined to form a new character reading *koto*, meaning "fact"; parts of the *hiragana* forms for *yo* and *ri* are combined to form a new character reading *yori*, meaning "from," and the radical for "tree" is combined with the character for "deity" to render the character for *sakaki*, the tree sacred to Shiñtō.

Describing uses of the Chinese characters in the Nara period, Sansom refers to "devices in the script comparable to the riddle, the rebus, the acrostic, and the palindrome,"[28] and gives examples. In the *Mañyōshū* three characters that are usually read *hachijūichi*, "eighty-one," are given the pronunciation *kuku* because the element *ku* may mean "nine" and *kuku* or "nine times nine" is eighty-one. Many similar examples suggest that there was probably more playfulness on the part of the Japanese with respect to the characters, and by implication less reverence for the Chinese tradition, than on the part of the Koreans.[29]

VI

The foregoing discussion has touched upon some of the reasons why the writing systems took different courses of development in Korea and Japan. Korea's proximity to China and closer dependence on Confucianism and on other forms of Chinese thought, expressed in the Chinese language and charactery, served to dominate Korean thought and delayed invention of the *han'gŭl*. The larger role in social, and even in political life, which the Japanese women enjoyed, helped to popularize use of the *hiragana* even among the men. The *katakana*, too, became important because in the very process of learning about Confucianism and Buddhism the Japanese used them in their *kuñteñ* markings. Greater distance from China and a stronger sense of independence from Chinese

[28] *Op. cit.*, pp. 25-26. Ueda Kazutoshi and others, *Daijiteñ* (A Large Dictionary of Characters) (Tōkyō, Keiseisha, 1917, etc.), under character number 2262, *ko* (child), gives a run of six uses of the same character, with the reading *shishi no ko no kojishi* (a baby lion which is the child of a lion), or *neko no ko no koneko* (a kitten which is the child of a cat).

[29] In poetry, a similar playfulness is found in the use of *kakekotoba*, "pivot words," which terminate one phrase or clause and at the same time begin another, *makura-kotoba* or "pillow-words," which are fixed modifying forms attached to particular nouns, and *eñgo* or "associated words"whose use is suggested by somewhat forced association, with emotional overtones, with a word that has previously been used in the same poem, and in the category of poems known as *mono no na* (the names of things) in which one or more words are punningly concealed in other words and phrases. In these cases, however, the playfulness consists more in wordplay than with written forms and their pronunciations.

political and intellectual dominance made the Japanese attempt Japanized reading of Chinese texts.

Korea's cultural dependence on China was relatively long-lived, Japan's less so. Beginning with the *Wei shu* or Dynastic History of the Wei Dynasty, which was written in the third century, A.D., a number of Chinese histories refer to Korea and Japan and render Korean and Japanese words, mainly place and personal names, in phonetic notation, with the Chinese characters used phonetically.

Korea was first peopled by Tungusic tribes from Siberia and Manchuria; its legendary founding goes back to 2333 B.C. In 1122 B.C. Kija, a Chinese sage, is said to have emigrated into northern Korea with 5,000 followers. In the year 108 B.C., under the Han dynasty, four Chinese colonies were established in northeastern Korea. However, three kingdoms which were descended from their Tungusic ancestors maintained their independence in the south; these were Koguryŏ (?37 B.C.–668A.D.), Paekche (?18 B.C.–660 A.D.), and Silla (?57 B.C.–935 A.D.). It was Koguryŏ which conquered the last of the four Chinese colonies, Lo-lang, and was in turn overcome by Silla, which had allied itself with the T'ang dynasty of China. In the early tenth century one of Silla's generals, Wang Kŏn, revolted and ultimately became head of an independent state, Koryŏ, which lasted till 1392 despite invasions by the K'itan, Jürčen, and Mongols in the preceding centuries. The Wang dynasty was replaced by the Yi. Throughout this history Korea remained steadfast in preserving the Chinese part of its heritage. Particularly in the Koryŏ period, complete acceptance of Confucianism and absorption in the study of Chinese literature were accompanied by a belief that educated men should write only in Chinese. Since this also meant rejection of ways of thought other than Confucianism, such as Buddhism, and rejection too of widespread adoption of the *idu* which had developed in Silla, a vernacular literature of high quality could scarcely develop.[30]

In Japan, too, Chinese influence was felt in many ways. The Taika reforms of 645–650 remodeled the governmental structure along Chinese lines. Confucianism and Buddhism, which entered Japan through Korea, ameliorated the more animistic nature worship that was Shiñtō. The vogue enjoyed by Chinese artifacts in early Japanese history is today attested most graphically at the Shōsōiñ, the great storehouse at Nara which contains numerous

[30] Lee, *op. cit.*, pp. 15-16.

articles of Chinese origin—household implements, pieces of cloth, weapons, writing implements, and documents—from the reign of Emperor Shōmu (724–748). The site of the capital at Heiañ was determined by the Chinese theories of geomancy, which prescribed that the palace should be at the north, mountains at the north, east, and west, and a river flowing through the town, which was open to the south. But it was quite evident that, in spite of the organization of the Japanese government on Chinese models, the nation was ruled by Emperors governing by what was claimed to be divine right and not because of their virtue, as was supposed to be the case in China. Similarly, the Jiñgikañ or Department of Shiñtō had no counterpart in China. The civil service examinations for which China was famous were adopted by the Japanese as they were by the Koreans, but these examinations could not be taken by everyone; only the sons of men holding fifth court rank or higher and exceptionally brilliant sons of those holding sixth, seventh, and eighth court rank were eligible to take them. In the ninth century Japan swerved in other ways from China. This was due in part to the political decay of the T'ang dynasty and in part to intellectual, artistic, and political growth within Japan itself. The last embassy to China left Japan in 839 and returned in the same year. One of the members, Ono no Takamura, appears to have distrusted the seaworthiness of the vessel to which he was assigned. He therefore refused to go on the pretext that he was ill, and furthermore wrote a sarcastic poem about the embassy. For his pains Takamura was exiled to the Oki islands. In 894 the sending of envoys to China was finally stopped because it was felt that the T'ang dynasty was approaching its end and nothing would be gained by maintaining official relations. Japan thus entered into an age of relative severance from Chinese models, one manifestation of which was the development of her own writing system. Cultural independence from China, it may be argued, played its role in the invention of the *katakana* and *hiragana*.

VII

The Chinese system of charactery was also taken to Vietnam. Vietnam was a province of China from 207 B.C. to 939 A.D. and for a few years in the fifteenth century. Catholic missionaries from Europe appeared in the sixteenth and seventeenth centuries. At the end of the eighteenth century French influence began to be felt, first in Annam, that is, in central Vietnam; it became decisive in the latter part of the nineteenth century with the establishment of the colony of Cochin China in 1862 and the protectorates of Annam and of Tonkin in 1884. Vietnamese desire for independence is evidenced in a series of uprisings. These were encouraged during World War II by the Japanese, who sponsored an independent government under Bao Dai, Emperor of Annam, in 1945, but Bao Dai's regime was quickly replaced in the same year by a republic under Ho Chi Minh. In November, 1946, began the long war between the Vietnamese and the French which was terminated only by the Convention of Geneva of 1954. The further history of Vietnam needs no recounting.

The differences between the Vietnamese language and Chinese, Japanese, and Korean may be stated as follows:

a. In Vietnamese, modifiers follow the words that they modify, whereas in Chinese they precede these words.
b. In Vietnamese as in Chinese the words are basically monosyllabic and not polysyllabic. Nouns are distinguished with respect to whether they point to living or non-living things.
c. The words are non-inflecting, as is true of Chinese but not of Japanese and Korean.
d. In Vietnamese the lexicon is heavily influenced by Chinese and by Tai, that is, by two of the languages belonging to the Sino-Tibetan group. But the words for the numbers and for parts of the body show a relationship with the Mon-Khmer languages. Sentence-ending particles mark questions or serve to express doubt.
e. Distinctions of accent depend on pitch-height and pitch-contour within the syllables, which is truer of Chinese and of Korean than it is of Japanese.

The first writings in Vietnam appear to date from the third century, with both the Chinese language and charactery serving as vehicles of communication. By the thirteenth century came a new system known as *chữ' nôm*, "southern writing,"[31] in which the

[31] See n. 2, above.

[31] For descriptions in detail of the Vietnamese language see Laurence C. Thompson, *A Vietnamese Grammar* (Seattle, University of Washington Press, 1965); also, Mineya Tōru, "Añnañgo (The Annamese Language)," in Ichikawa Sañki and Hattori Shirô, *Keñkyūsha sekai geñgo gaisetsu* (Keñkyūsha Outline of the Languages of the World) Vol. 2 (Tōkyō, Keñkyūsha, 1955), pp. 833-870. For *chữ' nôm*, a brief description of which follows, see the article by Nguyễn Đình Hoà, cited in n. 2.

characters were used in much the same way as in Korea and Japan. A single character could thus represent a single monosyllabic morpheme in Annamese, whether this morpheme was a borrowing from Chinese or a morpheme more native to the Annamese language. In the former case, the pronunciation carried in Annamese was similar to that carried in the Chinese language, and in the latter the Annamese morpheme was identical or similar in meaning but not in pronunciation to its Chinese equivalent. Sometimes a Chinese character was used to represent a second, homophonous or almost homophonous Annamese morpheme which was quite unrelated in meaning to the first. Sometimes, also, two Chinese characters were combined to form a new character not found in Chinese. In this case both components could carry the same meaning, or one could indicate the general area of meaning into which a word fell, that is, act as a radical, and the other, its pronunciation. Although the Koreans and Japanese also originated a few characters of this type, the Vietnamese gave a very special flavor to *chữ' nôm* not found in Korean and Japanese writing. In the monosyllabic structure of its lexicon the Vietnamese language was more like Chinese than Japanese and Korean were, and could therefore be more easily accommodated to representation in the Chinese characters than could Japanese and Korean. But, compared with *han'gŭl* and even with *kana*, *chữ' nôm* was an imperfect system as far as representing the phonemes of the Annamese language was concerned. The advent of Catholic missionaries in the seventeenth century gave impetus to writing Vietnamese in the letters of the alphabet. This system, which was largely phonemic and included indications of tone, was called *quôc* ngữ*, "the national language." Adopted under French rule in 1910, it is now used throughout Vietnam for all purposes.

It is almost as an afterthought that we note: Annamese songs and stories existed, but could not be transcribed until the *chữ' nôm* were invented. In early Annamese history, no high literature, except in Chinese, could be written. The high prestige associated with knowledge of the Chinese language and charactery was reinforced by the same adoption of civil service examinations found in Korea and Japan. *Chữ' nôm* was therefore considered unfit for use in government or in literature, and writers in *chữ' nôm* usually refrained from signing their writings.

VIII

The problems faced by the nations now emerging in Asia and Africa with respect to their languages were to some degree faced by Annam, Korea, and Japan in the early centuries of their contacts with China. Encumbered with a difficult system of writing at a time when communication was slower, it took the Annamese some seventeen centuries and the Koreans some fourteen centuries of periodically turbulent history before the *chữ' nôm* and *han'gŭl* were devised, and the Japanese some four centuries of relatively peaceful political and cultural development before the *kana* were invented. Compared with Annam, Korea, and the countries that have recently gained their independence in Asia and Africa, Japan in particular enjoyed a history of autonomous growth. But, however strong the influence of China in government, law, thought, art, and literature, centuries of history prior to the modern era gave to Annam, Korea, and Japan their distinctive cultures, variegated, to be sure, in the different regions of their areas. In all three countries the vernaculars fought off the Chinese language when it was seen that the native languages could play the same roles assumed by the invader. The preponderant part of the Annamese, Korean, and Japanese populations remained monolingual because it was only the educated, relatively small in number, who learned the Chinese language and charactery. But even among the educated, the Chinese characters were not exclusively used; newly devised characters were invented, and, in the case of the Vietnamese, the letters of the alphabet were ultimately adopted. In modern times, the rate of literacy has shown a great increase, especially in Korea and Japan. In Korea the period of Japanese domination after 1910 brought the development of bilingual capacities, but in Japan the entire twentieth century became a period of rapid adoption of the standard language, based on the language of the middle and higher classes in Tokyo, and today disseminated in the schools, over radio and television, and in the public prints. Emphasis on the standard language now permits dialect speakers from various parts of the country to speak to each other in a series of common languages; writings in the standard language permit education to proceed to the highest levels. But even in Japan not all of the dialects are mutually intelligible.[32] Under present-day conditions, when

---

[32] See the present author's article, "On Dialect Intelligibility in Japan," *Anthropological Linguistics* (January, 1967), pp. 1–17.

North and South Korea are divided from each other, we may expect a further development of dialect differences between the two areas. The differences in phonology noted for the whole of Vietnam in *A Vietnamese Grammar*, by Laurence C. Thompson,[33] suggest that speakers of Vietnamese living in widely separated areas would most probably find considerable difficulty in speaking with each other.

No language used within their respective borders has really competed with the Vietnamese, Korean, and Japanese languages. Vietnamese nationalism today expresses itself in the closing of schools established by the French in the nineteenth century. In Japan, the Ainu language, spoken in close proximity to Japanese, was driven with its speakers to northern Hoñshū and to Hokkaidō. Intermarriage and the public schools, to which the Ainu children go, have almost wiped out the Ainu language. Chinese influence still remains strong in Vietnam, Korea, and Japan. In newspaper editorials in Japan, 56.3 per cent of the nouns are of Chinese origin.[34] With political independence and geography on their side, the Japanese were able to control the impact of Chinese influence even as early as the ninth century, and in Korea and Vietnam, too, the native language was kept by the populace. In Korea, Japanese, which was actively taught in the years of the Japanese occupation, remains now a second language only of the older generation.

The influence of the Chinese language on the Annamese, Korean, and Japanese elites may be compared with the influence of Pali in Indo-China or of Sanskrit among the speakers of Telegu in India. Among these speakers of Telegu, it is said that Sanskritization has contributed to the development among the upper class of a prestigious and formal written style.[35] In India the Brahmins are similarly said to be more receptive to English as well as to Sanskrit than are the members of any agricultural community; those living in rural areas simply do not have the same contacts with these

---

[33] Thompson, *op. cit.*, chap. 4, pp. 78-104.

[34] Kokuritsu Kokugo Keñkyūjo (National Language Research Institute), *Goi chōsa: geñdai shiñbuñ yōgo no ichirei* (Lexical Survey: an Example of Words Used in Modern Newspapers), *Kokuritsu Kokugo Kenkyūjo shiryōshū* (Materials Collection of the National Language Research Institute), 2 (Tōkyō, 1952), p. 104.

[35] Andrée J. Sjoberg, "Coexistent Phonemic Systems in Telegu: a Socio-cultural Perspective," *Word*, 18 (1962), pp. 269-279.

languages which the Brahmins enjoy.[36] In Europe, the situation has been different only because the foreign language that gained precedence for a time, Latin, was related to the vernaculars. But there too language became an instrument for the development of nationalism. As Deutsch has shown, the number of languages (and of dialects attaining standard status) in Europe increased from 16 to 53 between 1800 and 1937, paralleling the growth in number of modern sovereign states.[37] In each area it was the native language or dialect that has won out as nationalism developed.

One of the first changes noted in a country that has newly won its independence has been the adoption or readoption of its own vernacular name and of its other native place names. Study or knowledge of foreign languages permits the importation of foreign ideas, ease in dealing with foreign countries, increased commerce, and enhancement of national prestige on the international scene. But for basic day to day needs in a unified community, it is the native vernacular which has to be favored.

In the Annamese, Korean, and Japanese instances, it was a foreign system of charactery quite unsuited to the native language which was first adopted. With the languages of the northern half of India, which belong to the Indo-European family, the problem is relatively simpler because the Devanagari alphabet, proposed for the writing systems, is closely correlated with the phonetic structures of the languages concerned. Given political deftness and today's conditions of rapid communication, Piripino and Hindi should take something less than centuries to get established in the Philippines and India. The alternative in the Philippines and India is the kind of fracturing, seen in Europe, into smaller states, each with its separate tongue. Despite periods of domination by Western powers, independence and assertion of a national consciousness sufficient to make a native vernacular the accepted language of an Asian nation should in modern times take much less time than it took the Annamese, Koreans, and Japanese to achieve.

---

[36] William Bright, "Linguistic Change in Some Indian Caste Dialects," in Charles A. Ferguson and John J. Gumperz, eds., *Linguistic Diversity in South Asia: Studies in Regional, Social and Functional Variation, International Journal of American Linguistics* (Indiana University Research Center in Anthropology, Folklore, and Linguistics Publications, 13; 1960), Part 3, p. 363.

[37] Karl W. Deutsch, "The Trend of European Nationalism—the Language Aspect," *American Political Science Review*, Vol. 36 (1942), pp. 533-541.

American Oriental Society / Middle West Branch 1917-1967

by A. Kirk Grayson
University of Toronto

The title of this paper might suggest that this is a very insignificant subject indeed and hardly worthy of the attention of serious scholars. Certainly the history of the Middle West Branch is not characterized by monumental changes or exciting events. There are no economic upheavels, natural calamities, world wars, ideological revolutions, or major technical advances to narrate. In fact on the surface the history of this small society appears to be an uninspiring topic, of interest only to the handful of members who have worked so hard over the years on its behalf. Certainly this was the impression of the present writer when he was first asked to present such a paper as an introduction to the semicentenary celebrations. In going through past records, however, he found that certain features of the history of the society which were of considerable interest began to take form. Some of these features were noteworthy solely because of their antiquarian value, while others were relevant to problems facing the Branch today. The author has, therefore, approached the subject from the point of view of these themes. Inevitably there is some subjectivity involved in this kind of approach, but it is certainly a more meaningful and interesting form than a mere chronicle of events. One naturally hopes that members will follow in the author's footsteps and find that as they read farther they become involuntarily interested in the subject.

1. Purpose of the Branch

In April, 1916, the Directors of the American Oriental Society appointed a committee consisting of Professors Breasted, Olmstead, Morgenstern, Clay (secretary-treasurer of the A.O.S.) to consider the formation of a "Western Branch." The committee accordingly held a meeting on January 27, 1917, at Chicago to which all interested members of the society were invited. During the course of this meeting it was decided to form the "Middle West Branch of the American Oriental Society." This was, in fact, the first meeting of our Branch; it was attended by seventy-five members, and twelve papers were read. The first officers were: Breasted (president), Laufer (vice-president), Olmstead (secretary-treasurer). The purpose that the Branch was to serve was stated in an amendment to the parent society's constitution:

> To provide for scientific meetings of groups of members living at too great a distance to attend the annual sessions of the Society, branches may be organized with the approval of the Directors.

Over the years the original purpose of the society has become meaningless owing to the rapid development in swift forms of transportation and to the more liberal travel funds available from the employers of delegates. In 1966 a Special Committee was formed to investigate various problems facing the Branch, and in its report stated that one of the main functions of the Branch was to provide an opportunity for younger scholars and senior graduate students to present papers. Reference was also made to the informal nature of the meetings and the advantage this had over the larger sessions of the parent society.

2. *Meeting Times*

For the first few years (1917-23) the Branch normally held its meetings in the latter part of February, but in 1924 the first meeting held jointly with a society other than the parent society (the Central Section of the American Anthropological Association) took place at the end of March. Ever since that time the Branch has normally met during the latter part of March or early April.

3. *Attendance*

During the last few years the matter of diminishing attendance has been a real problem. It has been necessary to send out appeals shortly before recent meetings for members to attend and present papers. In looking through the files for the last fifty years, it is noteworthy that the highest recorded figure for attendance is 150. This is for the second annual meeting (in Cincinnati) in 1918. Over the years the figure has fluctuated considerably, going as low as 16 in 1919 (the year of the influenza epidemic), but it never again came close to 150. Diminishing attendance and general apathy is not an entirely new problem. In 1925 Professor T. George Allan as secretary sent out desperate appeals for people to attend and present papers.

4. Nature of Meetings

Formal papers have formed, from the start, the core of any meeting of our Branch. Informal discussion, however, has also been a highlight of most meetings. In this connection it is noteworthy that in the early years Informal Discussion Groups were held. For example, in 1922 such a discussion took place on the theme "Tenure of Land in the Ancient World," and among the participants were Breasted, Olmstead, and Rostovtzeff. Formal symposia have also been held from time to time, with such subjects as "Unity of Early History" (1921) and "The Sacred Book: Its Rise and its Religious and Cultural Role" (1949).

Frequently the Branch has met jointly with the parent society and with other societies—American Anthropological Association, Chicago Society for Biblical Research, American Historical Association (on one occasion Breasted was president of both groups). In 1943 we held our first joint meeting with the Mid-West Section of the Society of Biblical Literature and Exegesis (as it was called then), and we have regularly met with that group ever since.

5. "The Eastern Problem"

In the early years Middle West members apparently experienced some difficulty in gaining the recognition they felt they deserved in the East. This problem became obvious when it was proposed that the parent society meet in Chicago one year with the Middle West Branch. Many easterners objected strongly to this departure from tradition, but eventually the Middle West won, and in 1922 the first joint meeting of the parent society and the Middle West Branch was held in Chicago. The Middle West members patted themselves on the back over this victory and there is a letter from Olmstead in which he is positively jubilant:

> In spite of all the bad luck croakers, the Chicago meeting *was* a success, but didn't we have to hustle! Of course, the east did pretty badly, but I am pleased at the way our people turned out and read papers. And if

I do say it myself, our papers mostly had point and pep. The easterners who did come heard and saw some things to take back.

Subsequently such joint conventions have been held frequently. The Western Branch of this society might well be encouraged by this precedent.

6. *Sitz im Leben*

The activities of the Middle West Branch have inevitably been affected over the past fifty years by what has been going on in the world in which the Branch exists. Traces of the influence of "outside" events are to be found in the archives, and it is worthwhile to note these briefly. The first such instance is found at the third annual meeting, at Urbana, Illinois, in 1919. Influenza had swept across the land and the catastrophic effect of this epidemic is reflected not only in direct reference to it in the correspondence of the time—even the executive of the Branch was affected—but in the pathetically small attendance figure for the 1919 meeting—sixteen. There were few formal papers at this meeting since very few of the scheduled speakers came, and most of the time was spent in informal discussion. The meeting was considered a particularly successful one by those who attended.

The fluctuations in the economy of the half century are best illustrated by the prices quoted for hotels. In 1922 one could have a single room without bath at the Hotel Windermere in Chicago for $2.50. Then came the depression, and in the 1930's the same accommodation was priced at $2.00. It is hardly necessary to quote 1967 hotel prices to illustrate the price spiral over the last few decades.

When discussing the meetings of the Branch in relation to their environment, one must refer to a problem which plagued executives of the society for many years. For some time after its founding the society was wooed like any convention by enterprising city officials and businessmen. Thus one finds in the files engraved invitations from such urban centres as the City of Chicago to hold the next convention in that city. Hotels are represented among these invitations, as well as professional photographers who felt that every delegate would want a picture of the whole group for his mantelpiece. Even theatrical and entertainment agencies regarded our Branch as fair game. The Shubert Vaudeville Booking Exchange wrote to the society shortly before its 1922 meeting in Chicago offering the services of various entertainment groups including the "Last Waltz" and the "Rose Girl." The problem of these invitations was finally solved by one of my harassed predecessors who, in 1940, wrote to the people responsible for drawing up the list of conventions to be held in Chicago, pointing out what kind of a group we were ("small potatoes" he called us) and asking that our meetings no longer be mentioned in the convention literature. A polite reply was received and this kind of correspondence came to an abrupt halt.

The Second World War had a disastrous effect on the Branch. The correspondence of the early 1940's refers more and more to the number of members and officers of the society who had been called up to active service; it soon became a problem to find replacements for the decimated executive. Then, because of a United States government restriction on conventions of fifty or more persons, the 1945 meeting was cancelled. This is the only time that the Middle West Branch failed to hold its annual meeting, and it is because this one meeting was not held that we are celebrating our fiftieth anniversary this year and not last.

In our semi-centenary year two events of major significance for the Branch are taking place. Since most members find the spring an inconvenient time to meet (the parent society has its annual meeting within a few weeks of our own), it has been decided to experiment with other times of the year. Thus, in 1969 our annual meeting will be held in October (at Madison, Wisconsin), and in 1970 in November (at Bloomington, Indiana). The other momentous occurrence is the publication of the present volume. This book serves both as a fitting tribute to the past achievements of the Branch and as an indication that this organization is still a vital, scholarly body.

APPENDIX A: SOURCE MATERIAL

The only source material available to the writer was the records found in the archives and the proceedings published in The Journal of the American Oriental Society. These documents are not very illuminating since they consist mainly of minutes, financial reports, and correspondence dealing with the arrangement of meetings. Nor are the archives complete despite an attempt over the last year to bring together and put in order all the files of the Branch. A brief sketch of the nature of the archives follows.

The constitution of the society is incorporated into the constitution of the parent society, which is published, from time to time, in JAOS. There is a complete record of the Proceedings of the Branch in the appropriate volumes of JAOS. The oldest document in the archives is the program for the meeting in Evanston in 1920. Then from 1920 to 1925 we have very full records. On the basis of these records it appears that Professor Olmstead was the individual most interested in the welfare of the Branch in its early years. He would certainly win an award for the most colorful correspondence in the archives. Records diminish in 1926 and for 1927-35 there are virtually no documents. In 1937 records begin to increase and for 1938-41 there is full documentation. Then there is another decline in 1942 and a dearth for 1943-45 due to the war. In 1946 records again become full (except for a lapse in 1958-60) and take the form which they have maintained to the present day. Before leaving this subject, the name of Professor Kraft should be mentioned. If Olmstead deserves a reward for colorfulness, Kraft deserves one for the industry and diligence he displayed on behalf of the Branch, which is evident from the archives of the period when he was secretary-treasurer.

APPENDIX B: ANNUAL MEETINGS

Number	*Year*	*Place*
1	1917	Chicago, Illinois
2	1918	Cincinnati, Ohio
3	1919	Urbana, Illinois
4	1920	Evanston, Illinois
5	1921	Madison, Wisconsin
6	1922	Chicago, Illinois
7	1923	Chicago, Illinois
8	1924	Ann Arbor, Michigan
9	1925	Evanston, Illinois
10	1926	Chicago, Illinois
11	1927	Cincinnati, Ohio
12	1928	Urbana, Illinois
13	1928 (Dec. 28-29)	Indianapolis, Indiana
14	1930	Toronto, Ontario
15	1931	Oberlin, Ohio
16	1932	Chicago, Illinois
17	1933	Toledo, Ohio
18	1934	Evanston, Illinois
19	1935	Ann Arbor, Michigan
20	1936	Chicago, Illinois

Number	*Year*	*Place*
21	1937	Cleveland, Ohio
22	1938	Chicago, Illinois
23	1939	Chicago, Illinois
24	1940	Lexington, Kentucky
25	1941	Chicago, Illinois
26	1942	Oberlin, Ohio
27	1943	Evanston, Illinois
28	1944	Chicago, Illinois
29	1946	Chicago, Illinois
30	1947	Ann Arbor, Michigan
31	1948	Evanston, Illinois
32	1949	Cincinnati, Ohio
33	1950	Cincinnati, Ohio
34	1951	Evanston, Illinois
35	1952	Lexington, Kentucky
36	1953	Evanston, Illinois
37	1954	Chicago, Illinois
38	1955	Toronto, Ontario
39	1956	Chicago, Illinois
40	1957	Dubuque, Iowa
41	1958	Chicago, Illinois
42	1959	Ann Arbor, Michigan
43	1960	Chicago, Illinois
44	1961	Madison, Wisconsin
45	1962	Chicago, Illinois
46	1963	Ann Arbor, Michigan
47	1964	Chicago, Illinois
48	1965	Chicago, Illinois
49	1966	Detroit, Michigan
50	1967	Holland, Michigan